MARTA HØYLAND LAVIK, Dr. theol. (2004), University of Oslo, is Associate Professor in Old Testament Studies at School of Mission and Theology, Stavanger. Her publications show an exegetical interest, and also hermeneutical issues are attended to in her scholarly contributions.

A People Tall and Smooth-Skinned

Supplements to
Vetus Testamentum

VOLUME 112

A People Tall and Smooth-Skinned

The Rhetoric of Isaiah 18

by

Marta Høyland Lavik

BRILL

LEIDEN • BOSTON
2007

This book is printed on acid-free paper.

Library of Congress Cataloging-in-Publication data

LC Control No.: 2006051754

ISSN 0083–5889
ISBN 90 04 15434 5

PRINTED IN THE NETHERLANDS

For Hallvard and Jenny

To my husband, Ørjan Lavik, whose support and encouragement
were vital to the completion of this book

CONTENTS

PREFACE

The present book is a revised version of my doctoral thesis presented to the University of Oslo in November 2004. The research project on the rhetoric of Isaiah 18 was made possible by a scholarship from the Research Council of Norway, and a scholarship from the School of Mission and Theology, Stavanger. The thesis was directed by Prof. Knut Holter, School of Mission and Theology, to whom I am indebted for his kind support and helpful suggestions. My thanks go further to the Faculty of Theology, University of Oslo, and to the opponents at the disputation, Prof. Kirsten Nielsen (Aarhus) and Prof. Karl William Weyde (Oslo). Let me also express thanks to the editors of the *Supplements to Vetus Testamentum* for accepting this book in the series.

Many people have inspired me in my work on Isaiah 18, and they are all included when I now single out only a few of them. Through some years in which pregnancies and the demands of the birth of two children competed with the thesis, Prof. Knut Holter guided me along the way with a combination of patience and insistence upon excellence. I am of course myself fully responsible for the results of this book, and for any mistakes. Other colleagues at the School of Mission and Theology who have given me helpful comments are Prof. Magnar Kartveit and Ph.D. student Ingeborg A.K. Kvammen. I am also grateful to Prof. Hans M. Barstad (Oslo/Edinburgh), Prof. Helge S. Kvanvig (Oslo), Prof. emeritus Martin Ravndal Hauge (Oslo), Prof. Terje Stordalen (Oslo), and Prof. John Barton (Oxford), whose insightful comments made me think differently about several parts of the project. Colleagues and friends participating in various research seminars in Oslo/Granavolden, Aarhus, Oxford and Stavanger deserve thanks for valuable advice on earlier drafts of the thesis. The staff of the library at the School of Mission and Theology, headed by Rev. Arne B. Samuelsen, have also been very helpful. My thanks goes further to some friends, and also members of my family who have communicated significant observations about literary devices of Isaiah 18 to me. One of my sisters, Brita Høyland, made constructive comments to several parts of the earlier drafts of this book.

Last, but not least, my husband Ørjan Lavik deserves thanks. I am very grateful indeed for his supportive attitude in the process of writing this book. I dedicate this book to Ørjan, Hallvard and Jenny.

Marta Høyland Lavik
Spring 2006, Stavanger, Norway

ABBREVIATIONS

The abbreviations follow S.M. Schwertner, *Abkürzungsverzeichnis, Theologische Realenzyklopädie (TRE)*, Berlin: Walter de Gruyter 1994². When not found in *TRE*, abbreviations are made by me.

ABD	*The Anchor Bible Dictionary*. Ed. by D.N. Freedman et al. (New York: Doubleday 1992)
Ac.B	Academie Books
AfrCSt	African Christian Studies
AmUSt.TR	American University Studies. Theology and Religion
AnBib	Analecta biblica
AncB	Anchor Bible
ANET	J.B. Pritchard, (ed.), *Ancient Near Eastern Texts Relating to the Old Testament*. Third Edition with Supplement (Princeton: Princeton University Press 1950/1969).
ANETS	Ancient Near Eastern Texts and Studies
Arch.	*Archaeology*
ATD	Das Alte Testament Deutsch
AthD	Acta Theologica Danica
ATJ	*Africa Theological Journal*
AUL	Acta Universitatis Lundensis
BAT	Botschaft des Alten Testaments
BBB	Bonner biblische Beiträge
BC	Biblischer Commentar über das Alte Testament
BDB	F. Brown, S.R. Driver, C.A. Briggs, *The New Brown—Driver—Briggs—Gesenius Hebrew and English Lexicon with an Appendix Containing the Biblical Aramaic* (Peabody: Hendrickson Publishers 1979).
BEAT	Beiträge zur Erforschung des Alten Testaments und des antiken Judentums
BET	Beiträge zur biblischen Exegese und Theologie
BEThL	Bibliotheca Ephemeridum Theologicarum Lovaniensium
BevTh	Beiträge zur evangelischen Theologie
BHS	K. Ellinger & W. Rudolph (eds.), *Biblia Hebraica Stuttgartensia* (Stuttgart: Deutsche Bibelgesellschaft 1984).
Bib.	*Biblica*

BibIS Biblical Interpretation Series
BibMF Bibelen med forklaringer
BibThA Bible and Theology in Africa
Bijdr. *Bijdragen. Tijdschrift voor philosophie en theologie*
BiLiSe Bible and literature series
BiSe Biblical seminar
BJSt Brown Judaic studies
BJudSt Biblical and Judaic Studies
BK *Biblischer Kommentar*
BN Biblische Notizen
BRBS Brill's Readers in Biblical Studies
BRL Biblisches Reallexikon
BS Bibliotheca sacra
BVC Bible et vie chrétienne
BZ Biblische Zeitschrift
BZAW Beihefte zur Zeitschrift für die alttestamentliche Wissenschaft
CBET Contributions to Biblical Exegesis and Theology (Kampen: Kok Pharos)
CBETh Contributions to Biblical Exegesis & Theology (Leuven: Peeters)
CB.OT *Coniectanea biblica. Old Testament series*
CBQ Catholic Biblical Quarterly
CBQ.MS *Catholic Biblical Quarterly. Monograph Series*
CNEB Cambridge Bible Commentary on the New English Bible
CThM Calwer theologische Monographien
CThMi *Currents in Theology and Mission*
CuBi Cultura biblica
DCH D.J.A. Clines (ed.), *The Dictionary of Classical Hebrew.* Vols. 1–5. (Sheffield: Sheffield Academic Press 1993 ff.).
DicBI L. Ryken, J.C. Wilhoit et al. (eds.), *Dictionary of Biblical Imagery* (Downers Grove & Leicester: Inter Varsity Press 1998).
EB Die Heilige Schrift in deutscher Übersetzung. 'Echter Bibel'
EdF Erträge der Forschung
EHAT Exegetisches Handbuch zum Alten Testament
EJ *Encyclopaedia Judaica*
ET *Expository times*
EThL Ephemerides Theologicae Lovanienses
EvTh *Evangelische Theologie*
FAT Forschungen zum Alten Testament

FB   Fontana Books
FOTL   The Forms of the Old Testament literature
FRLANT   Forschungen zur Religion und Literatur des Alten und
              Neuen Testaments
FThL   Forum theologiae linguisticae
FuSt   Fuldaer Studien
FzB   Forschung zur Bibel
GBS.OT   Guides to Biblical Scholarship. Old Testament Series
GrJ   *Grace Journal*
GrSt   de Gruyter Studienbuch
GS.AT   Geistliche Schriftlesung. AT
HALAT   L. Koehler & W. Baumgartner, *Hebräisches und Aramäisches*
              Lexikon zum Alten Testament (Leiden: E.J. Brill 1967).
HAT   Handbuch zum Alten Testament
HBib.   Handledning vid bibelstudium
HEp.   Handbuch der althebräischen Epigraphik; 1 Text und
              Kommentar
Hermeneia   Hermeneia
HK   Handkommentar zum Alten Testament
HOr.   Handbuch der Orientalistik. Erste Abteilung, Der Nahe
              und der Mittlere Osten
HSAT   Die Heilige Schrift des Alten Testaments
HSM   Harvard Semitic Monographs
HThK.AT   Herders Theologischer Kommentar zum Alten Testament
HThR   Harvard Theological Review
HUCA   *Hebrew Union College Annual*
ICC   International Critical Commentary
IDB   *The Interpreter's Dictionary of the Bible*
IDB.S   *The Interpreter's Dictionary of the Bible. Supplementary volume*
IEJ   Israel Exploration Journal
Interp.   *Interpretation*
IntB   *The Interpreter's Bible*
IRT   Issues in Religion and Theology
ISBL   Indiana Studies in Biblical Literature
ISP   International Scholars Publications
ITC   International Theological Commentary
ITP   Interpretation, A Bible Commentary for Teaching and
              Preaching
JAOS   *Journal of the American Oriental Society*
JARP   *Journal of African Religion and Philosophy*

JARSt	*Journal of Arabic and Religious Studies*
JBL	Journal of Biblical Literature
JITC	Journal of the Interdenominational Theological Center
JL.SM	Janua Linguarum. Series Minor
JLT	Journal of Literature and Theology
JNES	Journal of Near Eastern Studies
JQR.S	*Jewish Quarterly Review. Supplement*
JRT	Journal of Religious Thought
JSNT.S	*Journal for the Study of the New Testament. Supplement Series*
JSOT	Journal for the Study of the Old Testament
JSOT.S	Journal for the study of the Old Testament. Supplement Series
JSSt	Journal of Semitic Studies
JThS	Journal of Theological Studies
JThS.NS	The Journal of Theological Studies. New Series
KAT	Kommentar zum Alten Testament
KEH	Kurzgefaßtes exegetisches Handbuch
KHC	Kurzer Hand-Commentar zum Alten Testament
LAI	Library of Ancient Israel
MzE	Monographien zur Erdkunde
NCBC	The New Century Bible Commentary
NIC	New International Commentary on the Old Testament
NIntB	*The New Interpreter's Bible*
NMES	Near and Middle East series
NTOA	Novum testamentum et orbis antiquus
OBO	Orbis biblicus et orientalis
OTL	Old Testament Library
OTMes	Old Testament Message
OTS	Oudtestamentische Studiën
PEQ	*Palestine Exploration Quarterly*
POS	Pretoria Oriental Series
PrOT	De Prediking van het Oude Testament
RExp	*Review and Expositor*
RNBC	Readings: A New Biblical Commentary
SBBS	*Soncino Books of the Bible (Series)*
SBEC	*Studies in the Bible and Early Christianity*
SBL.DS	*Society of Biblical Literature. Dissertation Series*
SBL.SP	Society of Biblical Literature. Seminar Papers. Annual Meeting
SBL.SS	Society of Biblical Literature. Semeia Studies

SBONT	Sacred Books of the Old and New Testaments
SBT	Studies in Biblical Theology.
SC	Sources chrétiennes
SchL	Schweich Lectures
Semeia	*Semeia*
Semitics	*Semitics*
SEÅ	*Svensk exegetisk årsbok*
SJOT	*Scandinavian Journal of the Old Testament*
SJTh	*Scottish Journal of Theology*
Skr.K	*Skrif en Kerk*
SLittG	Societatis Litterarum Gottingensis
SPHS	Scholars Press Homage Series
SSN	Studia semitica neerlandica
SubBi	Subsidia biblica
Syr.	*Syria. Revue d'art oriental et d'archéologie*
TEJTM	*Theological Educator: A Journal of Theology and Ministry*
THAT	*Theologisches Handwörterbuch zum Alten Testament*
ThWAT	*Theologisches Wörterbuch zum Alten Testament*
ThZ	*Theologische Zeitschrift*
TI	Theological Inquiries
TOTC	The Tyndale Old Testament Commentaries
TTK	*Tidsskrift for teologi og kirke*
TWOT	*Theological Wordbook of the Old Testament*
UBL	Ugaritisch-biblische Literatur
UF	*Ugarit-Forschungen*
UTBW	UTB für Wissenschaft, Uni-Taschenbücher
VT	*Vetus Testamentum*
VT.S	Supplements to Vetus Testamentum
WBC	Word Biblical Commentary
WO	*Die Welt des Orients*
WoW	*Word and World*
WUNT	Wissenschaftliche Untersuchungen zum Neuen Testament
ZAW	*Zeitschrift für die alttestamentliche Wissenschaft*
ZBK.AT	Zürcher Bibelkommentar. Alten Testament
ZDMG	*Zeitschrift der Deutschen Morgenländischen Gesellschaft*
ZDPV	*Zeitschrift des Deutschen Palästina-Vereins*
ZEthn.	*Tribus. Zeitschrift für Ethnologie und ihre Nachbarwissenschaften*

CHAPTER ONE

INTRODUCTION

Isa 18 is found within a group of texts, Isa 13–23, that—for the most part—deal with nations other than Israel/Judah.[1] The majority of these texts open with a מַשָּׂא X, "pronouncement concerning X", and they are often interpreted as messages of judgement towards specific nations. Isa 18, however, opens with a הוֹי to a land מֵעֵבֶר לְנַהֲרֵי־כוּשׁ, "from along the rivers of Cush", and הוֹי seems to be a weaker pronouncement than מַשָּׂא. At a first glance at the text, one realises that Isa 18 opens and closes by mentioning the remote African nation Cush. Does this then mean that the text predicts judgement over Cush? As this work will show, Isa 18 is open to various interpretations. When it comes to the scholarly treatment of Isa 18, this text has traditionally been studied with view to whether v. 7 can be considered "original" or added to vv. 1–6 at a later stage.[2] However, by focusing on questions about "authenticity", scholars have overlooked features that bind the text together. In terms of contents, Isa 18:1–7 opens and closes by describing גּוֹי מְמֻשָּׁךְ וּמוֹרָט, "a people tall and smooth-skinned", whereas vv. 3–6 does not mention this people. The question is then whether there are any connections at all between 18:1–2 and 7 on the one hand, and vv. 3–6 on the other hand. Suggesting features of a deliberate rhetoric of the chapter as a whole, this work

---

[1] In this study, the form critical terminology "oracles against the nations", abbreviated as OAN, applied about chs. 13–23 and related material will be avoided as the present research is not done within a traditional form critical approach. The preferable terminology is "the nations material", cf. G.I. Davies, "The Destiny of the Nations in the Book of Isaiah", *The Book of Isaiah* (1989) 93–120, 114.

[2] Cf. H. Wildberger, *Jesaja 13–27* (1978) 682, who argues that the "original" parts of Isa 18 are 18:1, 2a, 2bα, and 4–6a. For a similar view, see J. Jensen, *Isaiah 1–39* (1984) 164: "Verse 7 is without doubt a later addition and in all probability v. 3 and v. 6b are also later additions." Cf. also G.R. Hamborg, "Reasons for Judgement in the Oracles Against the Nations of the Prophet Isaiah", *VT* 31 (1981) 148, who writes: "[. . .] there is little continuity between xviii 7 and xviii 6. xviii 7 should therefore be seen as an addition [. . .]". A division between "authentic" and "original" material in Isa 18 is also referred to by B.M. Zapff, *Schriftgelehrte Prophetie* (1995) 289–290, who (with Wildberger) regards the following of Isa "[. . .] 18,1f.4f.6a jesajanisch, V 3.6b und 7 später Ergänzungen."

will address the question of unity. By pursuing a literary reading of Isa 18, proposals will be made about an intentional rhetoric of the chapter as a whole through observations of textual design and motifs.

Introductory to the analysis of Isa 18, some words need to be said about: (i) the nations material in the book of Isaiah to which this text belongs, (ii) some preliminary observations of Isa 18, and (iii) some methodological questions.

1.1. THE NATIONS MATERIAL IN THE BOOK OF ISAIAH

As in other prophetic books, the book of Isaiah, too, contains texts that concern peoples other than Israel/Judah.[3] These texts deal with neighbouring nations to Israel/Judah, and with more remote peoples. In addition to what is found in chs. 13–23, there are numerous texts in the book of Isaiah that mention the nations. This has resulted in many exegetical studies of these texts. The present section will first give a brief outline of *what* is called the nations material in the book of Isaiah, and then show *how* this material has been treated.

---

[3] Similar collections of texts concerning foreign nations appear in Jer 46–51, Ezek 25–32, Amos 1:3–2:16 and Zeph 2:4–15. Furthermore, the prophecies of Nahum towards Niniveh, and Obadiah towards Edom can also be regarded as belonging to this category. An exception is the book of Hosea where the nations theme is absent. What is here referred to as the nations material in the book of Isaiah is part of a huge research field on the so-called "oracles against the nations" (OAN) in the Old Testament in general. As this chapter is restricted to how the Isaianic nations texts have been treated, it will go beyond the limits of this chapter to enter into the general debate about nations texts in other Old Testament books. The brief history of research to the Isaianic nations texts given in this chapter is however relatively representative for how the nations material in other books of the Old Testament has been treated. For some recent contributions to the nations material in other books than the book of Isaiah, see the following selected chronological listing: J.W. Watts, "Text and Redaction in Jeremiah's Oracles Against the Nations", *CBQ* 54 (1992) 432–447, D.J. Reimer, *The Oracles Against Babylon in Jeremiah 50–5* (1993), A.R. Ceresko, "Janus Parallelism in Amos's 'Oracles Against the Nations' (Amos 1:3–2:16)", *JBL* 113 (1994) 485–490, A. Berlin, "Zephaniah's Oracle Against the Nations and an Israelite Cultural Myth", *Fortunate the Eyes that See* (1995) 175–184, J.H. Hayes, "Amos's Oracles Against the Nations (1:2–2:16)", *RExp* 92 (1995) 153–167, H.R. Mosely, "The Oracles Against the Nations", *TEJTM* 52 (1995) 37–45, R. Nysse, "Keeping Company with Nahum: Regarding the Oracles Against the Nations as Scripture", *WoW* 15 (1995) 412–419, P.R. Raabe, "Why Prophetic Oracles Against the Nations?", *Fortunate the Eyes that See* (1995) 236–257, D.H. Ryou, *Zephaniah's Oracles Against the Nations* (1995), J. Barton, *Understanding Old Testament Ethics* (2003).

1.1.1. *Texts*

Generally speaking, the nations material has traditionally not been an area of great concern in Old Testament scholarship.[4] For Isaianic studies, however, the recent interest in the composition and unity of the book has caused a growing interest in this area. This book does *not* focus on features that might bind the book of Isaiah together as the investigation concentrates on one text only. Still, as long as Isa 18:1–7 mentions a foreign nation, it is important to briefly present the nations material in the book of Isaiah and this material's scholarly treatment in order to illustrate the context of Isa 18.

Texts concerning the nations can be found in all three divisions that the book of Isaiah is customarily divided into (1–39, 40–55, 60–66). The book of Isaiah is framed by two rather similar eschatological texts; 2:2–4 and 66:18–24. These two texts contain positive views of the nations' ultimate role alongside Israel. The next nation text is found in 5:26–30. The enemy (MT has "the nations", plural, in v. 26) is not identified. In chapters 7 and 8 it is said that YHWH rules over the world and threatens both individuals and nations (7:5–9, 16; 8:1–4). The nations will submit under the rule of the Davidic line (9:6–7). Chapter 10 exemplifies how nations on the one hand are seen as enemies of YHWH (vv. 12–19), and on the other hand as tools YHWH uses to punish Israel/Judah (v. 6). 11:1–16 presents a picture of the end-time that is close to what is presented in 2:2–4. 12:4–6 contains the proclamation of YHWH's deeds to the nations. Leaving Isa 1–12, the next main section in the Isaianic corpus is chapters 13–23. This section does almost entirely contain texts concerning nations other than Israel/Judah. The prophetic pronouncements are clearly demarcated by the common introductory super-scriptions, משא X, "pronouncement concerning X" (13:1; 14:28; 15:1; 17:1; 19:1; 21:1; 21:11; 21:13; 22:1; and 23:1). The Isaianic apocalypse which follows in chapters 24–27 mentions only one foreign nation by name: Moab (25:10b–12). Nations other than Israel/Judah are only vaguely mentioned in 25:1–5, which is a thanksgiving on behalf of the community. 25:6–10a is a passage which—in the form of a

---

[4] G.I. Davies, "The Destiny of the Nations in the Book of Isaiah", *The Book of Isaiah* (1989) 93: "The neglect of this material [. . .] has long been a feature of the study of the Old Testament prophecy in general."

banquet—speaks positively about the future destiny of the nations.[5]
26:7–19, which contains a community lament, is more vague concerning the nations. The next subdivision of the book (Isa 28–35) opens
with a foreign army used by YHWH to threaten Ephraim (28:2ff.).
This subject is continued in 28:11–13. The latter part of the chapter reintroduces the theme of misplaced trust in foreign alliances.
Chapters 34–35 open with a proclamation of judgement upon all
the nations. 35:4b might refer to 34:8 in that it speaks about YHWH's
revenge. The next section comprises chapters 36–39. In 36–37, the
pride of Assyria is in view, and in 39:5–7 Babylon appears.

The prominence of the nations material in the next main section
of the book (Isa 40–55) is well known. These chapters contain references to both a positive and a negative destiny for the nations.[6]
Isa 40–55 tends to treat the nations material in a more general way
than what is the case for chs. 13–23, and the noun גוים and close
synonyms occur no less than 24 times in these chapters. Still, among
the nations, Babylon is specified (41:11–13; 43:14; 47:1–3.5–15; 49:26;
51:8.12.23; 54:15), and some texts also speak of YHWH's choice and
elevation of Cyrus of Persia (41:2–6; 44:28; 45:1–7; 46:11; 48: 14–15).

In the final section of the book, 56–66, some of the teaching of
chapters 40–55 is reaffirmed. Like 40–55, this section also contains
contrasting views about the nations. Negatively, YHWH will judge
the nations after their deeds (59:18–19). Positively, a central idea in
this part of the book is that the peoples will approach Zion (56:1–7).
Along these lines, chs. 56–66 express the idea that the scattered people of YHWH will be transported back to Zion by the nations (Isa
60; 62:10–12).[7]

Summing up, as the following selected examples show, the nations
material appears in the book of Isaiah in the context of YHWH's
dealings with Israel/Judah—in judgement or salvation.[8] The way of

---

[5] It has been customary to treat 25:9–10a as "Israel's song of thanksgiving", cf.
O. Kaiser, *Der Prophet Jesaja* (1983) 163–164, "das Danklied Israels", and R.E.
Clements, *Isaiah 1–39* (1980/1994) 209–210, "Israel's final song of thanksgiving".

[6] For an analysis of the different positions see D.W. van Winkle, "The Relationship
of the Nations to Yahweh and to Israel in Isaiah 40–55", *VT* 35 (1985) 446–458.
The article is a summary of van Winkle's unpublished Ph.D. dissertation, which
has the same title (1983).

[7] For a recent contribution to a reading of Isa 60 and its function in the book
as a whole, see G.J. Polan, "Zion, the Glory of the Holy One of Israel: A Literary
Analysis of Isaiah 60", *Imagery and Imagination in Biblical Literature* (2001) 50–71.

[8] There has for some time been an assertion that the nations material functions

describing foreign nations with opposite signs is not exclusive for the book of Isaiah, as all prophetic books show this ambiguity towards foreign nations. Israel/Judah is warned against going into political coalitions with foreign powers (7:1–17; 18:1–7; 28:15–16; 30:1–7, 15–17; 31:1–3). Foreign nations are sometimes used as a tool of YHWH in the punishment of Israel/Judah (5:26–30; 10:6; 28:1–13, 14–22; 29:1–4; 39:5–7), and sometimes the nations are described as YHWH's enemies (10:12–19). YHWH rules over the world and threatens both individuals and nations (7:5–9, 16; 8:1–4; 17:1–3; 23; 37:26–29; 45:20–21; 47:1–3, 5–15). The nations must submit the rule of the Davidic line (9:6–7; 11:10), and will give praise to YHWH's redemption of his people by bringing in the diaspora (11:11–12; 49:22–23; 60:8–9; 66:20) and by giving their tribute to Jerusalem (14:1–2; 18:7; 23:15–18; 45:14; 60:5–7, 11, 13, 16; 61:6; 66:12).

1.1.2. *Interpretative perspectives*

The modern history of research of the book of Isaiah can roughly be divided into three phases. Simplistically said, the first phase considered the book to be one, the second phase treated the book as three separate books, whereas the third phase—although with different presuppositions—went back to the idea of one book.[9]

---

as a form of salvation prophecy for Israel, so for example C. Westermann, *Basic Forms of Prophetic Speech* (1991) 205, who writes: "[t]hey [the oracles against the nations] belong in the line of salvation-speeches because they imply salvation for Israel in the light of the situation in which they were uttered." This assertion will be argued against as the interpretation of Isa 18 shows that this speech seems not to function as a form of salvation prophecy.

[9] The idea that chs. 40–66 of the book of Isaiah was attributed to other hands than that of the eight century Isaiah from Jerusalem was first suggested by J.C. Döderlein. Throughout the 1770 and 80s, Döderlein questioned the traditional view, and suggested a limit between chs. 39 and 40 in the book of Isaiah. For references to his works and analysis of his observations, see M. Mulzer, "Döderlein und Deuterojesaja", *BN* 66 (1993) 15–22. The delimitation of Isa 40–55 was one of the suggestions from B. Duhm in 1892, cf. B. Duhm, *Das Buch Jesaia übersetzt und erklärt* (1892) cf. p. xiii. His commentary has had an immense influence on subsequent interpretation of the book of Isaiah. As far as the question of the unity of the book is concerned, Duhm's delimitation of distinct units were widely accepted, and gave rise to the presupposition that the book is a more or less accidentally combination of three originally quite separate works. Cf. R.H. Pfeiffer, *Introduction to the Old Testament* (1953) 447–448, who states: "It was only because sufficient space remained on the scroll that the final editor [...] copied Is. 40–66 (then circulating as a separate book) after Is. 1–39."

In recent years, an increasing number of studies have been published that rather describe features that bind the parts of the book together than focusing on what

The scholarly treatment of the Isaianic nations texts reflects this development. Two main perspectives can be seen: a traditional and a more recent. The traditional perspective consists of studies done mostly within the framework of historical critical methods. A characteristic feature of these studies is that motifs and themes present in all three divisions of the book are not studied other than within the respective parts. The more recent perspective comprises of studies done within various approaches all with the overarching aim of reading the book with view to its unity. Alongside with what appears in the form of articles and monographs, also commentators must— for obvious reasons—deal with the nations material. Commentaries will however not be included in this presentation.[10] Let us proceed by briefly introducing these two perspectives on the Isaianic nations material.

a) *Traditional perspective: Divisions of the book*

As just mentioned, one characteristic feature of Isaianic studies done within the framework of historical critical methods is that the nations material is treated within one part of the book at the time. In consequence with this strong tradition, the present discussion will follow the traditional divisions of the book, and will, for pragmatic reasons, limit itself to chs. 13–23, and chs. 40–55. The hesitation to cross the "borders" between the different parts of the book reflects on the one hand the traditionally strong position historical critical methods have had in Old Testament scholarship, and on the other hand a lack of a more convincing theory about the book's composition and redaction than that suggested by Duhm.[11] In practice, this means that Isa 13–23 has not been studied with relation to chs. 40–55, and the other way round.

---

might divide them. Cf. J. Vermeylen, "L'unité du livre d'Isaïe", *The Book of Isaiah* (1989) 11–53, and R. Rendtorff, "The Book of Isaiah: A Complex Unity: Synchronic and Diachronic Reading", *Prophecy and Prophets* (1997) 109–128. Cf. also the canonical approach of B.S. Childs, *Introduction to the Old Testament as Scripture* (1979) 311–338, and J.D.W. Watts' commentaries *Isaiah 1–33* (1985), and *Isaiah 34–66* (1987). Cf. in addition the work of K. Jeppesen, *Græder ikke saa saare* (1987) 63–84, whose ideas were further developed by H.G.M. Williamson, *The Book Called Isaiah* (1994).

[10] J.D.W. Watts is a commentator who, according to Davies, is "[. . .] a rare case of a commentator who *over*-stresses the importance of the 'nations' theme!" cf. G.I. Davies, "The Destiny of the Nations in the Book of Isaiah", *The Book of Isaiah* (1989) 110. (Davies' italics and quotation mark). Cf. J.D.W. Watts's commentaries *Isaiah 1–33* (1985), and *Isaiah 34–66* (1987).

[11] B. Duhm, *Das Buch Jesaia übersetzt und erklärt* (1892), cf. p. xiii.

Isaiah 13–23

An example of an early scholar who discusses a nations text with geographically oriented questions in mind is H. Winckler, who addresses the matters of the history and geography of Cush in his analysis of Isa 18.[12] In his reading of Isa 18, Winckler argues—on the basis of history and geography—various solutions to where Cush may be located, and he concludes that: "[. . .] kann Kuš-Nubien nicht in betracht kommen [. . .] wol aber das von Kaš-Südbabylonien gelten."[13] A more recent scholar who has an historical focus when analysing a nations text, is S. Erlandsson. In his analysis of Isa 13:2–14:23, Erlandsson's major concern is to address the question of dating of this particular text.[14] He argues against the position that the text should be read as a text from the sixth century. His main point in the analysis of Isa 13:2–14:23 is that this text belongs to Proto-Isaiah and the eighth century. Another recent example is H.J. Katzenstein who—as the title of his book indicates—attempts to sketch the history and geography of Tyre.[15] Building the history of Tyre, Katzenstein uses—in addition to other sources—the Old Testament, arguing that: "[. . .] in this respect one cannot overstate the importance of the Bible [. . .]".[16] An outline of the history of Tyre could not have been given, he says, without paying attention to the "[. . .] very intricately interwoven history of Tyre and her neighbours, especially Israel and Judah." Katzenstein regards the nations text of Isa 23 as primarily an historical source, and this leaves out a discussion of the text's literary features: "Despite its poetic character, this chapter [Isa 23] may be regarded as a historical source [. . .]".[17] Other examples of scholars following the same lead are many.[18]

---

[12] H. Winckler, *Alttestamentliche Untersuchungen* (1892) 146–156.

[13] *Ibid.* 151.

[14] S. Erlandsson, *The Burden of Babylon. A Study of Isaiah 13:2–14:23* (1970). Erlandsson does not keep strictly to the Proto-Isaianic texts as he discusses texts from other parts of the book, too. However, as his main point is the dating of Isa 13:2–14:23, he belongs to this category.

[15] H.J. Katzenstein, *The History of Tyre* (1973).

[16] *Ibid.* vii.

[17] *Ibid.* 249.

[18] Cf. this selected chronological listing: F. Buhl, "Jesaia 21, 6–10", *ZAW* 8 (1888) 157–167, T.K. Cheyne, "The Nineteenth Chapter of Isaiah", *ZAW* 13 (1893) 125–128, V. Zapletal, "Der Spruch über Moab: Is. 15 und 16", *Alttestamentliches* (1903) 163–183, E. Power, "The Prophecy of Isaias against Moab (Is. 15:1–16:5)", *Bib.* 13 (1932) 435–451, B. Alfrink, "Der Versammlungsberg im äussersten Norden (Is. 14)", *Bib.* 14 (1933) 41–67, J. Begrich, "Jesaja 14:28–32. Ein Beitrag zur Chronologie der israelitisch-judäischen Königszeit", *ZDMG* 86 (1933) 66–79, R.B.Y.

Isaiah 40–55

Isa 40–55 tends to treat the nations material in a more general way than what is the case for chs. 13–23. However, among the nations, Babylon is specified, and some texts even speak about an individual, Cyrus, who is chosen and elevated by YHWH. This dissimilarity between Isa 13–23 and 40–55 concerning the number of nations explicitly mentioned does not prevent scholars from suggesting who is alluded to in Isa 40–55. Y. Gitay is an example of a scholar who—though analysing the texts' rhetoric—relates history and exegesis in his study of Isa 40–55.[19] The assumed historical situations lie as a foundation upon which the exegetical interpretations are placed, cf. what is said about Isa 47:1–15: "[. . .] DI's intention is to illustrate the historical changes which are a divine response to the people's political expectations and their feelings towards Babylon, their great and powerful enemy."[20] The following selected chronological listing shows that the studies are many in number also in this section of the book of Isaiah.[21]

Scott, "Isaiah XXI 1–10; The Inside of a Prophet's Mind", *VT* 2 (1952) 278–282, A.H. van Zyl, *The Moabites* (1960), W. Rudolph, "Jesaja xv–xvi", *Hebrew and Semitic Studies* (1963) 130–143, H. Donner, *Israel unter den Völkern* (1964), D.L. Petersen, "The Oracles Against the Nations: A Form-Critical Analysis", *SBL.SP* 1 (1975) 39–61, W. Vogels, "L'Égypte mon peuple—l'universalisme d'Is 19, 16–25", *Bib.* 57 (1976) 494–514, F. Huber, *Jahwe, Juda, und die anderen Völker beim Propheten Jesaja* (1976), W.G.E. Watson, "Tribute to Tyre (Is. 23:7)", *VT* 26 (1976) 371–374, G. Hamborg, "Reasons for Judgement in the Oracles Against the Nations of the Prophet Isaiah", *VT* 31 (1981) 145–159, T. Fischer & U. Rüterswörden, "Aufruf zur Volksklage in Kanaan (Jesaja 23)", *WO* 13 (1982) 36–49, R.D. Weis, "A Definition of the Genre Massa' in the Hebrew Bible" (1986), J.F.A. Sawyer, "'Blessed be my People Egypt', (Isaiah 19:25): The Context and Meaning of a Remarkable Passage", *A Word in Season* (1986) 57–71, R.H. O'Connell, "Isaiah XIV 4B-23: Ironic Reversal through Concentric Structure and Myth Allusion", *VT* 38 (1988) 407–418, J. Høgenhaven, *Gott und Volk bei Jesaja* (1988), J.H. Brangenberg, "A Reexamination of the Date, Authorship, Unity and Function of Isaiah 13–23" (1989), A.K. Jenkins, "The Development of the Isaiah Tradition in Isaiah 13–23", *Le livre d'Isaïe* (1989) 237–251, B. Gosse, "Isaïe 14:24–27 et les oracles contre les nations du livre d'Isaïe", *BN* 56 (1991) 17–21, B. Gosse, "Isaïe 17:12–14 dans la rédaction du livre d'Isaïe", *BN* 58 (1991) 20–23, B.M. Zapff, *Schriftgelehrte Prophetie* (1995), B.C. Jones, *Howling over Moab* (1996).

[19] Y. Gitay, *Prophecy and Persuasion. A Study of Isaiah 40–48* (1981).

[20] *Ibid.* 206–207.

[21] R. Kittel, "Cyrus and Deuterojesaja", *ZAW* 18 (1898) 149–162, M. Haller, "Die Kyros-Lieder Deuterojesajas", *EYXAPIΣTHPION* (1923) 261–277, C.C. Torrey, *The Second Isaiah* (1928), R. Marcus, "The 'Plain Meaning' of Isaiah 42:1–4", *HThR* 30 (1937) 249–259, E. Jenni, "Die Rolle des Kyros bei Deuterojesaja", *ThZ* 10 (1954) 241–256, G. Fohrer, "Zum Text von Jes. xli 8–13", *VT* 5 (1955) 239–249, L.G. Rignell, *A Study of Isaiah ch. 40–55* (1956), P. Auvray, "Cyrus, instrument du Dieu unique. Isaie 45:1–8", *BVC* 50 (1963) 17–23, R. Davidson, "Universalism in

Common for many of the above mentioned works to both Isa 13–23 and 40–55 is the historical manner in which the nations material is studied. A traditional historical orientation reveals itself in that the exegetical findings seem to answer questions such as what did happen, where did it happen, when did it happen, and who are the ones described, etc. When a nations text mentions a specific people, this seems to inaugurate a discussion of geography and chronology. Subsequently, a discussion of the texts' literary qualities is left out. This leads to the next paragraph.

b) *Recent perspective: Unifying features in the book*

Two things can be said about what characterises recent studies of the nations material in the book of Isaiah. First, generally speaking, recent studies do not focus on historical matters to such an extent as was the case for what is here labelled traditional studies. Second, recent Isaianic studies of the nations material seem to have the book in its final form as its object of investigation. Connections between various parts of the book are uncovered, and features that bind the book together are observed. This is done within the framework of various methodological approaches, but the overarching aim seems

Second Isaiah", *SJTh* 16 (1963) 166–185, M. Smith, "II Isaiah and the Persians", *JAOS* 83 (1963) 415–421, C. Westermann, "Das Heilswort bei Deuterojesaja", *EvTh* 24 (1964) 355–373, D.W. Thomas, "'A Drop of a Bucket?' Some Observations on the Hebrew Text of Isaiah 40:15", *In Memoriam Paul Kahle* (1968) 214–221, D.E. Hollenberg, "Nationalism and 'the Nations' in Is. 40–55", *VT* 19 (1969) 23–36, R.E. Manahan, "The Cyrus Notations of Deutero-Isaiah", *GrJ* 11 (1970) 22–33, W.A.M. Beuken, "The Confession of God's Exclusivity by All Mankind: A Reappraisal of Is. 45: 18–25", *Bijdr.* 35 (1974) 335–356, H. Leene, "Universalism or Nationalism? Isaiah 45:9–13 and Its Context", *Bijdr.* 35 (1974) 309–334, W. Dietrich, *Jesaja und die Politik* (1976), G. Cañellas, "El universalismo en el Deuteroisaias", *CuBi* 35 (1978) 3–20, R.W. Klein, "Going Home—A Theology of Second Isaiah", *CThMi* 5 (1978) 198–210, B.J. Oosterhoff, "Tot een licht der volken (Is 42:6)", *De Knecht* (1978) 157–172, R. Martin-Achard, "Esaïe 47 et la tradition prophétique sur Babylone", *Prophecy* (1980) 83–105, C. Westermann, *Sprache und Struktur der Prophetie Deuterojesajas* (1981), L.R. Bailey, "Isaiah 14:24–27", *Interp.* 36 (1982) 171–176, A.S. Kapelrud, "The Main Concern of Second Isaiah", *VT* 32 (1982) 50–58, O.H. Steck, "Aspekte des Gottesknechts in Deuterojesajas 'Ebed-Jahwe-Liedern'", *ZAW* 96 (1984) 372–390, A. Wilson, *The Nations in Deutero-Isaiah* (1986), R.G. Kratz, *Kyros im Deutero-Jesaja-Buch* (1991), O.H. Steck, *Gottesknecht und Zion* (1992), J. van Oorschot, *Von Babel zum Zion* (1993), J.P. Fokkelman, "The Cyrus Oracle (Isaiah 44:24–45:7) from the Perspectives of Syntax, Versification and Structure", *Studies in the Book of Isaiah* (1997) 303–323, R.F. Melugin, "Israel and the Nations in Isaiah 40–55", *Problems in Biblical Theology* (1997) 249–264.

to be the same, namely to address the question of unity. Much has
been done in this area, but those who most explicitly treat this topic
are G.I. Davies, R.E. Clements, and H.G.M. Williamson. In order
to illustrate how scholars within this perspective work, let us give an
example of one theme they have treated.

   G.I. Davies was one of the first to emphasise the nations material in the affirmation for the unity of the book of Isaiah: "[. . .] this
material contributes to the unity of the book of Isaiah as a whole
[. . .]."[22] However, the unity discovered is not of total consistency as
there are harsh contradictions between positive and negative passages.[23] A feature of the nations material that by Davies is seen to
support the view that Isa 40–55 was composed with specific allusion
to parts of chs. 1–39, is the raising of a נס לגוים "a standard for the
nations" (5:26; 11:10–12; 49:22; 62:10—cf. 13:2 and 18:3, without
לגוים). Davies argues that these passages are related. One indication
is that each continues with a reference to "prey" which can only
with great difficulty be rescued from a strong enemy.[24] The fact that
the words for "prey" vary is according to Davies only a sign of
"[. . .] the freshness of Deutero-Isaiah's poetry, even where he is
dependent on older materials."[25] R.E. Clements sees this theme as
being developed from an initially hostile sense (5:26) to becoming
an expression about the role of the nations in the return of the exiles
to Jerusalem (49:22): "Yet the theme of this 'signal flag' evidently
became one of importance to the later, more deeply eschatological
development, of the prophetic theme of the great 'return' from the
nations."[26] Another scholar who has contributed to the use of the
expression נס לגוים throughout the book of Isaiah is H.G.M. Williamson.
Williamson's overall aim is to inquire the role of Isa 40–55 in the
final composition of Isa 1–39. In this context, he argues that נס לגוים
is a theme of "[. . .] God himself (in either the first or the third person) raising a signal to the nations in order to summon them for
some special purpose."[27] Unlike Davies and Clements, Williamson

---

   [22] G.I. Davies,"The Destiny of the Nations in the Book of Isaiah", *The Book of
Isaiah* (1989) 93–120, 105.
   [23] *Ibid.* 106.
   [24] *Ibid.* 115.
   [25] *Ibid.* 115.
   [26] R.E. Clements, "Beyond Tradition-History. Deutero-Isaianic Development of
First Isaiah's Themes", *JSOT* 31 (1985) 95–113, 109.
   [27] H.G.M. Williamson, *The Book Called Isaiah* (1994) 63–67, 64.

restricts his commentaries to three passages only: 5:26; 11:12 and 49:22. Williamson's purpose is to show how this theme is closely related from one part of the book to the other, and he acknowledges 11:12 to be evidence of Deutero-Isaiah's influence on later editing. Arguing that 11:12 derives from a time much later than Isaiah of Jerusalem, he holds that "[. . .] this verse manifests a knowledge of both the other two passages [. . .]".[28] Williamson's purpose seems to be twofold. On the one hand, he emphasises that the theme of נס לגוים is present in Isa 1–39 and 40–55. On the other hand, his endeavour seems to be to suggest the dating of the different texts in order to show the development of the theme, and the Deutero-Isaianic redaction of chs. 1–55. In addition to what has already been mentioned, the following studies are examples of works that relate nations texts from one part of the book to the other.[29]

To be briefly mentioned here is also recent studies of the nations material that not necessarily draw lines between various parts of the book of Isaiah, but rather study such texts from a literary and/or linguistic perspective. J.P. Fokkelman can here represent this way of treating nations texts. In his article he does not discuss unifying features in the book of Isaiah as such, rather, he is concerned about one text, Isa 44:24–45:7. As this text is studied from a perspective of syntax, versification and structure, and not from the perspective of history and geography, it represents a recent way of reading the nations material in the book of Isaiah. In his search for the servant's identity, Fokkelman does *not* go into a discussion of political matters at the time the text refers to, but strictly keeps to forms and structures in the text.[30]

---

[28] *Ibid.* 66.

[29] Not all these scholars go deeply into the nations material as a unifying feature of the book of Isaiah, but they touch upon it in various ways. Cf. W.A.M. Beuken, *Jesaja deel 2A* (1979), B.S. Childs, *Introduction to the Old Testament as Scripture* (1979) 325–338, esp. 329–330, W.A.M. Beuken, *Jesaja deel 2B* (1983), A. Wilson, *The Nations in Deutero-Isaiah* (1986), B. Gosse, *Isaïe 13:1–14:23* (1988), W.A.M. Beuken, *Jesaja deel 3A* (1989), W.A.M. Beuken, *Jesaja deel 3B* (1989), B. Gosse, "Isaïe 21: 11–12 et Isaïe 60–62", *BN* 53 (1990) 21–22, B. Gosse, "Isaïe 17:12–14 dans la rédaction du livre d'Isaïe", *BN* 58 (1991) 20–23, W.A.M. Beuken, "Jesaja 33 als Spiegeltext im Jesajabuch", *EThL* 67 (1991) 5–35, D. Carr, "Reaching for Unity in Isaiah", *JSOT* 57 (1993) 61–80, R.J. Clifford, "The Unity of the Book of Isaiah and Its Cosmogonic Language", *CBQ* 55 (1993) 1–17, B. Gosse, "Isaiah 8:23b and the Three Great Parts of the Book of Isaiah", *JSOT* 70 (1996) 57–62, C.R. Seitz, "How is the Prophet Isaiah Present in the Latter Half of the Book? The Logic of Chapters 40–66 within the Book of Isaiah", *JBL* 115 (1996) 219–240, M.A. Sweeney, *Isaiah 1–39* (1996), B.S. Childs, *Isaiah* (2001).

[30] J.P. Fokkelman, "The Cyrus Oracle (Isaiah 44:24–45:7) from the Perspectives

Common for many of the above mentioned studies to the nations
material is their focus on the question of unity. Works referred to
here as belonging to the recent perspective do not focus on historical matters to such an extent that is the case for the more traditionally oriented studies. Although their methodological approaches
vary, recent Isaianic studies of the nations material all seem to have
the book in its final form as their object of investigation.

1.2. Isaiah 18:1–7

Of all the nations material in the book of Isaiah presented in 1.1.,
this study will concentrate on chapter 18. Isa 18:1–7 belongs to the
nations material as it opens and ends with a reference to a remote
nation to Israel/Judah: Cush. As a whole, however, the text could
be likened with a collection of loosely connected film-shots. Different
scenes are described from strophe to strophe, and it is not always
clear how the scenes are related, and how the text in its final form
should be perceived.

There are several reasons why Isa 18 deserves an analysis. First,
not only has the nations material in general received little scholarly
attention, among this material, Isa 18 in particular has not been
studied to any certain extent.[31] Although J.D.W. Watts exaggerates,
he is right when it comes to the lack of attention Isa 18 has met
within the scholarly milieu: "There is a remarkable *lacuna* in the literature on this passage."[32] Second, as Isa 18 contains a number of

---

of Syntax, Versification and Structure", *Studies in the Book of Isaiah* (1997) 303–323,
320: "[. . .] I do not mean the historical Cyrus here, but rather the object of the
song, the character in the universe evoked by the lyric." Only vaguely, Fokkelman
refers to history, p. 323: "[. . .] God's creating the universe and writing history."

[31] Isa 18 has of course been dealt with by commentators, but no monograph has
been published with view to this text. Cf. G.I. Davies, "The Destiny of the Nations
in the Book of Isaiah", *The Book of Isaiah* (1989) 93: "There is very little in the
standard textbooks on prophecy about the oracles against foreign nations and related
material, despite their evident theological interest, and even detailed studies in this
area are rare [. . .]". An example of a scholar who neglects Isa 18 in his study of
Isa 1–39 is R. Kilian, *Jesaja 1–39* (1983). His study does not have any references
to Isa 18 although one of his main chapters, pp. 40–97, deals with Zion (cf. 18:7).

[32] Cf. J.D.W. Watts, *Isaiah 1–33* (1985) 243. (Watts' italics). It should be mentioned that works concerned about Africa and Africans in the Old Testament of
course include a reading of Isa 18. Such studies do however not insist on being
detailed investigations of individual texts—they have a wider perspective, cf. for
instance D.T. Adamo, *Africa and Africans in the Old Testament* (1998), and R.S. Sadler,
"Can a Cushite Change His Skin? An Examination of Race, Ethnicity, and Othering
in the Hebrew Bible" (2001).

unresolved textual, translational, methodological and interpretative problems, it deserves a thorough investigation.[33]

Isa 18 has puzzled scholars working either as textual critics, literary critics or redaction critics. On a textual critical level, the Hebrew witnesses vary.[34] Further, scholars working within the framework of literary criticism or redaction criticism have suggested that the text in its final form lays bare signs of a compositional growth. Many of the problems have not been resolved despite much careful study pursued by commentators. Even on a thematic level, there are several suggestions to what the text is all about. Isa 18 is also difficult to translate as it contains some *hapax legomena*. In its beginning and ending (18:1–2 and 7), there is a rather detailed description of the foreign nation Cush, and this has lead scholars to read the text as an oracle of judgement against this nation. The text itself, however, does not explicitly reveal the name of the nation that will be judged (18:5–6).

In order to present the subject of investigation in this work, this entry comprises three parts: (i) an establishing of the boundaries of the text, (ii) a brief history of research to Isa 18:1–7, and (iii) some preliminary observations.

1.2.1. *The text*

The delimitation of the text will be done from two angles: an external and an internal. The external delimitation suggests how Isa 18:1–7 relates to the broader context of the nations material in the book of Isaiah (chs. 13–23), whereas the internal delimitation describes features within chapter 18 that seem to shape the text as an organic whole. First, however, a brief summary of the text's contents.

Isa 18 opens with a הוֹי directed to a land of buzzing wings along the rivers of Cush. Messengers are then commanded to go to this land far away—a land where "a people tall and smooth-skinned" lives (vv. 1–2). Then follows a general address for "all who live on earth" to be attentive when a standard is raised on the mountain, and a signal is heard (v. 3). A message from YHWH to "me" is reported in v. 4. Vv. 5–6 describe YHWH at work in the vineyard destroying twigs with grapes before the grapes are mature. The end

---

[33] This study provides a reading that differs from the "mainstream" interpretations of this text both methodologically and as far as exegetical results are concerned. More about this in sections 1.3.3. and 1.3.4.

[34] In the present study, the textual critical discussion will be done in footnotes alongside the translation of Isa 18:1–7.

of the text foresees representatives from the Cushites bringing a gift
to YHWH on Mount Zion.

In order to describe and make distinctions between the different
parts of the text, this study applies the terms "stanza" and "strophe".[35] Stanza refers to the main divisions of the text, whereas strophe refers to the subdivisions of the text. Each strophe is again made
up by one or several line(s). In Isa 18 there are three stanzas which
will be referred to by roman numbers I, II and III. The three stanzas accommodate all of chapter 18. The first stanza contains the
two first verses of chapter 18, whereas the second stanza comprises
vv. 3–6. The third stanza consists of 18:7. Altogether, there are 6
strophes of Isa 18. The strophes of the text do not fuse with the
verse divisions. The text is divided into stanzas and strophes the following way:

Stanzas	Strophes	Verses
I	1	vv. 1–2
II	2–5	vv. 3–6
III	6	v. 7

The analysis below is pursued verse by verse in order to make the
reading easy.

External delimitation
How does Isa 18:1–7 relate to the broader context of chapters 13–23?
First, chapter 18 is an example of a nations text as it mentions the
remote Cush. The collection of prophecies concerning the nations
(Isa 13–23) is characterised by mentioning foreign entities by name.
Chapters 13–14 concern Babylon, chapters 15–16 Moab, the beginning of chapter 17 starts with addressing Damascus, chapter 18 mentions Cush, chapters 19–20 Egypt, chapter 21 concerns "the Desert
by the Sea", whereas chapter 23 concerns Tyre. In between the
mentioning of foreign nations, the collection also contains words
directed to Israel/Judah, cf. parts of chapters 17 and 22.

---

[35] I have not attempted to make new definitions of the terms "stanza" and "strophe" as I find W.G.E. Watson's elementary definitions sufficiently adequate for my
analysis of Isa 18, cf. W.G.E. Watson, *Classical Hebrew Poetry* (1984/1986) 160–163.
Watson materialises the terms by relating them to house, room and furniture. The
analogy is then: poem = house, stanza = room, and strophes = furniture, see pp.
161–162. Strophe is throughout this study not linked to the rhythm, but simply
used to refer to various parts of Isa 18.

Second, as we have already touched upon, Isa 18:1–7 differs from the majority of addresses in chs. 13–23 by its lack of the common superscription מַשָּׂא X, "pronouncement concerning X". There are ten occurrences of this formula within Isa 13–23 (13:1; 14:28; 15:1; 17:1; 19:1; 21:1; 21:11; 21:13; 22:1; 23:1). Isa 18:1 interrupts this structure by opening with the interjection הוֹי—which seems to be weaker than מַשָּׂא. The הוֹי of Isa 18:1 is the twelfth occurrence of in all twenty-one in the book of Isaiah, but only the second הוֹי out of two that occur within Isa 13–23. The other הוֹי of Isa 13–23 is found in the immediate preceding context, Isa 17:12. Following the הוֹי in 17:12 is a general vision of the destruction of the enemies of YHWH's people, whereas the הוֹי of 18:1 is directed to the land "along the rivers of Cush." There is a shift in addressee from 17:12–14 to 18:1–2. Further, the perspective shifts from the general to the specific, and this together with a shift in scene underlines that a new textual unit is starting by 18:1. In 17:12–14 nations in general are addressed, whereas 18:1–2 describe one specific nation, Cush. Isa 17 has caused great problems to interpreters, and has often been fragmented into a variety of smaller parts that have sometimes been assessed as independent oracles.[36] M.A. Sweeney argues that Isa 17 and 18 are closely related as he sees the overarching structure of the unit extending from 17:1 to 18:7.[37] 17:1 and 19:1 have the common superscription מַשָּׂא X, "pronouncement concerning X", whereas this heading lacks in 18:1. Sweeney also considers chapter 17 and 18 closely related thematically by a common agricultural imagery (17:4–6, 10–11; 18:3–6), and he regards ch. 18 as a typical reference to YHWH's action in human affairs—characteristic for the מַשָּׂא sections.

Third, what follows immediately after Isa 18:1–7 is a מַשָּׂא concerning Egypt (19:1ff.). Again, the heading common for chs. 13–23 opens a new unit. Although the superscription מַשָּׂא X, "pronouncement concerning X", lacks in 18:1 and is present in 19:1, there are thematic similarities between ch. 18 and 19–20 as they all mention nations belonging on the continent of Africa.

---

[36] Cf. O. Kaiser, *Der Prophet Jesaja* (1983) 63–74, and R.E. Clements, *Isaiah 1–39* (1980/1994) 156–163.
[37] M.A. Sweeney, *Isaiah 1–39* (1996) 252–262.

Internal delimitation

I am aware that most scholars working within the framework of traditional historical-critical methods would not regard Isa 18:1–7 as
an integral unit (see 7.1.2. in this research).[38] As this research has
the text in its final form as its point of departure, it is interesting to
see whether or not there are features in the text—as it has been
handed over to us—that delimitate the text. A formal literary device
is the most evident sign of consistency of Isa 18:1–7 as some of v. 2
is repeated in 18:7. In that the text opens and ends with almost the
same wording (vv. 2 and 7), the boundaries of Isa 18:1–7 are thus
set by an *inclusio*. The literary device *inclusio* may have several functions,
and an obvious one is to tie the first and last part of the text together.
In addition, the *inclusio* here seems to gather also the various scenes
of the text together with the opening and ending of the text. As the
audience might be confused by the seemingly lack of order between
the different scenes of Isa 18:1–7, the *inclusio* creates a feeling of stability when collecting the bits together by linking the ending scene
to the beginning scene.[39] Worth noting is that the ending (v. 7) is
not an identical repetition of the opening (v. 2) as the last scene
(v. 7) develops the ideas from the first scene and brings eschatology
into the message.

1.2.2. *Interpretative solutions to Isa 18*

Isa 18:1–7 has almost without exception through the times of scholarly
research been interpreted as an independent oracle of judgement
against either Assyria or Cush/Ethiopia.[40] This research will argue
against the idea that Isa 18 judges Assyria or Cush/Ethiopia (see
the analysis of vv. 5–6 in this book), but it supports the suggestion
that Isa 18:1–7 is a text that pronounces a consistent message (of
judgement). As already mentioned, no monograph has been published
on Isa 18. Two things can be said about the major lines in the his-

---

[38] The repetition of parts of v. 2 in v. 7 would by scholars working within the
framework of *Literarkritik* be just as much an indication of *Fortschreibung* of (parts of)
vv. 1–6 as of the literary device of *inclusio*. As the aim of this study is to contribute
to a literary reading of Isa 18 in its final form, it is not adequate to go into the
debate of the text's eventual process of growth.

[39] By "audience", this work refers to readers at the time when the Old Testament
was completed. See 1.3.2. in this book for a discussion about the text's historical
meaning.

[40] For references, see the analysis of Isa 18:5 in this book.

tory of interpretation of Isa 18. First, the majority of scholars interpret Isa 18 as a message of judgement against a specific nation.[41] Second, when commentators encounter the term Cush (18:1), most of them go into questions about the historical and geographical background of this entity—at the expense of a discussion of how Cush functions as a literary motif.[42] This entry contains two main parts. First, I will briefly refer to the various solutions to whom the metaphoric language of vv. 5–6 is understood to hit—regardless of their interpretative point of departure. Second, I will notice whether or not there are any relations between traditional historical critical readings of Isa 18, on the one hand, and contributions from the perspective of various recent approaches, on the other hand.

The diverging interpretative solutions of Isa 18 all depart from an understanding of Isa 18:5–6, as these two verses contain important information to the understanding of the text. Isa 18:5–6 contains a scene of judgement, but it is not explicitly stated to whom the doom is directed. Commentators can be categorised into four groups according to their interpretation of vv. 5–6—and subsequently of Isa 18 as a whole. Let me briefly refer to the solutions from these groups.[43] The majority of commentators see Isa 18:1–7 as an independent oracle of judgement against Assyria. A smaller group of commentators—and not the majority, as B.S. Childs claims—proposes the remote nation Cush to be doomed by YHWH.[44] Some scholars in this group define the term Cush as Egypt *and* Cush, whereas others do not include Egypt when they refer to Cush. A third group of scholars sees the judgement referred to in Isa 18:5–6 as directed towards the Judeans. The fourth and last group of scholars hesitates to suggest any addressee at all for YHWH's judgement as described in 18:5–6. What can be said about these four solutions? First, in all

---

[41] The nation that is to receive judgement according to Isa 18:5–6 is not necessarily the same as the addressee of the message as a whole. The addressee of the message is by most scholars seen as Judah, whereas the judged nation is regarded to be found outside the borders of Judah, cf. H. Wildberger, *Jesaja 13–27* (1978) 690, and U. Becker, *Jesaja* (1997) 276.

[42] As will be evident, this study emphasises how Cush is applied as a literary motif, and will as such contribute with another perspective on the text. Later in this study it is appropriate to present and discuss how commentators have treated the term Cush.

[43] References to scholars belonging to each group will be given in the analysis of vv. 5–6 in this book.

[44] B.S. Childs, *Isaiah* (2001) 136.

four groups one finds the presupposition that Isa 18 refers to political alliances in the eighth century B.C. Reading Isa 18 as an historical record implies that elements *outside* the text serve as a basis
for drawing conclusions about the textual meaning. The dating of
the text (or the dating of the events the text is seen to refer to)
stands out as more central than an analysis of motifs and themes
present in the text.[45] Second, in all four groups of commentators,
one can thus find that there is a disparity between analyses and conclusions about the textual meaning. My impression is that conclusions
about the textual meaning are drawn on the basis of insufficient
exegetical discussion. This focus on events outside the text is probably
due to (i) the strong position of historical critical methods in Old
Testament studies, and to (ii) the fact that Isa 18 is a difficult text to
translate, and that it at a first glance seem to be a collection of loosely
connected scenes—difficult to perceive as related to one another.

Turning to the second entry of this section, are there any relations between traditional historical critical readings of Isa 18 on the
one hand, and contributions from the perspective of various recent
approaches to Isa 18, on the other hand? Somewhat surprisingly,
also quite recent commentators (to Isa 18) emphasise discussions of
history/geography. This can on the one side be due to the fact that
not *all* recent contributions make use of recent approaches. In addition, the reason why elements outside the text seem to be of importance to the understanding of this text is (i) the reference to the
remote nation Cush (18:1), and (ii) a metaphoric language in vv.
5–6. With the exception of those not wanting to propose any specific
nation at all, all scholars include a discussion of who the metaphoric
language of vv. 5–6 is meant to hit (for references, see my analysis
of vv. 5–6). The difference between traditional and recent interpretations of Isa 18, however, is that the latter group of scholars are *less
certain* about factors outside the text than what seems to be the case
for their former colleagues. To illustrate what has just been said, let
us look at a few examples. Of recent contributions to the understanding of Isa 18, W. Brueggemann talks about the rhetoric of the

---

[45] Gottwald is an example of this as he concludes without giving any textual evidence for his view: "Isaiah alludes to the defeat of Egypt and her allies without
actually stating it." Cf. N.K. Gottwald, *All the Kingdoms of the Earth* (1964) 163.
Gottwald uses historical knowledge of the Ancient Near East in combination with
theological exegesis of the Old Testament to illuminate the text, cf. N.K. Gottwald,
idem, xi.

text, but seems at the same time to wish that the text were more accurate about historical information: "The oracle is exceedingly obscure, both because of the elusive images that are used and because we do not know enough to grasp any historical allusions that may be offered."[46] Even though Brueggemann has published his commentary in recent years, he is still occupied with the text's relations to historical events. However, one change between older and younger commentaries to Isa 18 is that recent commentators are less conclusive compared to their former colleagues, and that recent contributors seem to look for a textual basis for their conclusions: "We may assume, in context, that the campaign concerns Ethiopia, but nothing is said of that."[47] Another late current commentator, B.S. Childs, affirms both synchronic and diachronic dimensions in his commentary on the book of Isaiah.[48] In his analysis of the final form of Isa 18, he criticises solutions from form critics and redaction critics, nevertheless, his analysis draws insights from traditional historical critical approaches.[49] Childs credits M.A. Sweeney for assuming an overarching structure of chapter 17 alongside with chapter 18, and applies the same delimitation as Sweeney in his own analysis. Sweeney regards Isa 17–18 as presupposing specific historical events, and working within the framework of form criticism, his study belongs to the traditional historical critical mode of reading even though his contribution is quite recent.[50]

This similarity between traditional and recent approaches when it comes to the understanding of Isa 18 is, as already said, probably due to the enigmatic nature of the text. Being enigmatic, the text invites the reader to speculate in questions such as who are described, what is their mission, who is to be judged, etc.? If one can find adequate answers to questions, one can come close to what the text as a whole is all about. In my view, the understanding of vv. 5–6 is vital for the understanding of the text as a whole. However, as the text never expresses explicitly who are to be judged, one can never be absolutely sure about *who* were meant to be hit by the harsh message

---

[46] W. Brueggemann, *Isaiah 1–39* (1998) 152.

[47] *Ibid.* 153.

[48] B.S. Childs, *Isaiah* (2001) 133–139.

[49] *Ibid.* 133–139. This is seen both in his use of traditional historical critical terminology (First, Second and Third Isaiah), and that his final insights would not be meaningful without the earlier discussions.

[50] M.A. Sweeney, *Isaiah 1–39* (1996) 252–262.

of doom (18:5–6). My solution to the problem can therefore be regarded as just as hypothetical by nature as any other solution put forward. Nevertheless, I will in the following bring arguments that Judah is above all the *most probable* goal for YHWH's punishment as referred to in Isa 18:5–6. The major difference between my understanding of Isa 18, on the one hand, and previous and recent commentators' interpretations as referred to above, on the other hand, is that my understanding is based on an analysis of the text's design, motifs, and rhetoric, and *not* by factors outside the text (such as geography and history).[51] This work will show that Isa 18 is designed this particular way in order to entrap the audience to think that somebody else will be judged, and not themselves. The next paragraph will point at some preliminary textual observations, and the ambition throughout the work is to put forward *arguments* for the present interpretative stance.

1.2.3. *Some preliminary observations*

So far in 1.2., we have looked at the delimitation of Isa 18, and at some interpretative solutions this text has been subject to. Let us now give some indications to how the present work understands this text.

As already said, a preliminary reading of Isa 18 shows that this chapter contains several scenes showing a variety of episodes. At a first glance, the text seems not to embody a unified message—rather it looks disordered and enigmatic, and it is difficult to defend that the text as a whole makes sense.[52] However, I will suggest that the key to understanding the text as a whole lies in the interpretation of

---

[51] I will not be able to divorce the analysis completely from factors outside the text as long as the text seems to refer to relations between nations, and evidently describes one foreign nation vividly. However, my project is not to reconstruct historical events the text might refer to, rather my emphasis lies on textual design, literary motifs and themes, and how these function to create a persuasive rhetoric.

[52] Cf. B.S. Childs, *Isaiah and the Assyrian Crisis* (1967) 45: "This oracle is one of the most perplexing in the whole Isaianic collection. It is filled with lexicographical and form critical problems which continue to resist a clear interpretation." See also H.M. Wolf, *Interpreting Isaiah* (1985) 121: "Although the prophecy is a short one, it probably ranks as the most obscure chapter in this entire section", W. Brueggemann, *Isaiah 1–39* (1998) 152: "The oracle is exceedingly obscure [. . .]", and H.T. Aubin, *The Rescue of Jerusalem* (2003) 228: "[. . .] the biblical passage, however, is genuinely puzzling." There are however voices who regard this text (at least vv. 1–6) as a magnificent poem both by means of form and content—one of the best of Isaiah, cf. Aa. Bentzen, *Jesaja* (1944) 143: "Med v. 6 er det pragtfulde digt, bade formelt og hvad indholdet angaar et av Jesajas bedste, klart afsluttet."

18:5–6. Could Isa 18:1–7 be understood as a warning to Judah against seeking human alliance partners, and a request to hold on to YHWH? Some clues seem to hint at a deliberate shape of the text. Vv. 5–6 show a dramatic scene with YHWH at work in the vineyard, and the understanding of these two verses is by this reader regarded as vital for the interpretation of Isa 18 as a whole. The various scenes find their place when vv. 5 and 6 are interpreted as YHWH's judgement of the Judeans, and not the Cushites or any other foreign nation. Let us briefly look at some signs to the text's consistency.

First, vv. 5–6 unfold a dramatic scene. The growth of the vine grapes from blossom to grapes just about ready to be harvested is described: כי־לפני קציר "For, at harvest time," כתם־פרח "when the bud has been completed," ובסר גמל יהיה נצה "and [the] sour grape[s] [are] ripen. . ." Then, three verbs are applied when the destruction of the parts of the vine are described: כרת qal, "cut off", סור hiphil, "turn aside", and חזז hiphil, "strike away." V. 5: "He will cut off the quivering tendrils with pruning knives, and he will turn aside [and] strike away the twigs." The subject is "he" for all three verbs. The shift from 1st person singular in v. 4 to 3rd person masculine singular in v. 5 underlines the drama described. The atmosphere created by these verbs is negative. Whether "he" is YHWH or not is not explicitly stated, but from the context it seems likely that the suffixes for 3rd person masculine singular refer to YHWH as the stanza as a whole (vv. 3–6) proposes to report a message from YHWH. This contrasting picture of growth and extermination in v. 5 becomes the dramatic centre of the text. V. 6 continues the negative scene of death (in v. 5) by describing how the birds of prey of heaven and the beasts of the earth shall be over the dead vine tendrils and twigs all year. This description of a destruction of parts of the vine (in v. 6) functions to strengthen the message of doom already given in v. 5.

Second, this text's scene of (swift) messengers travelling between Judah and Cush gives the impression not only of diplomacy, but of diplomacy of urgency (v. 2): "Go, swift messengers to a nation tall and smooth-skinned, to a people feared from that day and onwards, [to] a nation line upon line and down-treading, whose land rivers cut through." Much information (about the Cushites and their land) on few lines creates an hectic atmosphere. YHWH's calmness described in v. 4 contrasts the hurry of Cush (v. 1) and Judah (v. 2), and functions to show a great distance between YHWH and his people (v. 4):

"For thus says YHWH to me: I will be quite and gaze in my dwelling place, like glowing heat of [the] light, like a cloud of dew in [the] heat of harvest." From this follows that YHWH acts in a clear way to make Judah understand that her plans are wrong in the eyes of her deity. The devastating judgement (described through the ruining of grapes, vv. 5–6) functions to startle Judah, and to show her how total the catastrophe will be if she goes after human coalition partners, and not trusts YHWH.

Accordingly, having made a preliminary reading of this particular chapter, I have got the impression of a text with *one* superior aim, namely to persuade the Judeans to keep to YHWH and avoid the foreign people from Cush. It is my contention that the text— despite its focus on the remote nation Cush at the beginning and end—contains a message of judgement towards Judah. By letting the remote power frame the message as a whole, the audience is ensnared to believe that the message is directed towards the Cushites. However, the strong dramatic scene in vv. 5–6 puts the emphasis on the grapes, and brings the message of judgement towards someone else. Here, as many other places in the Old Testament, vine and vineyards are applied metaphorically for the relationship between YHWH and the people (cf. Isa 5:1–7; Jer 2:21; Ps 80:8–16).[53] The design of the text can best be described as a rhetoric of entrapment.[54] This rhetoric of entrapment has thus an overall theological aim; to persuade the Judeans to put their trust in YHWH only, and not in human powers. The theological message of Isa 18:1–7 is therefore: Disobedience has its dire consequences, and Judah has to choose YHWH as her alliance partner before it is too late. The textual observations referred to here concerning the rhetoric of entrapment of Isa 18:1–7, have not been touched on in previous studies on this chapter. A few commentators have suggested that the judgement described in 18:5–6 should be applied to Judah, rather than Cush, Assyria or other powers, but as long as they have not presented arguments for understanding the text this way, I believe there is need for a thorough

---

[53] Cf. C.E. Walsh, *The Fruit of the Vine* (2000) 2: "[. . .] images of vines, vineyards, and grape clusters throughout the Bible are used to convey the nature of relationships between Yahweh and his people [. . .]." For a presentation of how metaphoric speech about vine and vineyards are applied throughout the Old Testament, see the analysis of v. 5 in this study.

[54] The terminology is taken from R. Alter, *The Art of Biblical Poetry* (1985/1990) 144. For a definition of the terminology, see 1.3.4. in this study.

investigation. I will therefore in the following chapters make a closer
analysis of Isa 18:1–7, and this will, hopefully, shed some light on
what appears to me as a somewhat overlooked text in the book of
Isaiah.

1.3. METHOD

Before the detailed analysis of Isa 18 can start, it is necessary to make
some methodological considerations. This entry contains four parts
that all deal with methodological issues. Isa 18 is a rhetorical composition, and my aim is to see *how* the chapter is designed in order
to persuade an audience. Unfortunately, there is still little knowledge
about principles in ancient Semitic rhetoric. However, it is my contention that it *is* possible to make a rhetorical analysis of the text
even though the information about ancient Semitic rhetoric is meagre.

Although the study of rhetoric is a classical discipline, the contemporary methodologies of biblical rhetorical criticism are relatively
recent.[55] In the latter half of the twentieth century, an interest in
the rhetorical shape of Old Testament texts arose, and some of the
tools developed can be found within the framework of biblical rhetorical criticism. The term rhetorical criticism is used in many ways.[56]
I do not find it necessary to provide a full presentation of all the
different types of rhetorical criticism. Nor do I find it necessary to
present what provided the background of what came to be called
biblical rhetorical criticism.[57] What is important, however, is to sketch
some main principles of biblical rhetorical criticism in order to clarify my own rhetorical approach.

---

[55] The term "biblical" will not appear unless it is needed for emphasis, clarity,
or contrast with the classical discipline.

[56] Behind the label "rhetorical criticism", a diversity of more or less different
approaches are hiding, cf P. Trible, *Rhetorical Criticism* (1994) 61: "[. . .] the plural-
ism of contemporary rhetorical criticism resides in biblical scholarship."

[57] There are some examples of attempting to sketch the background and development of rhetorical criticism, one of them to be found in D. Patrick & A. Scult,
Rhetoric and Biblical Interpretation (1990). Another more systematic and more recent is
done by P. Trible, *Rhetorical Criticism* (1994) 5–23. The following presentation is
indebted to her overview. Other studies that discuss the various lines of rhetorical
criticism are C.C. Black, "Keeping up with recent studies XVI. Rhetorical criticism
and biblical interpretation", *ET* 100 (1989) 252–258, T.B. Dozeman, "Rhetoric and
Rhetorical Criticism. Old Testament Rhetorical Criticism", *ABD* 5 (1992) 712–715,
and J.R. Lundbom, *Jeremiah* (1997) xix–xliii.

1.3.1. *Two understandings of rhetoric*

J. Muilenburg's presidential address to the Society of Biblical Literature in 1968, together with other publications of his, inaugurated a new interest in the subject of rhetoric.[58] Muilenburg himself modestly wanted to suggest rhetorical criticism as a supplement to and an extension of the method form criticism. However, his address gave rise to a full-fledged Old Testament discipline that has later been practised in different ways.[59] The differences seem to relate to two distinct—although not incompatible—understandings of rhetoric. One understanding sees rhetoric as the art of composition, the other as the art of persuasion.[60] Both understandings exhibit different styles and emphases.

In the following, I will first present Muilenburg's ideas from his address in 1968 as these are the basis for the methodological approach of Old Testament rhetorical criticism that sees rhetoric as the art of composition. Second, Y. Gitay and R.J. Clifford will represent the part of Old Testament rhetorical criticism that understands rhetoric as the art of persuasion. Third, a synthetic approach of the two understandings will be suggested in order to put my own rhetorical approach on the map.

a) *Rhetoric as the art of composition*

In his presidential address at the annual meeting of the Society of Biblical Literature in 1968, J. Muilenburg presented his program of a "rhetorical criticism" that intended to supplement form criticism.[61] However, not only form criticism constituted the background for his SBL proposal.[62] Although the name of the endeavour was new, both Muilenburg and others had been occupied with the aesthetics of Old Testament texts long before the year of this address.[63]

---

[58] J. Muilenburg, "Form Criticism and Beyond", *JBL* 88 (1969) 1–18.

[59] Cf. P. Trible, *Rhetorical Criticism* (1994) 32.

[60] *Ibid.* 32–48.

[61] J. Muilenburg, "Form Criticism and Beyond", *JBL* 88 (1969) 1–18.

[62] Classical rhetoric, secular literary critical theories, biblical literary studies together with form criticism were components that made up the background for his proposal.

[63] Cf. the classic work of J.G. von Herder, *Vom Geist der ebräischen Poesie 1 & 2* (1827), which is an early example of the study on the "inner spirit" of ancient Hebrew poetry. What Muilenburg labelled "rhetorical criticism" had also earlier been done in the literary tradition of R. Lowth, *Lectures on the Sacred Poetry of the Hebrews* (1995), and R.G. Moulton, *The Literary Study of the Bible* (1895/1899), and

Muilenburg's enterprise opened for a new frontier where the text in its *final form* was emphasised more strongly than had been done earlier. By his reuse of the classical term rhetoric, Muilenburg inaugurated an interest in rhetoric that is still developing. However, the fact that Muilenburg never developed a comprehensive theory about rhetorical criticism, this has led rhetorical critics after him in different directions, and have caused confusion as to what can be called rhetorical criticism and what can not. This has again led to the situation that scholars, when defining rhetorical criticism, very often have defined what it is not, e.g. not classical rhetoric, not form criticism, not tradition history etc. P. Trible sums the situation after Muilenburg up well, stating that: "A plethora of rhetorical perspectives allows the Muilenburg mode a place to be without mandating that it stay in its place."[64]

What does the Muilenburg program consist of? Muilenburg's rhetorical criticism does not appear as a comprehensive system. As he proposed his method at a relatively late stage in his career, many of Muilenburg's works show how the methodological insights for a long time had evolved.[65] His commentary on Isaiah 40–66, published in 1956, applied rhetorical criticism extensively.[66] What, then, characterises Muilenburg's work with Old Testament texts? First, the task of the rhetorical critic is to define the limits of a literary unit by using the criteria of form and content. Discovering literary devices such as climax, *inclusio* and *chiasmus* assists the critic in this task. Second, the structure of the unit needs to be discerned. In order to describe the structure, the critic needs to delineate the overall design and individual parts of the unit, and to show how they relate. He/she also needs to identify literary devices and explicate their function within the unit.

---

in the stylistics of E. König, *Stilistik, Rhetorik, Poetik in Bezug auf die biblische Litteratur* (1900), and more recently L. Alonso Schökel, *Estudios de poética Hebrea* (1963), idem, *A Manual of Hebrew Poetics* (1988). For examples of scholars who proceed Muilenburg, and who—like him—are occupied with keywords, motifs, *inclusios, chiasmi* etc., see a listing in J.R. Lundbom, *Jeremiah* (1997) xxvi–xxxi.

[64] P. Trible, *Rhetorical Criticism* (1994) 62.

[65] For a report on selected works by Muilenburg, see T.F. Best (ed.), *Hearing and Speaking the Word: Selections from the Works of James Muilenburg* (1984).

[66] Cf. J. Muilenburg, "The book of Isaiah: Chapters 40–66", *Interpreter's Bible* 5 (1956) 381–419; 422–773. For a short presentation of Muilenburg's rhetorical analysis of Isa 40–66, see P. Trible, *Rhetorical Criticism* (1994) 29–31.

Muilenburg's rhetorical approach to Old Testament texts came to be a pattern for scholars succeeding him. One example of a scholar working within the Muilenburg mode is J.R. Lundbom, who completed his thesis under the direction of Muilenburg.[67] Other examples of scholars following the Muilenburg mode are T. Craven in her study of the Book of Judith,[68] and A.R. Ceresko on 1 Sam 17:34–37.[69] These three studies exhibit different styles and emphases in the study of Old Testament texts, but have in common an understanding of rhetoric as the art of composition. Examples of studies within this methodological framework continue to appear.[70]

b) *Rhetoric as the art of persuasion*

The second understanding defines rhetoric as the art of persuasion. Within this understanding, some scholars accentuate the classical model of rhetoric, while others do not. For both groups, the interest lies in author, text, and audience, and in how a speaker or writer shapes discourse to affect an audience.[71] Y. Gitay's and R.J. Clifford's Isaianic studies will stand as two distinct samples of how Old Testament texts can be analysed with view to an understanding of rhetoric as the art of persuasion.[72] This section will in addition include a brief

---

[67] See J.R. Lundbom, *Jeremiah* (1997). His thesis was first published in 1975.

[68] T. Craven, *Artistry and Faith in the Book of Judith* (1983). Craven diverged from Muilenburg in that she considered rhetorical analysis a complete approach divorced from form criticism.

[69] A.R. Ceresko, "A Rhetorical Analysis of David's 'Boast' (1 Sam 17:34–37)", *CBQ* 47 (1985) 58–74.

[70] Cf. J.K. Kuntz, "The Contribution of Rhetorical Criticism to Understanding Isa 51:1–16", *Art and Meaning* (1982) 140–171, G.J. Polan, *In the Ways of Justice Toward Salvation* (1986), L.C. Allen, "Ezekiel 24:3–14: A Rhetorical Perspective" *CBQ* 49 (1987) 404–414, C.C. Black, "Keeping up with Recent Studies XVI. Rhetorical Criticism and Biblical Interpretation", *ET* 100 (1989) 252–258, R.H. O'Connell, "Deuteronomy 8:1–20: Asymmetrical Concentricity and the Rhetoric of Providence", *VT* 40 (1990) 437–452, R.H. O'Connell, *The Rhetoric of the Book of Judges* (1996), D.J. Reimer, *The Oracles against Babylon in Jeremiah 50–51* (1993), C. Franke, *Isaiah 46, 47, and 48* (1994), P.A. Smith, *Rhetoric and Redaction in Trito-Isaiah* (1995), P. van der Lugt, *Rhetorical Criticism and the Poetry of the Book of Job* (1995).

[71] At this point it is important to stress that rhetoric as the art of composition and rhetoric as the art of persuasion not necessarily excludes one another. On the one hand, it is possible to study a text's composition without studying its persuasion. However, one cannot study a text's persuasive character without saying something about its composition. For the sake of clarity, the two approaches are distinguished in this presentation.

[72] Y. Gitay, *Prophecy and Persuasion* (1981), and R.J. Clifford, *Fair Spoken and Persuading* (1984).

presentation of a few other scholars who see rhetoric as the art of persuasion.

Ten years after Muilenburg's presidential address, Y. Gitay completed his thesis about Isa 40–48. And in his book *Prophecy and Persuasion*, Gitay has developed the views from his thesis about rhetoric as the art of persuasion.[73] In his Aristotelian system of rhetoric he is concerned with the communicative relationship between sender, message and receiver. The study of rhetoric involves these three dimensions, and aims at exploring their mutual relationship in their orientation toward a pragmatic goal.[74] The prophet or rhetor persuades the audience by clothing the message in particular garments. According to Gitay, the literary approach for prophetic material should be rhetoric as this discipline provides literary criteria for exploring the nature and structure of the prophetic addresses.[75] Throughout his textual analysis, Gitay quotes classical rhetoricians, and contemporary rhetoricians who follow the Aristotelian system. This, together with the omission of form critical insights, detaches his analysis from that of Muilenburg.[76]

With his emphasis on persuasion, R.J. Clifford's approach can be aligned with that of Gitay. However, though having "[. . .] learned much from the approach of Gitay [. . .]",[77] Clifford differs from him in that he does not invoke the classical Aristotelian system of rhetoric. The adjective "persuading" applied to the prophet (cf. the title of his commentary on Deutero Isaiah: *Fair Spoken and Persuading*) is by Clifford defined as "[. . .] practical, given to sustained argument to move people to specific action [. . .]".[78] In Clifford's opinion, the

---

[73] Y. Gitay, *idem*. His thesis has the title: "Rhetorical Analysis of Isaiah 40–48: A Study of the Art of Prophetic Persuasion" (1978).

[74] *Ibid.* 35.

[75] *Ibid.* 26–27: "Since DI's [Deutero-Isaiah's] prophecy is a public address, it should be studied as a communicative discourse designed to appeal to its audience." According to Gitay, classical rhetoric from Aristotle on is of course not used by the prophet. However, if the prophetic speech is seen as a communicative discourse, Gitay argues, one can apply principles of selection used to appeal to an audience. In his study of Isa 40–48, Gitay pursues an analysis of four steps. The first step has the headline "Rhetorical Unit", the second "Invention", the third "Organisation", and the fourth "Style". There is little doubt that these headings are influenced by the classical rhetorical scheme where *inventio, dispositio* and *elocutio* are integral parts.

[76] It should here be noted that Gitay applied this approach for prophetic literature only.

[77] R.J. Clifford, *Fair Spoken and Persuading* (1984) 6.

[78] *Ibid.* 4.

prophet is an orator more than a lyric poet: "His eloquent monotheism, his skill in consoling, the force of his ideas and images, long celebrated by commentators, are all subordinate to his task of persuading."[79] In his analysis of Deutero-Isaiah, Clifford's focus lies on showing how the prophet through persuasion wants to make the people of YHWH return to Zion. Though acknowledging a debt to Muilenburg, Clifford has an accent on persuasion rather than on aesthetics and composition. His analysis is separated from that of Muilenburg also by his omission of form criticism.

Although different from each other, the following selected examples of scholars share the principal understanding of rhetoric as the art of persuasion. One example is J. Barton. Even though Barton's article does not include a discussion of theory, his exegetical aims reflect an understanding of rhetoric as the art of persuasion.[80] Another scholar, M.V. Fox, argues that: "Rhetoric is persuasive discourse [. . .]".[81] Rhetorical criticism should, according to Fox, focus on the analysis of "[. . .] the suasive force of discourse rather than on its formal literary features or its structure."[82] Fox does however not have a preference for classical rhetoric: "[. . .] in Israel we have a well-documented major rhetorical movement entirely independent of the classical tradition from which Western rhetoric and rhetorical criticism descend."[83] In his deconstructionist reading of the Book of Job, D.J.A. Clines uses the general concept of rhetoric as the art of persuasion. He sees persuasion as the overarching effect in the book of Job that triumphs over logic and fact.[84] D. Patrick and A. Scult also advocate a rhetorical model that has an accent on persuasion rather than on structure and style.[85] Works within the understanding of rhetoric as the art of persuasion continue to appear.[86]

---

[79] *Ibid.* 4.

[80] J. Barton, "History and Rhetoric in the Prophets", *The Bible as Rhetoric* (1990) 51–64, 52: "The genius of the classical prophets was to take the highly recalcitrant facts of history, [. . .] and to give an account of these facts which would *convince* people [. . .] that the hand of God could be seen in them [. . .]" (My italics).

[81] M.V. Fox, "The Rhetoric of Ezekiel's Vision of the Valley of the Bones", *HUCA* 51 (1980) 2.

[82] *Ibid.* 1.

[83] *Ibid.* 5.

[84] D.J.A. Clines, "Deconstructing the Book of Job", *The Bible as Rhetoric* (1990) 65–80.

[85] D. Patrick and A. Scult, *Rhetoric and Biblical Interpretation* (1990).

[86] Cf. J.H. Hayes & S.A. Irvine, *Isaiah, The Eight-century Prophet* (1987), L. Poland, "The Bible and the Rhetorical Sublime", *The Bible as Rhetoric* (1990) 29–47, R.K.

c) *Rhetoric as the art of composition and persuasion—a synthetic approach*

The paragraphs a) and b) above have showed that most scholars
define rhetoric *either* as the art of persuasion *or* as the art of composition. There are however examples of scholars who apply a combination of the two understandings of rhetoric in their studies. This
synthetic approach is my own way of pursuing rhetorical analysis,
and should therefore be presented.

P. Trible will here be singled out as a representative for the small
group of scholars who combine the two approaches of rhetorical criticism presented above. Other examples of scholars using a synthetic
method in their studies are B. Wiklander,[87] R.H. O'Connell,[88] B.C.
Jones,[89] and K. Möller.[90] Although Trible considers herself as belonging to the Muilenburg mode of rhetorical criticism, she differs from
Muilenburg in various ways. First, she does not work within the
framework of form criticism, rather she consults this and other historical critical methods when she finds them illuminating.[91] Second,
although departing from Muilenburg's accent on the aesthetics of
the text, she goes beyond him by focusing on the text's persuasiveness, too.

Her book on rhetorical criticism comprises of two main parts. Part
one sets the context of rhetorical analysis in the past and present,
whereas part two presents the method and her own close reading
of the book of Jonah. Trible's rhetorical analysis of the book of
Jonah, and even the way her book *Rhetorical Criticism. Context, Method,*

Duke, *The Persuasive Appeal of the Chronicler* (1990), adheres to the Aristotelian tradition (cf. pp. 37–39), whereas C.S. Shaw, *The Speeches of Micah* (1993), follows Fox's
definition of rhetoric (see p. 22, footnote 3 in Shaw). See also K. Möller, *A Prophet
in Debate* (2003) 2, who examines "[. . .] the communicative function of the *book* of
Amos" (his italics), and further, on p. 294, where he states that the texts in the
book of Amos have been compiled "[. . .] for a specific persuasive purpose."

[87] B. Wiklander, *Prophecy as Literature* (1984).

[88] R.H. O'Connell, *Concentricity and Continuity* (1994).

[89] B.C. Jones, *Howling over Moab* (1996).

[90] K. Möller, *A Prophet in Debate* (2003). Although Möller is already included in
the group of scholars that regards rhetoric as the art of persuasion, he is at the
same time occupied with what he calls "rhetorical structure" in the book of Amos,
and therefore he also needs to be mentioned here (p. 49): "[. . .] any structural
investigation must consider not only a text's structure per se, but also what purpose it is meant to be serving."

[91] P. Trible, *Rhetorical Criticism* (1994) cf. 107–108, and 161 where she briefly consults several historical critical methodologies in order to examine how they contribute to the analysis of the book of Jonah.

and the Book of Jonah is structured shows that she is influenced by
both Muilenburg's rhetorical approach and by classical rhetoric.[92]
Some chapters are chiastically structured, and the whole of part two
is shaped as an *inclusio*. She explains what she is doing in terms of
the classical categories of rhetoric.[93]

Trible works along the lines of a synthetic approach regarding
rhetoric as both the art of composition and persuasion. She even
proposes that the Old Testament text uses parts of the classical scheme
of rhetoric. This is explicitly stated in the last of her many summaries:
"Through "artful words" Yhwh seeks to persuade Jonah, judge and
complainant, to make a right decision about past events. [. . .] In
shaping the rhetoric Yhwh appropriates the five skills of the classical orator."[94]

As will be evident later (see 1.3.3. and 1.3.4. in this research), the
synthetic approach pursued in this work is not identical with Trible's.
However, her focus on the text's persuasiveness *alongside* with her eye
for the text's aesthetics is what will be sought for in the present study
of Isa 18:1–7.[95]

1.3.2. *Presuppositions of the following rhetorical analysis*

Four presuppositions of rhetorical criticism need to be uncovered before
I can present the rhetorical model applied in this work.[96]

First, this book presupposes the assumption that there is something
that can be called *an Old Testament rhetoric*. For Europeans, the classical
or Graeco-Roman rhetoric is the prevailing rhetoric. However, the
lack of a textbook in the fashion of Aristotle in Old Testament
rhetoric does not mean that an Old Testament rhetoric does not
exist. Much has been done in this area over the years, even though

---

[92] Trible is however closer tied to the Muilenburg mode than to the classical
rhetoric. This is evident from the many explicit and implicit references throughout
her work to Muilenburg's way of pursuing rhetorical criticism.

[93] Cf. for example P. Trible, *Rhetorical Criticism* (1994) 121.

[94] See *ibid.* 224. Her point is not that the book of Jonah is shaped from the pattern of classical rhetoric, rather she exemplifies the universal nature of rhetoric by
showing how certain rhetorical clues existed in Old Testament rhetoric—long before
the classical rhetoricans systematised them.

[95] Cf. *ibid.* 107–244, 225: "In teaching rhetoric as the art of composition, the book
of Jonah unfolds rhetoric as the art of persuasion. What more can the reader want?"

[96] Although his rhetorical analysis differs from mine, R. Meynet points to some
of the same presuppositions of rhetorical analysis in his study of biblical texts, cf.
R. Meynet, *Rhetorical Analysis* (1998) 168–181.

the historical critical methods did not make Old Testament rhetoric a prioritised field of investigation. R. Lowth's lectures on the Hebrew poetry in 1753 inaugurated an interest in Old Testament rhetoric—which is still only in its infancy.[97] Since the 1960s, biblical studies have moved from an orientation where the historical critical methods were dominating, to an openness for more literary oriented approaches, and "[. . .] this development constitutes a paradigm shift."[98] It is however not a shift into something new, rather it is a return to an activity that extends "[. . .] from the time of Jerome and before and continuing on with the rabbis and until modern times [. . .]".[99] Throughout the last two or three decades a large number of studies of poetic and narrative Old Testament texts have been published. These studies reflect innumerable methods and points of views, still, they increase our general knowledge of Old Testament rhetoric.[100]

When scholars try to define Old Testament rhetoric they often compare it with classical rhetoric, and looks for similarities or dissimilarities between the two.[101] Some of these findings are the following: Old Testament rhetoric tends to be more concrete than abstract, it uses parataxis[102] more than syntax(is), and it is more involutive than

---

[97] R. Lowth, *Lectures on the Sacred Poetry of the Hebrews* (1995).

[98] P. Trible, *Rhetorical Criticism* (1994) 73.

[99] J. Muilenburg, "Form Criticism and Beyond", *JBL* 88 (1969) 8.

[100] Cf. for example the following selected studies, chronologically listed: J. Muilenburg, "The book of Isaiah: Chapters 40–66", *IntB* 5 (1956) 381–419, 422–773, M. Weinfeld, *Deuteronomy and the Deuteronomic School* (1972), S.A. Geller, *Parallelism in Early Biblical Poetry* (1979), R.J. Clifford, "Rhetorical Criticism in the Exegesis of Hebrew Poetry", *SBL.SP* 19 (1980) 17–28, R. Alter, *The Art of Biblical Narrative* (1981), J.L. Kugel, *The Idea of Biblical Poetry* (1981/1998), A. Berlin, *Poetics and Interpretation of Biblical Narrative* (1983), A. Berlin, *The Dynamics of Biblical Parallelism* (1985), R. Alter, *The Art of Biblical Poetry* (1985/1990), S. Prickett, *Words and The Word* (1986/1989), W.G.E. Watson, *Classical Hebrew Poetry* (1984/1986), J. Barton, "Reading the Bible as Literature", *JLT* 1 (1987) 135–153, D.N. Freedman, "Another Look at Biblical Hebrew Poetry", *Directions in Biblical Hebrew Poetry* (1987) 11–28, L. Alonso Schökel, *A Manual of Hebrew Poetics* (1988), R. Rendtorff, "Between Historical Criticism and Holistic Interpretation: New Trends in Old Testament Exegesis", *Congress Volume Jerusalem 1986* (1988) 298–303, R. Alter & F. Kermode (eds.), *The Literary Guide to the Bible* (1989), S. Bar-Efrat, *Narrative Art in the Bible* (1989), H. Fisch, *Poetry with a Purpose* (1988/1990), J.L. Ska, *"Our Fathers Have told Us"* (1990), C. Westermann, *Basic Forms of Prophetic Speech* (1991), H.C. Brichto, *Toward A Grammar of Biblical Poetics. Tales of the Prophets* (1992), W.G.E. Watson, *Traditional Techniques in Classical Hebrew Verse* (1994), A. Berlin, "Introduction to Hebrew Poetry", *NIntB* 4 (1996) 301–315.

[101] An example here is R. Meynet, *Rhetorical Analysis* (1998) 172–177.

[102] The latin term *parataxis* is taken from the Greek *paratassein*, which literally means "to arrange side by side." *Collins English Dictionary* (1979/1994) 1132, defines the term as follows: "The juxtaposition of clauses without the use of a conjunction."

linear.[103] According to classical rhetoric rules of composition, the Old
Testament texts seem badly constructed, or not reflecting a clear
structure at all. As most scholars have been trained in a milieu where
classical rhetoric has been part of the philosophical framework, this
has mislead some Old Testament scholars to think that biblical texts
are inorganic and that they lack an inner logic. The increasing knowledge about Old Testament rhetoric, however, shows that there is an
inner logic to be found in the texts, even though it is somewhat
different from that of the classical rhetoric. When analysed with adequate tools, Old Testament texts seem to be—for the most part—
well composed. This is why it is important to do a rhetorical analysis
on the basis of Old Testament rhetoric, and not on the basis of classical rhetoric. However, I will of course not be able to escape my
cultural heritage, and I thus make use of the classical rhetorical idea
that rhetoric is persuasive. How does my rhetorical analysis relate
to the situation of a not clearly defined Old Testament rhetorical
scheme? In the study of the composition of Hebrew poems, L. Alonso
Schökel suggests the following to be the most appropriate procedure:
"[. . .] the most fruitful approach is to see how clear-sighted and
experienced experts analyze poems and learn by imitation."[104] My
analysis will be but just one little contribution to the still rather unex-
posed field of Old Testament rhetoric.

A second presupposition is that *the text is designed*, and that it for
the most part is well designed.[105] This contrasts some of the presuppositions of historical critical methods. These methods sometimes—
generally speaking—regard biblical texts as inorganic, consisting of
scattered collections of pieces with few links between them.[106] My
presupposition is not that all biblical texts are designed with the same
skilful art, or with the same regularity. However, my contention is
that Isa 18 in its final form is designed in a way that is possible to
describe, and that the text is shaped this way consciously.

---

[103] For an exposition of these points, see R. Meynet, *Rhetorical Analysis* (1998)
172–177.

[104] L. Alonso Schökel, *A Manual of Hebrew Poetics* (1988) 200. He then lists a small
number of scholars, including himself.

[105] Design is here—and throughout this study—defined as the overall architecture of the text, and the organising of the various elements of the text, cf. 1.3.4 in
this study.

[106] It must here be noted that I work with only one relatively short text, and do
neither take into consideration longer units, nor the composition of the whole of
the book of Isaiah.

A third presupposition is that *form and content* are inseparable. There is an inextricable relationship between form and content, just as between the two sides of a coin: "No form appears without content, and no content without form."[107] Throughout the present work, form is defined as the text's design, i.e. how the text is shaped. Content is understood as the meaning of the text, i.e. the unique configuration of details that the interpreter perceives from the text. This interpretation of the text involves the following three elements: authorial meaning, textual meaning, and reader's meaning.[108] The present work has an emphasis on tracing *the text's* meaning. Before this is more explicated (see 1.3.3.), the term *meaning* needs some further definition.

As a text does not speak, it needs a reader to give it a voice. The analogy from P. Ricoeur is helpful at this point: "The text is like a musical score and the reader like the orchestra conductor who obeys the instructions of the notation."[109] The conductor is not to change the notes, but he/she can produce multiple interpretations of one single score. The different interpreters bring various skills, knowledge and sensitivities to the text. The meaning of the words in Isa 18 can only be suggested from their use in the Hebrew language, and the primary source for the Hebrew language in such an endeavour is the Old Testament. The Old Testament is written in the span of several hundred years, and there have been linguistic changes over the years. This makes it difficult to say anything definite about the text's meaning. Can one still search for the text's historical meaning?[110] It may sound naïve that I as a contemporary reader aim at

---

[107] P. Trible, *Rhetorical Criticism* (1994) 92. J. Muilenburg goes as far as stating that form and content are one, cf. J. Muilenburg, "Form Criticism and Beyond", *JBL* 88 (1969) 5. I differ from Muilenburg in the definition of the terms. For Muilenburg, form corresponds with the form critical term *Gattung(en)*, and content has to do with authorial intent.

[108] Throughout this work the terms author, text, and reader are applied alternately with the terms rhetor, message, and audience.

[109] P. Ricoeur, *Interpretation Theory* (1976) 75.

[110] In the search for an historical meaning of Isa 18, I have chosen to place myself among the audience of Isa 18 at a point when the Old Testament was (about to be) completed. For the audience of Isa 18, this means that they knew and could draw on the whole of the Old Testament in their understanding of this specific text. For me as a modern interpreter placing myself among this audience, this enables me to bring in various Old Testament texts—without going into the complex and complicated discussion of every relevant text's dating. This corresponds with the method of literary analysis that the present research has chosen as its point of departure. I am however aware that this position is not uncomplicated. First, as my second opponent at the disputation, Prof. Karl William Weyde, pointed at, one

searching for meaning of an ancient text. I am aware that I can never discern exactly what the text meant for the first listener or reader of Isa 18, neither can I be sure of what the author intended. All interpretations that aim at tracing the historical meaning(s) are hypothetical by nature, and can never be other than possible suggestions of meaning(s). What one can do, however, is to describe what is perceived by the modern reader as the text's meaning, and try to get as close as possible to an historical meaning. My emphasis lies therefore on reader's meaning and textual meaning, with an emphasis on the latter. In other words, in the search for the text's historical meaning, it is impossible to escape the fact that I am a modern reader. It is however my hope that I can suggest (some of) what the historical readers who knew the Old Testament perceived when they read Isa 18. As will be evident from the analysis, the main focus is on the text, rather than on author or reader. Nevertheless, the author and reader are still essential elements in an interpretation of the text simply because there is an author who has composed the text, and because I encounter the text as a contemporary "flesh-and-blood-reader".[111]

The fourth presupposition in my rhetorical analysis has to do with a preference for *the text in its final form*. Isa 18:1–7 will be interpreted as it now appears. Such a synchronic approach does however not exclude a diachronic reflection.[112] This work will evaluate the findings of historical critical disciplines in light of the synchronic findings. Every Old Testament text has both literary and historical qualities in that they are texts from the past.[113] Although an analysis of the final

---

could ask if this stance of mine implies that the earlier audience(s) of Isa 18 were unable to understand the text—as it can look as if one needs to know *all* of the Old Testament in order to comprehend Isa 18. I will stress that it is my opinion that Isa 18 expressed its message also before the Old Testament was (about to be) completed. Second, one could also argue that the modern reader who applies all of the Old Testament in searching for the meaning of one specific text, works under the risk of reading too much into the text in question. There is always a danger of "over-interpretation", and I am aware that I belong in the 21st century, and that I encounter the text with different presuppositions than those in the centuries B.C.E. However, it is my contention that for a modern interpreter, the danger of reading too little into the text/not grasping all that the text communicates, is larger than the danger of reading too much into the text.

[111] An expression borrowed from P. Trible, *Rhetorical Criticism* (1994) 99.

[112] That diachronic and synchronic approaches can supplement each other is recently suggested by L.C. Jonker, *Exclusivity and Variety* (s.a.) [1996], and also by the historical critical scholar R.G. Kratz, *Die Komposition der erzählenden Bücher des Alten Testaments* (2000) 5.

[113] Cf. T. Stordalen, "'Bibel og litteratur' i nyere GT-forskning", *TTK* 2 (1992) 124.

form of Isa 18 is the main task, this study will nevertheless show that others have seen *features in the text* that—in their view—show the text's development through time. These features are pointed at by scholars working within the framework of traditional historical critical approaches, and as long as I go into a dialogue with scholars before me who have studied Isa 18, I will encounter some diachronic questions.

This study does not work along the lines that want to improve the Masoretic Text by means of correcting it or remove "later additions" in order to establish an "original" text. MT is not always intelligible—sometimes it is obscure, and there can be disruptions and oppositions that seem difficult to explain for a reader living in a different culture from the Semitic, and in a different time. However, unlike scholars working within the approach of tradition-history, I do not examine development and transmission. And unlike literary critics/source critics, I do not examine antecedent literary strands. Here it must be added that I do not deny that there most likely has been a process of composition of Old Testament texts and books— often at several hands. What I resist doing in my study of Isa 18 is to trace its eventual compositional process. Having said this, I do not, however, reject the historical critical undertaking of textual criticism. Sometimes, the witnesses are ambiguous and obscure to such an extent that a textual critical discussion is demanded. Textual criticism should be applied in order to decide and be definite about *which* text is studied.

1.3.3. *The rhetorical model pursued in this book*

So far in chapter 1.3. we have touched methodological considerations for a rhetorical analysis. Now, it is time for presenting the rhetorical model that is pursued in the present work. I am engaged in studying the aesthetics of Isa 18. At the same time, however, I want to seize the text's persuasive power. In my opinion, the text is a piece of *persuasive artistry*.[114] In my view, design and persuasiveness are two sides of the same coin. This study will subsequently *combine* the two understandings of rhetoric referred to above in order to address the text with adequate questions.

---

[114] The wording is borrowed from the book title: D.F. Watson (ed.), *Persuasive Artistry* (1991).

The reading method practised in this book owes much to the literary approaches to the Bible published in the last three decades.[115] However, as this work pursues a synthetic approach of rhetoric, the relations to the Muilenburg program on the one hand, and to the classical rhetoric on the other hand need to be defined. Some will argue that rhetorical criticism from Muilenburg on is already outdated, and that my reading of Isa 18 does not reflect the contemporary methodological development in Old Testament studies. In my choice of a methodological approach, it implicitly lies an exclusion of other approaches.[116]

Muilenburg inaugurated an interest in the *final form* of the text that had not been the case to such an extent earlier. As I do an analysis of the text with view to its design and motifs, I am in that respect close to Muilenburg's program. However, as my reading is a way of approaching the text with regard to how the text implies persuasive elements, I differ from Muilenburg at several points. First, my synthetic approach to Isa 18 goes "beyond" Muilenburg in that it combines the two main understandings of rhetorical criticism. Second, I do not work as a form critic, although I gain insights from form criticism and other historical critical methodologies.[117] Third, I

---

[115] Cf. P. Trible, *Rhetorical Criticism* (1994) 73–80, who provides a brief overview of these approaches until the beginning of the 1990s.

[116] What is the relation between my mode of rhetorical criticism and reader response criticism? Regarding the text as a piece of aesthetic was typical for early studies within rhetorical criticism. This way of pursuing the textual analysis differed from form criticism (which it succeeded), and was indebted to New Criticism. The reader response methodology, however, sprang up as a reaction to the objective ideals of analysis of New Criticism. Subjectivity became a decisive premise for understanding the text. As I define rhetoric as both the art of composition and as the art of persuasion, I need to go into a dialogue with the text, and do a reading of it. As an exegete I become the text's reader, or audience. Although I am aware that I encounter the text as a contemporary reader with specific prejudices and a specific world-view, my aim is to put in focus the text as a historical document, and not myself as a modern reader. My emphasis is therefore more on the text than on the reader. What can turn out to be a problem with a hermeneutic that focuses on the reader and his/her response, is a moving away from the text, and a moving away from the world-view the text holds. I do not consider myself as an advocate for reader response criticism, rather I belong to the group of readers who want to trace the text's historical meaning. What is obvious, however, is that the reading process is an interaction between text and reader. In this study, the main emphasis is on the text. Cf. W. Iser, *The Act of Reading* (1978) 170–179, 107–134, who describes the reading process as "[. . .] a *dynamic* interaction between text and reader". (The quote is taken from p. 107, his emphasis).

[117] The literary context of Isa 18 (Isa 13–23) has by form critics been classified

am not concerned with authorial intent, but with textual meaning.[118] Where Muilenburg stressed authorial intention as the aim of the process, this research accents a text-centred focus. Muilenburg's definition of meaning as authorial intent needs some further reflections.

Is meaning restricted to authorial intention? I agree with P. Trible when she states that "[t]he intention of an author does not determine the meaning of a text."[119] In my analysis of Isa 18 I do not intend (!) to divorce author and text, as texts do reveal authors. "Yet authorial intention constitutes a part, not the whole, of meaning. Texts [. . .] may reveal more or less or other than their flesh-and-blood authors intend."[120] For a modern reader, authorial intent is neither possible, nor desirable to discern.[121] Instead of focusing on an author's intentions, this research prefers speaking about the text's design or shape. The text of Isa 18 has a shape that is perceived as persuasive. Implicit in this hermeneutical stance lies the view that searching for a single meaning can no longer be the aim of the interpretation as meaning vary as long as interpreters are not identical. This leads to the rather complex discussion of whether or not unfixed meanings

---

as OAN (oracles against the nations). Although I do not consider this designation a genre (it rather consists of several genres), the form critical approach can serve as a background for a rhetorical study of the final form of the text.

[118] Cf. J. Muilenburg, "Form Criticism and Beyond", *JBL* 88 (1969) 7.

[119] Cf. P. Trible, *Rhetorical Criticism* (1994) 96.

[120] Cf. *ibid.* 96–97. See also K. Nielsen, "Intertextuality and Hebrew Bible", *International Organization for the Study of the Old Testament: Congress Volume 1998* (2000) 18, for a similar view: "The meaning of a text cannot be limited to its author's intention. The text contains meaning potentials that are only realized in the meeting with its readers—both readers of its own time and those much later."

[121] If the author's intention were available, hypothetically speaking, this would nevertheless not have been helpful as long as the text can reveal more or less or other than the author intended. I am however concerned about the text's persuasiveness. My conviction that the text is designed in a specific way in order to persuade an ancient audience causes a methodological problem. As long as I consider the text as shaped in a certain way in order to persuade, do I not then speak of an author's intention? And, is it not most likely an author who has deliberately given the text its shape? First, it is very probable that an author deliberately has given the text its shape in order to persuade an audience. However, to me it is not desirable to go beyond the text and search for this authorial intention. As has already been said, in my study, the emphasis lies on the text more than on the author or reader. Second, what is possible, however, is to describe the ways in which the text is designed. As a modern reader I can for obvious reasons never figure out *exactly* what the text was meant to communicate to an ancient audience. What I as a modern reader can do, however, is to describe how the text is shaped, and subsequently what this shape or design communicates to me. Hopefully, this is not too far from how the ancient audience of Isa 18 perceived the text's message.

of a text open for a potential literary chaos. It will go beyond the limits of an introductory chapter to go into that discussion here. However, having said this, it is still my contention that the understanding of Isa 18 presented in this research is a legitimate and reasonable understanding of the text. The point at this stage is to show that the analysis pursued in this research works at the boundary of text and reader, with emphasis on the former.[122]

Isa 18 does not follow an Aristotelian convention of rhetoric, and will not be analysed by applying a classical rhetorical scheme.[123] What is the relation, then, between classical rhetoric and the analysis pursued in this book? Although there is no direct use of classical rhetoric in this work, the synthetic approach of rhetorical criticism pursued here has relations to classical rhetoric in two respects. First, my rhetorical model is related to the classical rhetoric as it is concerned with a message delivered from a sender to a receiver. The actual message is here the subject of analysis, and not only is "what is said" sought answered, but also "how is the message said". The rhetor knows how to reach the audience by using specific words and by omitting others. Second, the analysis pursued in this book has a relation to classical rhetoric as it is occupied with the text's persuasive character. Apart from this, it has no explicit relations to classical rhetoric.

1.3.4. *Application of the model*

Let us now proceed by looking at how the actual reading of Isa 18 will be pursued in this book. The overall aim of the analysis of Isa 18 is to show the persuasive artistry of the text. Isa 18 shows several signs of persuasion—signs that might not be perceived by the audience before the argumentative piece is brought to an ending. The present study offers an interpretation of Isa 18 premised both on its integrity and on its rhetoric of entrapment.[124] In the course of this interpre-

---

[122] This way of applying rhetorical criticism is also done by P. Trible, *Rhetorical Criticism* (1994).

[123] The classical rhetorical scheme was intended for extensive texts, and even if desirable, it would not be adequate to apply this scheme on the few verses that constitute Isa 18. A recent example where elements from the classical rhetorical scheme are applied on the study of Old Testament texts, is K. Möller's study on the rhetoric of persuasion in the book of Amos, cf. K. Möller, *A Prophet in Debate* (2003).

[124] The term is taken from R. Alter, *The Art of Biblical Poetry* (1985/1990) 144, cf. section 1.2.3. in this study.

tation, indications to support both of these premises will be offered. Practically, the analysis of the text will be pursued from four angles.

First, the *textual design* of Isa 18 will be observed.[125] By textual design I here—and throughout this book—refer to both the arrangement and the interrelation of explicit linguistic and literary elements in the text. Textual design has to do with the architecture of the text. Features that are more or less directly observable from the text's design can for instance include: *inclusio*, parallelism, assonance, alliteration, *onomatopoeia, chiasmus*, play with words, rhyme, enjambment, gapping, poetic technique, etc. Obviously, not all strophes of Isa 18 contain all such characteristics. It therefore varies what features are described from strophe to strophe.

Second, Isa 18 will be analysed with view to its *motifs*. Three literary terms—some have already been used to a certain extent—need to be defined at this stage: text, motif, and theme.[126] The term "text"

---

[125] The technical term "textual design" is here applied about what others would label surface structures, or even *ipsissima verba*. The definition of the term "structure" varies from one methodological approach to the other. On the history of the word "structure", see J.C. Rowe, "Structure", *Critical Terms for Literary Study* (1995) 23–38. As said elsewhere, rhetorical criticism in the Muilenburg mode went beyond form criticism. However, the word "structure" is used with different meanings by both form critics and rhetorical critics, and these meanings differ from the term as used by structuralists. When defining textual design, I am influenced by definitions of "surface structures" done by L. Alonso Schökel, *A Manual of Hebrew Poetics* (1988) 190–193, and W.G.E. Watson, *Classical Hebrew Poetry* (1984/1986) 21 and 88. Under the heading "Obvious composition—The Surface Structure", Alonso Schökel defines surface structures as something that is "clear from explicit linguistic signs, and is therefore neither hidden nor completely absent". As examples of such surface structures, he lists a) alphabetic composition, b) numerical composition, c) *inclusio*, d) refrain, e) concentric structure, and f) key word/root, see pp. 190–193. Watson relates his definition to W. Vogels' definition of "surface structures". Cf. W. Vogels, "A structural analysis of Ps 1" *Bib.* 60 (1979) 411: "Exegetes are familiar with searching for the surface-structure of texts. Based upon some syntactic elements and upon the thought-development of a text, one can seek its "structure". Strictly speaking, this is not structural analysis. In French, this is referred to as "l'analyse structurelle", as opposed to "l'analyse structurale", which considers the deep structures of a text." (Vogels' quotation marks). P. Trible, *Rhetorical Criticism* (1994) 92, somewhat surprisingly defines "structure" as the *ipsissima verba* of the text. In my opinion, this terminology would have been suitable were it not for its traditional use as the "original" words of the prophet in contrast to words that were not considered "original". Trible does not refer to the traditional use of the expression. I hesitate to use the expression as it can give the wrong associations for the reader. In order to avoid misunderstandings concerning the relations between surface structures and deep structures on the one hand, and between surface structures and the traditional meaning of *ipsissima verba* on the other hand, I prefer the terminology textual design.

[126] For the definitions of "motif" and "theme", see Å. Svensen, *Tekstens mønstre* (1985) 15, L. Alonso Schökel, *A Manual of Hebrew Poetics* (1988) 182–185, and E. Vinje, *Tekst og tolking* (1993) 31.

is here used in a strict literary sense. Text is understood as a *literary
product*, conveying written letters. Subsequently, the term text is not
used in a wider sense, such as a designation for communities and
the like.[127] A "literary motif" is throughout this book defined as a
concrete, sometimes trivial phenomenon taken from the world outside
the text.[128] The motif(s) can either be mentioned briefly or described
thoroughly in the text. Likewise, there can be subordinate motifs and
primary motifs. The literary motif is what the text *mentions*.[129] It is
not unconcerned what motifs are applied in a text as "[. . .] motifs
are effective tools in the hands of authors only as long as they evoke
a clear echo in their audiences' minds."[130] The motif analysis in this
book will be done in three steps. First, the motif will be identified.
Second, as the motifs of Isa 18 are reflected also elsewhere in the
Old Testament, the second step is to show how the motif is applied
(in the Old Testament) in general.[131] On this background, the third
step is to see how the motif is applied in Isa 18 in particular.

As motifs hold thematic perspectives of the text, a "literary theme"
is what the text—on a deeper level—is all about. The theme is what
the text *says* about what it mentions, and this leads to the third angle
from which the text will be studied. Third, the text will be analysed
with view to how textual design and motifs together create the rhetoric

---

[127] For a broader use of the term, cf. L.C. Jonker, "Communities of Faith as
Texts in the Process of Biblical Interpretation", *Skr.K* 20 (1999) 79–92.

[128] In the consulted literature, "motif" is sometimes mixed up with "motivation",
i.e. the intention of somebody.

[129] For a brief outline of the history of application of the term motif to the study
of literature generally, and especially to biblical literature, see S. Talmon, "Har and
Midbār: An Antithetical Pair of Biblical Motifs", *Figurative Language in the Ancient Near
East* (1987) 120–121, cf. especially footnote 12 for references to biblical motif analyses.

[130] *Ibid.* 123.

[131] The first to introduce the actual concept of intertextuality was J. Kristeva,
Desire in Language (1980). Her ideas were quickly adopted and reinterpreted by others. K. Nielsen has given a sufficient definition for the application of intertextuality as pursued in this study. According to Nielsen, the main idea of intertextuality
is that "[. . .] no text has come into being or is ever heard as an independent unit;
it is always part of a network of texts. [. . .] Each and every text has arisen out of
a network of texts which the author deliberately draws on, and indeed wishes the
reader to notice." K. Nielsen, "Old Testament Imagery in John", *New Readings in
John* (1999) 69–70. For other recent contributions to the field of Old Testament
intertextuality, see the special issue of *Semeia* 69/70 (1995), and K. Nielsen, "Intertextuality and Hebrew Bible", *International Organization for the Study of the Old Testament:
Congress Volume 1998* (2000) 17–31, J. Barton, "Intertextuality and the 'final form'
of the Text", *International Organization for the Study of the Old Testament: Congress Volume
1998* (2000) 33–37, and M. Fishbane, "Types of Biblical Intertextuality", *International
Organization for the Study of the Old Testament: Congress Volume 1998* (2000) 39–44.

of the text. By *rhetorical analysis* this book refers to the way the text's theme(s) is (are) presented. What is mentioned (the motif) is in one or the other way bound to what is the text's deeper message (theme).[132] The rhetorical analysis pursued here includes three steps: (i) rhetorical features in the text's design, (ii) rhetorical features in the text's motifs, and (iii) how do textual design and motifs together create the strophe's rhetoric? As will be evident, this research separates *what* from *how*. In other words, the description of *what* features are present (textual design and motifs), is separated from the discussion of *how* these same features function (rhetorical analysis).

Fourth, at the end of each stanza (except the first), there will be a discussion of how the different strophes within a stanza relate to one another, and to the foregoing stanza(s). This endeavour is labelled *contextual analysis*. Each stanza will be seen in relation to the foregoing stanza(s) in order to see whether or not there are any links between them. The central question here is: Are there any connections at all by means of textual design, motifs or rhetorical drive between strophes and/or stanzas in Isa 18? Under the headline *contextual analysis*, Isa 18 will not be related to other texts, but the analysis will be strictly kept to the relationship between these three stanzas and their strophes.

---

[132] Very few scholars have defined the terms *motif* and *theme* understood as literary devices in Old Testament rhetoric. W.G.E. Watson is right when he sums up the situation: "It must be admitted, though, that so far little work has been done in the area of theme in Hebrew poetry." W.G.E. Watson, *Classical Hebrew Poetry* (1984/1986) 81. He does not contribute to a more consistent and precise use of the term as he lends himself to Culley's definition of "theme" as "[...] an intermediate structural device between the line and the poem itself", cf. R.C. Culley, *Oral Formulaic Language in the Biblical Psalms* (1967) 100. If one finds "theme" vaguely defined, "motif" is even more vaguely defined by Watson: "Related to the theme, as Culley has pointed out, is the motif which is, in fact, a smaller component than the theme." See W.G.E. Watson, *Classical Hebrew Poetry* (1984/1986) 81.

CHAPTER TWO

STROPHE I: 18:1–2

The introductory chapter of this book has treated questions about
the nations material in the book of Isaiah, and given some preliminary
observations about Isa 18. Further, chapter 1 contained a methodological discussion. From the present chapter and onwards, each
strophe of Isa 18 will be approached from the following four angles:
(i) text and translation, (ii) textual design, (iii) motifs, and (iv) rhetorical analysis. As the present chapter begins the analysis of the text,
definitions of central vocabulary—that will be applied throughout
the analysis of Isa 18—will be given here.

2.1. Text and Translation

As Isa 18 (especially vv. 1–2) contains several difficult words, there
is need for a supplement to a mere traditional textual critical discussion before the analysis can start. Under the headline *text and
translation*, the Hebrew text will appear first, followed by my own
translation into English with a textual critical discussion in footnotes.[1]
Then follows a discussion of translational challenges.[2]

---

[1] I am aware that it is impossible entirely to separate textual criticism from interpretation when producing a translation. Nevertheless, the discussion of textual variants will be kept in the footnotes to my English translation in an attempt to distinguish
the two tasks.

[2] To the syntax of vv. 1–2, it has been remarked by the American Jewish translation *Tanakh—The Holy Scriptures* (1988) 653, that the qal participle masculine singular absolute הַשֹּׁלֵחַ, "sending" (v. 2aα) does not correlate in gender with the noun
אֶרֶץ, "land" (v. 1a): "The Hebrew verb for "sends" agrees in gender with "nation",
not with "land"." According to this observation, a radical emendation is therefore
done by *Tanakh* as MT's (v. 2aα–2aβ) הַשֹּׁלֵחַ בַּיָּם צִירִים וּבִכְלֵי־גֹמֶא עַל־פְּנֵי־מַיִם, "sending envoys by sea and in vessels of paper-reed over the waters" (my translation) is
moved to the end of v. 2—for the sake of clarity. By this reconstruction of MT's
text, *Tanakh* claims to improve the sense of the text by making it clearer. However,
this emendation is not necessary for the following reasons. First, the criterion "clarity"
is not a valid argument for moving lines from one part to the other of the MT.
Second, if correspondence in gender is what is sought from *Tanakh*'s side, the emendation suggested is not necessary as אֶרֶץ, "land", also can be perceived as a masculine noun, cf. *BDB* (1979) 75–76, which refers to Ezek 21:24. Third, discrepancy

2.1.1. *Textual criticism*

A number of textual problems occur in Isa 18:1–2 and this influences the translation and interpretation of the strophe.[3]

Text	Verse
הוי ארץ צלצל כנפים	v. 1a
אשר מעבר לנהרי־כוש	v. 1b
השלח בים צירים	v. 2aα
ובכלי־גמא על־פני־מים	v. 2aβ
לכו מלאכים קלים	v. 2aγ
אל־גוי ממשך ומורט	v. 2aδ
אל־עם נורא מן־הוא והלאה	v. 2aε
גוי קו־קו ומבוסה	v. 2bα
אשר־בזאו נהרים ארצו	v. 2bβ

Verse	Text
v. 1a	Ah! land of buzzing[4] wings
v. 1b	from along the rivers of Cush,
v. 2aα	sending envoys by sea
v. 2aβ	and in vessels of paper-reed over the waters.
v. 2aγ	Go, swift messengers
v. 2aδ	to[5] a nation tall and smooth-skinned,[6]
v. 2aε	to a people feared from that day and onwards,
v. 2bα	[to] a nation line upon line[7] and down-treading,
v. 2bβ	whose land rivers cut through.[8]

in gender is a common phenomenon in Hebrew, and does not qualify for moving lines from one part to the other of the MT. For examples of discrepancy in biblical Hebrew, cf. J. Levi, *Die Inkongruenz im biblischen Hebräisch* (1987).

[3] The text that is translated and analysed in this work is the Masoretic text (MT), Codex Leningradensis, as printed in *BHS* (1984). With a few exceptions, 1Q Isa[a] and MT are identical, and one could ask why the textual basis of this analysis is the MT, and not the older 1Q Isa[a]. In favour of 1Q Isa[a] is its closeness in time (compared to the MT) to both the origin of the book of Isaiah, and to the climax of Kush's history. In favour of MT is its established Tiberian vocalisation system that enables the modern reader to make proposals about the (though insecure) field of pronunciation of ancient Hebrew. In addition, if E.Y. Kutscher is right when he suggests that MT was the textual basis for 1Q Isa[a], this is yet another reason for using MT as the textual basis for the present analysis of Isa 18, cf. E.Y. Kutscher, *The Language and Linguistic Background of the Isaiah Scroll (1Q Isa[a])* (1974) 2–3: "[. . .] the 1Q Isa[a] reflects a later textual type than the Masoretic Text". The Isaiah text from Qumran, 1Q Isa[a], is taken from D.W. Parry & E. Qimron (eds.), *The Great Isaiah Scroll (1Q Isa[a])* (1999). The references to LXX throughout this work are all taken from *Septuaginta. Vetus Testamentum Graecum. Isaias*, ed. by J. Ziegler (1939), and *Septuaginta*, ed. by A. Rahlfs (1979).

[4] The word צלצל has a difficult textual history. 1Q Isa[a] has צל צל, while MT has one word, and the scribe of 1Q Isa[a] has probably had the word צל in mind

2.1.2. *Translation*

The translation of הוֹי

Isa 18 opens with the interjection הוֹי to the "land of buzzing wings from along the rivers of Cush".[9] הוֹי can be rendered "Ah", "Alas",

---

("shadow" or "darkness", cf. Isa 30:2; Ps 17:8 & al.). The Vulgate has *cymbalum* probably relating it to the Hebrew צְלָצְלִים, "cymbals" (2 Sam 6:5; Ps 150:5). Targum renders "ships", and the LXX translates אֶרֶץ צִלְצַל כְּנָפַיִם γῆς πλοίων πτέρυγες, "land of the boats of wings". For my suggestion, see the section that follows this textual critical discussion.

[5] 1Q Isaᵃ reads לְנוֹי where MT has אֶל־גּוֹי. Other examples of the same difference of אֶל and לְ between 1Q Isaᵃ and MT are attested in 37:6 and 37:7.

Generally speaking, it is difficult to determine anything with certainty when it comes to variations concerning the interchanging of prepositions between MT and 1Q Isaᵃ. More important than the variations between אֶל and לְ, are the אֶל/עַל changes. A number of variation of the preposition occurs between the MT's עַל and the אֶל of the 1Q Isaᵃ (10:20; 14:2; 22:15; 29:12; 30:16; 31:1; 37:9; 53:1; 56:6; 60:5). However, the more common difference appears to be that of MT having the preposition אֶל, where 1Q Isaᵃ has עַל (2:2; 3:8; 6:9; 17:7; 17:8; 22:5; 22:11; 36:7; 36:12; 37:21; 37:33; 46:7; 65:6; 66:20). If one presupposes, like E.Y. Kutscher, *The Language and Linguistic Background of the Isaiah Scroll (1Q Isaᵃ)* (1974) 403–410, that MT was the textual basis for 1Q Isaᵃ, one may say that the scribe of the 1Q Isaᵃ acted relatively free as far as changing of prepositions were concerned. According to Kutscher, most of the אֶל/עַל changes are probably due to the weakening of the pharyngeals. Even though these substitutions are common in the Old Testament, the phenomenon can be explained as Aramaic influence.

[6] MT has a rare form of the root מרט, "make smooth/bald", "polish". Most likely, מוֹרָט (also found in v. 7) is a pual participle of מרט, where the normal variant is מְמֹרָט (cf. 1 Kgs 7:45). Further examples of pual without preformative מ are: Exod 3:2; Judg 13:8; 2 Kgs 2:10; Isa 30:24; 54:11; Eccl 9:12. Cf. Ges-K (1910/1970) 143 § 52-s: "The rejection of the מ may be favoured by an initial מ, as in Isa 18²·⁷[. . .]."

Some Hebrew manuscripts and 1Q Isaᵃ have the normal variant of the pual participle (with or without the waw). The apparatus of *The Hebrew University Bible* (1995), reveals a correction in 1Q Isaᵃ from prima manus וממרט (defective spelling) to secunda manus וממורט (plene spelling). The MT's וּמוֹרָט is plene spelled, but lacks the preformative מ. The reason why 1Q Isaᵃ is different from the MT is not evident. According to E.Y. Kutscher, *The Language and Linguistic Background of the Isaiah Scroll (1Q Isaᵃ)* (1974) 344, the מוֹרָט (of the MT) is the qal passive participle which gradually went out of use. 1Q Isaᵃ has chosen the normal form ממרט (ממורט), with or without the waw, which is pual participle. Basing his analysis of the 1Q Isaᵃ on the hypothesis that 1Q Isaᵃ corrected the MT, Kutscher finds it likely that the word מְמֻשָּׁךְ, which appears in the context of Isa 18:2, 7, probably was influential for the 1Q Isaᵃ emendation of MTs מוֹרָט. Also the explanation given by G.R. Driver is coloured by the supposition that MT was the textual basis for 1Q Isaᵃ: "The Scroll further confirms a considerable number of emendations which have been proposed by various scholars to improve the sense or to obtain sense", G.R. Driver, "Hebrew Scrolls", *JThS* 2 (1951) 25. For a similar explanation of why the normal variant of the pual participle of מרט was preferred by the scribes of some Hebrew manuscripts and of 1Q Isaᵃ, see H. Wildberger, *Jesaja 13–27* (1978) 680, who states that "[. . .] die ungewohnte Form wurde später wie oft normalisiert."

"Ha", and although it usually expresses some kind of dissatisfaction and pain, it is not as strong as אוֹי, "woe".[10] Despite its complexity, הוֹי seems to occur in the Old Testament in three different forms of

---

We do not know why MT has an uncommon form of the pual participle, however, MT has further examples of the same rare form, and it can thus be accepted. Most likely, the scribe of the 1Q Isa^a has chosen the word ממרט or ממורט (with or without the waw) to avoid confusion about the form. Whether 1Q Isa^a knew or not knew MT, there is no doubt that the form chosen by 1Q Isa^a was the most common to express a pual participle of מרט.

[7] The reduplicated form קַו־קָו of MT occurs only here and in 18:7. 1Q Isa^a and Ketib Orientales read קוקו (one word), probably relating to Arabic *qwy*, "to be or become strong". Both the Vulgate (*expectantem* x2) and LXX (ἀνέλπιστον) derive קַו־קָו from קוה^I, "hope".

[8] בָּזְאוּ occurs only here and in 18:7. Both times MT has בָּזְאוּ which is qal perfect 3rd person plural, while 1Q Isa^a has בּוֹזֵי which is either qal participle active status construct or a misspelling. One part of the Hexaplaric and Lucianic recension reads בֹּזֵי "to spoil"/"to take as spoil"/"plunder", and renders διηρπασαν, "they plundered". The same is also done by some of the versions (Targum, Syriac, Jerome, Vulgate), cf. Isa 42:22; Jer 50:37; Ezek 26:12; 39:10. The LXX has ignored בָּזְאוּ both here and in v. 7 and not given a translation of the word.

[9] There are three main suggestions to trace the origin and development of the so-called woe oracles in the prophets. In his book first published in German in 1960, C. Westermann, *Basic Forms of Prophetic Speech* (1991) 190, proposes הוֹי to be the most common woe to announce judgement, and its origin is by Westermann seen as covenant curses. This would carry the view that the woe oracle was a by-form of the curse. Further, E. Gerstenberger, "The Woe-Oracles of the Prophets", *JBL* 81 (1962) 249–263, states that the word הוֹי originated in popular sayings, in lists of acceptable and unacceptable conduct. A different line of explanation is that of R.J. Clifford, "The Use of *Hôy* in the Prophets", *CBQ* 28 (1966) 458–464, who argues that since the funeral lament is the only attested non-prophetic use of הוֹי in the Old Testament, it is more likely that הוֹי has its origin in the funeral lament than in the popular saying. This latter suggestion that the prophetic הוֹי most likely originates from the use of the identical cry (הוֹי) in funerary lamentation (cf. Jer 22:18) has received a considerable measure of support, cf. for instance G. Wanke, "אוֹי und הוֹי", *ZAW* 78 (1966) 215–218, H.W. Wolff, *Dodekapropheton 2. Joel und Amos* (1969) 284–287, W. Janzen, *Mourning Cry and Woe Oracle* (1972) 40–49, and H.-J. Zobel, "הוֹי", *ThWAT* 2 (1977) 384–386. According to Clifford, all but two passages in the book of Isaiah (29:15 and 33:1) have a clear lament context. Clifford argues that הוֹי has developed into a curse-like formula in the late prophets. This development is by Clifford seen as moving away from its origin of being a funeral lament. Clifford argues this on the basis of having examined all the הוֹי formulas in their approximate chronological order. There are a few major problems about Clifford's explanation, however. First, basing the argument on a chronological study is insecure as the exact chronology of the different books of the Old Testament is not possible to trace. Second, in terms of syntax, there are differences between the funerary and the invective usage of הוֹי. In the funerary usage, the הוֹי is followed by the vocative, whereas in the prophetic invective the הוֹי is followed by an impersonal third-person formulation. This is regarded a major objection by H.-J. Krause [sic], "*hôj* als prophetische Leichenklage über das eigene Volk im 8. Jahrhundert", *ZAW* 85 (1973) 15–46. Tracing the origin and development of the prophetic הוֹי

usage.[11] First, הוֹי occurs in funeral laments (cf. 1 Kgs 13:30, Jer 22:18; 34:5).[12] In such lamentations הוֹי is usually followed by a noun indicating the relationship between the person who mourns and the one who is dead, cf. 1 Kgs 13:30: הוֹי אָחִי "alas my brother." Second, הוֹי can be found in vocative appeals or addresses functioning as a way of getting the attention and expressing either an invitation (Isa 55:1), a moan (Jer 47:6) or a warning (Zech 2:10 (x2), 11).[13] Third, הוֹי appears in prophetic indictments (Isa 10:5; 17:12; 28:1). This latter usage seems to be limited to the prophets.[14] Common for all three forms of usage is the onomatopoetic nature of this interjection. According to the three ways of applying הוֹי, it expresses grief, alarm, or anger—or a mixture of these emotions.[15]

The book of Isaiah contains the highest frequency of the heading הוֹי.[16] Of altogether 51 occurrences of הוֹי in the Old Testament, the

---

oracles is not pursued by R.E. Clements, "OT 'Woe' Oracles", *ABD* 6 (1992) 946: "The use of a very simple onomatopoetic particle to express both emotions [grief and anger] have given rise to the notion that the one originated from the other. In reality the two originally separate cries have come to be associated with each other." In my judgement, the interesting task is not to determine the origin and development of the various הוֹי formulas found in the Old Testament, but rather to analyse how these function within their literary contexts.

[10] As the LXX uses the same word to translate both הוֹי and אוֹי, this might suggest that there is no essential difference between the two interjections. This is however contradicted by the different syntax of the two words, cf. the statistical survey of G. Wanke, "אוֹי und הוֹי", *ZAW* 78 (1966) 215–218, which is rechecked by C. Hardmeier (in H.W. Wolff, *Dodekapropheton 2. Joel und Amos* (1969) 284–287). See H.-J. Zobel,"הוֹי", *ThWAT* 2 (1977) 382–383, for a presentation of the statistical survey from Wanke and Hardmeier.

[11] This is also suggested by R.J. Clifford, "The Use of *Hôy* in the Prophets", *CBQ* 28 (1966) 458–464. For the meaning and application of הוֹי, see also E. Jenni, "הוֹי", *THAT* 1 (1971) 474–477.

[12] For this usage, cf. J. Scharbert, *Der Schmerz im Alten Testament* (1955) 71.

[13] For a study of the presence or absence of a vocative element after the הוֹי, see D.R. Hillers, "*Hôy* and *Hôy*-Oracles: A Neglected Syntactic Aspect", *The Word of the Lord Shall Go Forth* (1983) 185–188.

[14] There is a formal similarity between הוֹי used in laments and הוֹי in indictments as both contexts contain a nominal construction after the initial הוֹי. In indictments, however, the relationship of the mourner to the subject of his/her lament is not present. Instead, indictments describe the conduct of men towards YHWH in order to motivate the threat that follows. Another bond between laments and indictments opening with הוֹי is that a human being formulates and pronounces the cry in both cases. The threat, however, is often spoken by YHWH in indictments, cf. H.-J. Zobel,"הוֹי", *ThWAT* 2 (1977) 384–385.

[15] Cf. R.E. Clements, "OT 'Woe' Oracles", *ABD* 6 (1992) 945–946.

[16] In the first part of the book of Isaiah, series of הוֹי are found in 5:8–24 and in chs. 28–31, whereas scattered occurrences are found in 1:4, 24; 10:1, 5; 17:12; 18:1.

book of Isaiah carries 21. There is an accumulation of this term in
chapter 5, and Isa 1–39 has 18 occurrences altogether, whereas the
remaining three instances of the term in the book of Isaiah are to
be found in chapters 45:9 and 10, and 55:1. The הוֹי oracles in the
Old Testament are addressed to all realms of life (social, cultic and
political spheres) and all classes of people, and even to Jerusalem
(Isa 29:1; Zeph 3:1) or Israel as a whole (Isa 1:4).[17]

What, then, is the most likely use of הוֹי in Isa 18:1? All three
uses of the word הוֹי may have passed through the minds of the audience. In Isa 18:1 a noun follows immediately after the הוֹי, and this
could indicate that what follows should be understood as a funeral
lament.[18] However, as Isa 18 does not describe a typical funeral, the
audience most likely would not perceive this הוֹי as a mourning cry.
Could the הוֹי then be taken as a vocative appeal or address, as is
the case in Isa 55:1; Jer 47:6 and Zech 2:10 and 11? The lack of
a negative description of the land and inhabitants of Cush could
indicate that the opening הוֹי is not used in terms of judging, but
simply as an exclamation arousing attention: "Ha!".[19] Or would the
audience most likely perceive this הוֹי as a prophetic indictment as
long as a nation is mentioned explicitly? I would say that this latter solution is the most convincing one.[20] By the opening הוֹי the
audience recognizes straight away that the genre of the speech is a
word of doom. It has been stated that the participle (here הַשֹּׁלֵחַ,
"sending", at the beginning of v. 2) is an element typically found in
woe oracles.[21] The classical woe oracle includes an identification of
the person (or nation) being addressed after the initial הוֹי, and links

---

[17] H.-J. Zobel, "הוֹי", *ThWAT* 2 (1977) 387.

[18] הוֹי is followed by a noun or proper noun in 7 instances (Isa 1:4; 10:5; 18:1;
28:1; 29:1; 30:1; Nah 3:1).

[19] Cf. *BDB* (1979) 222–223, and W. Gesenius, *Handwörterbuch* (1995) 271, where
הוֹי of Isa 18:1 are suggested to have this latter meaning. *BDB* even proposes the
interjection to have a touch of sympathy or pity in Isa 18:1; 55:1; Jer 47:6; and
Zech 2:10, 10, 11. Gesenius also includes Isa 17:12 in the list. Koehler-Baumgartner,
HALAT (1967) 232, relates the Hebrew הוֹי to the Syriac *hāwāy* and lists the interjection in Isa 18:1 under the heading "aufmunternd".

[20] This is however not understood the same way as is suggested by W. Janzen,
Mourning Cry and Woe Oracle (1972) 60–61. Janzen holds that YHWH's messengers
are sent to Assyria (v. 2), and that this nation is the agent of punishment: "The
hôy against Ethiopia/Egypt, then, introduces the announcement of the Lord's Day
(cf. Ez 30:9)".

[21] Cf. H. Wildberger, *Jesaja 1–12* (1980) 182. Wildberger takes vv. 4–6a as a
threat addressed Cush.

this to a participial clause that briefly identifies the sinful action (here v. 2aα etc.). Following this scheme, the sinful action would here be the alliance making between the two groups of messengers referred to (i.e. Cushites and Judeans). Taking into account the immediate preceding verses of vv. 1–2, Isa 17:12–14, it would make sense that the land of Cush should be cursed—as a representative for the nations, but is this what the text says? From the heading הוי together with the participle השלח, "sending", at the beginning of v. 2, it is clear that the genre of Isa 18 is that of doom. What is not clear, however, is the question about who is judged. As the description of the Cushites is positive where one would expect the negative, the audience might feel confused. In my view, three options are possible: (i) Cush is judged,[22] (ii) Judah is judged, (iii) both Cush and Judah are judged as they commit a sinful action by negotiating with one another about making an alliance against a greater power. This uncertainty when it comes to who is judged is not solved before vv. 5–6, and הוי is here used ambiguously in order to leave the audience in confusion for a while.

The translation of צלצל

צלצל is a word of uncertain meaning which has evoked several interpretations. The word as it stands is unintelligible. Among the many renderings of צלצל three appear to be prominent. First, צלצל is suggested to refer to a locust-like creature.[23] Of the older commentaries,

---

[22] This view is held by G.R. Hamborg, although he argues that the judgement does not have to do with any sin committed by Cush, cf. G.R. Hamborg, "Reasons for Judgement in the Oracles Against the Nations of the Prophet Isaiah", *VT* 31 (1981) 155: "In a number of instances (xix 1–15, xviii 1–6, xiv 28–32, xv–xvi) Isaiah announces judgement on a foreign nation because of Judah's possible reliance on or alliance with that nation, and not for any sin of the nation itself."

[23] Cf. the rendering in W. Gesenius, *Thesaurus* (1842) 1167f., W. Gesenius, *Handwörterbuch* (1962) 684–685, ("Land des Flügelgeschwirres"), and Koehler-Baumgartner, *Lexicon* (1958) 805, ("country of winged crickets"). This view is supported by the fact that הצלצל in Deut 28:42 is used to designate insects, see for instance H. Seidel, *Musik in Altisrael* (1989) 77, footnote 35. There is a debate, however, about what kind of insect הצלצל refers to. In Deut 28:38–42 three terms are referred to as decimating the wheat, vine, trees, and fruit of the land: התלעת, הארבה and הצלצל. Traditionally, *both* the first and last mentioned creatures (הארבה and הצלצל) are translated "locust". A recent contribution however, argues that הצלצל in Deut 28:42 refers to "beetles", cf. M. Lubetski, "Beetlemania of Bygone Times", *JSOT* 91 (2000) 3–26. Through an analysis of ancient Egyptian texts, classical literature, Aramaic and rabbinic sources, post-biblical texts and archaeological material, Lubetski suggests that ארץ צלצל כנפים in Isa 18:1 most likely means "land of

B. Duhm suggests צלצל to be rendered "Geschwirr", pointing at
tsetseflies of the Nile area.[24] K. Marti and O. Procksch translate
"Flügelgeschwirrs."[25] Of more recent works, O. Kaiser renders צלצל
"Flügelgeschwirrs", relating to the Arabic *salla* and *salsalla*, "clinking" and "jingling."[26] Together with a literal translation of the word
that follows צלצל in Isa 18:1, כנפים, "wings", צלצל can in this
approach be understood as onomatopoeia for the buzzing or jingling
sound made by insects. A second suggestion is that צלצל is a derivation
of the word צל, "shade" or "shadow". Of older works, this translation is suggested by M. Luther, J.A. Alexander, and A. Dillmann.[27]
The idea that "shade" or "shadow" allude to protection, is referred
to by M. Goshen-Gottstein.[28] If כנפים, "wings" is not taken literally,
but rather represents protection, the phrase ארץ צלצל כנפים is understood in the meaning "most sheltered land" or "a land in the shadow
of wings". The third view relies on the LXX and the Targum which
take צלצל as referring to ships.[29] Of older commentaries, F. Buhl
renders צלצל "Landet med de vingede Skibe" ("the land of the
winged boats").[30] More recently, H. Wildberger translates the phrase

---

the winged beetle". According to Lubetski, this land is Egypt. *Idem*, 16: "The beetle in Egyptian literature is not only the dung beetle but also the young rising sun
god known as *Ḫprr*" *Idem*, 18: "[. . .] from the XXII Dynasty onwards, the deity is
viewed in many instances not merely as the winged solar Horus but also as a divine
winged beetle."

[24] B. Duhm, *Das Buch Jesaja* (1892) 113–114.

[25] Cf. K. Marti, *Das Buch Jesaja* (1900) 147–148. Marti reads צלצל in comparison with Deut 28:42 and Ps 150:5. O. Procksch, *Jesaja I* (1930) 237–238, translates
צלצל "Flügelgeschwirrs", relating to the insects of the Nile region.

[26] Cf. O. Kaiser, *Der Prophet Jesaja* (1983) 74–80. Of other commentators suggesting a similar translation, cf. G. Fohrer, *Das Buch Jesaja Kapitel 1–23* (1960/1966)
222–224, F. Delitzsch, *Jesaja* (1984) 221, and J. Jensen, *Isaiah 1–39* (1984) 162–164.

[27] Cf. Martin Luther, *Die heilige Schrift* (1929) 758, J.A. Alexander, *The Prophecies
of Isaiah* (1870) 343, and A. Dillmann, *Der Prophet Jesaja* (1890) 167.

[28] M. Goshen-Gottstein, *R. Judah Ibn Bal'am's Commentary on Isaiah* (1992) 98.

[29] Cf. Koehler-Baumgartner, *HALAT* (1983) 966, "Land der geflügelten Boote".
See also J.V. Kinnier Wilson, "A Return to the Problems of behemoth and leviathan",
VT 25 (1975) 11, footnote 1. For a suggestion to why the LXX translators rendered
ארץ צלצל כנפים, "land of the boats of wings" and in M. Lubetski's view mislead
many commentators, see M. Lubetski, "Beetlemania of Bygone Times", *JSOT* 91
(2000) 21–22: "[. . .] צלצל was no longer the holy beetle in his sacred ship but rather
the boat in the mundane sense. [. . .] what impressed the Jewish LXX translators
as distinctive of Egypt in the third or second century B.C.E., was the country of the
winged sailing boats, and not the land of the holy beetle, as Isaiah had known it."

[30] F. Buhl, *Jesaja* (1894) 280–281. The second edition of F. Buhl, *Jesaja* (1912)
229, has changed the translation of צלצל כנפים from "vingede Skibe" ("the winged
boats") to "den vingede Sværm" ("the winged swarm"). This amendment is not
reflected in Buhl's comment on the phrase in question.

אֶרֶץ צִלְצַל כְּנָפַיִם "Land der geflügelten Boote."[31] Dependent on
Wildberger, J.D.W. Watts renders אֶרֶץ צִלְצַל כְּנָפַיִם "land of winged
boats".[32] When צִלְצַל according to this approach is rendered "boat",
כְּנָפַיִם, "wings" are understood as the sails of the boat.[33] What seems
to be clear, is that the word צִלְצַל does not reveal a certain meaning neither to the scribes of ancient times nor to the modern reader.
E.Y. Kutscher describes the situation well as he designates the word
an enigma.[34]

The chosen translation, "buzzing", to the noun צִלְצַל is conventional, and it is related to the root צלל[I].[35] צלל[I] seems to have various functions in Biblical Hebrew, cf. the tingle of ears at horrid
sound (1 Sam 3:11; 2 Kgs 21:12; Jer 19:3), and the tingle of lips or
quiver in terror (Hab 3:16). However, despite its broad usage, צלל[I]
always refers to the phenomenon of something clinking or tingling.[36]
In Isa 18:1 צִלְצַל is found immediate before the noun in dual, כְּנָפַיִם,
"wings", and צִלְצַל should be seen in relation to this word. I would
therefore argue that the rendering "buzzing wings" is preferable for
four reasons: (i) it obviates an emendation of כְּנָפַיִם, "wings", (ii) it

---

[31] Cf. H. Wildberger, *Jesaja 13–27* (1978) 678–679. Wildberger gives a thorough
analysis of צִלְצַל. Incorrectly, Wildberger renders Buhl's translation of צִלְצַל to be
"Schatten" ("shadow"), while Buhl as cited above has "winged boats" or "winged
swarm", cf. F. Buhl, *Jesaja* (1894) 280–281, and *Jesaja* (1912) 229. For other examples of scholars translating צִלְצַל "boat" or "ship", cf. G.R. Driver, "Difficult Words
in the Hebrew Prophets", *Studies in Old Testament Prophecy* (1957) 56, J. Barr, *Comparative
Philology and the Text of the Old Testament* (1968) 334, number 270, "boat", G.R.
Driver, "Isaiah 1–39: Textual and Linguistic Problems", *Journal of Semitic Studies* 13
(1968) 45, A.S. Herbert, *The Book of the Prophet Isaiah* (1973) 117–118, T. de Cyr,
Commentaire sur Isaïe (1982) 122–123, E. Strömberg Krantz, *Des Schiffes Weg mitten im
Meer* (1982) 61–66, J.H. Hayes & S.A. Irvine, *Isaiah* (1987) 254, and J.N. Oswalt,
The Book of Isaiah (1986) 357–360.

[32] J.D.W. Watts does not even discuss the different solutions presented by
H. Wildberger, as he designates his work an "exhaustive description", and finds his
presentation convincing, J.D.W. Watts, *Isaiah 1–33* (1985) 243–244.

[33] For an example of a scholar who lately has advocated this translation, see R.S.
Sadler, "Can a Cushite Change His Skin? An Examination of Race, Ethnicity, and
Othering in the Hebrew Bible" (2001) 114.

[34] E.Y. Kutscher, *The Language and Linguistic Background of the Isaiah Scroll (1Q Isaᵃ)*
(1974) 279.

[35] It is unlikely that צִלְצַל in Isa 18:1 is related to צלל[II], "sink"/"be submerged"
or צלל[III], "be or grow dark" as these two roots' functions seem not compatible with
the other words of Isa 18:1. The listing of the roots of צלל vary from lexicon to
lexicon, here the numbering from *BDB* is followed.

[36] The various meanings derived from the root צלל[I], "tingle", "quiver", all describe
a buzzing, clinking or clashing sound: "harpoon" (cf. Job 40:31) = "whizzing fish-
spear", "cymbal" (cf. 2 Sam 6:5; Ps 150:5), "bell" (cf. Zech 14:20).

takes seriously the dual form of כנפים as "wings" appear in pairs, (iii) the rendering "buzzing" is close to the root צלל[1]—referring to something that is clinking or tingling, and (iv) "buzzing wings" mimicries the sound of wings of insects. The opening of Isa 18 should thus be rendered: "Ah! land of buzzing wings", suggesting צלצל as an onomatopoeia for the sound of whirring or buzzing, pointing to the wings (כנפים) of insects.[37]

The translation of מעבר

The rendering of the phrase מעבר לנהרי־כוש (v. 1b) needs to be discussed as מעבר is central to the understanding of the text. מעבר appears to have more nuances of meaning than is commonly referred to, and מעבר is here given a translation that differs from most commentators' renderings.[38] מעבר consists of a preposition מן, "from", and a noun, עבר (masculine singular absolute), which is often rendered "region across or beyond".[39] Most translators therefore render מעבר לנהרי־כוש of Isa 18:1 "beyond the rivers of Cush/Ethiopia" without any discussion.[40] In addition to this most common rendering, however, מעבר can also be translated "along", or "on the side of", cf. 1 Sam 14:4, 40; 1 Kgs 5:4; 7:20, 30.[41]

---

[37] For the suggestion that the root צלצל is onomatopoetic, see A. Parmelee, *All the Birds of the Bible* (1959) 182, and E. Firmage, "Zoology", *ABD* 6 (1992) 1159, footnote 69. Suggesting *what* kind of insect צלצל in Isa 18:1 refers to is however not of interest here. For the opposite view on this question, see M. Lubetski, "Beetlemania of Bygone Times", *JSOT* 91 (2000) 3–26, 26, who argues that צלצל in Isa 18:1 refers to beetles as the deity in ancient Egypt is viewed as a divine winged beetle: "[. . .] Isaiah utilized Egyptian symbolism in his oracles to Egypt. I do not share Lubetski's optimistic view that it is possible for a modern reader to identify what—in this case—insect the ancient text Isa 18 describe. I believe that accurate knowledge about ancient fauna is impossible to attain for the modern interpreter.

[38] An identical phrase is found in Zeph 3:10: מעבר לנהרי־כוש. A discussion of Zeph 3:10 will be done under the analysis of Isa 18:7.

[39] Cf. H.-P. Stähli, "עבר", *THAT* 2 (1976) 200–204.

[40] Some scholars treat v. 1b as a gloss, cf. B. Duhm, *Das Buch Jesaia* (1892) 137–139, K. Marti, *Das Buch Jesaja* (1900) 147, and H. Donner, *Israel unter den Völkern* (1964) 122. J.P.U. Lilley, "By the River-side", *VT* 28 (1978) 165–171, makes a systematic examination of the use of עבר, supporting and extending the conclusions of B. Gemser, "Be'ēver hajjardēn: In Jordan's borderland", *VT* 2 (1952) 349–355. Lilley translates מעבר in both Isa 18:1 and Zeph 3:10 "beyond", but regards "beside" acceptable, see p. 167. Lilley, concludes that מעבר, *ibid.* p. 171: "[. . .] normally means 'beyond', unless the force of min = 'from' predominates [. . .]".

[41] This is also argued by B. Gemser, "Be'ēver hajjardēn": In Jordan's borderland", *VT* 2 (1952) 351: "Thus 'ēber signifies undoubtedly 'region across, other side' but just as well 'region alongside, side'. For the translation of מעבר in Isa 18, see

B. Gemser shows that the word עבר is applied especially of a riverside region, and argues that in Isa 18:1 מעבר לנהרי־כוש has to be translated "alongside the rivers of Ethiopia" to give an appropriate meaning.[42] Along the same lines is the argument from E. Vogt. According to Vogt, (מ)עבר is usually rendered "on the other side of". Often, however, Vogt stresses, (מ)עבר has one of the following nuances of meaning: *iuxta*, "by", "along", *prope*, "near", "close by", *adiacentem*, "adjacent to", *latus*, "side" (right or left).[43] Vogt holds that (מ)עבר הירדן can be translated "*in regione Iordanis*", ("in the region/territory of the Jordan"), and in accordance with this, he translates מעבר לנהרי־כוש in Isa 18:1: "*in regione iuxta flumina Kuš*", "in the region by/along the rivers of Cush".[44] Of the commentaries, O. Procksch renders מעבר לנהרי־כוש, "ein Zugang zu den Strömen von Kusch", referring to Isa 16:2 and Gen 32:23.[45] More recently, J.D.W. Watts, following H. Wildberger, takes the phrase מעבר לנהרי־כוש as an obvious reference to the African nation Cush.[46] This is also presupposed by T. Stordalen who renders מעבר לנהרי־קוש [*sic*], "from the region of the rivers of Cush".[47] Agreeing with those who take לנהרי־כוש מעבר as an obvious reference to the ancient African nation Cush, the translation favoured here is "from along the rivers of Cush". From the above mentioned nuances of meaning of מעבר, this rendering is conventional.

The translation of ממשך and מורט

The words ממשך and מורט are not difficult to translate. However, applied about human beings, the combination of ממשך and מורט is unusual. The verb משך have the meaning "draw", "drag", "seize".

BDB (1979) 719. See also Koehler-Baumgartner, *HALAT* (1983) 738, who puts Isa 18:1 under the heading 'Seite', and translates מעבר לנהרי־כוש 'im Umkreis der Ströme von Kusch'".

[42] B. Gemser, "Be'ēver hajjardēn: In Jordan's borderland", *VT* 2 (1952) 352.

[43] E. Vogt, "'ēber hayyardēn = regio finitima Iordani", *Bib.* 34 (1953) 118–119.

[44] *Ibid.* 118.

[45] O. Procksch, *Jesaia I* (1930) 236–238.

[46] See H. Wildberger, *Jesaja 13–27* (1978) 678–679, who renders מעבר, "im Umkreis", and J.D.W. Watts, *Isaiah 1–33* (1985) 244, who translates מעבר "in the region of" the rivers of Cush. Wildberger and Watts both follow Vogt's suggestion. Their reference to Vogt's critical note to מעבר is however incorrect. It is found in *Biblica*, and not in *Biblische Zeitschrift* as Wildberger and Watts inform.

[47] T. Stordalen, *Echoes of Eden* (2000) 280. See also H.T. Aubin, *The Rescue of Jerusalem* (2003) 172, footnote 32 for the same view.

The noun מַשְׂכֵּת is applied in Job 38:31 with the meaning "cord". In Isa 18:2 מְמֻשָּׁךְ, pual participle masculine singular absolute, is rendered "tall". Literally, it means "drawn out". מוֹרָט, pual participle masculine singular absolute, is here translated "smooth-skinned". Literally, the verb מָרַט means "make smooth/bald", "polish". 1 Kgs 7:45 speaks about נְחֹשֶׁת מְמֹרָט, "burnished bronze", and Ezek 21:14–16 of חֶרֶב הוּחַדָּה וְגַם־מְרוּטָה, "a sharpened and polished sword".

The use of the two words in this sense is without parallel, and it is thus difficult to know how they are best rendered in Isa 18:2. As usually understood, these two terms are assumed to refer to the tallness and bronzed skin of the people described.[48]

The translation of קַו־קָו

קַו means "line", "measuring-line", "cord" (cf. Isa 28:10, 13; 34:11; 44:13).[49] The reduplicated form קַו־קָו, however, appears only in Isa 18:2, 7 and is of doubtful meaning.[50] The following five renderings of קַו־קָו have been suggested.

First, קַו־קָו is understood as a reduplication of קַו, "line", "measuring-line", "cord". Second, קַו־קָו in Isa 18 is not regarded a measuring line, but rather seen as an instrument for the destruction.[51] Third, קַו־קָו is suggested to be a reduplicated noun form of קָוָה[I] ("wait for", "look for", "hope").[52] Fourth, the obscurity of the form קַו־קָו has led some to the assumption that it is onomatopoetic for a foreign nation's speech.[53] Fifth, most modern critics favour a linking

---

[48] Cf. H. Wildberger, *Jesaja 13–27* (1978) 678, who renders גּוֹי מְמֻשָּׁךְ וּמוֹרָט "hochgewachsenen, blanken Nation". Wildberger explains how these words most likely were perceived by the Judeans, p. 689: "Den eher kleinen Bewohnern Judäas [. . .] sind sie durch ihre Schlankheit aufgefallen", and further: "Jesaja dürfte also die gränzende Glätte des mit Öl abgeriebenen Körpers im Auge haben, was bei der dunklen Haut der Kuschiten besonders auffallen mußte."

[49] In Isa 28:10 and 13 קַו is perhaps senseless, or it might mimicry the prophet's words.

[50] On reduplication in general, cf. R. Meyer, *Hebräische Grammatik* (1992) 151–152, § 39–3, and Ges-K (1910/1970) 396 §123–e. Ges-K explains the phenomenon of repetition as due "[. . .] to express an exceptional or at least superfine quality [. . .]." According to Ges-K, repetition serves to intensify the expression to the highest degree.

[51] Cf. V. Tanghe, "Dichtung und Ekel in Jesaja 28:7–13", *VT* 43 (1993) 253: "Wie auch immer, *qw* kann im Zusammenhang mit Zerstörung niemals eine Meßschnur sein, sondern ein Instrument der Vernichtung, wie wohl auch aus dem Parallelismus in *gwy qw-qw mbwsh*, Jes xviii 2, 7 zu entnehmen ist."

[52] Cf. the already mentioned rendering of the Vulgate (*expectantem*) and the LXX (ἀνέλπιστον) that both derive קַו־קָו from קָוָה[I], "hope".

[53] Cf. for example H. Donner, *Israel unter den Völkern* (1964) 122, who suggests

to Arabic *qwy*, literally "he was strong", or "he became strong".[54]

Traditionally, lexicons and concordances to the Old Testament have frequently used comparative etymological research results concerning Arabic to make the Hebrew קַו־קָו make sense.[55] However, after J. Barr's studies in the 1960s and 70s, few Old Testament scholars would trust results from etymological research based on comparative Semitics alone, as the field is considered insecure when it comes to deriving the meaning of words from one language to another.[56] Words with equal spelling (in two languages) do not necessarily have the same origin or the same meaning. There is no reason to think differently about the Hebrew language and languages from areas surrounding the ancient Israel. Basing the discussion of meaning of Hebrew words exclusively on lexical discussions on comparative etymology is therefore, in my opinion, insecure.[57]

---

that קַו־קָו is an incomprehensible onomatopoetic lallation or babble, to denote a foreign language. Seen in relation to Isa 28:10, B.S. Childs, *Isaiah* (2001) 134–135, suggests the rendering "a nation of strange speech". For a similar assertion, see A. Laato, "*About Zion I will not be silent*" (1998) 72: "[. . .] a people of strange language."

[54] This is also done earlier, cf. the choice of 1Q Isaᵃ and Ketib Orientales, קָוקָו (one word), that might relate to the Arabic *qawiya*, "he was strong", or "to be or become strong", or the noun *quwatun*, "strength"/"power" (1st derivation)—both derived from the root *qwy*. According to this, the Hebrew קָוקָו (one word) would then mean "might" or "strength". F. Huber, *Jahwe, Juda und die anderen Völker beim Propheten Jesaja* (1976) 130 (footnote 189), translates קַו־קָו "kraftvoll": "Ich lese *qāwqaw* und verstehe das Wort als ein von der Wurzel *qwh* abgeleitetes Nomen (mit KBL)." A similar proposal is made by O. Kaiser, *Der Prophet Jesaja* (1983) 74, "[. . .] dem Volk voller Kraft und Gewalt".

[55] Of the lexicons, W. Gesenius, *Handwörterbuch* (1883) 729, compares the Hebrew with Arabic and translates קַו־קָו "ein Volk von enormer Kraft". The 17th edition of W. Gesenius *Handwörterbuch* (1962) 705, has the same Arabic word in mind, and suggests the reduplicated קַו־קָו to be read קָוקָו and thus be rendered "sehnige Kraft." *BDB* (1979) 875–876, translates גּוֹי קַו־קָו, "a mighty nation", understanding קַו־קָו as a reduplicated adjective. The rendering from Koehler-Baumgartner, *Lexicon* (1958) 830, and Koehler-Baumgartner, *HALAT* (1983) 1011, is also influenced of the Arabic language ("strength"). G.R. Driver, "Isaiah 1–39: Textual and Linguistic Problems", *Journal of Semitic Studies* 13 (1968) 46, supports *BDB* in rendering קַו־קָו as a reduplicated adjective with intensive significance, meaning "very strong." Related to this is that of J. Fischer, *Das Buch Isaias* (1937) 138, who understands קַו־קָו as onomatopoetic for the sound of marching feet.

[56] Cf. J. Barr, *The Semantics of Biblical Language* (1961) 107–160, and J. Barr, "Etymology and the Old Testament", *Language and Meaning* (1974) 1–28. Barr holds that etymology can be applied when there are no other possibilities left for attaining meaning of a word.

[57] One representative lexicon for this more sceptical trend is that edited by D.J.A. Clines, *DCH* (1993ff.). The lexicon of Clines is not yet completed, but the trend is exemplified for instance in the discussion of the word בָּזָא, cf. below.

As the reduplicated form is found only in Isa 18:2 and 7, other Old Testament texts cannot provide help. Still, the meaning of קָו is known: "cord", "line" or "measuring-line", so is also the meaning of קָוָה¹: "wait for", "look for", "hope". Most likely, קַו־קָו of Isa 18:2, 7 relates in one or the other way to one or both of these words.[58] My translation of קַו־קָו is "line upon line". As קַו־קָו comes immediately after גּוֹי it should be seen in relation to this word as קַו־קָו most likely points to a feature of גּוֹי. Here, קַו־קָו is taken to mean "line upon line" in the sense of people lined up in rows.

The translation of בָּזְאוּ

בָּזְאוּ occurs only here and in v. 7. Of the lexicons and concordances, previous editions of Gesenius have "durchschneiden"[59], whereas the recent 18th edition has "fortschwemmen"—"[. . .] ein Volk dessen Land Flüsse fortschwemmen".[60] "Fortschwemmen" is also suggested by Koehler-Baumgartner.[61] Koehler-Baumgartner's lexicon refers to Arabic *bazza*, "pull along forcibly", and renders "pull along by floating".[62] G. Lisowsky translates בָּזְאוּ "to wash away."[63] S. Mandelkern suggests *diripere*, "to tear asunder", *findere* "to divide", or *prorumpere*, "to clear the way" "break through".[64] *BDB* also suggests the traditionally accepted rendering "divide", "cut through" in dependence on Syriac *bz'* "tear apart", "cut apart".[65]

Of other works, L. Köhler—comparing with the Arabic *bazza*—argues against the common rendering "durchschneiden", "divide" or "cut through", holding that this solution is dependent on an intimate knowledge of the map of the landscape.[66] However, his own rendering "pull along by floating" is just as problematic. Of the commentaries, H. Wildberger suggests the rendering "durchschneiden", "cut through", following the Syriac *bz'*, "tear apart", "cut apart".[67]

---

[58] In Isa 18:2, 7 קַו־קָו probably plays on the meanings of both קָו and קָוָה¹, but this suggestion belongs under the headline *rhetorical analysis*, and will be taken up later, see 2.4.

[59] Cf. W. Gesenius, *Handwörterbuch* (1962) 90.

[60] Cf. W. Gesenius, *Handwörterbuch* (1987) 134.

[61] Cf. Koehler-Baumgartner, *HALAT* (1967) 113.

[62] Cf. Koehler-Baumgartner, *Lexicon* (1958) 115.

[63] Cf. G. Lisowsky, *Konkordanz* (1981) 205.

[64] Cf. S. Mandelkern, *Veteris Testamenti Concordantiae* (1971) 182.

[65] Cf. *BDB* (1979) 102.

[66] L. Köhler "Baza' = fortschwemmen", *ThZ* 6 (1950) 316–317.

[67] H. Wildberger, *Jesaja 13–27* (1978) 680.

As pointed at earlier, J.D.W. Watts, without any discussion, takes the same position as that of Wildberger.[68]

The critical and sceptical standpoint towards comparative etymology is difficult to hold when one discovers that almost every lexicon and concordance consulted is dependent on comparative etymology, and thus relates the rendering of בזאו to the Arabic or the Syriac. An exception, however, from following the comparative etymological path to the word בזאו is D.J.A. Clines.[69] As Clines does not relate his suggested translation of בזאו ("divide" or "wash away") to the Arabic or Syriac, one could then ask from where he gets his information. Most likely, he builds his translation on earlier lexicons and is probably in the end himself dependent on comparative etymology. The rare occurrence of בזאו forces the translator to do a rendering on a very limited basis. As בזאו occurs only in Isa 18:2 and 7, comparative biblical material can not be consulted, and one can never be assured about having made a valid solution. However, to be able to translate בזאו, it is here considered together with the following word נהרים, "rivers". As בזאו both in 18:2 and 7 occurs together with נהרים "rivers", the most convincing translation of בזאו is "cut through", in the meaning rivers dividing the landscape.

2.2. Textual design

As addressed in the introductory chapter, *textual design* is throughout this book defined as the arrangement and the interrelation of explicit linguistic and literary elements in the text.[70] As listed in chapter 1.3.4., features that are more or less directly observable from the text's design can for instance include: *inclusio*, parallelism, assonance, alliteration, *onomatopoeia*, *chiasmus*, play with words, rhyme, enjambment, gapping, poetic technique etc.

Under the headline *textual design* a set of linguistic and literary questions will be asked to all strophes of Isa 18:[71] How is each strophe

---

[68] J.D.W. Watts, *Isaiah 1–33* (1985) 244.

[69] Cf. D.J.A. Clines, *DCH* 2 (1995) 132.

[70] The present study is an analysis of the rhetoric of Isa 18, and as such, it is a literary study. However, as rhetoric uses language in a variety of ways, the textual observations make use of terms taken from the field of linguistics, such as the area of phonetic, syntax and semantic.

[71] As will be evident throughout the analysis, not *all* strophes of Isa 18 will be asked *all* questions. The observations made depend on the textual design of the individual strophe.

arranged phonetically,[72] syntactically,[73] and semantically?[74] And further, what poetic techniques are observable from strophe to strophe?[75] Common for all strophes of Isa 18 is the occurrence of parallelism of some kind.[76] Syntactic and semantic parallelisms are the most

---

[72] In this study, the analysis of phonetic patterns will observe rhyme, alliteration (repetition of consonants) and assonance (repetition of vowels). This is a broader understanding than that of A. Berlin who defines sound pairs as: "[. . .] the repetition in parallel words or lines of the same or similar *consonants* in any order within close proximity", A. Berlin, *The Dynamics of Biblical Parallelism* (1985) 104. (My italics).

As the Hebrew language developed, evolved and changed over the centuries, it could be argued that it is *impossible* to say anything at all about phonetic patterns of a text. It is therefore with hesitation I include phonetic observations as part of the analysis of Isa 18. However, although there is no such thing as *the* pronunciation of Hebrew, the Tiberian vocalisation of the Hebrew consonant text does convey how the words were heard at a certain period in time, and is thus presupposed in the present study. For this view, cf. W.G.E. Watson, *Classical Hebrew Poetry* (1984/1986) 222: "[. . .] the Masoretic vocalization is very reliable—any alternation must be vouched for."

[73] Syntactic analysis will observe the constituent parts' organising. Occurrences of parallelism, *chiasmus*, enjambment, transformation of grammatical mood, gapping etc. will be identified here.

[74] Semantic analysis deals with observing whether or not lines (or half-lines) express the same meaning. The phenomenon of similes, play with words and word-pairs etc. will be discussed here—although word-pairs not necessarily are semantically parallel.

[75] Under the heading poetic technique, two questions will be asked to each strophe of Isa 18: (i) Does the strophe convey direct speech?, and (ii) in what way is (are) the character(s) of the strophe referred to?

[76] The notion that Hebrew poetry is organised in parallel lines was first systematised by R. Lowth in his *Lectures on the Sacred Poetry of the Hebrews*, originally published in latin in 1753. The present understandings of parallelism are in one or the other way related to Lowth's distinguishing of three basic types of parallelism (synonymous, antithetic and synthetic). However, Lowth's broad definition lacked precision, and the development since the 1980s is largely made possible by the disposal of linguistics tools that were not available in the eighteenth century. In the early 1980s, one of the important insights was that the second half of a parallelistic couplet is not merely a repetition of the first, but that there is a dynamic movement from the first to the second, cf. J.L. Kugel, *The Idea of Biblical Poetry* (1981/1998) 1–58, 8, schematised as follows: "A is so, and *what's more*, B is so" (his italics), and R. Alter, *The Art of Biblical Poetry* (1985/1990) 3–26. Other important contributors to the debate of Old Testament parallelism throughout the 1980s include: S.A. Geller, *Parallelism in Early Biblical Poetry* (1979), M. O'Connor, *Hebrew Verse Structure* (1980/1997), A. Berlin, *The Dynamics of Biblical Parallelism* (1985), W.G.E. Watson, *Classical Hebrew Poetry* (1984/1986), D. Pardee, *Ugaritic and Hebrew Poetic Parallelism* (1988), L. Alonso Schökel, *A Manual of Hebrew Poetics* (1988), H. Fisch, *Poetry with a Purpose* (1988/1990), and W.G.E. Watson, "Internal or Half-line Parallelism in Classical Hebrew again", *Poetry in the Hebrew Bible* (2000) 198–220. Although W.G.E. Watson's handbook is illuminating in many respects, it sometimes seems to uphold a mechanical contention from the past that there is some kind of automatism or inertness in biblical parallelistic poetry: "Quite often *only one element of a word-pair is intended* by the author." Cf. W.G.E. Watson, *Classical Hebrew Poetry* (1984/1986) 139, (Watson's italics).

obvious in Old Testament texts, but other means of correspondences occur as well.[77] In Isa 18, word-pairs are observable in vv. 2, 3, 6 and 7. Chiastic patterns are present in vv. 1–2, direct speech occurs only in v. 4, and the poetic technique shifts as scenes change from one strophe to the next. The text as a whole is created as an *inclusio*.[78] Important to have in mind—the features of the text's design commented upon here are only *some* of what can be said about how the strophes of Isa 18 are designed. In the following, observations about phonetic, syntactic, and semantic features will be presented. Further, the poetic technique will be looked at. The way these linguistic and literary features function, however, will not be dealt with here, but will be argued for under the heading *rhetorical analysis* to each strophe.

During the 1990s, two features of parallelism have come to be firmly grasped: (i) parallelism is an organising principle the biblical poets used flexibly, and (ii) parallelism involves the interaction of various aspects of language, and is thus not limited to semantics. Already in 1971, B. Hrushovski (now Harshav), "Prosody, Hebrew", *EJ* 13 (1972/1974) 1200–1203, defined parallelism along these lines, but was for some reason overlooked by biblical scholarship. Following R. Jakobson and other linguistics, A. Berlin, *The Dynamics of Biblical Parallelism* (1985), speaks in terms akin to those of Harshav about equivalence in biblical parallelism—not just limited to the field of semantics. The same is the case for L. Alonso Schökel, *A Manual of Hebrew Poetics* (1988) 51, 57, and R. Alter, "The Poetic and Wisdom Books", *The Cambridge Companion to Biblical Interpretation* (1998) 228–230. For other selected contributions to parallelism from the 1990s, see W.G.E. Watson, *Traditional Techniques in Classical Hebrew Verse* (1994) 104–391, and A. Berlin, "Introduction to Hebrew Poetry", *NIntB* 4 (1996) 301–315.

Although the term "parallelism" continues to be used by the majority of scholars to describe the relationship between lines, new terms such as "matching", "intensifying", and "seconding" are applied to describe the kind of correspondence between the lines. The definition of parallelism in this work is broader than that of R. Lowth, and corresponds better with that of A. Berlin *The Dynamics of Biblical Parallelism* (1985) 1–3. Where R. Lowth, *Isaiah* (1795) 14, speaks of the correspondence of one verse, or line, with another, this work includes analyses of smaller segments than lines, too, e.g. consonants and words.

[77] Recent works have advanced our understanding of linguistic parallelism. Such studies have identified syntactic, morphologic, and phonetic forms of parallelism, cf. S.A. Geller, *Parallelism in Early Biblical Poetry* (1979), M. O'Connor, *Hebrew Verse Structure* (1980/1997), E.L. Greenstein, "How Does Parallelism Mean?", *A Sense of Text* (1983) 41–70, A. Berlin, *The Dynamics of Biblical Parallelism* (1985), D. Pardee, *Ugaritic and Hebrew Poetic Parallelism* (1988), P.R. Raabe, *Psalm Structures* (1990), and P.E. Dion, *Hebrew Poetics* (1992).

[78] The classical definition of *inclusio* is that there exists a verbal identity at the extremities of a literary unit. This identity could comprise a repetition of one single word or entire lines. In our text, the idea of the opening phrase of verses 1 and 2 is restated in verse 7.

2.2.1. *Phonetic observations*

Alliteration and assonance

From the diagram on page 41, it is apparent that four of the nine lines of Isa 18:1–2 begin with an א. An alliterative or quasi-acrostic pattern is created by the lines 1b, 2aδ, 2aε and 2bβ as they all start with an א.[79] Vv. 1a and 2aα both start with a ה. The two consonants ה and א both belong to the group of larynxes. Another consonantal pattern of this opening strophe of Isa 18 is made by the first letter of the last words of v. 2aδ, v. 2aε, and v. 2bα. All three lines have ו as the first consonant of the last word. Verse 2bβ however, has א as the beginning consonant in the first and last words, whereas the last word ends with ו. Looking at the strophe as a whole, the consonant א is present in all verse lines except in 2aα and 2bα. V. 2aε and v. 2bβ shows to have an accumulation of א.

Another alliterative pattern is the consonant צ that is found both at the beginning of v. 1 in ארץ, "land" and at the close of verse 2 (and ארצו). In addition צ is found in two other words of vv. 1–2, twice in צלצל, "buzzing", and once in צירים, "envoys". The consonant צ takes place three times in two words (ארץ and צלצל). This accumulation of צ within these two words create an explosion of sound when uttered.

In vv. 1–2 a pattern is created by the consonant ם. There are altogether eight occurrences of the final consonant ם in vv. 1–2. The following diagram shows only the words that have final ם:

Final ם	*Verse*
כנפים	v. 1a
בים צירים	v. 2aα
מים	v. 2aβ
מלאכים קלים	v. 2aγ
עם	v. 2aε
נהרים	v. 2bβ

---

[79] Alliteration is throughout this work defined as consonant repetition within lines, strophes or the text as a whole, and is not restricted to word-initial repetition. Although quasi-acrostic patterning often is defined as texts using only half of the alphabet (in contrast to the whole alphabet), quasi-acrostic patterns can also designate "[. . .] sequences of lines (though often not more than two) beginning with the same letter." Cf. W.G.E. Watson, *Classical Hebrew Poetry* (1984/1986) 111.

The consonants of the sentence לְכוּ מַלְאָכִים קַלִּים, "Go, swift messengers" (v. 2aγ), show to have the following relationship: The two כ (velar fricative) in the words לְכוּ מַלְאָכִים, and the ק (uvular plosive) in the word קַלִּים are uttered by the root of the tongue, and constitute an alliteration. However, the adjective sounds sharper than the imperative לְכוּ and the noun מַלְאָכִים as the ק has a plosive pronunciation, whereas the two כs have a fricative pronunciation. All three words contain the consonant ל (double consonant in קַלִּים). מ occurs at the beginning and end of מַלְאָכִים and once at the end of קַלִּים, and forms alliteration. The vowels of מַלְאָכִים קַלִּים create the following pattern: מַלְאָכִים /a-a-î/, קַלִּים /a-î/. By applying the same vowel-sounds (/a-î/) in these two words, assonance is created.

The reduplicated form of קוּ־קָו contains the consonant ק (uvular plosive) twice. This consonant is pronounced by the root of the tongue. At a phonetic level, the two קs of קוּ־קָו give emphasis to this reduplicated word.

Rhyme
Another phonetic observation is the end-rhyme of the phrase קַלִּים לְכוּ מַלְאָכִים, "Go, swift messengers" (v. 2aγ). The ending with the consonants ים and the vowel î of the two last words create an end-rhyme: îm îm.

2.2.2. Syntactic observations

Two patterns of chiasmus
In verses 1–2 there are two chiastic patterns.[80] One of them is made up by the repetition of the words for "land", "rivers" and "messengers/envoys" as the words (A) אֶרֶץ (B) לִנְהָרִי (C) צִירִים is reversed by (C') מַלְאָכִים (B') נְהָרִים (A') אַרְצוֹ. Even though there are different terms used in C and C', both terms cover the rendering "messengers." Schematically, the chiastic pattern can be showed as follows:

A	אֶרֶץ	מַלְאָכִים	C'
B	לִנְהָרִי	נְהָרִים	B'
C	צִירִים	אַרְצוֹ	A'

---

[80] "By chiasmus is meant a series (a, b, c. . .) and its inversion (. . .c, b, a) taken together as a combined unit", W.G.E. Watson, *Classical Hebrew Poetry* (1984/1986) 201.

The repetition of terms related to water (מִים, "waters", יָם, "sea", and נָהָר, "rivers"), is another chiastic feature of the opening strophe of Isa 18. Vv. 1–2 open with a הוֹי to "the land of buzzing wings from along the rivers of Cush", and ends with a command to messengers to go to a people "whose land rivers cut through." This creates a chiasmus as נָהָר, "rivers" occurs twice—once in the beginning, and once at the end of strophe 1—while יָם, "sea", and מִים, "waters", occur in the middle of strophe 1. The chiasmus can be schematised as AB//B'A', where A = נָהָר, "rivers", B = יָם, "sea", B' = מִים, "waters", and A' = נָהָר, "rivers".

Text	Verse	Chiasmus
הוי ארץ צלצל כנפים אשר מעבר לנהרי־כוש	v. 1a–b	A
השלח בים צירים ובכלי־גמא על־פני־מים [...]	v. 2aα–2aβ	B//B'
[...] אשר־בזאו נהרים ארצו	v. 2bβ	A'

Enjambment

The first sentence of Isa 18 does not end when the first verse ends, but runs into the next. This is called enjambment or "run-over line".[81] Here, the type of enjambment is an integral enjambment as the four short lines of vv. 1–2aβ form a single sentence:

Text	Verse
הוי ארץ צלצל כנפים	v. 1a
אשר מעבר לנהרי־כוש	v. 1b
השלח בים צירים	v. 2aα
ובכלי־גמא על־פני־מים	v. 2aβ

Gapping[82]

The first strophe of Isa 18 shows an instance of gapping as the preposition אֶל, "to", is not found in v. 2bα where one would expect its presence:

Text	Verse
אל־ גוי ממשך ומורט	v. 2aδ
אל־ עם נורא מן־הוא והלאה	v. 2aε
גוי קו־קו ומבוסה	v. 2bα

---

[81] Cf. *ibid.* 333: "Enjambment [...] is present when a sentence or clause does not end when the colon ends but runs over into the next colon."

[82] Gapping (also called ellipsis or deletion) is here and throughout this book defined as the omission of en element (sound, particle, word, or group of words) within a unit where its presence is expected.

Transformation of grammatical mood

In Isa 18:1–2 there is a transformation of grammatical mood between indicative and imperative. The first sentence of Isa 18 is held in indicative (vv. 1a–2aβ). The continuing of verse 2 (v. 2aγ–2bβ) how-ever, comprises an imperative. The command "go, swift messengers" (v. 2aγ) contains four descriptive subordinate lines that characterise the inhabitants and geography of Cush.

2.2.3. *Semantic observations*

Semantically, most of vv. 1–2 characterises the land "from along the rivers of Cush". The only line that does not mention the land or inhabitants from Cush is 2aγ. The imperative לכו, "go", of verse 2aγ is directed to the קלים מלאכים, "swift messengers" who seem not to be from Cush. Where are the messengers sent? The answer is given by four descriptive sentences (v. 2aδ-2bβ, the three first lines describ-ing the people, and the last describing the land). The first descrip-tion gives information about anthropological features of the people in question. They are described as ממשך ומורט, "tall and smooth-skinned". The second description focuses on the people's reputation as a people who is נורא מן־הוא והלאה, "feared from that day and onwards". The third description is along the same lines and says that the people is קו־קו ומבוסה, "line upon line and down-treading". After these three descriptions of the people's characteristics and rep-utation, the fourth description defines the destination for the swift messengers by describing the geography of the land in which the down-treading tall and smooth-skinned people live, אשר־בזאו נהרים ארצו, "whose land rivers cut through".

Word-pairs[83]

A striking feature of v. 2 is the pattern made by the word-pair גוי and עם. The nouns "nation"/"people" occur three times in verse 2

---

[83] What is here and throughout this book labelled word-pairs is by modern schol-ars used interchangeably with other terms: standing pairs, fixed pairs, A–B pairs, paralleled pairs etc. According to W.G.E. Watson, *Classical Hebrew Poetry* (1984/1986) 128, parallel word-pairs can be recognised as such if they fit the following three requirements: (i) each must belong to the same grammatical class (verb, noun, etc.), (ii) the components must occur in parallel lines, and (iii) such word-pairs must be relatively frequent. Throughout this work, Watson's three requirements have been understood only as a guide, as word-pairs are designated in this research even though not all three criteria are present.

(2aδ, 2aε, 2bα), where the first and third is גוי and the second is עם.
Linked to the first and second noun is the preposition אל, while the
third גוי does not have neither this nor any other preposition (v.
2bα). The two אל, verse 2aδ and 2aε are instrumental prepositions
as they introduce the people to whom the messengers are sent.

Another word-pair is found in v. 2aα and v. 2aγ where two terms
for messengers are applied: צירים, "envoys", and מלאכים, "messengers". צירים is applied about messengers *from* the remote nation Cush,
whereas messengers who are commanded to go *to* Cush are referred
to as מלאכים.

Play with words
According to J.J. Glück, "[e]xcept for the word גוי, "people", all the
other words are problematic, indeed vague."[84] Although this is an
exaggeration, it is correct that many words of Isa 18:1–2 are difficult
to translate. There are some words that play on the meaning of
other words in v. 2.[85] The verb משך have the meaning "draw",
"drag", "seize". The noun משכה is applied in Job 38:31 with the
meaning "cord". In Isa 18:2 ממשך, pual participle masculine singular
absolute, is rendered "tall". Literally, it means "drawn out", "long",
or "lined". As has been dealt with above, the meaning of קו־קו, is
insecure, too. Here, the translation "line upon line" is preferred. As
referred to above, other possible renderings of קו־קו are: "hope",
onomatopoetic for a foreign people's speech, "strong" or "mighty".

All possible meanings might have passed through the minds of the
ancient audience, connecting ממשך and קו־קו, but bringing no
clarification. The word מורט can be translated "torn", "shiny", or
"smooth-skinned". These words that are used to describe the inhab-

---

[84] J.J. Glück, "Paronomasia in Biblical Literature", *Semitics* 1 (1970) 71.
[85] By *play with words* is here and throughout this book meant an application of
words which meaning(s) is (are) uncertain, or words which meaning(s) is (are) clear,
but used deliberately with ambiguity. By playing with words, the text masks other
meanings, and when used frequently within close proximity it can confuse readers
to interpret in ways that might mislead, see S.B. Noegel, "Drinking Feasts and
Deceptive Feats: Jacob and Laban's Double Talk", *Puns and Pundits* (2000) 163. Cf.
the definition of pun by J.J. Glück, "Paronomasia in Biblical Literature", *Semitics* 1
(1970) 53. I agree with J.J.M. Roberts, "Double Entendre in First Isaiah", *CBQ* 54
(1992) 40, when he says: "While one must remain aware of the danger of over-
reading, however, it is far more likely that our lack of familiarity with the wider
connotations of classical Hebrew words and phrases will result in underreading, of
missing intentional double entendres."

itants of the remote land can all have several meanings. However, all possible renderings give the impression of a strong and handsome people as "line" can draw the association to military operations where soldiers are lined up, and "smooth-skinned" can point to shiny and attractive bodies. However, describing a people as "smooth" can also be associated with something polished and slippery, and can create a feeling of uncertainty when political alliances are in question.[86] Will this people be trustworthy, or will they slide out of our hands? This vagueness of meaning serves to leave the audience in perplexity about the appearance and attributes of the exotic people from "along the rivers of Cush".

The words ממשך and קו־קו, both having to do with something that is lined or long is further related to the rivers that בזא, "cut through" the area described in vv. 1–2. By the word בזא, "cut through", the text describes a pattern in the landscape drawn by the rivers, seen from above, it would look like several long lines. The text plays with words that are linked to each other by the associations to lines. The audience might have had all the various renderings at its disposal.

2.2.4. Poetic technique

Direct speech?
How is the first strophe of Isa 18 designed with view to poetic technique? Direct speech is not straightforwardly applied in vv. 1–2.[87] However, the style of what is said points to a situation where one could imagine one character bringing out a message to an audience. From the linguistic analysis above, this is clear in v. 2aγ. By the imperative לכו "Go!", (qal imperative masculine plural), there is an implicit address to a group of people. Whether or not there were

---

[86] A.L. Sachar, *The History of the Jews* (1966) 56, alludes to "smooth" in Isa 18:2, and regards it as not referring to a physical characteristic, but rather to the people's way of performing diplomacy: "The arguments were plausible and were presented with the glibness and smoothness of practiced diplomats." See also H.L. Aubin, *The Rescue of Jerusalem* (2003) 229, who goes against those who find a double (negative) meaning by the word that is translated "smooth" in Isa 18:2: "The context [. . .] suggests that the word "smooth", as we saw in Chapter 13, is not meant to convey unctuous, insincere talk but rather a physical characteristic [. . .]".

[87] Direct speech is here understood as situations described in the text where (i) a character is cited, or (ii) where a conversation between two or more characters is referred to.

swift messengers who heard the message when it was said is another question, what is clear from the text is that a group of מלאכים, "messengers", is given a command: "Go, swift messengers [. . .]", (v. 2aγ).

Thoroughly described characters
Another central poetic technique that is applied in vv. 1–2 is the focusing on the characters from Cush at the expense of the other group of characters mentioned, the מלאכים, "messengers" (v. 2aγ).[88] In this first strophe of Isa 18, all lines—except v. 2aγ—portray the people and land "from along the rivers of Cush". The only other group of characters that is mentioned in addition to the Cushites are the messengers that are commanded to go to the people from Cush, לכו מלאכים קלים. Indirectly, this other group also makes Cush stand in the centre of attention, as they are sent to Cush. These characters (מלאכים) are described only briefly as being מלאכים קלים, "swift messengers". This technique of briefness contrasts the detailed portrayal of the physical appearance (together with the reputation) of the Cushites, and lets the focus be on the Cushites. In sum, the characters who occupy most of the space in vv. 1–2 are the people living in a land that is divided by rivers: the Cushites.

Summing up the features in the text's design
The features in the text's design can be summarised as follows: First, there are phonetic patterns observable in vv. 1–2. Alliteration, assonance, and rhyme have all been attended to in the analysis above. Second, the syntactic observations have showed that vv. 1–2 contain two patterns of chiasmus, and that enjambment, gapping, and transformation of grammatical mood are also at work in this strophe. Third, semantically speaking, it has been observed that all lines except one (v. 2aγ), describe the land or inhabitants of Cush. Further, semantically, word-pairs and play with words have been described. Fourth, observations about the poetic technique of vv. 1–2 have showed that this strophe contains a command, and that one group of characters is thoroughly described (the Cushites) at the expense of the other group of characters mentioned (the "swift messengers").

---

[88] Participant reference is here and throughout this book applied about the various characters (individuals or groups) playing major or minor roles in the text.

2.3. Motifs

So far, some observations about the textual design of Isa 18:1–2 have been made. Now it is time for presenting the motifs of vv. 1–2.[89] This will be done in three steps. First, the central motifs of Isa 18:1–2 will be identified. Then, as each motif of Isa 18:1–2 is reflected also in other texts, the second step is to show how the motif is applied in the Old Testament in general.[90] On this background, the third step is to see how the motif is applied in Isa 18 in particular.[91] In

---

[89] As remarked in 1.3.4., a motif is throughout this book defined as a concrete, sometimes trivial phenomenon taken from the world outside the text, i.e. what the text *mentions*.

[90] There will not be a discussion of each motif's growth (diachronic perspective) throughout the Old Testament.

[91] Some of the motifs of Isa 18 are applied metaphorically, while others are not. As the present work is not a study of metaphors as such in the Old Testament, but an analysis of the rhetoric of Isa 18 where metaphorical speech occurs, there is not a need for a thorough discussion of metaphor theories. For recent contributions, cf. K. Nielsen, *There is Hope for a Tree* (1989) 25–42, C.G. Müller, *Gottes Planzung—Gottes Bau—Gottes Tempel* (1995) 5–44, G. Eidevall, *Grapes in the Desert* (1996) 19–46. Cf. also M.C.A. Korpel, *A Rift in the Clouds* (1990) 35–54, and P.W. Macky, *The Centrality of Metaphors to Biblical Thought* (1990) 4–8.

Let me give a brief survey, in order to determine the terminology applied in this work. I.A. Richards, *The Philosophy of Rhetoric* (1936/1965) 96, provides the impetus to the modern study of metaphor, and suggests that the meaning of a metaphor is the interaction between vehicle and tenor. M. Black, *Models and Metaphors* (1962/1981), develops Richards' interactionist insights, but suggests the terms principal subject and subsidiary subject as more adequate than vehicle and tenor. In the example: "Man is a wolf", "man" is principal subject, and "wolf" subsidiary subject. According to Black, interaction differs from substitution or comparison. The interaction between principal and subsidiary subjects has to do with knowing the system of associated commonplaces of the two subjects. In Black's view, the metaphor "Man is a wolf" organises our view of man, and fosters insight into this principal subject, *ibid*. 38–47. In the 1980s, the works of G. Lakoff & M. Johnson, *Metaphors We Live By* (1980), and G. Lakoff, *Women, Fire, and Dangerous Things* (1987), demonstrate how extensively metaphorical our ways of describing common realities are. They apply the terminology source domain and target domain. For the metaphor: "Man is a wolf", "wolf" is source, and "man" is target. This is further developed in G. Lakoff & M. Turner, *More than Cool Reason* (1989). Within biblical studies, the following works are central: J.M. Soskice, *Metaphor and Religious Language* (1985), P.W. Macky, *The Centrality of Metaphors to Biblical Thought* (1990), and M.C.A. Korpel, *A Rift in the Clouds* (1990). Most recent biblical scholars—including this writer—tend to take an interactionist view (proposed by Richards and developed by Black) as a point of departure. However, no uniform terminology exists, and scholars fill old terms with new content, cf. T. Stordalen, *Echoes of Eden* (2000) 51–53, who, like Lakoff and Turner, would call "David" target, and "wolf" source in the statement "David is a wolf." However, *seeing David as a wolf* is by Stordalen called tenor (my italics), *ibid*. 52. His definition of tenor is not the same as Richards' of the same term.

Isa 18:1–2, Cush is the primary motif. Of the subordinate motifs of
vv. 1–2, messengers and rivers (together with sea and waters) will
be dealt with here. Let us start with the subordinate motifs.

2.3.1. *Messengers*

One of the motifs of Isa 18:1–2—that partly describes the primary
motif Cush—is the motif "messengers". In Isa 18:2 the description
of the Cushites is given through a reference to צִירִים, "envoys", and
further through a command to a group of מַלְאָכִים, "messengers".

Concerning the meaning of the two terms, מַלְאָכִים is a common
term applied for messengers, whereas צִירִים is used more rarely. The
noun צִיר¹ means "envoy" or "messenger" and is applied six times
throughout the Old Testament.[92] The plural, צִירִים, "envoys", is found
only in Isa 18:2 and in Isa 57:9 (the latter with suffix for 2. person
feminine singular). In Jer 49:14, Prov 13:17; 25:13, and Obad 1:1
it is applied in singular, צִיר. In Prov 13:17 צִיר is paralleled with
מַלְאָךְ: "A wicked messenger (מַלְאָךְ) falls into trouble, but a faithful
envoy (צִיר) brings healing."[93] The two terms are applied synony-
mously in Isa 18, in the meaning "messengers"/"envoys".[94]

The word מַלְאָךְ, "messenger", occurs 213 times in the Old
Testament.[95] מַלְאָךְ has two forms of usage in the Old Testament: (i)
human envoys or (ii) divine envoys. First, the term מַלְאָךְ, "messenger", is applied either about a personal messenger (cf. Gen 32:4, 7
[ET: 32:3, 6]; Job 1:14; Prov 13:17;), or a political envoy (cf. Isa
14:32; 30:4; 37:9, 14; Jer 27:3; Ezek 17:15; 2 Chr 35:21). In singular מַלְאָךְ is employed 16 times, in plural 89 times. 72 of the 89
occurrences refer to political envoys.[96] These political מַלְאָכִים brought

---

A metaphor is not a word, but figurative speech. The definition of metaphor
applied in this work is based on the interactionist view of (Richards and) Black,
and the terminology is taken from Lakoff and Turner: source domain and target
domain—a terminology commonly applied by scholars today. Subsequently, the
metaphorical speech of Israel/Judah as the vineyard (in Isa 18:5) can be described
as follows: Israel/Judah is target domain, and vine/vineyard is source domain.

[92] Cf. *BDB* (1979) 851, and Koehler-Baumgartner, *HALAT* (1983) 960, "Bote".
The listing of the roots of צִיר vary from lexicon to lexicon, here the numbering
from *BDB* is followed.

[93] Cf. D.N. Freedman & B.E. Willoughby, "מַלְאָךְ", *ThWAT* 4 (1984) 890 and
893, who refer to Prov 13:17 and Isa 18:2 as instances where these two words are
paralleled.

[94] As will be argued below, this does however not mean that the two groups of
messengers are *identical*.

[95] Cf. R. Ficker, "מַלְאָךְ", *THAT* 1 (1971) 901.

[96] Cf. D.N. Freedman & B.E. Willoughby, "מַלְאָךְ", *ThWAT* 4 (1984) 892.

messages either intrastate (Josh 7:22; 1 Sam 6:21) or international (Judg 11:17; 2 Sam 5:11; 1 Kgs 20:2; 2 Kgs 16:7; 17:4; 19:9). The frequent use of the term in political contexts suggests that מלאכים designates government officials. Second, included in the group of divine messengers who are sent by God are both prophets (2 Chr 36:15; Isa 44:26; Jer 1:4–10; Ezek 30:9; Hag 1:13), priests (Mal 2:6–7; Eccl 4:17–5:6 [ET: 5:1–7]), and angels (Gen 28:12; 32:2; Ps 91:11; 103:20; 148:2).[97] The various groups of messengers referred to in the Old Testament by the term מלאך have one thing in common: they do not report their own message. Their function and message are dependent upon the will of the one/those who sent them.[98]

What does the motif "messengers" refer to in Isa 18:2? As already said, two words for messengers are applied in Isa 18:2: צירים and מלאכים. The first group travel *from* the "land along the rivers of Cush" (v. 2aα–2aβ):

> השלח בים צירים ובכלי־גמא על־פני־מים [. . .]

> [. . .] sending envoys by sea and in vessels of paper-reed over the waters.

The other group of messengers is ordered to go *to* the land of Cush (v. 2aγ–2aδ):

> לכו מלאכים קלים אל־גוי ממשך ומורט [. . .]

> Go swift messengers to a people tall and smooth-skinned [. . .]

The צירים travel to an unspecified place: על־פני־מים "[. . .] over the waters". The מלאכים are given a definite destination (v. 2): "to a people tall and smooth-skinned, to a people feared from that day and onwards, [to] a people line upon line and down-treading, whose land rivers cut through." Most likely, the messengers referred to in Isa 18:2 describe human envoys.[99] However, do these two terms for

---

[97] For the prophet as YHWH's messenger, see the work of R. Then, *"Gibt es denn keinen mehr unter den Propheten?" Zum Fortgang der alttestamentlichen Prophetie in frühjüdischer Zeit* (1990) 143–161, with further references.

[98] Cf. D.N. Freedman & B.E. Willoughby, "מלאך", *ThWAT* 4 (1984) 888.

[99] This view has its opponents, cf. W. Janzen, *Mourning Cry and Woe Oracle* (1972) 60: "[. . .] the Lord takes counter-measures in his Divine Council by sending his own messengers." It seems as Janzen assumes the messengers to be heavenly. This interpretation of Janzen is followed by R.E. Clements, *Isaiah 1–39* (1980/1994) 164. Another scholar who suggests מלאכים to be heavenly messengers is C.R. Seitz, *Isaiah 1–39* (1993) 148: "[. . .] the swift messengers are probably sent from the divine council itself." However, of all the 120 occurrences of מלאך as a divine messenger, the singular form clearly predominates (only 15 plural forms occur). In Isa 18:2

messengers designate *one* delegation from Cush?[100] The adjective קלים,
"nimble" (thus "swift"), accords with the portrayal of the Cushites
provided by vv. 1–2 as a whole, and could suggest that the two
groups of messengers refer to *one* Cushite delegation.[101] The following five observations make this unlikely, however, and argue for two
distinct delegations described in the text. First, as two terms are
applied (צירים and מלאכים), this could indicate a reference to two
distinct groups of messengers. Second, if the delegation from Cush
(צירים) is to return to their own land, the detailed description of the
people and land of Cush provided in vv. 1–2 is not needed.[102] Third,
the verb לכו, "go" does not carry the meaning of "return", which
would be expected if the מלאכים were referring to the Cushites.[103]
Fourth, as the Cushite delegation is not explicitly said to arrive in
Jerusalem, this could indicate that the command to go to Cush
(מלאכים) is given to a group of messengers present in Jerusalem. Fifth,
in Isa 30:16 the same adjective קל, "swift", is applied about horses
that the people of YHWH want to ride in search for a coalition
partner: "We will ride off on swift horses". From this, the most likely
interpretation is that מלאכים is a Judean delegation distinct from the
Cushite delegation, צירים.

מלאכים is applied in plural which could suggest that human messengers most likely
are described in this verse. For regarding the messengers as human, cf. Koehler-
Baumgartner, *HALAT* (1974) 554, and D.N. Freedman & B.E. Willoughby, "מלאך",
ThWAT 4 (1984) 892–893.

[100] This is suggested by H. Donner, *Israel unter den Völkern* (1964) 121–126, N.K.
Gottwald, *All the Kingdoms of the Earth* (1964) 163, H. Wildberger, *Jesaja 13–27* (1978)
689: "Die Boten von Kusch sind 'leicht' (קל) und also schnell", J. Jensen, *Isaiah
1–39* (1984) 164, K. Jeppesen, *Jesajas Bog fortolket* (1988) 125, D.T. Adamo, *Africa
and Africans in the Old Testament* (1998) 104, and R.S. Sadler, "Can a Cushite Change
His Skin? An Examination of Race, Ethnicity, and Othering in the Hebrew Bible"
(2001) 115. Cf. in addition B.S. Childs, *Isaiah and the Assyrian Crisis* (1967) 45, who
is not clear about whether the text describes one or two groups of messengers: "It
is not at all obvious why the prophet should describe to the messengers a people
to which they themselves belong. [. . .] And why is the term 'go' used, if the messengers are to return to Ethiopia?".

[101] For the description of messengers as being "swift", see S.A. Meier, *The Messenger
in the Ancient Semitic World* (1988) 25, who shows how ancient Semitic writers often
refer to a messenger's speed.

[102] Cf. M.A. Sweeney, *Isaiah 1–39* (1996) 257: "Clearly one cannot identify the
messengers described here [מלאכים] with those sent by Cush along its rivers [צירים],
as the latter messengers are sent to a nation described by the characteristics of the
land of Cush [. . .]".

[103] This is also noticed by E.J. Kissane, *The Book of Isaiah* (1960) 198, and B.S.
Childs, *Isaiah* (2001) 138.

2.3.2. *Rivers*

Another subordinate motif of Isa 18:1–2—that partly describes the primary motif Cush—is נָהָר, "rivers". In v. 1b and v. 2bβ the motif Cush is related to rivers (and also to sea and waters, v. 2aα and 2aβ). This section therefore includes the motifs "sea" and "waters" in the presentation of the subordinate motif "rivers".

The noun נָהָר, "river", occurs 110 times in the Old Testament and means "river", "flow" or "stream". In contrast to a נַחַל which flows only during the rainy season, the נָהָר is a perennial river that unusually dries up (cf. Nah 1:4 and Ps 74:15).[104]

In the Old Testament, the motif "river" has both a literal and non-literal meaning.[105] In its literal meaning, the motif "rivers" is applied about natural phenomena. Literally, rivers can be travelling routes, and often represent barriers to caravans and armies (cf. Josh 24:11; Isa 43:2; 47:2). "Rivers" can also function as boundaries (Ps 89:26 [ET: 25]).[106] In its metaphorical meaning however, the motif "rivers" has one of the following three functions: (i) as living water, (ii) as sacred places, or (iii) as destructive. First, water stands for blessing (Num 24:6). An increase in prosperity is sometimes likened to a river: "I will extend peace to her like a river, and the wealth of nations like a flooding stream" (Isa 66:12, cf. also Isa 48:18). Salvation is often likened to the water in the rivers (Isa 33:21; 43:20; 66:12; Ps 105:41). The rivers from Eden flow to the four corners of the earth and brings growth and fertility to the whole world (Gen 2:10–14). Interestingly for this study, in Gen 2:13 it is said that one נָהָר winds through the entire land of Cush. Second, rivers are applied in the meaning of sacred places. By the river Chebar, Ezekiel has a heavenly vision (Ezek 1:1, 3; 10:15; 43:3). Daniel, too has visions on the bank of a river, Ulai (Dan 8:2), and Tigris (Dan 10:4). Third, the motif "river" is metaphorically applied in contexts of destruction. When YHWH appears in judgement, the rivers are dried up (Isa 19:5; 50:2; Nah 1:4; Ps 107:33–34), and people are deprived a necessity of life. Rivers can be threatening, cf. Isa 43:2. YHWH's wrath is like a river (Isa 30:28; 59:19). The devastating rivers flood the land in

---

[104] Cf. L.A. Snijders, "נָהָר", *ThWAT* 5 (1986) 283.

[105] Cf. *ibid.* 281–291, where some of the following functions of the motif "rivers" are listed. Snijders does however not distinguish between literal and metaphorical application of the motif in the Old Testament.

[106] Cf. *ibid.* 284.

judgement (Hab 3:8–9; Nah 2:7 [ET: 2:6]). Job 22:16 speaks about a river that washes away the secure foundation of the wicked.

In addition to נהר, "river", Isa 18:1–2 apply two other words for the element of water: ם', "sea" and מים, "waters". מים, "waters" occurs only in plural in the Old Testament. As is the case for נהר, these terms too are applied either literally or non-literally in the Old Testament. Let us here briefly refer to the metaphorical applications of waters and sea in the Old Testament. Water is one of the basic elements from which the universe is formed (cf. Gen 1:9–10). ם', "sea" is in the Old Testament viewed with ambivalence.[107] On the one hand, ם' stands for fullness and regularity (cf. Isa 48:18), on the other hand the sea with its roaring and churning has a dangerous power, much greater than that of mankind (Ps 93:3–4). Accordingly, marine imagery is sometimes applied when enemies' attacks are described (cf. Isa 17:12; Jer 6:23). Metaphorically, enemies are described as "mighty waters" or "deep waters" (Ps 18:4, 17 [ET: 18:3, 16]; 69:16; 2 Sam 22:4, 17; Isa 8:7–8; 17:12–13). Egypt is portrayed as a sea monster troubling the water (Ezek 29:3; 32:2).[108] YHWH tames and overcomes the chaos (the sea monster), cf. Ps 77:17 [ET: 16]; 78:13; 93:3–4.

From this, it is clear that the texts referred to suggest that "rivers", "sea" and "waters" are parallel concepts.[109] Further, in the Old Testament the element of water stands for both the negative and the positive. On the one hand, the chaotic and devastating is associated with rivers, sea and waters. On the other hand, water is a necessity to all life, and is used in contexts of salvation.

What, then, does the motif נהר, "river" (together with "waters" and "sea") refer to in Isa 18? נהר occurs three times within the seven verses of Isa 18. In v. 1 נהר is found in plural construct, נהרי, whereas in vv. 2 and 7 it is found in plural absolute, נהרים. In v. 1 נהר is linked to Cush: לנהרי־כוש, "the rivers of Cush". In v. 2 it is linked to "land", נהרים ארצו (suffix for 3. person masculine singular), and as v. 2 is repeated in v. 7 the same wording is found there: נהרים ארצו. The masculine plural absolute of נהר occurs only 6 times in the Old

---

[107] Cf. E.R. Follis, "Sea", *ABD* 5 (1992) 1058–1059.

[108] "The connection with water may have suggested the comparison of Egypt with a river monster (30.6–8, 28)", cf. K. Koch, *The Prophets* (1982) 146.

[109] The same contention is also held by L.A. Snijders, "נהר", *ThWAT* 5 (1986) 289: "Aus den oben angeführten Stellen ergibt sich, daß die Begriffe Meer und Fluß parallel sind [. . .]".

Testament—two of these to be found in Isa 18 (vv. 2 and 7). נהר
is applied twice in 18:1–2 (and once in v. 7), and is thus a central
element in the description of the land.

Rivers and water/sea have the following five meanings in Isa
18:1–2. First, in its literal sense, it describes the geography of Cush
as divided by rivers. Second, literally, the reference to a nation that
travels over the waters shows a people in (diplomatic) activity—crossing the waters in order to establish contacts with other nations. Third,
the notion that rivers—as natural phenomena—are boundaries is
also echoed in Isa 18:1–2. Israel's ancestors dwelt beyond the Euphrates
(Josh 24:2), and beyond the rivers is also the place of exile (1 Kgs
14:15). The phrase מעבר לנהרי־כוש in Isa 18:1 refers to a distant foreign land at the borders of the world (cf. similar phrases, Isa 7:20;
Ezra 8:36; Neh 2:7, 9; 3:7). Fourth, Isa 18 plays on the metaphorical meaning of rivers/waters as life-giving (cf. Gen 2:13 and Zeph
3:10). As the terms for river, sea and water is mentioned four times
within vv. 1–2, this shows that the motif is central in the description
of Cush. As the portrayal of Cush in 18:1–2 strongly associates this
land with the element of water (rivers, waters and sea), this gives associations to an area of wealth and abundance. Fifth, the Old Testament
notion of rivers as destructive has been proposed for Isa 18:1 as the
rivers of Cush are seen as part of a negative context: "Schauderhaft
ist das Volk auf der anderen Seite der Ströme von Kusch (Jes
18,1)."[110] In my view, however, the people from Cush in Isa 18:1–2
is not portrayed as a horrifying people. Rather, the attributes chosen to describe the Cushites reveal admiration and respect.

2.3.3. *Cush*

The primary motif of Isa 18:1–2 is Cush. Except for one line (v.
2aγ: לכו מלאכים קלים), all of Isa 18:1–2 describes either the geography or the inhabitants of the land of Cush.[111] The literal meaning

---

[110] Cf. *ibid.* 285.

[111] Not all scholars would agree that Isa 18:1–2 describes Cush. A quite common suggestion is that Isa 18:2 describes Assyria, cf. R.E. Clements, *Isaiah 1–39*
(1980/1994) 164, who cites W. Janzen, *Mourning Cry and Woe Oracle* (1972) 60–61.
See also A. Gileadi, *The Literary Message of Isaiah* (1994) 149. H. Wildberger, *Jesaja
13–27* (1978) 689, however, proposes Cush, and M.A. Sweeney, *Isaiah 1–39* (1996)
257, suggests Egypt. Another suggestion is that the Medes are referred to in Isa
18:2, cf. E.J. Kissane, *The Book of Isaiah* (1960) 198, who suggests that the people
referred to in Isa 18:2 is described in Isa 13:17 (the Medes): "[. . .] there is nothing

of the motif Cush points to an African nation known as Kush in
Ancient Near Eastern sources, and as Ethiopia in Graeco-Roman
sources.[112] This land was located south of Egypt between the first
and sixth cataracts of the Nile, and throughout the third and second
millennia B.C. there were close relations between Cush and Egypt.[113]
In the first millennium B.C. Cush established a kingdom reaching
from central north-east Africa to the Red Sea in the east and the
Mediterranean in the north. For approximately one hundred years
(from ca. 760 to 656 B.C.) Cush governed Egypt in what is known
as the 25th Kushite dynasty. This climax of the history of Cush is
close in time to the origin of most of the Old Testament, and it
should therefore not be irrelevant to ask whether or not this military and politically achievement of Cush is reflected in one or the
other way in the Old Testament portrayal of Cush.[114]

---

in the description here which is out of harmony with this [Isa 13:17]." J.N. Oswalt
The Book of Isaiah (1986) 361, also suggests the Medes to be portrayed in 18:2.

[112] For surveys of the history of the ancient Kush, see B.C. Trigger, B.J. Kemp
et al., *Ancient Egypt. A Social History* (1983), D. O'Connor, *Ancient Nubia* (1993), T.G.H.
James, *A Short History of Ancient Egyp* (1995/1998), J.D. Hays, "The Cushites: A Black
Nation in Ancient History", *BS* 153 (1996) 270–280, and L. Török, *The Kingdom of
Kush* (1997). For examples of textual references to the ancient Kush, cf. J.B. Pritchard,
(ed.), *ANET* (1950/1969) 290–297, 316, W.W. Hallo (ed.), *The Context of Scripture.*
Vol. 1 (1997) 46a, 403c, W.W. Hallo, (ed.), *The Context of Scripture.* Vol. 2. (2000) 6d,
16d, 159, 300, W.W. Hallo (ed.), *The Context of Scripture.* Vol. 3 (2002) 243a, T. Eide
& T. Hägg et al. (eds.), *Fontes Historiae Nubiorum.* Vol. 1 (1994) 187, 232–234, 237,
240–241, 261–262, T. Eide & T. Hägg et al. (eds.), *Fontes Historiae Nubiorum.* Vol. 2
(1996) 603, 699, and T. Eide & T. Hägg et al. (eds.), *Fontes Historiae Nubiorum.* Vol. 3
(1998) 970, 979, 983. In the literature, the historical Cush is often referred to as
Kush, whereas the Old Testament Cush is referred to as Cush. In this work, the
same spelling is used about the historical and literary Cush.

[113] Traditionally, this relationship has been explained in terms of a superior Egypt
and an inferior Cush. Recently, however, it has been argued that the two should
be seen as more equal rivals, as "[. . .] two major powers competing for resources
and lands of the Lower Nile." Cf. D. O'Connor, *Ancient Nubia* (1993) 2.

[114] Scholars have emphasised the relationship between ancient Egypt and the
Ancient Near East. The approximately 680 Old Testament references to Egypt
show that Egypt was a well-known entity for the ancient Israelites. In sum, these
references reflect a dual picture of this north-African nation. On the one hand,
Egypt is the place of suffering and humiliation (see Deut 4:20; 1 Sam 10:18), on
the other hand Egypt is an asylum for refugees (see 1 Kgs 11:40; 2 Kgs 25:26),
and a coalition partner for the king in Jerusalem (2 Kgs 18:21, 24). As Cush ruled
Egypt for approximately one hundred years, it is not peculiar that this power's reputation would reach parts of the Mediterranean area, and be referred to in the
Old Testament. Isa 18 most likely alludes to pre-exilic political conditions, and as
a text dealing with political alliances presumably in the eighth century B.C. it might
indirectly refer to the Cushite control over Egypt. By this stance, I put my self in
an opposite position from the so-called "minimalists" who hesitate to draw lines

The Old Testament contains 56 references to the motif Cush.[115] It should here be emphasised that not all of the 56 references to Cush/Cushite necessarily refer to the African nation, or to individual members of that nation.[116] Some may refer to the Kassites in Babylon, or to a tribal group presumably living on the south-western border of Judah.[117] Still, the majority clearly refer to the African nation. References to Cush are found in all three divisions of the Hebrew canon: the Law, the Prophets, the Writings. Starting with the Law, the motif Cush appears six times in the Pentateuch, of which four are to be found in Genesis (Gen 2:13; 10:6, 7, 8), and two in Numbers (Num 12:1,1). It is used once as a geographical location (Gen 2:13), and five times as personal names. Gen 2:13 reads: "The name of the second river is Gihon; it winds through the entire land of Cush". As Gihon is the name of a spring in Jerusalem, the reference to the African Cush seems odd. The second river has traditionally been located in Mesopotamia—like the location of the third and the fourth rivers (Tigris and Euphrates)—linking Cush to the Kassites. However, an African location is not impossible as there is a strong tradition for relating the name Gihon to the river Nile (cf. LXX Jer 2:18; Ben Sira 24:27).[118] The geographical reference to Cush in Gen 2:13, accordingly, most likely indicates that Africa is included in the world map reflected in Gen 2:13.[119]

In the Law there are five more occurrences of Cush, first, three in the Table of nations (Gen 10:6, 7, 8), where Cush is mentioned

---

between any Old Testament text and what could be called historical conditions outside the texts. My contention is that the Old Testament texts in some or the other way relate to the milieu in which they originated.

[115] כוש occurs 30 times, and כושי 26 times in the Old Testament. For a survey of the references, cf. A. Even-Shoshan, *A New Concordance of the Bible* (1983) 527.

[116] This opinion is not shared by D.T. Adamo, "Ethiopia in the Bible", *AfrCSt* 8 (1992) 51, who emphasises the African location of Old Testament Cush arguing that: "Everywhere the word 'Cush' is used with a clear cut identification, it refers to Africa."

[117] Cf. S. Hidal, "The Land of Cush in the Old Testament", *SEÅ* 41–42 (1977) 97–106. See also R.W. Anderson, "Zephaniah ben Cushi and Cush of Benjamin", *The Pitcher is Broken* (1995) 45–70, and R.D. Haak, "'Cush' in Zephaniah", *ibid.* (1995) 238–251.

[118] Cf. T.K. Cheyne, *The Book of the Prophet Isaiah* (1899) 108–109, and E. Ullendorff, *Ethiopia and the Bible* (1968) 2–3. Cf. the discussion in C. Westermann, *Genesis 1–11* (1974) 297–298, where an African location of Cush is suggested.

[119] Cf. S. Hidal, "The Land of Cush in the Old Testament", *SEÅ* 41–42 (1977) 97–106, K. Holter, "Africa in the Old Testament", *Yahweh in Africa* (2000) 100–101, and T. Stordalen, *Echoes of Eden* (2000) 279–281.

first in a series of Ham's four sons. Cush is here applied as a personal name.[120] Further, vv. 10–12 list several places and cities that the son of Cush established. Of Cush's stock comes one who is said to be the first to have a great dominion on the earth. Although Cush is here a personal name, Cush is mentioned first in Gen 10:6 probably due to a geographical orientation starting from the far south.[121] The two last references to Cush in the Law are found in a narrative in Numbers 12 about Moses and his Cushite wife.[122]

The former prophets comprises eight references (2 Sam 18:21 (x2), 22, 23, 31, 32 (x2); 2 Kgs 19:9), and the latter prophets twenty-five (Isa 11:1; 18:1; 20:3, 4, 5; 37:9; 43:3; 45:14; Jer 13:23; 36:14; 38:7, 10, 12; 39:16; 46:9; Ezek 29:10; 30:4, 5, 9; 38:5; Amos 9:7; Nah 3:9; Zeph 1:1; 2:12; 3:10). The eight references in the former prophets are found in two different narratives, both alluding to the military ability of the Cushites. The first narrative (2 Sam 18) depicts a Cushite officer in king David's army (vv. 21–33) reporting Absalom's death to the king (vv. 32–33). The other narrative (2 Kgs 19) gives the Cushite king Tirhakah a central role in the deliverance of Jerusalem (v. 9). Both narratives implicitly refer to Cushites in relation to the people of YHWH, and portray the two individuals from Cush as having central roles in society.

From the 25 references to Cush in the latter prophets, the Cushites are featured in various ways. In Isaiah 18 and Jer 13:23 Cushites are described in anthropological terms. The wealth of Cush is alluded to in Isa 43:3 and 45:14. In Isa 20, YHWH's people is warned against trusting Cush. The allusion to a military reputation of Cush is reflected in lists (Ezek 38:5 and Nah 3:9), and in the narrative about the officer Ebed-Melech (Jer 38–39). A comparison between Cush and Israel is done in Amos 9:7 where Israel's exodus from Egypt is compared to other peoples' similar experiences:[123]

---

[120] E.A. Speiser, "The Rivers of Paradise", *Festschrift Johannes Friedrich* (1959) 475, states that Cush in the Table of Nations is an eponym of the Kassites in Mesopotamia. For the same opinion, see J.D. Levenson, *Sinai and Zion* (1985) 131.

[121] Cf. D.T. Adamo, "The Table of Nations Reconsidered in African Perspective (Genesis 10)", *Journal of African Religion and Philosophy* 2 (1993) 138–143. The table of nations is repeated in 1 Chr 1.

[122] For solutions to why Miriam and Aaron criticises Moses, see D.T. Adamo, "The African Wife of Moses: An Examination of Numbers 12:1–9", *ATJ* 18 (1989) 230–237, J.D. Hays, "The Cushites: A Black Nation in Ancient History", *BS* 153 (1996) 270–280, and K. Holter, "Africa in the Old Testament", *Yahweh in Africa* (2000) 101.

[123] Cf. D.T. Adamo, "Amos 9:7–8 in an African Perspective", *Orita* 24 (1992)

Are not you Israelites the same to me as the Cushites? declares YHWH.
Did I not bring Israel up from Egypt, the Philistines from Caphtor
and the Arameans from Kir?

Cush is sometimes used as a limit of the borders of the world, such
as in Ezek 29:10. The opening verse of Zephaniah (1:1) introduces
the prophet as the son of Cushi.[124] Further, Cush represents the far
south in the prophet's geographical orientation (Zeph 2:4–15, v. 12).
Cush is mentioned in the context of salvation (Zeph 3:10).[125] This
is also reflected in Isa 18:7. Some of the same thought is reflected
in Isa 11:11. YHWH will collect his people from the corners of the
earth (v. 12). Cush is the most remote and southern place of those
mentioned.

The Writings have seventeen references to Cush and Cushites, three
of these are found in the Psalms (7:1; 68:32; 87:4), one in Job (28:19),
two in Esther (1:1; 8:9), one in Daniel (11:43), three in 1 Chronicles
(1:8, 9, 10), and seven in 2 Chronicles (12:3; 14:8, 11, 12 (× 2); 16:8;
21:16). Ps 68:32 [ET: 68:31] probably alludes to the motif of Cushites
bringing gifts to YHWH in Jerusalem: "Envoys will come from Egypt;
Cush will quickly stretch out her hands to God." Ps 87:4 mentions
pilgrims from different nations, including Cush. Job 28:19 alludes to
the wealth of Cush. The two references to Cush in Esther (1:1; 8:9)
refers to Cush as the south-western border of the world. In Dan
11:43 Cushites are mentioned in the context of wealth and riches.
The narrative in 2 Chr 14:8–14 [ET: 14:9–15] is typical for the
way the holy war is described, as it exaggerates the number of soldiers involved: "Now Zerah the Cushite came out against them with
an army of a million men and 300 chariots, and he came to Mareshah"
(2 Chr 14:8).

From this Old Testament survey it is clear that the motif Cush
literally refers to an ancient African nation that was located south
of Egypt. Non-literally, the motif Cush is in the Old Testament associated with the following: Richness, military reputation, abundance,

76–84, R. Smith, "A New Perspective on Amos 9:7a", *JITC* 22 (1994) 36–47,
K. Holter, "Is Israel Worth More to God than Cush? An Interpretation of Amos
9:7", *Yahweh in Africa* (2000) 115–125.
    [124] R.W. Anderson argues that this reflects a Cushite presence in the land of
Israel, cf. R.W. Anderson, "Zephaniah ben Cushi and Cush of Benjamin", *The
Pitcher is Broken* (1995) 45–70, while others argue for an African origin of the prophet
Zephaniah, cf. G. Rice, "The African Roots of the Prophet Zephaniah", *JRT* 36
(1979) 21–31, and D.T. Adamo, "The Black Prophet in the Old Testament", *JARSt*
4 (1987) 1–8.
    [125] Zeph 3:10 will be briefly discussed under 7.3. when Isa 18:7 is analysed.

remoteness, and relation to Zion in eschatological times. The references to Cush/Cushi in the Law either refer to a geographical location (Gen 2:13), a personal name (Gen 10:6, 7, 8), or an individual (Num 12). In Gen 2:13 the mentioning of Cush in connection with water functions to relate Cush to abundance. In addition, Cush is in Gen 2:13 referred to as one of the corners of the world. In the Table of Nations, Cush is associated with strength as Nimrod is a mighty warrior on the earth (Gen 10:6–9). The references to Cush in the Prophets describe the Cushites in terms of anthropological features (Jer 13:23), economic wealth (Isa 43:3; 45:14), military reputation (2 Sam 18; 2 Kgs 19; Isa 20; Ezek 38:5; Nah 3:9), and remoteness (Ezek 29:10; Zeph 2:4–15, v. 12). In addition, there are some examples of texts that relate Cush to Zion in eschatological times (Isa 11:11; 18:7; Zeph 3:10). In the Writings, the military reputation of the Cushites is strongly resonated (2 Chr 12:3; 14:8–14; 16:8), and the remoteness of Cush is also referred to as Cush is seen as the south-western limit of the world (Esth 1:1; 8:9), and richness is associated with Cush (Job 28:19; Dan 11:43). Cush is also in this part of the Old Testament referred to as being related to Zion in eschatological times (Ps 68:32 [ET: 31]; 87:4).

The third step in the motif analysis is to see how the motif Cush is applied in Isa 18:1–2. As these two verses depict both the land, and the inhabitants of Cush, the following section comprises two parts: one on the geography of Cush, the other on the people of Cush.

The land of Cush
In Isa 18, the geography of the region of Cush is described in the beginning of v. 1, and at the end of v. 2:

v. 1a Ah! land of buzzing wings   הוי ארץ צלצל כנפים
v. 1b From along the rivers of Cush,   אשר מעבר לנהרי־כוש
v. 2bβ [. . .] whose land rivers cut through. אשר־בזאו נהרים ארצו [. . .]

The land of Cush is in 18:1–2 poetically described by highlighting two features of the region: it is a land of buzzing wings, and of rivers. It is evident that Isa 18:1 alludes to other texts where rivers and Cush are mentioned, cf. Gen 2:13 and Zeph 3:10. For all three texts (Gen 2:13; Isa 18:1; Zeph 3:10), the connection between rivers and Cush has a positive function of associating Cush with abundance. At the same time, Cush is in all three texts seen as representing one of the corners of the world. Zeph 3:10 has the same wording as is found in Isa 18:1: מעבר לנהרי־כוש. This phrase speaks about Cush as the most remote nation in the world (cf. Esth 1:1; 8:9).[126] The poetic wording ארץ צלצל כנפים, "land of buzzing wings", does not appear elsewhere in the Old Testament, and there is no consensus among scholars how this expression of v. 1a is best rendered. What is clear though, is that כנף has two meanings, "wing" and "extremity".[127] In Isa 11:12 and 24:16, כנף is applied in the meaning "extremity". In 11:12 כנף is applied to designate the four corners of the earth. As in Isa 18:1, Cush is also here mentioned in connection with what is far away—as among those places from where the remnant of YHWH's people will come (Isa 11:11). The beginning of Isa 24:16 also applies כנף in the meaning of the extremity of the earth.

כנף in Isa 18:1 probably plays on both meanings of the word: "wing" and "extremity". First, being connected to the word צלצל, the literal meaning of כנפים, "wings" makes sense, as צלצל refers to something whirring or buzzing. Second, by paralleling כנפים and כוש, the meaning "extremity" is activated:

v. 1a Ah! land of buzzing wings	הוי ארץ צלצל כנפים
v. 1b From along the rivers of Cush	אשר מעבר לנהרי־כוש

The people of Cush
In Isa 18:1–2, the characters are not referred to explicitly. When the people living in the land of Cush are introduced, they are not referred to as "Cushites", but described in a threefold way: (i) by their habit of sending envoys by sea (2aα–2aβ), (ii) by how their bodies look (2aδ), and (iii) by what their reputation is like (2aε–2bα). The following diagram has singled out the lines of vv. 1–2 that explicitly describe the people of Cush:

השלח בים צירים	v. 2aα
ובכלי־גמא על־פני־מים	v. 2aβ
אל־גוי ממשך ומורט	v. 2aδ
אל־עם נורא מן־הוא והלאה	v. 2aε
גוי קו־קו ומבוסה	v. 2bα

---

[126] J.N. Oswalt *The Book of Isaiah* (1986) 360, argues that the meaning of Cush in Isa 18:1 is metaphorical: "[. . .] Cush was used as a metaphor for the ends of the earth."

[127] Cf. *BDB* (1979) 489, and Koehler-Baumgartner, *HALAT* (1974) 463.

v. 2aα   sending envoys by sea
v. 2aβ   and in vessels of paper-reed over the waters.
v. 2aδ   to a nation tall and smooth-skinned,
v. 2aε   to a people feared from that day and onwards,
v. 2bα   [to] a nation line upon line and down-treading,

The first of the threefold description says that this land has the habit
of השלח בים צירים ובכלי־גמא על־פני־מים "sending envoys by sea and
in vessels of paper reeds over the waters". The next description portrays the people as looking ממשך ומורט, "tall and smooth-skinned".
The two last lines focus on the people's reputation as אל־עם נורא
מן־הוא והלאה, "feared from that day and onwards", and גוי קו־קו ומבוסה,
"line upon line and down-treading". From this, the way the Cushites
are described in Isa 18:2 highlights the following features of the people: They are known as mastering the element of water ("sending
envoys by sea"), they have a characteristic look—as if their bodies
are shining—they are feared, and they are down-treading.

From what has been said about the motif Cush's application in
the Old Testament in general, and in Isa 18 in particular, three
observations are essential. First, besides its literal meaning as an
ancient African power, the motif Cush in Isa 18:1–2 is also applied as
an exotic representative for the nations at the outskirts of the world
(cf. Esth 1:1; 8:9). Second, from the survey of Old Testament texts
that refer to the motif Cush, it is evident that the Writings emphasises
more strongly military reputation when Cush is referred to than what
is the case in the Law and in the Prophets (cf. 2 Chr 14:8–14). Third,
Isa 18:1–2 (together with v. 7) accumulates some of the central Old
Testament associations to this motif. Isa 18:1–2 describes Cush as
associated with abundance (cf. Gen 2:13; Zeph 3:10, here: "whose
land rivers cut through"), as the most remote part of the world (here
"from along the rivers of Cush"), in anthropological terms (cf. Jer
13:23, here: "tall and smooth-skinned"), and as having a military
reputation (cf. 2 Kgs 19:9; Isa 37:9, here: "down-treading").

Summing up the features in the text's motifs
From the observations above, it has been observed that Cush is the
primary motif of Isa 18:1–2. The subordinate motifs discussed above are
"messengers" and "rivers". First, it has been argued that the messengers
referred to in Isa 18:1–2 most likely describe human envoys. Further,
we have seen that the two words for messengers applied in Isa 18:1–2
(צירים and מלאכים), most likely refer to two groups of messengers

(one Cushite and one Judean delegation). Second, among other meanings, the motif "rivers" (together with "waters"/"sea") is applied literally about the geography of Cush and about the travelling route of the Cushites. Further, the motif "rivers" play on the Old Testament associations to rivers/waters as life-giving (cf. Gen 2:13). Third, the motif Cush in Isa 18:1–2 literally refers to the ancient African power that is a potential ally for Judah. Non-literally, Cush is in Isa 18:1–2 an exotic representative for the outskirts of the earth.

2.4. RHETORICAL ANALYSIS

So far, observations about textual design and motifs have been given. The important task now is to see how these work together to create the rhetoric of Isa 18:1–2.[128] This will be done in three steps: (i) rhetorical features in the text's design, (ii) rhetorical features in the text's motifs, and (iii) how textual design and motifs together create the strophe's rhetoric. However, in order to describe the rhetoric of this strophe, it is necessary to grasp the theme of Isa 18:1–2, i.e. what the strophe is all about.[129]

From what has been noted about messengers travelling in different directions, and a remote nation described in positive terms, the theme of vv. 1–2 is clearly that of diplomacy—more closely Judah's search for a coalition partner.[130] First, this is seen by the reference to two groups of messengers (צירים and מלאכים) travelling in different directions. Further, the references to rivers, sea and waters in Isa 18:1–2 show that the element of water is suitable as a travelling route for these envoys. Last, the application of the primary motif Cush indicates that this African nation is a potential alliance partner for Judah. From several Isaianic texts, Assyria figures as the strong power against

---

[128] For a presentation of how the term "rhetoric" is applied in this study, see the introductory chapter.

[129] As defined in the introductory chapter, a literary motif is what the text *mentions*. The theme is what the text *says* about what it mentions.

[130] Cf. H. Wildberger, *Jesaja 13–27* (1978) 683, who argues that the Cushite delegation arrives in Jerusalem in order to discuss a political-military alliance with Judah. That the phenomenon of making journeys in search for protection is a "central theme" in the book of Isaiah, cf. W.A.M. Beuken, "Isaiah 30: A Prophetic Oracle Transmitted in Two Successive Paradigms", *Writing and Reading the Scroll of Isaiah* 1 (1997) 374. For a general introduction to the politics of ancient Judah and Israel, see N.K. Gottwald, *The Politics of Ancient Israel* (2001).

which Judah rebels by going into alliances with other powers. If one presupposes that Isa 18 refers to pre-exilic times, it is well attested that in the eighth century B.C., the power in the Near East is Assyria. Isa 18:1–2 might refer to Cush and Judah who try to provide themselves against this power.[131] References to journeys—with the purpose of seeking support from foreign alliances—are known from other texts in the book of Isaiah, too. Cf. Isa 30:1–2 where the people of YHWH is reported as travelling to Egypt in search for protection: "Woe to the stubborn children [. . .] who set out to go down to Egypt, without asking for my counsel."[132] Accusation of the Judean leaders who make plans without involving YHWH is an integral part of the prophetic warnings about coalitions with foreign powers (cf. 20; 28:14–16; 30:1–5; 31:1–9).[133] Such expeditions are results of lack of confidence in YHWH (Isa 31:3):[134]

> But the Egyptians are men and not God, their horses are flesh and not spirit. When YHWH puts forth his hand, the helper will stumble, the one helped will fall, and both will perish together.

This prophetic denunciation of entering into coalitions (cf. Isa 7:9; 14:32; 30:15) is inspired by a kind of "[. . .] political quietism based on uncompromising and absolute trust in the protection of Yahveh."[135]

---

[131] Cf. H. Wildberger, *Jesaja 13–27* (1978) 683, who argues along these lines.

[132] "The journey as such is the dominating concern of the entire passage. Reference is made to pointless negotiations with envoys from the Egyptian cities of Zo'an and Ha'nes [. . .]", W.A.M. Beuken, "Isaiah 30: A Prophetic Oracle Transmitted in Two Successive Paradigms", *Writing and Reading the Scroll of Isaiah* 1 (1997) 374.

[133] Cf. R.F. Melugin, "The Conventional and the Creative in Isaiah's Judgement Oracles", *CBQ* 36 (1974) 301. To the analysis of Isa 30, cf. B.S. Childs, *Isaiah and the Assyrian Crisis* (1967) 33: "The message sets forth clearly the contrast between Israel's plan for herself and Yahweh's plan". See also H. Wildberger, *Jesaja 28–39* (1982) 1155: "Längst hatte Jesaja mit dem Einsatz seiner ganzen prophetischen Autorität versucht, die selbstzerstörerische Politik der proägyptischen Kreise Jerusalems als solche zu entlarven, und man hätte sich sehr wohl vorstellen können, daß man sich mit all dem in den Augen anderer Völker nur blamieren würde", and M.A. Sweeney, *Isaiah 1–39* (1996) 399: "[. . .] the primary intention is to argue against Hezekiah's plans to ally with Egypt in preparation for a revolt against Assyria."

[134] There are several suggestions to what this lack of confidence in YHWH implies. For a recent contribution to the interpretation of Isa 31:1–3, cf. G.C.I. Wong, "Isaiah's Opposition to Egypt in Isaiah 31:1–3", *VT* 46 (1996) 392–401, 396: "Turning to Egypt for human help and resources was opposed by Isaiah primarily because it represented a human effort to avoid or counter the divine intention of bringing judgement upon Jerusalem."

[135] J. Blenkinsopp, *Isaiah 1–39* (2000) 412. For a different view on how the prophetic indictments should be perceived, see J. Høgenhaven, "The Prophet Isaiah and Judean Foreign Policy under Ahaz and Hezekiah", *JNES* 49 (1990) 351–354, 352. According

On this background, it is clear that Isa 18:1–2 has links to other texts in the book of Isaiah where political decisions concerning treaties are questioned.[136] The travelling of two groups of messengers described in Isa 18:2 refer to international missions of diplomacy.[137] This is generally acknowledged, cf. the following selected examples: "Vermutlich sollten sie [daß Boten aus Ägypten] mit den judäischen Führern über die Bildung einer antiassyrischen Koalition verhandeln".[138] Of the commentaries, see H. Wildberger who states that "[i]n Kap. 18 war von Gesandten die Rede, die von Kusch nach Jerusalem kamen, um dort für eine antiassyrische Front zu werben".[139] A recent commentary holds the same assertion: "Usually v. 2 is understood as a description of the exchange of envoys between the two countries, Judah and Ethiopia".[140] As the present work analyses the rhetoric of Isa 18, a reconstruction of historical events that might formed the background for Isa 18 will not be done here. What seems clear from the text of Isa 18:1–2, however, is that two groups of messengers are reported to travel in different directions, and this refers to diplomatic relations between Judah and Cush. Although there is no explicit accusation of the Judean leaders in 18:1–2, it will be asked later in this book whether or not Isa 18 as a whole is best understood as a warning against entering into political alliances.

2.4.1. Rhetorical features in the text's design

From the analysis above of the textual design we have seen that vv. 1–2 show several cohesive patterns, and that the poetic technique focuses on one group of characters at the expense of the other group mentioned in the text. Does the way the text is designed reveal any rhetorical features of Isa 18:1–2?

---

to Høgenhaven, texts like Isa 30:1–5, 6–7, and 31:1–3 do *not* warn against political alliances *as such*, but show the prophet's pro-Assyrian policy: "[. . .] there is no hint in the Isaiah oracles that the forming of alliances is particularly wicked."

[136] Cf. G. Stansell, "Isaiah 28–33: Blest be the Tie that Binds (Isaiah together)", *New Visions of Isaiah* (1996) 88, who—finding various links between Isa 13–23 and Isa 28–33—points to the relation of Isa 18 to other parts of the book: "[. . .] the series of woe-cries in chs. 28–33, in addition to the series in ch. 5, has a precursor in 18:1."

[137] Cf. G.R. Hamborg, "Reasons for Judgement in the Oracles Against the Nations of the Prophet Isaiah", *VT* 31 (1981) 149, and D.N. Freedman & B.E. Willoughby, "מלאך", *ThWAT* 4 (1984) 893.

[138] Cf. F. Huber, *Jahwe, Juda und die anderen Völker beim Propheten Jesaja* (1976) 132.

[139] Cf. H. Wildberger, *Jesaja 28–39* (1982) 1150.

[140] Cf. B.S. Childs, *Isaiah* (2001) 138.

Phonetic observations: Alliteration, assonance and rhyme

From the analysis of the textual design of vv. 1–2, it is apparent that an atmosphere of activity is created. First, at a phonetic level, the impression of hectic activity that is produced by the word צלצל is underscored and intensified by the צ in the foregoing word אׄרץ. These two words together create an explosion of sound when uttered, and the sense of the phrase is emphasised by the use of the phonetic qualities of the language. The onomatopoeia has here a descriptive function in that it can mean "buzzing" at the same time as it imitates the sound of insects.[141] צלצל points to the sound of insect wings. As insects sound hectic, this choice of sounds in v. 1 serves to create an atmosphere of business.

Further, on a phonetic level, the pattern of consonants and vowels in v. 2aγ sound soft and resolute at the same time, and creates a feeling of symmetry and consistency, and thus functions to underline the contents of the command. As noticed by L. Alonso Schökel, the reduplication of consonants together with the end-rhyme in this strophe portray "an easy movement"—just like the message of the command itself.[142] The swift messengers are commanded in a way that imitates their swiftness. The alliteration in לכו מלאכים קלים, "Go, swift messengers", formed by כ (velar fricative) and ק (uvular plosive) has a function of making the command sound firm and resolute. This is created by the consonants of the adjective קלים that sounds sharper than the consonants of the imperative לכו and the noun מלאכים (the ק in קלים has a plosive pronunciation, whereas the two כs in לכו and מלאכים have a fricative pronunciation). The plosive pronunciation of קלים serves to underline the adjective "swift", and gives the command a feeling of urgency and haste.

The reduplicated form of קו־קו (v. 2bα) creates a dramatic effect.

---

[141] Generally speaking, the function of onomatopoeia is to convey the meaning of a word by its sound, cf. L. Alonso Schökel, *A Manual of Hebrew Poetics* (1988) 26. However, the relationship between sounds and meaning is arbitrary. More or less the same concept can be signified by differing sounds in different languages, and my aim here is to suggest a possible meaning of a Hebrew word that—for the modern reader—no longer have a known meaning. For the arbitrariness of the relationship between sound and meaning, cf. M. Kienpointner, "Linguistics", *Encyclopedia of Rhetoric* (2001) 429.

[142] L. Alonso Schökel, *A Manual of Hebrew Poetics* (1988) 28: "The metaphor of sound imitates by means of sound sensations derived from the other senses [. . .] An easy movement: *l'kû mal'ākîm qallîm* Go, swift messengers (Isa 18,2)".

At a phonetic level, the two פs give emphasis, and serves to create an atmosphere of urgency and danger.[143]

Second, observations on textual design of 18:1–2 has revealed some cohesive features which underscores that both verse 1 and verse 2 deal with the same people, the Cushites. The principal function of alliteration is that of cohesion. The alliterative pattern of consonants described in the phonetic analysis has the function of linking the various lines of vv. 1–2 together. The following consonants have an outstanding cohesive function in the first stanza of Isa 18: The consonant ו features 15 times in the strophe, whereas א, occurring twelve times, and ה, featuring seven times, also serve to tie the lines of Isa 18:1–2 together. The alliteration of א highlights the preposition אל, "to", and serve to focus on the people to which the messengers from Jerusalem are commanded to go.

On a smaller scale, the accumulation of the consonant מ within a limited area ties the two words מלאכים קלים together (v. 2aγ). All three words of v. 2aγ contain the consonant ל (double consonant in קלים). מ occurs at the beginning and end of מלאכים and once at the end of קלים, and forms alliteration. Another small-scale observation is that of assonance. By applying the same vowel-sounds (/a-î/) in the two words מלאכים קלים, assonance is created. The vowels of מלאכים קלים create the following pattern: מלאכים /a-a-î/, קלים /a-î/. This also functions to bind words together.

Syntactic observations: Chiasmus, enjambment, transformation of grammatical mood, and gapping

In verses 1–2 there are two patterns of chiasmus. One of them is made up by the repetition of the words for "land", "rivers" and "messengers/envoys" as the words (A) ארץ (B) לנהרי (C) צירים is reversed by (C') מלאכים (B') נהרים (A') ארצו. The other chiastic pattern is created by the repetition of terms related to water (מים, "waters", ים, "sea", and נהר, "rivers"). First, these chiastic patterns function to open Isa 18. Second, on a small scale, the chiastic patterns are cohesive as they link words together. Third, on a larger

---

[143] See Watson on effects of immediate repetition, W.G.E. Watson, *Classical Hebrew Poetry* (1984/1986) 277, who lists examples such as Judg 5:12; Isa 52:1, and Lam 1:4: "[...] immediate repetition is used to convey a sense of *urgency* [...]" (Watson's italics).

scale, the chiastic patterns link verses 1–2 together. Fourth, the chiastic patterns highlight words that are important in the text's rhetoric:
"land", "rivers", "messengers", "waters" and "sea". These words help
the audience focus on diplomacy ("land", "messengers", "rivers") and
on the remote nation "whose land rivers cut through".

Another striking feature of 18:1–2 is that of enjambment. Here,
a single sentence does not end by v. 1, but continues into v. 2 (v.
2aβ). One effect of enjambment is that it ties vv. 1 and 2 closely
together. Another effect is variety as it breaks the monotony of end-
stopped lines.[144]

The transformation of grammatical mood from indicative in v.
1–2aβ to imperative in v. 2aγ–2bβ functions to create an atmosphere
of activity. From the descriptive sentence in vv. 1a–2aβ, the next sentence is a command (vv. 2aγ–2bβ) that underscores the feeling of
urgency and activity, and also functions as a way of keeping the
audience attentive.

The syntactic analysis above also showed an occurrence of gapping in v. 2. Verse 2aδ and 2aε both begin by a preposition, אֶל,
"to", whereas v. 2bα does not have this expected preposition. Gapping
functions to focus the attention on what comes where the expected
element is missing. Here, a concentration on the people from Cush
is attained.

Semantic observations: Word-pairs and play with words
A striking feature of verse 2 is the pattern made by the word-pair
גּוֹי (x2) and עַם (1x). The noun "people" occurs three times in verse
2 (2aδ, 2aε, 2bα), where the first and third is גּוֹי and the second is
עַם. The two initial אֶל, verse 2aδ and 2aε, are instrumental prepositions that introduce the people to whom the messengers are sent.
This structure of a mixing of the two nouns, together with the irreg-
ular use of the instrumental preposition אֶל is not seen as a limping
structure. Rather, the גּוֹי עַם גּוֹי creates an A-B-A pattern:

$$\text{אֶל־גּוֹי} \quad \text{A}$$
$$\text{אֶל־עַם} \quad \text{B}$$
$$\text{גּוֹי} \quad \text{A}$$

---

[144] Two other functions of enjambment as suggested by Watson are (i) to assist
the forward movement of a poem by creating tension between metre and grammar, and (ii) to bring verse closer to normal speech rhythms, cf. W.G.E. Watson,
Classical Hebrew Poetry (1984/1986) 333–335. Watson's examples are among others
Lam 1:7 and Job 4:8.

This changing of noun with its instrumental preposition אֶל has the following functions. First, it prevents a repetition of the same noun three times in one single verse. Second, the עַם גּוֹי גּוֹי pattern functions to parallel the descriptions of the Cushites. Third, the עַם גּוֹי גּוֹי pattern initiates descriptions of the people to whom the messengers are commanded to go, and functions to make vv. 1–2 concentrate on Cush.

As the semantic analysis showed there are two words for messengers applied in Isa 18:2: צִירִים, "envoys", and מַלְאָכִים, "messengers". In v. 1–2aβ, delegates that travel *from* Cush are described, whereas v. 2aγ demands a delegation to go *to* Cush. On a semantic level, a relationship between v. 2aα and 2aγ is created by the word-pair צִירִים and מַלְאָכִים as these two terms describe the same phenomenon of delegates travelling for diplomatic purposes. Another function is that the adjective, קַלִּים, "nimble", thus "swift", attached to מַלְאָכִים serves to highlight one quality of the messengers that are sent off to Cush, and thus underlines the hectic atmosphere of diplomatic activity.

Further, another semantic observation is that most of vv. 1–2 characterises the land and people "from along the rivers of Cush". The only part of vv. 1–2 that does *not* mention the land or inhabitants from Cush is v. 2aγ that reads: לְכוּ מַלְאָכִים קַלִּים, "go, swift messengers". However, even in this line the audience's attention is focused on the people and land of Cush as v. 2aγ is a command to go "to a people tall and smooth-skinned [. . .]", i.e. the Cushites.

The semantic analysis also showed that the words that have an uncertain or ambiguous meaning seem to play on each others' meaning(s). The play with words in this strophe functions to leave the audience in confusion and perplexity as some words have several possible meanings, or no known meaning at all. The verb מָשַׁךְ has the meaning "draw", "drag", "seize". The noun מֹשְׁכוֹת is applied in Job 38:31 with the meaning "cord". In Isa 18:2 מְמֻשָּׁךְ, pual participle masculine singular absolute, is rendered "tall". Literally, it means "drawn out", "long", or "lined". The meaning of קַו־קָו is here translated "line upon line". However, other possible renderings of קַו־קָו are: "hope", onomatopoetic for a foreign people's speech, "strong" or "mighty". This play with words functions to confuse the audience about how to perceive what is said, and to give a feeling of unattainableness when it comes to viewing the people from Cush.

Poetic technique: Over-focusing on the motif Cush
The analysis of some of the poetic techniques of Isa 18:1–2 can be
summarised in the following five points. First, although there is no
direct discourse referred to between two or more characters in Isa
18:1–2, the text contains a command given to a group of messengers לכו מלאכים קלים "Go swift messengers", (the verb "go" in qal
imperative masculine plural).[145] Second, as all of Isa 18:1–2 except
this command describe either the inhabitants or the geography of
Cush, the way vv. 1–2 is narrated functions to focus on this remote
people. Third, this way of narrating creates a contrast between the
over-focused Cushites, and the under-focused מלאכים קלים, "swift
messengers" who are given no names or identity, but simply a characterisation as "swift". Fourth, this somewhat exaggerated positive
portrayal makes the Cushites stand out as attractive alliance partners. Fifth, such an over-focusing on the physical appearance and
military reputation of the Cushites serves to mock an admiration of
the Cushites from the Judean side.

Summing up the rhetoric in the text's design
18:1–2 shows the first step in a rhetoric of entrapment. At first, by
the use of the construction הוי plus participle, the audience is led to
believe that what will come is a judgement over the Cushites. However,
the expected description of the Cushites' bad conduct is replaced by
a positive portrayal of them in v. 2.[146] What is then the sinful action
to which the הוי is spoken? The diplomatic relations between Cush
and Judah is put there instead of a judgement over Cush. Could
this indicate that the sin that is committed is the alliance making
itself? This feeling of confusion created by the opening lines of Isa
18 is not yet solved.

Through an analysis of the textual design of Isa 18:1–2 this beginning of a rhetoric of entrapment is revealed in the following ways.
First, *cohesion* between words and lines is created through the use of

---

[145] In general, participant references contribute to indicating paragraph boundaries.
In our case, Isa 18:1–2 provides a presentation of the Cushites, and thus serves to
introduce a new group of participants compared to the immediately foregoing verses
(17:12–14). Cf. L.J. de Regt, *Participants in Old Testament Texts* (1999) 1, 13–14.
[146] Other speeches of judgement in the book of Isaiah are more negative, cf. the
taunt song to the king of Babylon in Isa 14:3–23, the warning to the Philistines in
14:28–32, and the prophecies of judgement against Moab in 15–16 that are all
held in a negative tone.

phonetic patterns such as alliteration and assonance, through syntactic patterns such as enjambment, and through the chiastic patterns. Second, an atmosphere of *activity* and business is created through the use of phonetic patterns such as accumulation of the consonant צ within a limited area. Third, a feeling of *confusion* about what vv. 1–2 is all about is made by the use of semantic patterns of word-pairs and by the play with words. Fourth, *concentration* on Cush is attained through the use of phonetic patterns such as rhyme, through syntactic patterns of gapping and change of grammatical mood, and also through the poetic techniques applied.

2.4.2. *Rhetorical features in the text's motifs*

Messengers: Diplomatic relations between Judah and Cush

How does the mentioning of two groups of messengers function in Isa 18:1–2? By introducing these two groups of messengers, v. 2 is able to describe two movements that go in different directions. The first movement which is described in terms of the geography of the route, is referred to as continuing: i.e. the people's habit of travelling from Cush (הֹשֵׁלֵחַ is a qal participle, durative in aspect). The movement from Cush is referred to as going by sea, בַּיָּם and over waters, עַל־פְּנֵי־מַיִם, and functions to describe that the land of Cush is a powerful nation that masters the element of water, and that their travelling aims at diplomatic relations with other nations.[147]

The second movement is referred to as a single command to go to a land "[. . .] whose rivers cut through". In accordance with what has been noted about cohesive features of vv. 1–2, the description of "a people tall and smooth-skinned" refers to Cushites.[148] Those

---

[147] For an overview of travel and communication in the ancient Near East, cf. S.A. Meier, *The Messenger in the Ancient Semitic World* (1988), J.T. Greene, *The Role of the Messenger and Message in the Ancient Near East* (1989), L. Casson, *Travel in the Ancient World* (1994), and F.F. Bruce, "Travel and Communication", *ABD* 6 (1992) 649: "The great rivers of Egypt and Mesopotamia have provided convenient means of communication from time immemorial. [. . .] The Egyptians, the Cretans, the Phoenicians, and later Greeks undertook coastal voyaging and N–S crossing in the Mediterranean." See also E. Strömberg Krantz, *Des Schiffes Weg mitten im Meer* (1982), and L. Casson, *Ships and Seamanship in the Ancient World* (1971/1995).

[148] As mentioned in footnote 111 in this chapter, the most common suggestions to whom Isa 18:2 portrays are Assyrians, Cushites, Egyptians, or Medes. W. Janzen, *Mourning Cry and Woe Oracle* (1972) 60–61, H. Barth, "Israel und das Assyrerreich" (1974) 10, R.E. Clements, *Isaiah 1–39* (1980/1994) 164, J.D.W. Watts, *Isaiah 1–33* (1985) 246, A. Gileadi, *The Literary Message of Isaiah* (1994) 149, all suggest Assyria,

who are commanded to go are "swift messengers" from Judah: לכו
מלאכים קלים. This second movement differs from the first as there
is no description neither of the messengers' conveyance (cf. "and in
vessels of paper-reed"), nor of their route (cf. "over the waters"). This
imbalance in terms of what is referred to about the two movements
serves to focus on the movement that is most detailed described, that
from Cush. Only a description of the goal of the secondly referred
to journey is given: "to a people tall and smooth-skinned [. . .] whose
land rivers cut through". This again places the attention on Cush.
It is not clear whether the second journey comes about as a response
to the first journey. However, what is clear is that both movements
indicate diplomatic activities—between Cush and Judah.

Rivers: Activity, abundance, and remoteness

From the motif analysis, several forms of usage were presented as
common for the motif "rivers" (together with "water" and "sea") in
the Old Testament. Isa 18:1–2 plays on some of these (boundaries
and living water), in addition to remoteness.

First, by referring to rivers and waters Isa 18:1–2 echoes the notion
that rivers as natural phenomena are boundaries. Related to this is
the reference to צירים, "messengers" that travel upon the waters (v.
2). This shows activity—more closely defined as diplomacy. By relating the Cushites to rivers and water this serves to create the impression that this people masters the threatening waters, and uses them
for diplomatic purposes.

Second, the frequent mentioning of the element of water in Isa
18:1–2 strongly relates the motif Cush to water. Rivers as living
water is echoed in Isa 18:1–2 and the allusions to Gen 2:13 where
one of the rivers of Eden surround the entire land of Cush are clear.
Abundance is thus related to the motif נהר, "river" in Isa 18:1–2.
As pointed at in the motif analysis, the meaning of נהר is a perennial river that unusually dries up, cf. Nah 1:4 and Ps 74:15. The
function of twice in vv. 1–2 relating Cush to נהר, a river that usually do not get dry (a third time in 18:7) is to associate Cush with
abundance. Cush is related to rivers and waters in Isa 18:1–2 and

---

whereas H. Wildberger, *Jesaja 13–27* (1978) 689, proposes Cush, and M.A. Sweeney,
Isaiah 1–39 (1996) 257, suggests Egypt. E.J. Kissane, *The Book of Isaiah* (1960) 198,
and J.N. Oswalt *The Book of Isaiah* (1986) 361, suggest the Medes to be portrayed
in 18:2.

this serves to create associations to abundance and overflow. Most likely, נהר in plural (נהרים) is applied for the sake of amplification.[149] This is underscored also by the word ים, "sea" that might refer to the Nile in Isa 18:2 and 7.[150] Usually, the Old Testament calls the Nile יאר. However, the Nile is occasionally referred to as ים, "sea". In Isa 19:5 נהר, "river", seems to be equated with ים, "sea".[151]

Third, the rhetorical function of the phrase מעבר לנהרי־כוש, "from along the rivers of Cush" needs to be discussed. As I have pointed out previously, most scholars render מעבר "beyond" without any discussion. If the translation "beyond" is chosen, it becomes an open question whether the area מעבר לנהרי־כוש refer to the ancient African nation Kush, or to a region further south of Kush. This again causes confusion about what nation is described in v. 2. However, I have asserted that the meaning of מעבר can also be "along", and have argued that the expression מעבר לנהרי־כוש in Isa 18:1 most likely refers to the region of Kush, and that the people described in v. 2 refers to the Kushites. In a poetic way, Isa 18:1–2 describes the most remote south-east area known, and the accurate identifying of the actual boundaries of this area is secondary.[152] The expression מעבר לנהרי־כוש underscores the Old Testament conception that Cush is to be perceived as a river region on the borders of the known world (Esth 1:1; 8:9). מעבר then functions here as a designation of the most remote south-western area known to the Judeans, more than an accurate geographical location.[153]

---

[149] See Ges-K (1910/1970) § 124d–f. The same is suggested by L.A. Snijders, "נהר", *ThWAT* 5 (1986) 283.

[150] Cf. L.A. Snijders, "נהר", *ThWAT* 5 (1986) 283, cf. also p. 289.

[151] For a linking of the sources of water referred to in Isa 18 with the river Nile, see K. Koch, *The Prophets* (1982) 146.

[152] A comparable expression in Deut 30:13 (cf. עבר הים/מעבר לים), traditionally translated "beyond the sea", shows to have a similar function. According to H. Ringgren, "ים", *ThWAT* 3 (1982) 655, this expression refers to the greatest possible distance, comparable to "high in the heavens": "'Jenseits des Meeres' (*mēʿēbær hajjām*) ist die größte denkbare Entfernung, vergleichbar mit "hoch oben im Himmel" (Deut 30, 13).'

[153] In her work with the book of Ruth, K. Nielsen has been concerned with the names mentioned there, and she touches upon an idea that can also be applied to the understanding of מעבר לנהרי־כוש in Isa 18:1–2: "Geographical names do not necessarily point at real geographical conditions, but may very well be markers that point outwards to the narratives and traditions that are linked to the name in question." K. Nielsen, "Intertextuality and Hebrew Bible", *Congress Volume Oslo 1998* (2000) 23.

Cush: An attractive alliance partner

How is the beginning of a rhetoric of entrapment discernible through
the main motif of Isa 18:1–2? First, the following features are important when the land of Cush is portrayed in Isa 18:1–2:

(i) Activity is associated by the phrase ארץ צלצל כנפים. Though
suggesting a different translation, Wildberger touches upon a similar function of the expression suggesting the winged boats ("geflügelten
Boote") to point at the speed and maneuverability of the Cushite
boats.[154] Not only was it extraordinary that Jerusalem had visitors
coming from a nation located so far away, their means of travelling
was also out of the ordinary. The accumulation of terms having to
do with water (in vv. 1–2) functions to highlight an extraordinary
feature about the Cushites. The delegation from Cush does not come
by journey over land, but by boats over the waters. As they are
depicted as mastering the element of water, this makes them attractive as alliance partners. (ii) In addition to activity, extremity is related
to the land of Cush. As the root כנף can mean both "wing" (of bird,
insect, cherubim, seraphim, women) and "extremity" (of garment, or
of the earth), כנפים in Isa 18:1 most likely plays on both meanings.
According to its use in Isa 11:12 and 24:16, one can assume that
the audience of Isa 18 knew the two meanings of the word. The
description of Cush as ארץ צלצל כנפים serves therefore to underline
both the activity ("buzzing wings") of this country, and its remoteness as belonging to the extremes of the earth.

Second, by the way the people of Cush are portrayed in Isa 18:1–2
the following features are important. (i) There is an over-focusing on
Cush in this stanza at the expense of the other group mentioned. By
focusing to such an extent on Cush, the rhetoric of entrapment has
started. The space given the Cushites in v. 2 indicates who are the
main characters of the text so far, and who the audience are supposed
(or entrapped) to focus at. The detailed description of the Cushites
function to highlight several features about this people, and subsequently
to let the audience regard the Cushites as attractive alliance partners. Despite the lack of a message directed to the Cushites, the text
describes the people from Cush. The description of a tall and smooth-
skinned people living in an area where rivers cut through is textu-
ally connected to the term Cush.[155]

---

[154] Cf. H. Wildberger, *Jesaja 13–27* (1978) 688.
[155] A. Berlin, *Poetics and Interpretation* (1983) 34.

(ii) Isa 18:1-2 provides a rather detailed portrayal of the Cushites' anthropological features and their reputation. Inclusion of details about the bodies of the Cushites functions as a rhetorical strategy in order to make the audience create a certain picture of the Cushites. In addition, the mentioned anthropological features of the Cushites' bodies make the goal of the sent messengers' route seem exotic. By highlighting the physical appearance, the rhetorical effect is to portray a people far away with bodies that look differently from the audience's bodies. The description of the Cushites as tall and smooth-skinned, line upon line and down-treading can suggest that the device of hyperbole is at work. By focusing solely on positive features of the land and its people, the audience is entrapped to believe that it is a people worth trusting. The text reveals a certain measure of admiration for this exuberant people living at the borders of the world. Is the text genuinely positive, or does it play with the audience? If taken straightforwardly, the portrayal of the Cushites gives the audience reason for going into an alliance with them. However, if the way the Cushites are portrayed is one step in the text's rhetoric of entrapment, the audience is easily fooled. By highlighting some aspects of the Cushite characteristics (only the positive), and leaving out others, the Cushites' abilities as a coalition partner is exaggerated. Subsequently, the audience is ridiculed if they do not see through the tactics from the prophet. What the prophet aims at is to mock the audience that trust human coalition partners instead of trusting YHWH.

(iii) The apparent confusion about whether 18:1-2 speaks about one or two groups of messengers has a rhetorical function of making the audience wonder who the message in the end concerns. This is also an element in the rhetoric of entrapment. The function of gradually seeing the מלאכים קלים, "swift messengers" as Judah's envoys, is to make the audience starting to grasp that the message is not directed towards the Cushites, but towards themselves.[156]

Summing up the rhetorical features in the text's motifs
The over-focusing on the Cushites, together with the description of their bodies and their reputation, function as vivid and imaginative. It gives an impression of a strong and powerful nation that has an

---

[156] This is noticed by M.A. Sweeney, *Isaiah 1-39* (1996) 257, and picked up by B.S. Childs, *Isaiah* (2001) 138.

extraordinary and exotic physical appearance. When an information about their land is added, this emphasises and underlines the portrayal of them as even the word "river" used to describe their land have positive associations. The Cushites are portrayed in a way that make them admirable, and their land is described as mysterious—a land of buzzing wings, and a land that rivers cut through.

According to Wildberger, "die relativ ausführliche Einleitung (1f.) zum eigentlichen Jahwehwort 4–6 ist nötig, weil die Kuschiten in Jerusalem wenig bekannt gewesen sind."[157] In my view, the extensive introduction (vv.1–2) does not function to inform the Judeans about an unknown power.[158] From the altogether 56 Old Testament references to Cush, much seems to be known about them. Rather, the extensive portrayal seems to be a first step in the process of entrapping the audience. In Isa 18:1–2, only positive features about Cush are highlighted. Could this be a way of ridiculing the audience's reliance on strong human beings instead of in their deity, YHWH?

2.4.3. How do textual design and motifs together create the strophe's rhetoric?

Till now it has been noted that textual design and motifs, respectively, show signs of a deliberate rhetoric. However, in what way do they together create the rhetoric of Isa 18:1–2? By the way Isa 18 opens (v. 1) the audience can reasonably think that the nation addressed will be judged. However, as the speech continues (v. 2), this seems less likely. In the following, we will see how the textual design and motifs *together* form the beginning of a rhetoric of entrapment.

Cohesion: Vv. 1–2 forms a unity
Analyses of both textual design and motifs of Isa 18:1–2 have revealed several cohesive features that bind vv. 1–2 together. The following four points summarise such features and says how they function.

First, from the analysis of textual design, is has been showed that vv. 1–2 contains an instance of enjambment. Enjambment has a clear cohesive function as it links verses 1 and 2 of Isa 18 together.

---

[157] Cf. H. Wildberger, *Jesaja 13–27* (1978) 682.
[158] Cf. C.R. Seitz, *Isaiah 1–39* (1993) 148: "[. . .] the description of Cush as "a nation mighty and conquering, whose land the rivers divide" (18:2) is quite possibly a familiar epithet, as is the description of the Ethiopians as "a nation tall and smooth"—hence the use of this description in 45:14."

Further, the application of chiastic patterns indicates that vv. 1–2 should be perceived as one unity. One chiastic pattern of vv. 1–2 is made up by the words (A) אֶרֶץ (B) לִנְהֲרֵי (C) צִירִים reversed by (C') מַלְאָכִים (B') נְהָרִים (A') אַרְצוֹ. By applying a chiasmus, three elements of vv. 1–2 are linked together. First, אֶרֶץ (A) and אַרְצוֹ (A'), "land", referred to at the end of v. 1 and at the end of v. 2 are linked together, and indicates that the same land is described in the two verses. Second, by the chiasmus, נהר (B and B'), "rivers", mentioned in the opening and the closure of the stanza are related and indicates that the same region is described in v. 1 as in v. 2. Third, at the centre of the chiasmus some messengers are mentioned, צִירִים (C) and מַלְאָכִים (C'). Although these terms most likely refer to two different groups, their purpose for travel is the same—the diplomatic alliance making between Judah and Cush.

Second, the word-pairs serve to tie various parts of vv. 1–2 together. On a semantic level, it has been proposed that a relationship between v. 2aα and 2aγ is created by the word-pair צִירִים and מַלְאָכִים as these two terms describe the same phenomenon of delegates travelling for diplomatic purposes.

Third, the play with words also creates cohesion. The words מְמֻשָּׁךְ and קַו־קָו, both having to do with something that is lined or long is further related to the rivers that בָזְאוּ, "cut through" the area described in vv. 1–2. By the word בָזְאוּ, "cut through", the text describes a pattern in the landscape drawn by the rivers, seen from above, it would look like several long lines. The text plays with words that are linked to each other by the associations to lines.

Fourth, the way the motifs—messengers, rivers, and Cush—are presented in vv. 1–2 also shows cohesive features. The motif of messenger is referred to through two different terms in v. 2. צִירִים most likely refer to a Cushite delegation, and thus creates a link to the motif Cush. As mentioned above, some scholars suggest both terms for messengers, צִירִים and מַלְאָכִים to refer to the one delegation from Cush.[159] According to this view, *all* of Isa 18:1–2 would describe the motif Cush. Further, the motifs river (together with terms for sea

---

[159] This is—as already said—suggested by N.K. Gottwald, *All the Kingdoms of the Earth* (1964) 163, H. Wildberger, *Jesaja 13–27* (1978) 689: "Die Boten von Kusch sind "leicht" (קל) und also schnell." J. Jensen, *Isaiah 1–39* (1984) 164, K. Jeppesen, *Jesajas Bog fortolket* (1988) 125, D.T. Adamo, *Africa and Africans in the Old Testament* (1998) 104.

and waters) and Cush are also strongly connected in vv. 1–2. The motif Cush is described in all lines of Isa 18:1–2 except 2aγ—either in terms of the land of Cush or the inhabitants of Cush. In v. 1 the motifs river and Cush are connected, לנהרי־כוש, and in v. 2 the people described (the Cushites) live in a land that is divided by rivers, אשר־בזאו נהרים ארצו. By applying נהר, "river" twice in 18:1–2 in relation to כוש, this serves to connect these two motifs. In the first instance, the land is described as being located along the rivers. In the second instance, the rivers are described as cutting through the land. This reveals a textual development as the connection between rivers and land is intensified from v. 1 to v. 2. From both v. 1 and v. 2, the emphasis lies on the connections between rivers and land.

Activity: Diplomatic relations between Cush and Judah
Both textual design and motifs reveal that the feeling of urgency is created by references to messengers (Cushite and Judean) that travel in different directions. By applying the adjective קלים, "swift" to מלאכים, the impression is given that the mission from Judah's side cannot be effectuated quickly enough. In addition, on a syntactic level, the transformation of grammatical mood from indicative to imperative underscores this feeling of urgency.

By describing activity, textual design and motifs together make up the theme of vv. 1–2: Judah's search for an alliance partner. By focusing on activity, the first step in a rhetoric of entrapment is taken. The admirable way the Cushites are depicted functions to qualify for being a coalition partner for Judah. The command לכו מלאכים קלים, "go swift messengers", can be taken as a mimicry over what the Judean leaders say, and serves to mock those who eagerly look for an alliance partner instead of waiting for help from YHWH (cf. Isa 1:19–20; 2:22; 14:32; 31:1–9). The anonymous messengers from Judah are portrayed only by the adjective "swift", and this minimal characterisation informs the audience about the messengers' role as carrying messages from one party to another. This minimal information about the מלאכים keeps the action moving along and helps the audience focussing on the other characters of vv. 1–2.[160]

---

[160] For anonymity and characters in other texts in the Old Testament, cf. A. Reinhartz, "Anonymity and Character in the Books of Samuel", *Semeia* 63 (1993) 117–141.

Confusion: Who is judged?

Through observations of textual design and motifs of vv. 1–2 a feeling of uncertainty and confusion is created, and thus the contours of a rhetoric of entrapment is seen.

First, the function of הוֹי in this text is decisive. The הוֹי of Isa 18:1 functions to confuse the audience about who is judged, and is thus a step in the process of entrapping the audience.

Second, play with words functions here as a means of creating a feeling of confusion. As previously pointed at, the words applied to describe the inhabitants of the remote land can all have several meanings. For instance, describing a people as "smooth" gives both positive and negative associations. Positively, the shiny smoothness of the Cushites' skin is eye-catching. Negatively, smoothness gives associations to something slippery. When political alliances are in question, the description of the Cushites as "smooth" can create a feeling of uncertainty. Will this people be trustworthy, or will they slide out of our hands? This vagueness of meaning serves to leave the audience in perplexity and confusion about the appearance and attributes of the exotic people from "along the rivers of Cush".

Third, this confusing way in which the inhabitants of Cush are described serves to let the primary motif Cush be associated with a feeling of uncertainty. As the inhabitants are described in a way that play on several meanings, and as the description of their land is poetical this functions to create a picture of Cush as remote and enigmatic. In addition, by applying an infrequent word for the Cushite messengers, צִרִים, instead of the more common, מַלְאָכִים, a feeling of rarity and unusualness is created. All in all, this serves to leave the audience in confusion when it comes to how this delegation from the exotic Cush should be considered.

Concentration: Cush as an attractive alliance partner

From the analyses of both textual design and motifs of 18:1–2 it has been showed that there is a concentration on the motif Cush in these two verses.

First, the analysis of syntactic patterns showed that the instance of gapping functions to put the people from Cush in the centre. The missing preposition אֶל, "to" is instrumental, and by leaving out this preposition the text focuses on what is present: a description of the military reputation of the Cushites as גּוֹי קַו־קָו וּמְבוּסָה, "a people line upon line and down-treading".

Second, the effect of describing the inhabitants and geography of
Cush in a detailed way serves to let the audience focus on Cush. The
words that are chosen to describe Cush gives an impression of a
strong people that can become a suitable coalition partner, and reflect
an attitude of admiration from the Judean side.

Third, connected to observations from the semantic analysis, the way
vv. 1–2 is put together shows that the contrast between the over-
focusing on Cush at the expense of the unnamed and under-focused
מלאכים, "messengers", functions to make Cush stand out as an attractive alliance partner. It is apparent that such an exaggerated emphasis on Cush is part of a rhetoric of entrapment.

Fourth, all three motifs discussed under *motif analysis* relate in one
or the other way to the theme of Judah's search for a coalition partner. The messengers refer to diplomatic delegations. The command
interrupts ("go swift messengers") the description of Cush and Cushites,
and functions to speed up the action, and to give hints about urgent
diplomacy. The rivers (and sea and waters) function to underscore
the travelling of delegations for diplomatic purposes. In fact, the
Cushites are portrayed in a way that focuses on their attempts to
enter into coalitions (הׁשׁלח בים צירים, "sending of envoys by sea", v.
2aα). By underlining the urgency when the messengers are demanded
to go to Cush (לכו מלאכים קלים, "Go, swift messengers" v. 2aγ), the
text is sarcastic towards the Judeans, and the command sounds like
a repetition of what the leaders says to their officers.

Summing up the rhetoric in the text's design and motifs
Through the analyses of textual design and motifs of Isa 18:1–2 it
has been showed that these two verses form a unity. Further, this
first stanza of Isa 18 reveals a deliberate rhetoric that aims at entrapping the audience. This beginning of a rhetoric of entrapment is
observable in the following four ways.

First, a rhetoric of entrapment can only take place if what is said
hangs together. Therefore, *cohesion* of vv. 1–2 is made through alliteration, enjambment and *chiasmus*, and by the way primary and subordinate motifs of the stanza are interwoven. The motifs river and
Cush are described both in the beginning and end of this first stanza
(לנהרי־כוש, v. 1a and נהרים ארצו, v. 2bβ), and the motif messenger
is referred to twice in v. 2 (צירים, v. 2aα and מלאכים, v. 2aγ). Second,
an atmosphere of *activity* is created by several phonetic patterns, and
also as the motif "messengers" is applied in the sense of diplomatic

envoys. Observations about both textual design and motifs of Isa
18:1–2 have showed that the description of messengers travelling to
and from Judah functions to create an atmosphere of business and
activity. Third, the feeling of *confusion* is created by the play with words,
and by the way the motif Cush is applied. At first, it can seem as
if Cush will be judged (v. 1), but in the next moment (v. 2) positive
descriptions of Cush are given. Fourth, *concentration* on Cush is created by rhyme, gapping, change of grammatical mood, and poetic
technique. From the motif analysis it is clear that the primary motif
of Isa 18:1–2 is Cush. The extended description of the land and
people of Cush functions to let the audience concentrate on this
motif of Isa 18:1–2. However, this over-focusing on positive features
about Cush functions as an indirect critique of the Judean leaders
who eagerly seek help by human beings instead of putting their trust
in YHWH (cf. Isa 14:32; 30:1–5, 15–17).

CHAPTER THREE

STROPHE II: 18:3

As showed in the introductory chapter, the first stanza comprises 2 strophes, vv. 1–2, whereas the second stanza of Isa 18 is made up of 4 strophes (vv. 3, 4, 5, and 6). In order to make the reading easy, the analysis of this largest stanza of Isa 18:1–7 will be pursued verse by verse. Before the analysis can start, however, there is need for a clarification of why v. 3 is seen as opening a new stanza.

Three observations support the notion that vv. 3–6 forms a new stanza: the change of scene, characters, and style. First, a new series of *scenes* starts by v. 3. From portraying one nation (Cush) in stanza I, the perspective is suddenly widened as "all" peoples of the world are called to attention (v. 3). The Cushites are not on the scene again before v. 7. Second, the *characters* on the scene in stanza I are "a people tall and smooth-skinned", and a group of unidentified messengers who are given a command to go to Cush. In stanza II, on the other side, there are five different characters on the scene—two referred to as individuals, and three as collectives. As they are introduced in the text, they appear in the following order: (i) "all" (v. 3), (ii) those who bring a standard to the mountains (v. 3), (iii) those who blow the horn (v. 3), (iv) "me" (v. 4), and (v) YHWH (v. 4–5).[1] Whereas stanza I gives detailed descriptions of the physical features of the people presented, stanza II provides no characterisations of the participants' physical appearance. Beside these characters—all of them described with anthropological features—grapes, birds and animals are also referred to in stanza II. Third, there is a change of *style* from stanza I to stanza II. Except for the command "Go, swift messengers" (v. 2aγ), the first stanza of Isa 18 has a descriptive (though hectic) style, whereas stanza II—with its call for attention (v. 3), similes (v. 4) and metaphorical language (v. 5–6)—opens with a sense of expectance and excitement, continues with a sense of tenseness

---

[1] In v. 5 there are three verbs that all refer to a 3rd person masculine singular. From the context, "he" in these verbs most likely refers to YHWH. Subsequently, I argue that there are five, and not six groups of characters present in vv. 3–6.

(v. 4), and ends with devastation that can bring nothing other than
a feeling of despair and sorrow (vv. 5–6). This unsettled and tense
style is created by abrupt changes in scenes and temporal perspective from strophe to strophe, by the use of unidentified participants
that enter the scene unexpectedly, and by the gradually more and
more harsh message as the speech proceeds. At a first glance, there
seems to be no obvious connections between the scenes in stanzas
I and II, but as the analysis of Isa 18 proceeds, it will be made
clear how Isa 18 brings a unified message when regarded as a whole.

3.1. Text and translation

3.1.1. *Textual criticism*

Text	Verse
כל־ישׁבי תבל	v. 3aα
ושׁכני ארץ	v. 3aβ
כנשׂא־נס הרים תראו	v. 3bα
וכתקע שׁופר תשׁמעו	v. 3bβ

Verse	Text
v. 3aα	All who dwell in the world,
v. 3aβ	and who inhabit the earth,
v. 3bα	when a standard is raised [on the] mountains, you shall see,
v. 3bβ	and when a horn is blown, you shall hear.

The closest one comes a textual critical issue to v. 3 is the viewpoint from a commentator who argues that הרים, "mountain" is not
required neither by the parallelism, nor by the rhythm, and should
perhaps be omitted.[2] It is correct that an omission of the word הרים,
"mountain" would perfect the parallelism. However, as there are no
strong reasons—neither textual critical nor other—to leave out הרים,
"mountain", this proposal will not even be debated here. Instead, it
will be suggested that the phenomenon of gapping is at work. This
will be dealt with under the heading textual design, syntactic observations (3.2.2.).

---

[2] According to the apparatus of *The Hebrew University Bible. The Book of Isaiah*
(1995), the omission of הרים is done by Hebrew manuscripts (collated by Kennicott).
This omission is later taken up by G.B. Gray, *A Critical and Exegetical Commentary on
The Book of Isaiah* (1962) 313.

3.1.2. *Translation*

In contrast to vv. 1–2, v. 3 contains no examples of rare words, words that are difficult to render, or unusual combinations of words.[3] Only a few minor things need a comment.

The verbs נשא and תקע both have a prefixed כ. Preceding an infinitive construct, the particle preposition כ indicates time, whether of the past or the future.[4] As the verbs appear in imperfect, the time aspect of v. 3b most likely is future (תראו, qal imperfect 2nd person masculine plural, "you shall see", and תשמעו, qal imperfect 2nd person masculine plural, "you shall hear").

3.2. TEXTUAL DESIGN

3.2.1. *Phonetic observations*

In order to distinguish between the various phonetic observations in 18:3, v. 3a will be dealt with first, and then v. 3b. As will be evident, v. 3a and 3b can both be divided into two short lines. Accordingly, verse 3a comprises v. 3aα and 3aβ, and equally, v. 3b comprises v. 3bα and 3bβ. The two short lines of v. 3a and 3b are parallel, and will occasionally be referred to as AA', and BB'.[5]

Verse 3a: Assonance
The participles ישבי, "dwell", and שכני, "inhabit", found in v. 3aα and 3aβ, respectively, create an audible parallelism as they show

---

[3] Some interpreters regard v. 3 a later interpolation, and do not leave this strophe much attention, see for instance K. Marti, *Das Buch Jesaja* (1900) 148–149, H. Wildberger, *Jesaja 13–27* (1978) 681, R.E. Clements, *Isaiah 1–39* (1980/1987) 165, and J. Jensen, *Isaiah 1–39* (1984) 164.

[4] Cf. *BDB* (1979) 454, 3b. See also C.H.J. van der Merwe & al., *A Biblical Hebrew Reference Grammar* (1999/2002) 284: "כ + infinitive construct is used to indicate that an event referred to in the main clause following the temporal clause with the כ + infinitive construct, *immediately follows it in time.*" (His italics).

[5] The phenomenon of parallelism within a single verse line is by scholars called either internal parallelism or half-line parallelism. Internal parallelism will be used here and throughout this book. The most usual form for parallelism is however where the second line (often called B) is parallel to the first (often called A) of a couplet, cf. W.G.E. Watson, "Internal or half-line Parallelism in Classical Hebrew again", *Poetry in the Hebrew Bible* (2000) 198. Watson concludes that half-lines that are symmetrical parallel tend to be metrically interchangeable, *ibid.* 219. Cf. also Y. Avishur, "Addenda to the Expanded Colon in Ugaritic and Biblical Verse", *UF* 4 (1972) 4, for his study of repetition in various verse-halves.

resemblance both when it comes to both vowels and consonants.
The vowels in both participles are /o-ê/. The identical vowels from
יֹשְׁבִי to שֹׁכְנִי makes up a complete assonance.

When it comes to the consonants, the following are in common
between the participles יֹשְׁבִי, "dwell", and שֹׁכְנִי, "inhabit": Both participles have שׁ as one of their root consonants, and both have the
weaker spirantic pronunciation of ב and כ, respectively.[6] These shared
features between יֹשְׁבִי and שֹׁכְנִי can be showed the following way:

Participles	Verse
יֹשְׁבִי	v. 3aα
וְ שֹׁכְנִי	v. 3aβ

The nouns תֵּבֵל and אֶרֶץ in v. 3a also create an audible parallelism
in that three out of four vowels are /e-/ and /æ-/ sounds. The
vowel /e/ is found twice in the noun תֵּבֵל, /e-e/, and in אֶרֶץ the
vowels are /ā-æ/. The vowel /ā/ in the first syllable of אֶרֶץ, is darker
and uttered deeper into the mouth than the second vowel /æ/ of
אֶרֶץ and the two vowels /e/ of תֵּבֵל. However, the vowels /e/, /æ/
and /ā/ that are found in these two nouns do not sound very
different from one another, and thus create an audible parallelism.

The consonants of תֵּבֵל and אֶרֶץ do however not show the same
resemblance as did the consonants in יֹשְׁבִי and שֹׁכְנִי. Rather, the consonants of תֵּבֵל and אֶרֶץ form a contrasting sound picture. The two
first consonants of תֵּבֵל have a weak spirantic pronunciation, whereas
the last consonant ל is a dental. All in all, the consonants ת, ב, and
ל give the noun a gentle sound-picture. The noun paralleled to תֵּבֵל
does on the other hand not contain soft consonants. The two first
radicals of the noun אֶרֶץ belong to the group of larynxes, whereas
the third belongs to the group of emphatic consonants. Regarding
the sound-picture of אֶרֶץ, being an emphatic consonant, צ is pronounced with strong stress and thus creates a contrast to תֵּבֵל.

Rhyme
As pointed at above, there is a resemblance between the two participles of v. 3a in terms of both vowels and consonants. The iden-

---

[6] The final י's in both participles are *matres lectionis* for the vowel /ê/ (plene
written).

tical vowels from יֹשְׁבֵי to שֹׁכְנֵי creates a rhyme: /o-ê/, /o-ê/ and together with the consonants, the rhyme is as follows: yošbê—šoknê. Further, one can also see a rhyme (though weaker) from the vowels of תֵבֵל and אֶרֶץ: /e-e/, /ā-æ/.

Verse 3b: Assonance and alliteration
The two qal infinitive construct כִּנְשֹׂא, and כִּתְקֹעַ, (both with the particle preposition כ) together with the qal imperfect 2nd person masculine plural תִּרְאוּ and תִּשְׁמְעוּ found in v. 3bα and 3bβ, respectively, create an audible parallelism as they show a striking pattern of resemblance of both vowels and consonants. First, the vowels of כִּנְשֹׂא are: /i-o/, and the vowels of כִּתְקֹעַ are: /i-o-a/. Obviously, the two first vowels in כִּנְשֹׂא and כִּתְקֹעַ form an assonance from v. 3bα to 3bβ. (As is evident, כִּתְקֹעַ, v. 3bβ, has in addition the vowel /a/ that is not present in כִּנְשֹׂא, v. 3bα). Further, another assonance is made between v. 3bα and 3bβ as the vowels of תִּרְאוּ are: /i-û/, and those of תִּשְׁמְעוּ are: /i-ā-û/. Also in this case, the word belonging to v. 3bβ has one more vowel (/ā/ in תִּשְׁמְעוּ) than what is the case for תִּרְאוּ. Second, an alliterative pattern is created as two of the same consonants occur from v. 3bα to 3bβ. The first consonant in the words כִּנְשֹׂא and תִּרְאוּ (v. 3bα), כ and ת, are repeated in the corresponding words in v. 3bβ: כִּתְקֹעַ and תִּשְׁמְעוּ. This consonantal parallelism can be schematised the following way:

	Text	*Verse*
	כנשא־ . . . תראו	v. 3bα
	כתקע . . . תשמעו	v. 3bβ

Rhyme
The pattern of parallel vowels and consonants from v. 3bα to 3bβ forms then the following rhyme:

Verse	*Text*					
v. 3bα	/ki/	/o/	. . .	. . . /ti/	. . .	/û/
v. 3bβ	/ki/	/o/	/(a)/	. . . /ti/	/(ā)/	/û/

3.2.2. *Syntactic observations*

In order to distinguish between the various syntactic observations in 18:3, v. 3a will be dealt with first, and then v. 3b.

Verse 3a: Internal parallelism

As already said, Isa 18:3 is a strophe made up of four short lines where the two first (v. 3aα and 3aβ) and the two last (v. 3bα and 3bβ) are parallel (AA'//BB'). For v. 3a, this internal parallelism can be schematised as follows:

Text	Verse	
כל־ ישבי תבל	v. 3aα	A
ו־ שכני ארץ	v. 3aβ	A'

Syntactically, v. 3aα and 3aβ are identically constructed when it comes to word order as both contain a verb followed by a noun. The two participles (ישבי, "dwell" and שכני, "inhabit"), both appear in qal participle masculine plural construct, and the two nouns in v. 3aα and 3aβ appear in singular absolute (תבל, "world" and ארץ, "earth"). This makes a complete syntactic parallelism between v. 3aα and 3aβ. Only two elements are not present in both short lines: כל־ and ו.

Verse 3b: Internal parallelism

Also in v. 3b are the two short lines (almost) equally structured when it comes to word order. From v. 3bα to 3bβ, the internal parallelism can be schematised as follows:

Text	Verse	
כנשא־ נס הרים תראו	v. 3bα	B
ו־ כתקע שפר תשמעו	v. 3bβ	B'

From this table, it is evident that both v. 3bα and 3bβ contain a verb (qal infinitive construct), a noun (masculine singular absolute), and a verb (qal imperfect, 2nd person masculine plural). The two nouns form a gender-matched parallelism. Two elements, however, do not occur in both B and B': the particle conjunction ו, and the noun הרים, "mountains". This latter "omission" leads to the next paragraph.

Gapping

As already mentioned, v. 3bα contains the noun הרים, "mountains", whereas this word—or a corresponding one—is not present where it is expected in v. 3bβ. At a first glance, this lack of correspondence between these short lines seems to make the parallel less complete. However, what is at work is an instance of gapping. For the function of gapping here, see rhetorical analysis, 3.4.1.

Reappearance of grammatical mood
A striking feature of verse 3 is the extensive use of indicative. In contrast to vv. 1–2, where there is a transformation of grammatical mood between indicative and imperative, v. 3 shows the opposite as six out of six verbs appear in indicative. The six verbs in v. 3 have the following distribution:

	Verbs		*Verse*
	qal participle masc. pl. construct	ישבי	v. 3aα
	qal participle masc. pl. construct	שכני	v. 3aβ
qal imperfect 2nd person masc. pl. תראו	qal infinitive construct	נשא	v. 3bα
qal imperfect 2nd person masc. pl. תשמעו	qal infinitive construct	תקע	v. 3bβ

From this diagram, it is evident that each short line has either one or two verbs appearing in indicative.

3.2.3. *Semantic observations*

Parallelism
Semantically, every part of v. 3 addresses "all", and deals with events that will come.[7] The first line of v. 3 (v. 3aα and 3aβ) introduces and addresses "all", whereas the second line (v. 3bα and 3bβ) gives information about how "all" will respond when the standard is raised on the mountains, and when the horn sounds. Verses 3a and b, respectively, is organised in lines expressing the same meaning.

---

[7] Who are the receivers of this message? J.H. Hayes & S.A. Irvine regard this verse as containing the word the messengers (in v. 2) should proclaim on their way to Assyria. This suggestion refers to an interpretation of v. 2 where the swift messengers are seen as going to Assyria "[. . .] to make known that the Ethiopians are up to no good in Syria-Palestine", cf. J.H. Hayes & S.A. Irvine, *Isaiah* (1987) 254–255. The "people tall and smooth-skinned" (v. 2b), is here seen to refer to the Assyrians. Most likely, this is not an address to the envoys (v. 2), but rather a warning to the world at large, cf. G.B. Gray, *A Critical and Exegetical Commentary on The Book of Isaiah* (1962) 312–313, and E.J. Kissane, *The Book of Isaiah* (1960) 199. See also B.S. Childs, *Isaiah and the Assyrian Crisis* (1967) 45, who states that "[t]here is no indication in the text that v. 3 contains a message which the envoys are to take."

Semantically, the same meaning is expressed between A and A' (cf. 3.2.2.). Between B and B', however, the meanings are not quite the same. In B a *standard* shall be *seen* on the mountains, whereas in B' a *horn* will be *heard*. For both AA' and BB' there are degrees of developments between the respective lines. A is a general address to all who live on earth, whereas A' *specifies* A in terms of describing how and where (in general) "all" live. B informs that "you shall see" when a standard will be raised on the mountains, whereas B' adds that "you shall hear" when a horn sounds. B' *develops and complements* B as both the visible and the audible seems to be included in B'. B includes the place where this will happen (הרים "the mountains"), whereas B' does not, and one has to assume that the blowing of the horn will be heard from the mountains, too. In sum, by means of contents, A' continues and goes beyond A in terms of specificity, whereas B' shows a progression from only seeing to seeing *and* hearing.[8]

Word-pairs

The nouns תבל and ארץ occur in two parallel short lines (v. 3aα and 3aβ), and constitutes a synonymous word-pair. Generally speaking, the first element of a word-pair tends to be more well-known and more frequent than its counterpart.[9] This seems however not to be the case in this verse as ארץ occurs more frequently than תבל in the Old Testament (other examples of such a reversed order of ארץ and תבל are Pss 77:19 and 97:4). As synonyms are interchangeable in character, such a reversal as found here is made possible. Other instances in the Old Testament where ארץ and תבל are applied in one or the other kind of parallel lines are: 1 Sam 2:8; Ps 19:5; 21:4; 24:1; 33:8; 77:19; 89:12; 96:13; 97:4; 98:9; Isa 14:21; 18:3; 24:4; 26:18; 34:1; Jer 10:12; 51:15, Prov 8:26; Lam 4:12; and 1 Chr 16:30.

Another word-pair present in v. 3 is created by the verbs תראו, "you shall see", and תשמעו, "you shall hear", of v. 3bα and 3bβ. This word-pair is correlative as both verbs have to do with related senses. From the context, the counterpart to תראו, "you shall see":

---

[8] This corresponds with Kugel's idea about a kind of progression between the two lines A and B: "And this, it is suggested, corresponds to the expectations the ancient Hebrew listener, or reader, brought to every text: his ear was attuned to hearing 'A is so, and *what's more*, B is so.'" Cf. J.L. Kugel, *The Idea of Biblical Poetry* (1981/1998) 8 and 23, (Kugel's italics).

[9] Cf. W.G.E. Watson, *Classical Hebrew Poetry* (1984/1986) 129.

תשמעו, "you shall hear", indicates progression as "all" will *both* see and hear the coming events. Other Old Testament instances where ראה and שמע appear as correlated word-pairs are Isa 66:8 and Ezek 40:4.

3.2.4. *Poetic technique*

Direct speech?
It is not obvious whether or not all or parts or v. 3 contains direct speech. However, some indicators in terms of grammar (verb forms) and addressee ("all") might point towards a use of direct speech in this verse. The American Jewish translation *Tanakh—The Holy Scriptures* (1988) 653, has put v. 3 into quotation marks, and even added [Say this:] at the beginning of v. 3:

> ³[Say this:]
> "All you who live in the world
> And inhabit the earth,
> When a flag is raised in the hills, take note!
> When a ram's horn is blown, give heed!"[10]

In my view, however, v. 3 is not a clear instance of direct speech. Rather, this strophe refers to the prophet's or YHWH's words, and is as such an indirect occurrence of direct speech. This strophe does not refer to a conversation between two parts, but refers to an address to "all".

Unnamed characters
Verse 3 brings in three groups of characters: (i) "all", and (ii) those who will raise the standard on the mountains, (iii) and those who will blow the horn. Unlike the thoroughly described characters of vv. 1–2, the group of characters referred to in v. 3 are neither given names, nor any description of physical appearance. These groups are anonymous as they are left unidentified. However, the three groups have specific roles to fill: (i) "All" is encouraged to watch when (ii) the standard is raised on the mountains, and to listen when (iii) the horn is blown.

---

[10] As mentioned earlier, throughout the *Tanakh—The Holy Scriptures* (1988), every new line (in poetry) starts with a capital letter.

Summing up the features in the text's design
The textual features observed above can be summarised as follows:
First, there are striking phonetic patterns observable in v. 3 as vowels
and consonants are repeated from line to line. Second, the syntactic
observations showed that v. 3 is organised in four parallel short lines
where the two first and the two last lines have a parallel word order.
Third, semantically, the two first short lines of v. 3 show a synonymous parallelism as the same meaning is found in both lines. The
two last lines of v. 3 complement each other with view to meaning.
Fourth, observations about the poetic technique of v. 3 showed that
there can be discussed whether or not this verse should be regarded
direct speech or not. Further, the three groups of characters referred
to in v. 3 are neither given names, nor any description of their physical appearance as focus are given to the various roles they play.

From this, it is clear that the two first short parallel lines of v. 3
(v. 3aα and 3aβ) are homogeneous not only phonetically and syntactically, but also semantically.[11] Although the correspondence between
v. 3bα and 3bβ does not show the same degree of identification in
terms of semantics, also these lines are parallel with view to phonetics and syntax.

3.3. MOTIFS

3.3.1. *Standard*

In v. 3bα the little word סנ is noteworthy. סנ occurs only in the singular in the Old Testament.[12] The literal meaning of סנ indicates
"[. . .] a long pole enabling something set upon it to be seen at a
great distance (Num 21:8–9; Isa 30:17), or a pole for a banner (Isa
33:23; Ezek 27:7)."[13] Subsequently, סנ is rendered "standard", "banner", "flag", or "ensign" in the Old Testament.[14] In one instance in
the Old Testament, סנ is applied in the meaning "sign" or "won-

---

[11] This is a rare example of identical lines, cf. A. Berlin, *The Dynamics of Biblical
Parallelism* (1985) 31, who (though not speaking about this verse) says: "Those who
have studied the grammar of parallel lines are well aware that the surface structure of the lines is identical in only a small percentage of cases."

[12] Cf. H.-J. Fabry, "סנ", *ThWAT* 5 (1986) 470: "*nes* begegnet nur im Sing. und
steht fast durchwegs undeterminiert".

[13] Y. Zakovitch, "Miracle", *ABD* 4 (1992) 845.

[14] D.J.A. Clines (ed.), *DCH* 5 (2001) 697.

der": Num 26:10. As will be evident, נס is applied metaphorically in some texts.

The noun נס occurs 21 times in the Old Testament. The book of Isaiah contains 10 of these instances of נס, and the book of Jeremiah 5. The sites where the נס is raised are "mountain" (Isa 13:2; 18:3), "hill" (Isa 30:17), "land" (Jer 51:27), "city wall of Babylon" (Jer 51:12), "and toward Zion" (Jer 4:6).[15] A person or object can become a נס (Num 26:10; Ezek 27:7). The nations rally to the נס (Isa 11:10). Positively, one takes refuge in the נס (Ps 60:6 [ET: 60:4]), negatively, one flees from it (Isa 31:9). נס has three forms of usage in the Old Testament. First, in a military sense, the נס that is set up on a mountain or hill either provides orientation (Isa 13:2; 30:17), marks where the army is to assemble (Isa 5:26), or indicates where the attack is to be performed (Jer 51:12). The נס can also serve as a sign of the victor's claim to possession when the defeat is accomplished (Jer 50:2). In the military context, the setting up of a standard is sometimes accompanied by horns (Jer 4:21; 51:27), or battle cries (Isa 13:2). Just as the box-shaped ark could go forward as a military standard and emblem of YHWH, so could the נס be seen as a divine emblem endowed with leadership qualities.[16] Worth noticing is the fact that נס is not mentioned in any Old Testament descriptions of battles, it only appears in prophetic emulations of such.[17] Second, in a nautical sense, the נס denotes part of a ship's tackle (Isa 33:23; Ezek 27:7).[18] Although "sail" is the preferred rendering in both verses, this does not exclude the נס to have a signalling function.[19] Third, נס is applied metaphorically either as (i) a sign of protection or support, as (ii) a means of signalling judgement, or as (iii) a way of proclaiming restoration.

Let us briefly give some examples of these three forms of usage. The function of the נס as a support is evident from Num 21:8. In

---

[15] Cf. K. Goldhammer, "Die heilige Fahne", *ZEthn.* 4/5 (1954/1955) 34, and H.-J. Fabry, "נס", *ThWAT* 5 (1986) 470.

[16] See H. Weippert, "Feldzeichen", *BRL* (1977) 77–79, and M. Görg, "Der Altar—theologische Dimensionen im Alten Testament", *Freude am Gottesdienst* (1983) 291–306.

[17] Cf. H.-J. Fabry, "נס", *ThWAT* 5 (1986) 471: "Die Funktion militärischer Feldzeichen ist uns also nur bekannt durch die metaphorisierende prophetische Rezeption des Rituales vom Heiligen Krieg." In the ancient Near East, however, standards symbolise the gods advancing into battle. See M. Weippert, "'Heiliger Krieg' in Israel und Assyrien", *ZAW* 84 (1972) 477.

[18] Cf. H.-J. Fabry, "נס", *ThWAT* 5 (1986) 471.

[19] Cf. G.R. Driver, "Isaiah 1–39: Textual and Linguistic Problems", *JSSt* 13 (1968) 54, and E. Strömberg Krantz, *Des Schiffes Weg mitten im Meer* (1982) 126.

this text, the נס is the pole on which the snake is erected, and any-
one who sees the pole with the snake will be protected from the
bite of poisonous serpents. Another text where the protection form
YHWH is central is Exod 17:15, where it says: "Moses built an altar
and called it YHWH is my standard (יהוה נסי)."[20] The prophetic util-
isation of נס is important for the understanding of Isa 18:3. On the
one hand, נס is used in texts focussing on the impending end of
Israel, on the other hand, נס is applied in texts focussing on the
restoration of Israel after the exile. According to Isa 5:26, YHWH
raises a standard for a people far away about which they are to
assemble for their battle to destroy Israel. In another text, the נס
shows the enemy the way as it approaches Israel (Jer 4:6). The
judgement will be so devastating that the remnant will look like a
נס, a signal pole (Isa 30:17). When YHWH attacks Assyria, its officers
will flee from the נס (Isa 31:9). In Isa 13:2 the נס is applied in the
context of judgement against Babylon. Raising a נס against Babylon
means declaration of war (Jer 50:2; 51:12, 27). In contexts of salvation, however, the standard is an orientation signal for the expected
deliverance. The return from the exile is as an event a נס for the
nations (Isa 49:22; 62:10). According to Isa 11:10, the scion from the
root of Jesse will be the נס to which the nations will seek (cf. v. 12).

In 18:3 נס is the object of נשא, "raise", "set up". The place where
the נס is set up is the mountain (הר). From the Old Testament survey above, we have seen that נס is used in the prophetic books either
to denounce support/protection, or in contexts that speaks of judgement or restoration. The נס is raised on a mountain in order that

---

[20] It has been debated whether the expression יהוה נסי—applied to the altar Moses
is to build after the battle with the Amalekites at Rephidim—can be traced to the
southern tribes of the premonarchic period or to the later state. For the former suggestion, see, M. Weippert, "'Heiliger Krieg' in Israel und Assyrien", *ZAW* 84 (1972)
489, footnote 135. For the latter suggestion, see M. Görg, "Nes—ein Herrschaftsemblem?", *BN* 14 (1981) 4. More important, however, is suggestions to the understanding of Exod 17:15–16. R. Gradwohl, "Zum verständnis von Ex. XVII 15f.",
VT 12 (1962) 491–494, suggests a hand on a standard (Exod 17:16) to be a symbol
of the supporting hand of YHWH. M. Görg has showed that this designation of
the altar is a way of making an explicit reference to YHWH, see M. Görg, "Der
Altar—theologische Dimensionen im Alten Testament", *Freude am Gottesdienst* (1983)
302–303. H.-J. Fabry, "נס", *ThWAT* 5 (1986) 472, argues that just as the box-
shaped ark is a military standard and emblem of YHWH, so can a similarly shaped
altar be one. The designation of the Rephidim altar as both נס and כס is quite
possible, according to Fabry, as "[. . .] das eine sogar das andere aufgrund der
Assonanz erklären kann".

"all" will see it, and serves thus an orientation point. For what purpose is it an orientation point for "all"? As Isa 18 opens with a הוֹי, the גַם in v. 3 seems to be applied in the context of judgement. The setting up of a standard is in 18:3 accompanied by the blowing of a horn, and this leads to the next paragraph.

3.3.2. *Horn*

Another central motif of Isa 18:3 is שׁוֹפָר, "horn". The literal meaning of שׁוֹפָר is a foghorn that most likely belongs to a wild goat or a ram.[21] The שׁוֹפָר belongs to the group of aerophones, i.e. musical instruments, "[. . .] where the lips of the player produce the vibration of air."[22] The term שׁוֹפָר is together with הַחֲצֹצְרָה, "trumpet", the most common of instruments mentioned in the Old Testament primarily used for signals. However, the Old Testament distinction between שׁוֹפָר and הַחֲצֹצְרָה does not correspond to the modern distinction between "horn" and "trumpet".[23] Though the Old Testament does not contain detailed descriptions of the physical appearance and characteristics of the שׁוֹפָר, it does provide us with a wide range of conditions and ceremonies in which the instrument is used. Along with its literal meaning, the horn's non-literal meaning is being an instrument that signals danger, peace, or theophanies.

The term שׁוֹפָר occurs approximately 70 times.[24] Sometimes the שׁוֹפָר is used in peaceful settings, sometimes in settings associated with fear and danger.[25] The various contexts in which the שׁוֹפָר is mentioned have the following in common: The שׁוֹפָר is used to *signal*

---

[21] "Die Bestimmung der Tierart ist aber unsicher", cf. H. Ringgren, "שׁוֹפָר", *ThWAT* 7 (1993) 1195, see also J. Braun, *Music in Ancient Israel/Palestine* (2002) 26.

[22] Cf. I.H. Jones, "Musical Instruments", *ABD* 4 (1992) 936.

[23] Cf. K.D. Jenner, "The Big Shofar (Isaiah 27:13): A Hapax Legomenon", *Studies in Isaiah 24–27* (2000) 161.

[24] Cf. J. Braun, *Music in Ancient Israel/Palestine* (2002) 26: "With its seventy-four occurrences, the *šôp̄ār* is the most frequently mentioned instrument in the Old Testament."

[25] Cf. J.H. Eaton, "Music's Place in Worship: A Contribution from the Psalms", *Prophets, Worship and Theodicy* (1984) 92, who writes that the horn, according to its etymology and tradition, "[. . .] was peculiarly sacred to Israel, being the signal not only for holy seasons, but also for the revelations of God, evoking the tones of the voice from heaven [. . .]". Cf. also J. Braun, *Music in Ancient Israel/Palestine* (2002) 28: "In sixty-nine of its seventy-four Old Testament occurrences, the *šôp̄ār* appears as a solo-instrument, reflecting its unique position in the biblical world of sound. [. . .] the sound of the *šôp̄ār* could accommodate itself to a variety of situations, evoking a magical or even eschatological atmosphere, or functioning symbolically."

activities or events expected to be carried out in the (near) future.[26] From the Old Testament texts, the שׁופר has at least three interrelated areas of usage: war, warning, and worship.[27] In the context of war, the שׁופר is used for signalling (cf. Judg 3:27; 7:18; 1 Sam 13:3; Isa 27:13; Jer 4:5, 19, 21; 51:27; Zech 9:14), and it is used by the watchman (cf. Ezek 33:3–6; Neh 4:12,14 [ET: 4:18, 20]). Related to war is the use of שׁופר in the context of the day of YHWH (cf. Zech 9:14; see also Joel 2:1; Zeph 1:16).[28] Further, the שׁופר is used in the context of warnings—i.e. as a signal before the judgement so that the people have the opportunity to repent (cf. Isa 58:1; Jer 6:1, 17; Hos 5:8; 8:1; Joel 2:1, 15; Amos 2:2; 3:6). Last, in contexts of worship, the שׁופר sounds through the country on the Day of Atonement (cf. Lev 25:9), at the opening of the Jubilee Year (Lev 25:10), and when a holy fast is proclaimed (cf. Joel 2:15). Further, one blows the שׁופר in theophanies (cf. Exod 19:16, 19; 20: 18), in the bringing up of the ark of the covenant to Jerusalem (cf. 2 Sam 6:14–15; 1 Chr 15:28), in exaltation of YHWH (cf. Ps 98:6; 150:3), and in celebration of victory and blessing for the land (cf. Ps 47:6).[29] Related to worship is the use of שׁופר in connection with royal coronations (cf. 2 Sam 15:10; 1 Kgs 1:34, 39, 41; 2 Kgs 9:13), and in ceremonies of taking an oath (2 Chr 15:14).

How, then, is שׁופר applied in Isa 18:3? Having in mind the opening הוי of Isa 18 that indicates judgement, and what has just been said about the lifting of a standard, the blowing of the horn also seems to indicate something negative. Not only shall "all" lift their eyes to the mountain and see the standard, they shall in addition hear a horn being blown. Whether or not this announces a coming

---

[26] Cf. E. Kolari, *Musikinstrumente und ihre Verwendung im alten Testament* (1947) 43: "Man merkt, dass *š.* ein Signalinstrument war." For an attempt to classify the various forms of usage of the שׁופר, see *ibid.* pp. 43–49. In some instances, other musical instruments accompany the שׁופר, cf. H. Ringgren, "שׁופר", *ThWAT* 7 (1993) 1196.

[27] Most commonly, scholars distinguish between two forms of usage of the שׁופר, the military and the cultic, cf. I.H. Jones, "Musical Instruments", *ABD* 4 (1992) 936, and K.D. Jenner, "The Big Shofar (Isaiah 27:13): A Hapax Legomenon", *Studies in Isaiah 24–27* (2000) 162. Here, the category "warning" is added as the warning to repent seems different from clear contexts of war or worship. However, in a number of instances, all three categories are interrelated, and play on each other.

[28] For the interrelated forms of usage of the שׁופר, cf. H. Ringgren, "שׁופר", *ThWAT* 7 (1993) 1196: "In der Vorstellung vom Ertönen des Horns am Tage JHWHs verbinden sich Motive aus der Kriegserklärung und der Epiphanie."

[29] For more Old Testament references, see H.-M. Lutz, *Jahwe, Jerusalem und die Völker* (1968) 134.

war is not evident yet, but it is out of question that the שׁוֹפָר gives some sort of a warning to the listeners. Subsequently, in v. 3 the שׁוֹפָר is used as a signal to make "all" attentive of activities or events expected to be carried out in the (near) future.[30] The more detailed interpretation of what the signalling of events that will come implies must however wait until more of Isa 18 is analysed.

3.3.3. *Mountain*

The third central motif of Isa 18:3 is הַר, "mountain". הַר occurs approximately 550 times in the Old Testament.[31] In singular and plural הַר can refer to both individual mountain peaks and mountain ranges.[32] The word הַר often occurs in phrases "[. . .] denoting particular mountains or mountainous regions".[33]

The motif "mountain" has a wide range of usage in the Old Testament, and only a few areas of application can be briefly referred to here. In the Old Testament, הָרִים/הַר refers to: (i) the topography of Israel (cf. Gen 10:30; Josh 20:7; Amos 4:1; Mal 1:3),[34] (ii) territorial boundaries (cf. Judg 17–18; 19:1), (iii) lookout posts/focal points (cf. Isa 40:9; 42:11), (iv) asylum for fugitives (Josh 2:16, 22; 1 Sam 13:6; 14:22; Ezek 7:16), (v) the foundations of the earth (Job 9:5; Ps 90:2),[35] (vi) the connecting link between heaven and earth (Deut 32:22; Jonah 2:7; Ps 104:4–6), (vii) sites of theophanies (cf. Deut

---

[30] From the opening of Isa 18, vv. 1–2, the mentioning of the nation Cush could indicate that שׁוֹפָר (in v. 3) is used to warn Judah about Cush as an enemy. This is suggested by H.-M. Lutz, *Jahwe, Jerusalem und die Völker* (1968) 134, and H. Ringgren, "שׁוֹפָר", *ThWAT* 7 (1993) 1195. H. Seidel, *Musik in Altisrael* (1989) 112, lists Isa 18:3 under the heading "Militärische Signalgebung", but does not discuss how שׁוֹפָר is applied in this verse: "Da Jes 18,3 keine zusätzlichen Informationen zur Funktion des Horns als militärisches Signalinstrument liefert, kann die Frage nach der Echtheit dieses Textes ohne Schaden unbeantwortet bleiben."

[31] הַר does not occur in the books of Ruth, Ecclesiastes, Esther or Ezra. The most frequently used synonym for הַר is נִבְעָה. נִבְעָה occurs 60 times in the Old Testament, and in 31 of these cases it is applied in apposition or parallel to הַר. For a few examples, see S. Talmon, "הַר", *ThWAT* 2 (1977) 463–464.

[32] Cf. S. Talmon, "הַר", *ThWAT* 2 (1977) 462, and W. Gesenius, *Handwörterbuch* (1995) 284–285.

[33] D.J.A. Clines (ed.), *DCH* 2 (1995) 582.

[34] Cf. A.W. Schwarzenbach, *Die geographische Terminologie im Hebräischen des alten Testamentes* (1954), and Y. Aharoni, *The Land of the Bible* (1962/1967) 24–29.

[35] For a brief presentation of the same concept of mountains as foundations of the earth in the ancient Near East, cf. E.J. Hamlin, "The Meaning of 'Mountains and Hills' in Isa 41:14–16", *JNES* 13 (1954) 186, and H.G.Q. Wales, *The Mountain of God* (1953) 6–31.

4:11; 1 Kgs 19:11–14; Mic 1:3; Ps 18:7 [ET: 18:6]; 97:4–5),[36] and (viii) the place where (the name of) YHWH dwells (cf. Isa 18:7; Ps 68:16–17 [ET: 68:15–16]; 78:67–68; 132:13–14).[37] From this, it is clear that in its literal meaning, הר refers to the geography of the land with hills and mountains in contrast to lowlands and deserts. Further, mountains mark territorial boundaries, are suitable as look-out posts and focal points, and can serve as hiding places for fugitives. Non-literally, mountains are older than creation or are among the first to be created (Prov 8:25; Job 15:7), they are binding together the three strata: the netherworld, earth and heaven (Exod 20:4; Prov 8:22–29), and will last forever (Gen 49:26; Hab 3:6). These latter qualities of mountains culminate in the Old Testament notion of mountains as sacred places, and the "holy mountain"—which refers to Jerusalem and the temple mount.[38] The earliest Israelite sanctuaries were located upon mountains, and from the Old Testament it is evident that sanctuary and mountain came to be conceptually identical.[39] Subsequently, Sinai, and later Zion, play significant roles in Israel's religious life.[40] Zion is the place where the name of YHWH dwells (Isa 18:7), and the place where eschatological events will be fulfilled.[41]

---

[36] Apparently, non-Israelites perceived YHWH to be a typical "mountain-god", cf. 1 Kgs 20:23–28.

[37] Cf. for instance G. Westphal, *Jahwes Wohnstätten nach den Anschauungen der alten Hebräer* (1908). According to R.J. Clifford, the notion that YHWH dwell on mount Zion seems to be a direct borrowing from the Ugaritic epics, cf. R.J. Clifford, *The Cosmic Mountain in Canaan and the Old Testament* (1972) 131.

[38] Cf. A.J. Wensinck, *The Ideas of the Western Semites Concerning the Navel of the Earth* (1916) 11–12, and H. Schmidt, *Der heilige Fels in Jerusalem* (1933) 78–102. According to S. Talmon, "הר", *ThWAT* 2 (1977) 468, holy places are located on hills and mountains in order to reduce the distance between earth and heaven, "[. . .] die Spanne zwischen Erde und Himmel zu verkleinern."

[39] Cf. S. Talmon, "הר", *ThWAT* 2 (1977) 480, and S. Talmon, "Har and Midbār: An Antithetical Pair of Biblical Motifs", *Figurative Language in the Ancient Near East* (1987) 133.

[40] Cf. J. Jeremias, *Der Gottesberg* (1919) 134–141. See also B.S. Childs, *Myth and Reality in the Old Testament* (1960) 85, who writes: "Zion is a holy place because she belongs to God." R.J. Clifford, *The Cosmic Mountain in Canaan and the Old Testament* (1972) 98, points to the significance of mountains as holy places: "From her earliest life, around Sinai, through the time of her settled life, around Zion, sacred mountains played a significant role in Israel's religious life."

[41] Cf. S. Talmon, "Har and Midbār: An Antithetical Pair of Biblical Motifs", *Figurative Language in the Ancient Near East* (1987) 133: "After all previously chosen places had been rejected (Ps. 78.67; 68.15–16), God's presence finally and definitely came to rest upon Zion [. . .] which he had created for himself (Ps. 78.54)." Further considerations about Zion will be given in the analysis of Isa 18:7, chapter 7.

In Isa 18:3, הרים is applied in plural without the definite article, and is thus translated "mountains" with the article put in brackets. The location of the mountains is not specified in 18:3, and הרים seems here not to point to the specific dwelling place of YHWH (see v. 7). Rather, what is the main point in v. 3 is to regard the mountain as a focal point (cf. Judg 9:7; 2 Chr 13:4; Isa 13:2; 40:9; Nah 2:1 [ET: 1:15]).[42] The notions of mountains as a connecting link between heaven and earth, and mountains as sites of theophanies play together with the idea of the mountain as a focal point in Isa 18:3.[43]

Summing up the features in the text's motifs
From the observations above, it is first suggested that נס, "standard", is applied both as an orientation point and as a signal that warns about a coming judgement. Further, the motif שופר, "horn", is also applied in a negative way appearing along with the נס. Last, הרים "mountains", is the site where the lifting of the standard (and the blowing of the horn) will take place, and this suggests that mountain is here primarily applied in the meaning of a focal point. In addition, as it is not clear who speaks in v. 3 (the prophet or YHWH), the motif הרים also plays on the notions of being a connecting link between heaven and earth, and being used as sites of theophanies.

---

[42] Cf. E.J. Young, *The Book of Isaiah* (1965/1978) 476: "On the mountains a standard of assembly will be raised, for the mountains are a most conspicuous and visible spot." Further, הרים seems here to be applied in a cosmic way. In Old Testament references where the motif "mountain" has cosmic significance, it has been suggested that the Mesopotamian notion of "mountain" as the centre of the world has influenced Old Testament thought. This is however not convincing. According to S. Talmon, an almost exclusive use of the plural "mountains", rather than the singular "mountain", occur in Old Testament references with cosmic significance. Cf. S. Talmon, "הר", *ThWAT* 2 (1977) 471: "Das wird daduch angedeutet, daß sich die mythologischen Hinweise auf 'Berg' in kosmischer Bedeutung fast ausschließlich auf 'Berge' im Pl. beziehen und selten, wenn überhaupt, im Sing. stehen." Cf. Talmon for further references. Isa 18:3 falls into line with this as "mountain" here is found in plural. The present interpretation of Isa 18:3 supports Talmon's suggestion as the mountains (in plural) referred to here indicate a focal point for "all who dwell in the world and who inhabit the earth".

[43] That v. 3 expresses the presence of YHWH in one or the other way is also perceived by B.S. Childs, *Isaiah and the Assyrian Crisis* (1967) 45, as he regards this verse as communicating "[. . .] a picture of Yahweh's unruffled self-composure which arises from his sense of absolute sovereignty over the whole world." See also the recent commentary of B.S. Childs, *Isaiah* (2001) 138.

3.4. Rhetorical analysis

From what has been observed about the strophe's textual design and
motifs, the theme of Isa 18:3 is clearly that of summoning people
for signalling a coming judgement. (The judgement is not explicitly
communicated before vv. 5–6, though). First, the summoning theme
is seen as "all" nations of the world are addressed. Second, those
who are encouraged to see when a standard is raised on the mountains, and listen when a horn is blown, are "all", cf. the verbs forms
"see" and "hear" that are in 2nd person plural. Third, as the motifs
standard, banner, and mountains occur together, they are clearly signalling something for "all" who see and hear them. The theme of
summoning people has in principal three forms of usage in the Old
Testament: either for the purpose of war, warning or peace. Recruit-
ment for war is described with visible signs like standards, banners,
flags or gestures, and/or with audible signs such as shouting or blowing of horns and trumpets (cf. Isa 5:26; 13:2; 31:9). Summoning people in order to warn them before the judgement comes is known
from for instance Isa 58:1; Jer 6:1, 17; Hos 5:8; 8:1. Though, the
same visible and audible signs can also be used to summon people
for peaceful purposes (cf. Isa 11:10, 12; 49:22; 62:10). In Isa 18:3,
the purpose of summoning "all who dwell in the world" is to announce
a coming judgement (cf. the opening הוֹי, 18:1). The visible and audible signals that summons people (as referred to in v. 3) function here
to prepare for what will come.

3.4.1. *Rhetorical features in the text's design*

From the observations of the text's design, we have seen that every
line of Isa 18:3 shows some kind of parallelism. This entry will suggest
how the various elements observed above function in v. 3.

Phonetic observations: Assonance, alliteration and rhyme
On a phonetic level, vowels and consonants are repeated between
the two first and the two last short lines of v. 3, and create assonance and alliteration. In v. 3aα–3aβ, the participles יֹשְׁבֵי, "dwell"
and שֹׁכְנֵי, "inhabit" have identical vowels along with a resemblance
in consonants. These shared phonetic features serve to bind the two
first short lines of v. 3a closely together. Further, the vowels of the
two nouns תֵבֵל and אֶרֶץ also binds the two short lines together as

three out of four vowels are /e-/ or /æ-/ sounds. The contrast that
is created between the consonants of the nouns תבל and ארץ functions to underline the most emphatic consonants, namely those of
the noun ארץ. This growing crescendo from the consonants of תבל
to the consonants of ארץ serves to give a feeling of excitement and
worry. What starts as a quiet and calm address to "all who dwell
in the world", grows in intensity by the use of more emphatic consonants, and functions to sharpen the attention to what may follow.

In v. 3bα and 3bβ, there is also observed a striking pattern of
correspondence between vowels and consonants. Alliteration is created as the first consonant of כנשׂא and תראו (v. 3bα), כ and ת, are
repeated in the corresponding words in v. 3bβ: כתקע and תשׁמעו.
These instances of assonance and alliteration in v. 3b serve the function of being cohesive, and give a feeling of symmetry.

*Syntactic observations: Internal parallelism, gapping, and reappearance of
grammatical mood*
Syntactically, v. 3 shows an example of internal parallelism as the
two first and the two last short lines are parallel. As the word order
is identical from v. 3aα to 3bβ, this complete internal parallelism
functions to cohere the two lines, and also to give a unison message
to the audience. The (almost) identical word order from v. 3bα to
3bβ also serves to bind the lines together, and creates a feeling of
symmetry. A sense of balance is also created by the gender-matched
parallelism of נס (m.) and שׁופר (m.).

Further, the instance of gapping in v. 3b (where the noun "mountains" does not occur where it is expected) functions to intensify the
message as the focus is even more on what will *happen* than on the
mountains as such. On the one hand, if the word הרים were present in both lines, the syntactic parallelism would have been complete ("when a standard is raised [on the] mountains, you shall see,
and when a horn is blown [*on the*] *mountains*, you shall hear"). However,
on the other hand, when the expected word is not there, the focus
is on the other words in 3bβ. When the device of gapping is at
work, a repetition of the word הרים, "mountains", is regarded as
long-winded and merely a filler, and as diminishing the concentration about the future events that is now created by this gapping:
"when a standard is raised [on the] mountains, you shall see, and
when a horn is blown, you shall hear."

Another striking feature of v. 3 is that of the reappearance of grammatical mood from line to line. In contrast to vv. 1–2 where there was a transformation of grammatical mood between indicative and imperative, all verbs are held in indicative. This reappearance of grammatical mood functions to tie the four short lines of v. 3 together, and it also underlines an impression of a unison message as it gives a feeling of symmetry.

Semantic observations: Parallelism and word-pairs
Semantically, the two first lines of v. 3 are identical as the two participles and nouns correspond in meaning. However, v. 3aβ ארץ ושכני "and who inhabit the earth" seems to be a more closely description of v. 3aα כל־וישבי תבל "all who dwell in the world" as long as inhabiting seems to specify in what *way* "all" dwell.[44] In v. 3bα an 3bβ, the correspondence between the lines lays in complementing each other. The acts of raising a standard is complemented by the blowing a horn. Further, the guideline to the audience that they shall see is complemented by the hearing of these events The function of specificity and complementation is a feeling of symmetry. Further, this internal semantic parallelism serves to create a sense of excitement and worry as it is not revealed to the audience who will be judged.

Another semantic observation is that of word-pairs. The word-pair ארץ / תבל functions to express the totality, that all the world is addressed, and it underlines the symmetrical and homogenous way in which the message is expressed. The function of reversing the normal order of these elements of the word-pair is that of emphasis.[45] By reversing the order, the audience's attention is kept. In addition, the reversal underlines the crescendo from תבל to ארץ—as observed in the phonetic analysis. This crescendo serves to create the atmosphere of excitement and worry, and functions to sharpen the attention of what comes next.

Poetic technique: Direct speech and unnamed characters
Although there is no direct discourse referred to between two or more characters in v. 3, the text speaks to a group of unnamed

---

[44] Who are "all who dwell in the world, and who inhabit the earth"? E.J. Kissane, *The Book of Isaiah* (1960) 199, interprets "all" to be "[. . .] all the nations oppressed by Assyria". A more likely interpretation is that "all" includes the whole world, cf. C.R. Seitz, *Isaiah 1–39* (1993) 148, and B.S. Childs, *Isaiah* (2001) 138.

[45] Cf. W.G.E. Watson, *Classical Hebrew Poetry* (1984/1986) 135, for the function of reversing the elements of a word-pair.

characters ("all") that they shall pay attention when a standard will be raised and a horn will be blown. By not being clear about who is initiating the signals to be raised and blown (YHWH or human beings), the text leaves the audience in a state of confusion.

There are three groups of characters mentioned in v. 3. By neither describing "all", nor those who lift the standard, or those who blow the horn, the focus is directed towards these groups' roles rather than on the characters themselves.[46] The role of "all" is that of the spectator as "all" are encouraged to watch and listen—not more, not less.[47] The two other groups are simply described through the verbs (in qal infinitive construct) of raising and blowing. The acts of lifting a standard and blowing a horn create an atmosphere of expectance and worry as the audience senses that something is going to happen. What will happen is not yet revealed, and the way the characters are brought to the scene holds the audience caught in excitement and worry: Are there peaceful or disturbing events ahead? From the way the strophe is structured, it is clear that underlying the important message to the audience to watch and listen is the dramatic events that will *follow* the raising of the standard and the blowing of the horn. What will come is important to such a degree that כל־ישבי תבל ושכני ארץ "all who dwell in the world, and who inhabit the world" need to be aware and watch out.

Summing up the rhetorical features in the text's design
Through observations about the textual design of Isa 18:3, the rhetoric of entrapment seems to be continued in the following ways. First, *cohesion* between words and lines is created as almost every single word of v. 3 belongs in one or the other form of parallelism. Second, an atmosphere of *activity* is created through the accumulation of verbs that indicate actions. Third, v. 3 gives the audience a feeling of *confusion* about who will be judged, as this is not said. Fourth, *concentration* on the coming judgement is created by the device of gapping, and by the fact that four of the six verbs of v. 3 indicate future events.

---

[46] Although I interpret YHWH as the agent in v. 3, I will not propose ideas about *who* those who lift the standard and blow the horn might refer to as this only leads to speculations. There are suggestions, though, to whom these characters might be, cf. E.J. Kissane, *The Book of Isaiah* (1960) 199, who holds that the standard and horn summons "[. . .] His host to make ready for battle." See also P.D. Miscall, *Isaiah* (1993) 56: "The Lord's army is coming; it is seen and heard [. . .]."

[47] Cf. H. Wildberger, *Jesaja 13–27* (1978) 693–694, who regards "all" to have the function of being witnesses to the great events at the end of the age.

3.4.2. *Rhetorical features in the text's motifs*

Standard: Announcement of coming judgement

How does the mentioning of a standard function in Isa 18:3? In this strophe, the raising of a standard is paralleled with the act of blowing of a horn. In the book of Isaiah there seems to be a preference for using only the standard as a signal to get the people's attention.[48] Here, however, the visible (the lifting of a standard) together with the audible (the blowing of a horn) is applied in order to summon "all". This use of both a standard and a horn functions to warn the audience that something important and noteworthy is about to happen. By applying both visible and audible signs, a feeling of urgency and worry is created, and this functions to suggest that a situation of danger is approaching.[49] On the background of what has been said in vv. 1–2, the audience most likely expects the Cushites to be judged as a הוי is cried upon this nation (v. 1). As the analysis proceeds, however, it will be evident that this might not be the case, and that v. 3 is yet another step in the process of entrapping the audience to believe that they are safe when they as a matter of fact are not.

Horn: Announcement of a coming judgement

The blowing of a horn heightens the tension as the signalling is then *both* visible and audible. Most likely, the שופר here appears with the purpose of warning about a coming judgement, and the standard and horn function as signals that "[. . .] are employed as rhetorical strategies to indicate imminent danger."[50] Together with the raising of a standard, the blowing of the שופר creates an atmosphere of tenseness and worrying excitement. As it is not yet revealed to the

---

[48] Cf. K.D. Jenner, "The Big Shofar (Isaiah 27:13): A Hapax Legomenon", *Studies in Isaiah 24–27* (2000) 173: "[. . .] Isaiah shows the preference for the use of 'raising the banner'."

[49] Cf. however K.D. Jenner, *ibid.* 173, who interprets the blowing of the horn in Isa 18:3 as announcing "[. . .] that a present will be brought to Mount Zion." This interpretation will be dealt with under the analysis of 18:7.

[50] F.E. Deist, *The Material Culture of the Bible* (2000/2002) 208. The blowing of the horn and the raising of the signal as referred to in v. 3, is by G.R. Hamborg, "Reasons for Judgement in the Oracles Against the Nations of the Prophet Isaiah", *VT* 31 (1981) 149, interpreted as a battle-cry "[. . .] raised at the battle of the proposed coalition against the Assyrians [. . .]". R. Lowth, *Isaiah* Vol. 2 (1795) 149, suggests that what is meant by standard and horn is "[. . .] the meteors, the thunder, the lighting, the storm, earthquake, tempest, by which Sennacherib's army shall be destroyed".

audience *who* is going to be judged, the audience can believe that
this warning is meant for the Cushites.

Mountain: Focal point for the summoning of "all"
Verse 3 summons "all" the inhabitants on earth, and הרים functions
here as a focal point where "all" are encouraged to watch and listen when standards and horns will be visible and audible. Besides
being merely a focal point, the mountains referred to in Isa 18:3
also play on the meanings of being the connecting point between
heaven and earth (as long as it is not clear from v. 3 who initiates
the signalling, YHWH or human beings), and being sites for theophanies. Isa 18:3 gives associations to the Day of YHWH when the
horn will sound, and when every human being will focus on YHWH
(Joel 2:1–2).[51] This uncertainty about how to perceive the motif
mountain, and about *what* will happen when the signals have faded
out, is yet another step in the process of entrapping the audience.

Summing up the rhetorical features in the text's motifs
As the book of Isaiah shows a preference for using a standard as a
signal to get the people's attention, Isa 18:3 is important as it is one
out of two instances in the book of Isaiah where the שופר is used
as a warning signal (cf. in addition Isa 27:13).[52] In this light, the use
of the שופר serves here to emphasise the degree of seriousness of the
summoning of "all". When Isa 18:3 refers to *both* standard and horn
as ways of getting the attention from "all", this serves to underline
the importance of what follows v. 3. The mountains have the function of letting "all" take notice of what is going to happen, but does
in addition play on notions about mountains as connecting heaven
and earth, and as being sites of theophanies. Clearly, the standard
and horn visible and audible on the mountains give signals about a
coming judgement.[53] The strophe is ambiguous, however, when it

---

[51] For an association of Isa 18:3 to the holy war of YHWH, cf. S.H. Widyapranawa,
The Lord is Saviour (1990) 106: "The LORD of Hosts called upon all the nations to
participate in his holy war to aid Judah."

[52] Cf. K.D. Jenner, "The Big Shofar (Isaiah 27:13): A Hapax Legomenon", *Studies
in Isaiah 24–27* (2000) 173.

[53] Cf. H. Donner, *Israel unter den Völkern* (1964) 124–126, who states that the standard and horn mentioned in v. 3b are not signs for an impending battle, but an
emphatic assertion that YHWH is announcing his plans of judgement (vv. 4–5) to
all the world. Cf. also C.R. Seitz, *Isaiah 1–39* (1993) 148, who argues along the
same lines.

comes to the question about who is initiating the standard to be raised and the horn to be blown: is it YHWH or human beings?[54]

3.4.3. How do textual design and motifs together create the strophe's rhetoric?

Cohesion: V. 3 consists of parallel lines
Observations of both textual design and motifs of Isa 18:3 have revealed several cohesive features. The following three points summarises these features:

First, from the analysis of the textual design, it has been showed that v. 3 contains assonance, alliteration, rhyme, and internal parallelism. All these devices function to bind the lines together as they create a unison message and a feeling of balance.

Second, reappearance of grammatical mood also functions to tie the various parts of v. 3 together. Further, the word-pairs also have a cohesive function in that they link "all" to "seeing" and "hearing".

Third, the choice of the motifs standard and horn (v. 3b) is another cohesive element of v. 3 as these two motifs serve the function of complementing each other. The application of both standard and horn underline the symmetry (as they appear in parallel lines) and serves to pass on a unison message to the audience.

Activity: Standard and horn warn about a coming judgement
Both textual design and motifs reveal that an atmosphere of activity is created in v. 3. The focus on activities—at the expense of emphasis on characters (cf. v. 2)—serves to focus on what is going to happen. Four out of six verbs in v. 3 indicate activity, and this underlines the atmosphere. Further, a sense of excitement and worry is also created by the motifs as they function to signal activities that will be carried out in the future.

Confusion: Who is judged?
The way the text is designed, and the choice of motifs keep the audience in a state of confusion. This confusion started already in vv. 1–2

---

[54] My contention is that YHWH is the agent in this verse. The following selected previous and recent studies suggest the same: cf. R. Lowth, *Isaiah* Vol. 2. (1795) 149, Aa. Bentzen, *Jesaja* (1944) 141, E.J. Kissane, *The Book of Isaiah* (1960) 199, who writes "[. . .] when Jahweh gives the signal [. . .]", and W. Brueggemann, *Isaiah 1–39* (1998) 153: "Yahweh is about to give military signals [. . .]".

as the expected negative portrayal of Cush was never given. When the message of v. 3 is passed on to the audience, there is still no answer to the question about who will be judged. Confusion is created when it comes to understanding the motifs and their application in this verse. The audience most likely perceives that the signalling of a coming judgement has to do with the Cushites, but as this is not explicitly stated, one can assume a sense of insecurity about this among the listeners to the speech. It is hidden what will come next, but it is clear that dramatic events are ahead.

Concentration: "All" shall pay attention to the coming judging events
From both textual design and motifs, we have seen that the focus in v. 3 is on coming events—at the expense of the description of characters who are mentioned. This stands in sharp contrast to the detailed descriptions of both geography and physical appearance of Cush and Cushites in vv. 1–2. In this strophe, on the other side, there are no descriptions of the physical appearance of the characters mentioned as the focus is on the *actions* that the characters will carry out. From the text's design it has been showed that the device of gapping serves the function of focusing on the activities that are carried out. The motifs focus on the coming events as standard, horn and mountains are applied in order to announce judgement.

Summing up the rhetoric in the text's design and motifs
This strophe continues where vv. 1–2 started in showing signs of a deliberate rhetoric. This continuing rhetoric of entrapment is observable in the following four ways.

First, *cohesion* is created thorough the devices of assonance and alliteration in both 3a and 3b. V. 3aα and 3aβ make a complete parallelism as they are identical in terms of phonetics, syntax and semantic. This functions to give a unified message to the audience. Cohesion is also underlined by the motifs standard, horn and mountain as the way they are applied serves to underline that what "all" is encouraged to be attentive to is one thing, namely the coming events of judgement. Second, both textual design and motifs of Isa 18:3 have showed that an atmosphere of *activity* is created in v. 3. There is an accumulation of verbs that indicate activities, and four of six verbs clearly describe actions to be carried out. Third, the feeling of *confusion* is created by the various associations the motifs standard, horn and mountain carry. In v. 3, it seems clear that these motifs are applied as signals to announce a coming judgement, but over whom? This question is not yet answered, and v. 3 leaves the audience in excitement and worry about what the future events imply. Fourth, *concentration* on activities rather than on detailed descriptions of characters (cf. v. 2) functions to draw attention to why "all" nations are summoned, namely to give a signal about a judgement that will come. By creating an audible crescendo from soft to hard conso-nants in the two nouns of v. 3a, this intensifies the sound-picture, and creates an atmosphere of expectation. The identical form of the two short lines of v. 3a creates a prelude or colon to what comes in the next line and produces a feeling of excitement. As some of the verbs can indicate future, this creates an awareness of what will come. Also the choice of motifs makes the audience concentrate on forthcoming events as standard, horn and mountains are often asso-ciated with situations to come.

CHAPTER FOUR

STROPHE III: 18:4

4.1. Text and translation

4.1.1. *Textual criticism*

Text	Verse
כי כה אמר יהוה אלי	v. 4aα
אשקוחה ואביטה במכוני	v. 4aβ
כחם צח עלי־אור	v. 4bα
כעב טל בחם קציר	v. 4bβ

Verse	Text
v. 4aα	For thus says YHWH to me:
v. 4aβ	I will be quiet and gaze in my dwelling place
v. 4bα	like glowing heat of [the] light,
v. 4bβ	like a cloud of dew in [the] heat[1] of harvest.

4.1.2. *Translation*

The translation of בחם

When it comes to MT's בחם, "in [the] heat of", most commentaries are silent in the textual debate, and follow MT without any discussion.[2] There is however an exegetical tradition of emending the text

---

[1] At the end of verse 4 MT reads בחם קציר, "in the heat of harvest", a reading which is supported by 1Q Isaᵃ. Some Hebrew manuscripts read ביום קציר, "in the day of harvest", cf. the LXX, ὡς νεφέλη δρόσου ἡμέρασ ἀμήτου ἔσται, the Syriac version and the Vulgate. It is obvious that the orthographic variation (the resemblance between ח and ים) between the MT and the other Hebrew manuscripts is slight. On a textual critical basis I prefer the rendering בחם קציר, "in [the] heat of harvest", as the MT is not obscure, and as there exists no criteria for asserting the suggested reading more valuable than the MT. For a classification of what might be called errors in the Old Testament, see F. Delitzsch, *Die Lese- und Schreibfehler im Alten Testament* (1920). Delitzsch does not list בחם in Isa 18:4 among the errors.

[2] Nevertheless, when scholars make a fresh translation they always take a stance in the textual debate—even those who do not emend the MT, cf. B. Duhm, *Das Buch Jesaja* (1892) 114, K. Marti, *Das Buch Jesaja* (1900) 149, O. Procksch, *Jesaja 1* (1930) 236–241, O. Kaiser, *Der Prophet Jesaja* (1983) 74–80, and J.D.W. Watts, *Isaiah 1–33* (1985) 243–244, who all read MT's בחם.

of MT from קציר בחם, "in [the] heat of harvest", to ביום קציר, "in
[the] day of harvest", cf. the following three examples. F. Buhl, for
instance, suggests ביום קציר as original as it gives the expression more
variation: "Istedet for בחם have LXX Syr. Hier. ביום, der tydeligvis
er oprindeligere, da det giver en større Variation i Udtrykket."[3]
According to Buhl, repetition of a term within the same verse is
considered unfortunate as it does not bring variation into the text.
Further, without a textual critical discussion, H. Donner proposes
בחם קציר to be read simply as בקציר, "at harvest time".[4] H. Wildberger
is yet another example of a scholar who corrects the MT on the
basis of literary arguments more than textual critical analysis.
Wildberger suggests the reading ביום קציר as it is unlikely that Isaiah
would have used the same word twice in the same line of the verse:
"[. . .] da Jesaja kaum חם in derselben Verszeile wiederholt hätte."[5]
Common for these examples is (i) that this emendation is not argued
sufficiently for, and (ii) that the emendation reflects the literary ideal
of the commentator more than a sound textual critical argumenta-
tion. In my opinion, one should not force once own literary sense
upon texts that are clear as they stand.

4.2. Textual design

4.2.1. *Phonetic observations*

Alliteration

It is evident that an alliterative pattern is made by the consonant כ
that occurs in the beginning of v. 4aα, 4bα, and 4bβ. Further, כ is
the first consonant in the second word of v. 4aα. Although there is
no כ at the beginning of v. 4aβ, the consonant occurs at the end
of v. 4aβ, in במכוני.

Rhyme

A striking pattern of v. 4 is the accumulation of words that are short.
Lines one, three and four of v. 4 (v. 4aα, 4bα, and 4bβ) contain short
words, whereas the second line (v. 4aβ) contains longer words. The

---

[3] F. Buhl, *Jesaja* (1894) 287.
[4] H. Donner, *Israel unter den Völkern* (1964) 122.
[5] H. Wildberger, *Jesaja 13–27* (1978) 681.

first line of v. 4 (v. 4aα) has five short words, and the two last lines of v. 4 (v. 4bα and v. 4bβ) have both four short words. In terms of the length of the words, this accumulation of short words in v. 4 creates a staccato rhyme from v. 4aα to v. 4bα and 4bβ.

4.2.2. *Syntactic observations*

Verse 4 opens with the particle conjunction כִּי, "for", and this seems to be a motivation of what has been said, and of what will come.[6] As there are two occurrences of כִּי in Isa 18, the discussion about how these two function in the second stanza of Isa 18 (vv. 3–6) will be dealt with in the analysis of v. 5.

Internal parallelism
Syntactically, the two last lines of v. 4 (4bα and 4bβ) are nearly identically constructed when it comes to word order:

	Text				Verse
עֲלֵי־ אוֹר	צַח	חֹם	כְּ		v. 4bα
קָצִיר	חֹם	בְּ טַל	עָב	כְּ	v. 4bβ

Neither v. 4bα, nor v. 4bβ contain verbs. As is evident from the diagram, both lines open with the particle preposition כְּ followed by a noun in masculine singular absolute (חֹם and עָב, respectively). Further, where v. 4bα continues with an adjective, צַח (masculine singular), v. 4bβ has a noun טַל, (masculine singular absolute). Then both lines contain a preposition (עֲלֵי and בְּ, respectively), followed by a noun in masculine singular absolute (אוֹר and חֹם, respectively). Last, v. 4bβ has a noun in masculine singular absolute (קָצִיר) which has no counterpart in v. 4bα. From this, it is clear that when the nouns are parallel, they appear in the same number, gender and status from v. 4bα to v. 4bβ, and thus make a syntactic internal parallelism.

---

[6] Cf. C.H.J. van der Merwe & al., *A Biblical Hebrew Reference Grammar* (1999/2002) 302, § 40.9., who suggests the following as one of the ways in which the particle conjunction כִּי is applied in the Old Testament: "Speakers base their motivation for a *directive action* [. . .] on *what they or someone else is doing, has done, or will do.*" (His italics).

4.2.3. *Semantic observations*

Semantically, the first line of v. 4 reports that YHWH has given a message "to me". The remaining three lines of v. 4, then, refer in 1st person singular (v. 4aβ) to what YHWH has said "to me".

Similes

After the initial "for thus says YHWH to me" (v. 4aα), YHWH's words (in 1st person singular), "I will be quiet and gaze in my dwelling place" (v. 4aβ), are referred to in two similes: "like glowing heat of [the] light (v. 4bα), like a cloud of dew in [the] heat of harvest" (v. 4bβ).[7] The similes describe the way YHWH will be quiet and gaze. Although these two similes are not semantically parallel in the strict sense that the two of them comprise the same meaning, they show a resemblance in that they both describe *the ways in which YHWH will be quiet and gaze* in his dwelling place.[8] First, YHWH's quietness and gazing is likened with "glowing heat of [the] light", and then it is likened with "a cloud of dew in [the] heat of harvest". In order to understand the basic character of these similes, the technical terminology of tenor and vehicle can be applied.[9] The tenor is YHWH's quietness and gazing in his dwelling place, whereas the vehicle in the first simile (v. 4bα) is glowing heat of [the] light, and in the second simile (v. 4bβ) a cloud of dew in [the] heat of harvest. The tenor is clear, but the vehicles are not straight away easy to understand (see 4.3. Motifs). What is clear, though, is that the quietness and gazing of YHWH (tenor) are described by the use of meteorological phenomena of glowing heat and cloud of dew (vehicles). The semantic resemblance between these lines lies in the use of meteorological

---

[7] A simile is here understood as a comparison of two entities where the indicators of resemblance are "like" or "as". For a corresponding definition of simile, cf. W.F. Thrall & A. Hibbard, *A Handbook to Literature* (1962) 460, and D.L. Petersen & K.H. Richards, *Interpreting Hebrew Poetry* (1992) 50.

[8] Cf. H. Wildberger, *Jesaja 13–27* (1978) 691, who states that v. 4bα and 4bβ convey the same idea: "Das erste Bild muß sachlich dasselbe aussagen".

[9] Although the simile differs from the metaphor, the vocabulary applied about metaphors by I.A. Richards can also be used in order to describe the components of a simile: tenor and vehicle (cf. footnote 89, chapter 2 in this book). W.F. Thrall & A. Hibbard, *A Handbook to Literature* (1962) 281–282: "The tenor is the idea being expressed or the subject of the comparison; the vehicle is the image by which this idea is conveyed or the subject communicated." See also *idem* 460: "[. . .] in a simile both tenor and vehicle are clearly expressed and are joined by an indicator of resemblance, 'like', or 'as'."

phenomena to which YHWH's quietness and gazing are compared. It is impossible for the modern reader to know whether or not the audience was familiar with these different types of weather. The challenge lies therefore not in recognising the actual phenomena, but rather in perceiving the relation between YHWH's *attitude* and the atmosphere created by the similes. This will be suggested in 4.4.

4.2.4. *Poetic technique*

Direct speech
Verse 4 opens by referring to a message given to "me" from YHWH (v. 4aα). The remaining lines of v. 4 cite what YHWH has said "to me"—an audition. By the reference to YHWH and "me" a new strophe is introduced that shifts to direct discourse.[10] The formula כה כי אלי יהוה אמר, "for thus says YHWH to me" is found four times in the book of Isaiah (8:11; 18:4; 21:16; and 31:4). A more common formula in the book of Isaiah is יהוה אמר כה, "thus says YHWH". By using this poetic technique of letting "me" quote YHWH, the audience sees the following events from the perspective of "me". As will be evident from the analysis of v. 5, it is not obvious where the direct speech put in the mouth of YHWH ends, and where "me" continues. As the message from YHWH is referred to in the first person singular in verse 4, and in the third person singular (masculine) in verse 5, this could indicate that the direct speech ends by v. 4.

Characters
The appearance of the two participants YHWH and "me" is at a first glance somewhat sudden and unexpected, as the previous verses (vv. 1–3) do not refer to either "me" or YHWH. In this verse, the character YHWH is identified, whereas "me" is not. "Me" is not introduced more closely than through the preposition with a suffix for the 1. person singular, אלי "to me". In the Old Testament in general, such direct contacts with the deity are reserved prophets, priests or kings. Who is the most likely mediator in this instance? As the text is to be found in a prophetic book, the voice "me" most likely refers to the prophet. The fact that "me" makes an explicit reference to a message from YHWH supports this. Although it is

---

[10] Cf. L.J. de Regt, *Participants in Old Testament Texts* (1999) 23.

not directly stated in v. 4, we can assume that the message from
YHWH is brought to the audience through the mouth of the prophet.[11]

Summing up the features in the text's design
First, the phonetic analysis above displays that there is a clear alliterative pattern in v. 4. Further, at a phonetic level, there is an accumulation of short words in v. 4 (except in v. 4aβ that contains three
longer words) that makes a rhyme from v. 4aα to v. 4bα and 4bβ.
Second, the syntactic observations show that the two last lines of v. 4
are almost identically constructed when it comes to word order. The
words that correspond appear in the same number, gender and status.
Third, semantically, YHWH's quietness and gazing is described through
two similes that both borrow vocabulary from the sphere of meteo-
rology. Fourth, observations about the poetic technique show that
this verse comprises direct speech and that there are two participants
referred to in v. 4. YHWH is identified by name, whereas "me" is
anonymous—most likely referring to the prophet.

4.3. MOTIFS

4.3.1. *YHWH's dwelling place*

V. 4 makes use of two verbs in order to describe YHWH's dwelling:
אשקוטה, qal imperfect 1st person common singular cohortative, "I
will be quiet", and ואביטה, hiphil imperfect 1st person common singular cohortative "I will gaze". One of the motifs that play a significant
role in v. 4 is מכון, here rendered "dwelling place". מכון has in v. 4
the suffix of 1st person singular, and "my" refers to YHWH as the
immediately preceding line gives the signal that what comes is a
quote from YHWH: כי כה אמר יהוה אלי, "for thus says YHWH to
me" (v. 4aα). The attitude YHWH is said to have in his dwelling
place ("quiet" and "gaze") is central to the understanding of this
strophe. Subsequently, the treatment of the motif "dwelling place"
will be accompanied with suggestions about how YHWH's quietness
and gazing should be understood in this text.

---

[11] The word "messenger" is not applied about the character "me" in Isa 18:4.
However, the prophet here clearly appears as one who brings a message from
YHWH to the audience, cf. J.F. Ross, "The Prophet as Yahweh's Messenger",
Prophecy in Israel (1987) 118: "Thus the prophets, although they seldom called them-
selves 'messengers', [. . .] claimed that their authority was that of one sent by Yahweh
or from his council."

In the Old Testament, מכון, "place", appears seventeen times. The term מכון is often somewhat inadequately rendered as "dwelling place", as the word can be translated "fixed or established place", "foundation". In all but one occurrence (Ps 104:5), מכון refers to the dwelling place of God, either in heaven or in the temple.[12] The term is used about a place which is firmly fixed, which endures and cannot be shaken (Exod 15:17; Ps 89:15; 93:1–2; 97:2; 104:5; Isa 4:5).

Isa 18:4 does not reveal whether YHWH's dwelling place is in heaven, in the temple/Zion, but most scholars understand מכון in Isa 18:4 to refer to YHWH's heavenly dwelling.[13]

YHWH's attitude of being quiet and gazing from his dwelling place is explained through two similes. The first simile says that YHWH will be quiet and gaze "like glowing heat of light" (v. 4bα), the other that YHWH will be quiet and gaze "like a cloud of dew in the heat of harvest" (v. 4bβ). Let us briefly see how the verbs שקט, "be quiet", and נבט, "gaze", are applied in the Old Testament in order to suggest their usage in Isa 18:4.

In the Old Testament, שקט appears approximately 40 times, and may be used of YHWH's inactivity (Ps 83:2; Isa 62:1; Jer 47:6–7). It is also used to express freedom from annoyance or care (Ezek 16:42; Ruth 3:18), or it is applied to express a tense quietness (Ps 76:9 [ET: 76:8]).[14]

In Isa 18:4, שקט seems not to be applied in a positive way.[15] Rather, the verb is used about YHWH who is being observant and

---

[12] J.N. Oswalt, "מכון", *TWOT* 1 (1981) 434.

[13] Cf. the following selected examples, A. Knobel, *Der Prophet Jesaia* (1843) 124: "[. . .] in seinem himmlischen Wohnsitze [. . .]", F. Delitzsch, *Commentar über das Buch Jesaia* (1889) 242: "Ruhig sieht Jahve an der himmlischen Stätte [. . .]", F. Buhl, *Jesaja* (1894) 287: "Herren ser rolig til fra sin Himmel", O. Procksch, *Jesaia I* (1930) 240: "Sein Sitz [. . .] ist hier nicht der Zionsberg (8, 18), sondern der Himmel [. . .]", J. Fischer, *Das Buch Isaias* (1937) 138: "Jahves Wohnstatt [. . .] ist der Himmel", J. Ziegler, *Isaias* (1948) 62: "[. . .] in seiner himmlischen Wohnstatt [. . .]", H. Wildberger, *Jesaja 13–27* (1978) 691: "Jahwes Sitz, von dem aus er zuschaut, ist natürlich nicht der Zion [. . .], sondern sein himmlischer היכל", R.E. Clements, *Isaiah 1–39* (1980/1994) 165: "[. . .] from his heavenly dwelling", and B.S. Childs, *Isaiah* (2001) 138: "[. . .] God views the whole world in calm rest from his heavenly dwelling [. . .]." Others, for instance Aa. Bentzen, *Jesaja 1–39* (1944) 142, suggests the temple as YHWH's dwelling place, whereas I.W. Slotki, *Isaiah* (1949) 86, understands YHWH's dwelling place as Jerusalem.

[14] For the rendering of שקט, "be quiet", in 18:4, cf. Koehler-Baumgartner, *HALAT* (1990) 1514, "sich ruhig verhalten".

[15] In contrast to this interpretation of mine, cf. E. Bons, "שקט", *ThWAT* 8 (1995) 452, who suggests that YHWH's quietness is not of a negative kind: "Positiv sagt Jes 18,4 Gott von sich aus, er wolle ruhig bleiben [. . .] und zusehen auf seinem Platz, bevor er eingreift (v. 5)."

restless.[16] As the cohortative implies willingness, the form underlines this aspect of activity. From the context, it seems that YHWH is not inactive, rather, the verb implies that he follows what happens with a conscious eye. YHWH's quietness is likened with "glowing heat of [the] light", and "a cloud of dew in [the] heat of harvest", see 4.3.2. and 4.3.3. below.

The verb נבט, "gaze", appears 67 times in the Old Testament in the hiphil, and the verb means "[. . .] in eine bestimmte Richtung blicken, hinsehen, ausschauen u.ä.".[17] In hiphil it can mean "to look", "show regard to", "pay attention to", or "to look upon", and it implies an element of activity. Throughout the Old Testament, the verb נבט has either a human being or God as subject. According to H. Ringgren, when God is the subject, the hiphil of נבט is found in statements and petitions.[18] The verb is used of the divine observation of the world and its inhabitants (see Pss 33:13; 80:15, Lam 5:1, Isa 63:15; 64:8 [ET: 64:9]; 66:2). Frequently it appears in conjunction with ראה, "see", this is however not the case for Isa 18:4.

In 18:4 the verb נבט appears in hiphil imperfect 1st person singular cohortative, and it is rendered "I will gaze". Similarly to what is said above about שׁקט, the cohortative of נבט also implies willingness. Although the text says that YHWH will be quiet, he will at the same time look and thus be attentive to what is going on in the world. In 18:4 the subject is undoubtedly YHWH as שׁקט and נבט both are in 1st person singular, and as these verbs come immediately after the phrase: כי כה אמר יהוה אלי, "for thus says YHWH to me". Further, Isa 18:4 clearly belongs to the group of statements as YHWH proclaims through the voice of "me": "I will be quiet and gaze in my dwelling place".[19] In Isa 18:4, YHWH's quietness and gazing in his dwelling place express a tense quietness. This will be further argued for in 4.4.

---

[16] Cf. B. Huwyler, *Jeremia und die Völker* (1997) 166.

[17] Cf. H. Ringgren, "נבט", *ThWAT* 5 (1986) 137. See also Koehler-Baumgartner, *HALAT* (1974) 624: "ausschauen".

[18] Cf. H. Ringgren, "נבט", *ThWAT* 5 (1986) 139.

[19] For other examples of God as the subject of נבט in statements, cf. Job 28:24 where it is said that God looks from to the ends of the earth and sees everything, and Ps 104:32 where it is stated that when God looks at the earth, it trembles. In Hab 1:13 it is said that God cannot look on wrongdoing, and according to Amos 5:22 God will not look upon the offerings of the people.

4.3.2. *Glowing heat*

After the opening lines of v. 4 (4aα and 4aβ) a description is given—through two similes—of *how* YHWH is quiet and gazing in his dwelling place. The first simile is found in v. 4bα: "like glowing heat of [the] light". In order to understand what this simile says about YHWH's quietness and gazing, let us first comment upon the motif "glowing heat" by treating the terms חם, "heat", and צח, "glowing" separately.

The noun חם occurs twice in v. 4 (4bα and 4bβ), and means "heat".[20] In v. 4bα חם refers to the heat of light, whereas in v. 4bβ it refers to the heat of harvest. The Old Testament commonly uses the verb חמם to describe the period of the day that is warm or hot, cf. the heat of midday (see Gen 18:1; Exod 16:21; 1 Sam 11:9; 2 Sam 4:5; Job 6:17; Neh 7:3). Accordingly, the noun חם in Isa 18:4 refers to heat as a meteorological phenomenon.[21] However, the reference to heat in verse 4 has a function that goes beyond the meteorological, but this will be suggested under 4.4.2.

Further, the term צח, "glowing" needs to be commented upon. In the Old Testament, the term צח has the following meanings: "dazzling/glowing" (Isa 18:4),[22] "bright/white" (Cant 5:10; Lam 4:7),[23] and "arid/dry" (Isa 58:11; Jer 4:11).[24] In In Jer 4:11, צח is used about

---

[20] Cf. Koehler-Baumgartner, *HALAT* (1967) 312: "Hitze d. Sommers", W. Gesenius, *Handwörterbuch* (1995) 362, "Erntehitze", and D.J.A. Clines, *DCH* 3 (1996) 247, "heat".

[21] Cf. K.-M. Beyse, "חמם", *ThWAT* (1977) 1046 and 1047.

[22] I. Eitan, "A Contribution to Isaiah Exegesis. (Notes and Short Studies in Biblical Philology)", *HUCA* 12/13 (1937/38) 65, claims that צח means "sun" in this passage, but this seems less likely.

[23] Cf. R. Gradwohl, *Die Farben im Alten Testament* (1963) 7.

[24] Basing their interpretation on an inscribed jar stamp discovered in Arad (7th century B.C.E.), Aharoni and Amiran suggest צח to be the name of one of the ancient Hebrew-Canaanite months, cf. Y. Aharoni, & R. Amiran, "Arad: A Biblical City in Southern Palestine", *Arch.* 17 (1964) 43–53, and *idem*, "Excavations at Tel Arad. Preliminary Report on the First Season, 1962", *IEJ* 14 (1964) 131–147. That צח can be the name of a month is supported by J.A. Soggin, "Zum wiederentdeckten altkanaanäischen Monat צח", *ZAW* 77 (1965) 83–86, E. Koffmahn, "Sind die altisraelitischen Monatsbezeichnungen mit den kanaanäisch-phönikischen identisch?", *BZ* 10 (1966) 197–219, esp. 217, and S. Talmon, "צח", *ThWAT* 6 (1989) 983–986. Soggin and Talmon use this information about צח as the basis for a reinterpretation of Isa 18:4 and Jer 4:11. This reading can however not be demonstrated with complete certainty, and is speculative, cf. M. Weippert, "Archäologischer Jahresbericht", *ZDPV* 80 (1964) 150–193, esp. 183, J. Teixidor, "Bulletin d'épigraphie sémitique", *Syr.* 44 (1967) 163–195, A. Lemaire, "Note épigraphique sur la pseudo-attestation du mois 'ṣḥ'", *VT* 23 (1973) 243–245, and H. Wildberger, *Jesaja*

a wind coming towards Jerusalem, i.e. a judgement is to be expected (v. 12). Both in Isa 18:4 and Jer 4:11, צח evokes negative associations. In Isa 18:4, צח is understood as an adjective "glowing", that describes the חם, "heat".[25]

The translation "like the glowing heat of [the] light" needs some comments before we can suggest how the first simile (v. 4bα) is to be understood. Literally, עלי־אור means "above the light", and this has caused difficulties in understanding what is meant in Isa 18:4.[26] In the Old Testament, אור, "light", is on one occasion used specifically about the sun (Job 31:26), but in most cases it refer to "light." In Neh 8:3 אור is contrasted with mid-day in the meaning early morning or daybreak. However, אור can be rendered "sun" as the term occurs in contexts where the source of light seems to be what is meant.[27] In Isa 18:4 the phrase עלי־אור is rendered "of [the] light", and most likely אור here relates to the sunlight, cf. H. Wildberger's translation of the phrase.[28]

What, then, does this first simile (v. 4bα) say about YHWH's quietness and gazing? The expression כחם צח עלי־אור, "like glowing heat of [the] light" expresses the following: Although the heat is invisible, it is possible to see the shimmering and vibration of the hot air. In this simile, YHWH's quietness and gazing is likened with the intensity of the glowing heat. How this comparison functions in v. 4 will be taken up in 4.4.2.

13–27 (1978) 680. For a recent contribution to this discussion, see J. Renz, *Die althebräischen Inschriften* (1995) 386.

[25] S. Talmon, "צחה", *ThWAT* 6 (1989) 985, "In Jes 18,4 und Jer 4,11, kann *ṣaḥ* als Adj. 'flimmernd' oder als Subst im st. cstr. verstanden werden [. . .]". For the former, cf. H. Wildberger, *Jesaja 13–27* (1978) 680, and for the latter, cf. W. Rudolph, *Jeremia* (1958) 30.

[26] E. Baumann, "Zwei Einzelbemerkungen", *ZAW* 21 (1901) 266–268, suggests altering the text to read על יאור, "above the river" (Nile). Cf. also G.B. Gray, *A Critical and Exegetical Commentary on The Book of Isaiah* (1962) 314, who defines the dazzling heat as "[. . .] that which seems to be above the sun, not proceeding from it, but belonging to another sphere, and regarded by many people as the region of the highest gods."

[27] Cf. L.I.J. Stadelmann, *The Hebrew Conception of the World* (1970) 64, who refers to Isa 18:4 among other texts where אור might denote "sun".

[28] Cf. H. Wildberger, *Jesaja 13–27* (1978) 691: "Das schwierige עלי־אור muß wohl meinen "beim Sonnenlicht". I. Eitan, "A Contribution to Isaiah Exegesis. (Notes and Short Studies in Biblical Philology)", *HUCA* 12/13 (1937/38) 65, maintains that אור means "rain" or "dew" in this passage, but this seems less likely.

4.3.3. *Cloud of dew*

The second simile of v. 4 is found in v. 4bβ: "[. . .] like a cloud of
dew in [the] heat of harvest." Let us briefly comment upon the motif
"cloud of dew" in order to suggest what this second simile of v. 4
says about YHWH's quietness and gazing in his dwelling place.[29] As
was done in 4.3.2., the two terms that make up the motif, here עָב,
"cloud" and טַל, "dew", will be treated separately.

The Old Testament contains a considerable number of words for
"cloud", "fog", and similar phenomena.[30] When it comes to the term
עָב, "cloud", this occurs 30 times in the Old Testament.[31] Among
the prophetic books, עָב occurs only in the book of Isaiah (seven
times). According to J.C. de Moor, עָב designates the thick rain clouds
of the cumulus type: *strato-cumulus, cumulo-nimbus,* and *cumulus.*[32] From
the Old Testament texts, the עָב can on the one hand refer to something positive and pleasant: (i) it is associated with the spring rain
(Prov 16:15),[33] (ii) it is a blessing after the drought (1 Kgs 18:44–45),
(iii) it shelters against the summer heat (Isa 25:5),[34] (iv) it is one of
the blessings that will be taken away from the vineyard (Isa 5:6), (v)
it can refer to something moving rapidly and quickly across the sky
(Isa 19:1; 60:8), (vi) it is high in the sky (Isa 14:14; Job 20:6), (vii)
clouds are mentioned in contexts of YHWH's majesty and sovereignty (Job 26:8; 36:29; 37:16; 38:34; Ps 77:18 [ET: 77:17]; 147:8),
(viii) clouds and similar phenomena appear as divine messengers (Job
37:11–12; Ps 104:3–4), (ix) clouds appear in contexts of theophanies
(Exod 19:9; Judg 5:4; 2 Sam 22:12; [par. Ps 18:12]; Ps 104:3), and
(x) YHWH sweeps away the people's transgressions like a cloud (Isa
44:22). On the other hand, the עָב can bring something negative and
unpleasant: (i) powerful cloudbursts appear in the context of judgement (Judg 5:4), (ii) clouds are associated with "the days of trouble"
(Eccl 12:2), (iii) clouds refer to disruptive and distracting elements

---

[29] The motif קָצִיר, "harvest", appears also in v. 5, and will be discussed under 5.3.4.
[30] Cf. J.C. de Moor, "Cloud", *IDB.S* (1976) 168: "In the OT the most common
word for sky cover is *ʿānān* (עָנָן), which is used in prose and poetry alike."
[31] Half of the Old Testament occurrences attest עָב in the singular, the other
half in the plural. Of the 30 occurrences of עָב, only three are found in prose texts.
[32] Cf. J.C. de Moor, "Cloud", *IDB.S* (1976) 168. Cf. C. Schultz, "עָב", *TWOT*
2 (1981) 648, who states that עָב seems to designate a rain cloud.
[33] L.I.J. Stadelmann, *The Hebrew Conception of the World* (1970) 98.
[34] According to L.I.J. Stadelmann, *The Hebrew Conception of the World* (1970) 98,
עָב, "cloud", designates "[. . .] the 'cumulus' under whose shadow men seek solace
against the scorching heat during the summer."

(Eccl 11:3–4), and (iv) clouds are applied in order to describe something that vanishes (Job 30:15).

In Isa 18:4, עב, "cloud", appears in masculine singular absolute, and as it appears in relation to טל, "dew", the rendering of כעב טל is "like a cloud of dew".[35] The reference to עב in v. 4bβ gives associations along two lines. On the one hand, עב refers to the remoteness of YHWH as he is referred to as being quiet and gazing "[. . .] like a cloud of dew in the heat of harvest" (cf. the notion of clouds as high in the sky, Isa 14:14; Job 20:6). This evokes YHWH's lofty repose at a distance. On the other hand, more negative Old Testament associations to עב are also present here as v. 4bβ mentions the harvest, and thereby alludes to an approaching judgement (cf. v. 5 where harvest is mentioned again).[36]

The Old Testament occurrences of the term טל count approximately 30, and its semantic range includes "light rain" as well as "dew".[37] As a meteorological phenomenon, טל in the meaning "dew" is made the following way: As the wind brings moisture from the Mediterranean, this condenses under the action of the cool night air into a mist.[38] From the Old Testament texts, this moisture is seen as descending from heaven (Gen 27:28; Deut 33:28; Zech 8:12) by night (Num 11:9; Judg 6:36–40), returning (or vanishing) early in the morning (Exod 16:13–14; Hos 6:4). From the texts it is clear that the טל is regarded a gift from YHWH.[39] As YHWH is the giver of fertility, the dew is an expression of YHWH's blessing as there is no fertility without dew. However, there are two contexts in which the term טל appear. First, the promise of dew is found in contexts

---

[35] For the same understanding, cf. R.B.Y. Scott, "Meteorological Phenomena and Terminology in the Old Testament", *ZAW* 64 (1952) 25: "low stratus or dew-cloud", Koehler-Baumgartner, *HALAT* (1983) 730: "Tauwolke", and W. Gesenius, *Handwörterbuch* (1995) 423: "Taugewölk".

[36] For the same suggestion to the understanding of Isa 18:4, cf. B. Holmberg, "עב", *ThWAT* 5 (1986) 980.

[37] Cf. F. Zorell, *Lexicon* (1968) 284, who lists Gen 27:28, 39; Deut 33:28; Isa 18:4; Zech 8:12, and Prov 3:20 as examples where the word in its broader sense includes rain. See also Koehler-Baumgartner, *HALAT* (1974) 358–359: "Tau, sanfter Regen", and J. Katsnelson, "Dew", *EJ* 5 (1974) 1600–1602: "It should be noted, however, that in biblical Hebrew טל may also refer to rain", and M.D. Futato, "Sense Relations in the 'Rain' Domain of the Old Testament", *Imagery and Imagination in Biblical Literature* (2001) 93.

[38] Cf. J. Katsnelson, "Dew", *EJ* 5 (1974) 1600: "The conditions favoring the formation of dew are clear nights, moist air, and only light winds in the surface layers of the atmosphere." See also H. Wildberger, *Jesaja 13–27* (1978) 691, for an explanation of how the dew is made.

[39] Cf. P. Reymond, *L'eau, sa vie, et sa signification dans l'Ancien Testament* (1958) 25–27.

of blessings (cf. Gen 27:28). Second, the absence of dew is found in contexts of threats and punishments (cf. Gen 27:39). In the former usage, טל is a blessing that brings fertility (Deut 33:13–17, 28) and hope (Mic 5:6 [ET: 5:7]),[40] whereas in the latter form of usage, the deprivation of טל causes drought and despair (2 Sam 1:21; 1 Kgs 17:1; Hag 1:10). Hosea uses טל frequently in describing the relationship between Israel and YHWH.[41] Positively, if Israel will return to her God, YHWH will be like the dew to Israel, "he shall blossom as the lily [. . .]" (Hos 14:6 [ET: 14:5]). Negatively, like the quick vanishing of the dew in the morning, so is Israel's covenant love: "What can I do with you, Ephraim? What can I do with you, Judah? Your love is like the morning cloud, like the early dew that disappears" (Hos 6:4). In Hos 13:3 a threat is pronounced in terms of dew that vanishes: "Therefore they will be like the morning mist, like the early dew that disappears [. . .]."

What, then, does עב טל refer to in v. 4? Literally, "a cloud of dew" refers to the night mist that vanishes in the morning.[42] The expression "like a cloud of dew in [the] heat of harvest" may be based on the observation that dew increases in quantity as summer progresses.[43] However, is this second simile of v. 4 to be understood positively or negatively? The reference to "a cloud of dew" seems here to be used metaphorically to evoke negative associations along two lines.[44] First, in v. 4aα YHWH is referred to at a distance from the earth, and in this second simile of v. 4 (v. 4bβ) YHWH's distant quietness and gazing is compared to a cloud of dew (that vanishes) in the heat of harvest.[45] Just as the dew goes away in the morning, so will YHWH distance himself from whatever Judah is up to.[46] This

---

[40] In this text it is said that Israel will mediate the blessing that is granted to all nations, cf. A. Weiser, *Das Buch der zwölf kleinen Propheten* (1959) 275.

[41] טל also occurs in descriptions of various human relationships (Deut 32:2; Ps 133:3; Job 29:19; Prov 19:12).

[42] In its broader sense טל can mean "light rain", cf. the suggestion from F. Zorell, *Lexicon* (1968) 284. Cf. also M.D. Futato, "Sense Relations in the 'Rain' Domain of the Old Testament", *Imagery and Imagination in Biblical Literature* (2001) 93, who states that "[i]t remains to identify the texts where 'light rain' is the sense."

[43] See B. Otzen, "טל", *ThWAT* 3 (1982) 345, with references.

[44] According to B. Otzen, when טל is applied as a meteorological phenomenon, it is mostly used negatively, cf. *ibid.* 348.

[45] A different interpretation of these similes is that of W. Brueggemann, *Isaiah 1–39* (1998) 153–154: "Yahweh is as *constant* as hot sun or as summer cloud—ready, but not to be mobilized by any force or will other than Yahweh's own." (My italics).

[46] J.H. Hayes and S.A. Irvine *Isaiah* (1987) 256: "Yahweh [. . .], will keep his hands off and function as an observer."

understanding of Isa 18:4 has relations to the way Hosea likens
Israel's unfaithfulness to YHWH with dew that vanishes (cf. Hos 6:4
and 13:3). In Isa 18:4, however, it is not the people of YHWH who
are negatively described, it is *the help from YHWH* that disappears
from Judah—"like a cloud of dew in the heat of harvest". Second,
the likening of YHWH's attitude with "a cloud of dew" can also
suggest another interpretation. Just as the cloud of dew literally looks
as a veil between the air and the ground, so is it—metaphorically
speaking—a veil between YHWH and his people.[47] In both understandings of this second simile of v. 4, the description of YHWH as
being at a distance is what comes across to the audience.

Summing up the features in the text's motifs
First, it is said that YHWH will be quiet and gaze in his dwelling
place. In this text, the motif מכון most likely refers to YHWH's
dwelling in heaven, and not in the temple. Second, the way YHWH
is quiet and gazing is described through two similes. The motif "glowing heat" is here applied in a negative way as it compares YHWH's
attitude with a situation that meteorologically speaking makes the air
vibrate. Third, the second simile contains the motif "cloud of dew"
that is also applied negatively as it gives associations both to dew
that quickly vanishes in the morning, and to dew as a veil between
heaven and earth. In sum, the two similes of v. 4 have the following meanings: YHWH's quietness and gazing is not a mere observation of what is going on in the world, rather YHWH carefully
scrutinises Judah and looks at her in a way that can be likened with
the "glowing heat" that makes the air vibrate. Further, just as the
dew goes away in the morning, so will YHWH's support withdraw
from Judah if she seeks help from the Cushites and not take example of YHWH who is calm (cf. the attempt of diplomatic alliance
making between Judah and Cush as referred to in vv. 1–2).

4.4. RHETORICAL ANALYSIS

The theme of Isa 18:4 seems to be that of warning Judah against
entering into a coalition with Cush (cf. what is said about vv. 1–2).

---

[47] For the suggestion that "clouds of dew" can be compared with veil, see H. Guthe,
Palästina (1927) 49, who refers to Isa 18:4.

This theme is seen the following ways: First, the degree of importance of the message is high as the warning to Judah is put in the
mouth of YHWH. Referred to in 1st person singular, YHWH speaks
to his people through "me" (most likely the prophet). Second, the
warning from YHWH to his people comes from YHWH who "will
be quiet and gaze" in his dwelling place. Third, this implied distance between YHWH and Judah is further explained through the
two similes at the end of v. 4.

4.4.1. *Rhetorical features in the text's design*

Phonetic observations: Alliteration and rhyme
As pointed at under the headline phonetic observations, three of four
lines of v. 4 start with the consonant כ. The function of this alliterative pattern of v. 4 is to bind the various lines of the strophe
together.

In v. 4aβ there are three longer words applied that refer to
YHWH's attitude אשקוטה ואביטה במכוני. On a phonetic level, these
long words of v. 4aβ stand in contrast to all the short words of the
remaining three lines of v. 4. This staccato rhyme from line to line
(except v. 4aα) creates a feeling of restlessness and tenseness.

Syntactic observations: Internal parallelism
Syntactically, the two last lines of v. 4 are nearly identically constructed
when it comes to word order. By applying almost the same word
order from v. 4bα to v. 4bβ, the two lines are connected to each
other in a striking way. This internal parallelism has a cohesive function as it ties the two last lines of v. 4 together.

Semantic observations: Similes
When YHWH's quietness and gazing (tenor) is likened with two
meteorological phenomena (vehicles), this is creates a feeling of anxiety
and worry among the audience. The attitude of YHWH is not to be
understood in the sense of calmness, relaxation, and friendly interest
in what goes on on earth.[48] Rather, these types of meteorological

---

[48] For a contrasting interpretation, see G.B. Gray, *A Critical and Exegetical Commentary
on The Book of Isaiah* (1962) 313: "untroubled I will watch". See also M.A. Sweeney,
Isaiah 1–39 (1996) 257: "YHWH's 1st-person statement, 'I will be at rest and I will
look about in my habitation,' corresponds to that of a homeowner relaxing in the

phenomena evoke negative associations.[49] The semantic point of
resemblance between the two parallel lines lies in the similar atmosphere to which these meteorological descriptions refer, namely tenseness. It is obvious that "[. . .] similes, when combined with other
similes, work to create meanings different from situations in which
one simile stands by itself."[50] Here, the similes build upon each other
as they both use meteorological vocabulary. However, the second
simile allows progression as there is a change from the unmoving
glowing heat, to the quickly vanishing cloud of dew (which is one
of the aspects of this second simile).

Poetic technique: Direct speech and characters
The direct speech of v. 4 functions to let the audience pay attention
to what YHWH says.[51] By citing YHWH, the prophet brings YHWH's
opinion close to the audience. "Me" refers to an audition. This direct
speech of YHWH through "me" functions to bring the distant deity
a little closer to the situation of the Judeans. The distance between
YHWH as a sender of the message, and the audience as the receivers
of the message is further produced by the description of the view
from which YHWH sends the message. YHWH is referred to as
describing himself as being במכוני, "in my fixed place", watching
what is going on in the world. This perspective from above prevents
the closeness that could have been established by using direct speech.

Further, the poetic technique of identifying only one of the two
characters in v. 4 serves to let YHWH play the central role in v. 4,
and not the unidentified "me".[52] The important message from YHWH

---

garden and contemplating the trimming of decorative plants", and B.S. Childs,
Isaiah (2001) 138: "[. . .] God views the whole world in calm rest [. . .]."
   [49] Cf. D.F. Payne, "A Perspective on the Use of Simile in the Old Testament",
Semitics 1 (1970) 115: "[. . .] the effect and effectiveness of simile depends less on
the pictures utilized than on the aptness of their application, for a simple picture
may give a bizarre effect if placed in an unusual and unexpected frame [. . .]".
   [50] D.L. Petersen & K.H. Richards, *Interpreting Hebrew Poetry* (1992) 59.
   [51] H. Wildberger, *Jesaja 13–27* (1978) 689 and 690, states that the announcement is delivered to the Ethiopian messengers ("den ätiopischen Boten"/"den Boten
aus Kusch"), and not primarily to a Judean audience. However, as Wildberger
argues that this message to the Cushites is used to influence current decisions being
made in Judah, he indirectly includes a Judean element in the listening audience.
In my opinion, the audience most likely does not include the messengers from Cush
as they are no longer on the scene.
   [52] In general, "unnamed characters, [. . .] are among the minor participants." Cf.
L.J. de Regt, *Participants in Old Testament Texts and the Translator* (1999) 95.

comes across to the audience through the mouth of "me", but the prophet acts simply as a mediator between YHWH and the audience, and is not important compared to the other character who is named in v. 4, YHWH.

Summing up the rhetorical features in the text's design
Through observations about the textual design of Isa 18:4, the rhetoric of entrapment seems to be continued the following ways. First, *cohesion* between lines of v. 4 is created as all of this strophe deals with what YHWH says to Judah through the mediator "me". Second, YHWH's *lack of activity* stands in sharp contrast to the eager activity of Judah as referred to in vv. 1–2, and functions as a pattern that Judah should take the example of. Third, the text's design creates a feeling of *confusion* about what the similes mean as they give the impression that YHWH is quiet in a non-relaxing and tense way. As it is not yet revealed who this speech in the end will pronounce judgement over (cf. הוֹי in v. 1), a confusion about this is created in v. 4. Fourth, *concentration* on YHWH is made in v. 4 by the poetic technique of naming only YHWH, and by letting YHWH play the most significant role as the direct speech is put in the mouth of YHWH.

4.4.2. *Rhetorical features in the text's motifs*

YHWH's dwelling place: Important message from the distant YHWH
YHWH dwells in his fixed place having a panorama view over the world. From v. 3 to v. 4, the characters have changed from "all" to two (YHWH and "me"), and from an earthly to a heavenly scene where YHWH dwells at a distance. The actual place of YHWH's dwelling is not defined, but the text has moved away from the earthly surroundings where "all" see the standard and hear the horn. Most likely, YHWH speaks to the audience from his heavenly dwelling. From his dwelling place, YHWH watches down on the earth. The transcendence of YHWH is expressed through the reference to YHWH's dwelling place.

Glowing heat and cloud of dew: Tenseness
YHWH's quietness and gazing is first likened with a meteorological phenomenon that makes the air quiver, and then with a meteorological phenomenon where the dew is like a veil before it vanishes. These similes function to let YHWH's quietness and gazing be of a negative

kind as they function as threats.[53] YHWH watches over Judah and
her plans and wants his own calmness to set an example for Judah.

Summing up the rhetorical features in the text's motifs
The three motifs of v. 4 that have been discussed here are "YHWH's
dwelling place", "glowing heat", and "a cloud of dew". The fact
that the dwelling place of YHWH is not accurately described in this
verse serves to create a feeling of distance between YHWH and what
goes on on the earth. It has been proposed that in Isa 18:4 YHWH's
calmness is metaphorically equated with the fixed, peaceful course
of the agricultural year.[54] Rather, the quietness is not peaceful, but
tense and threatening. The first meteorological phenomenon evokes
a feeling of tenseness. The second meteorological phenomenon referred
to in v. 4 creates a feeling of anxiety as it creates associations to the
distant YHWH who will withdraw his help if Judah effectuates her
plans.

4.4.3. *How do textual design and motifs together create the strophe's rhetoric?*

Cohesion: Alliteration, short words, and similes
From the text's design we have seen that three of four lines start
with the same consonant. Further, it has been observed that v. 4
contains two lines that are parallel in terms of syntax (v. 4bα and 4bβ),
and that the accumulation of short words in v. 4 makes a rhyme
(except from v. 4aβ). Together, these features makes v. 4 hang
together. Semantically, the parallel lines consist of two similes that
explain *how* YHWH will be quiet and gaze, whereas the accumulation
of short words in three of four lines of v. 4 serves to make v. 4aβ
stand out: "I will be quiet and gaze in my dwelling place". The fact
that v. 4aβ does not contain short words—different from the remaining three lines of v. 4—focuses the attention on what is said in this

---

[53] For a more positive interpretation of the comparisons, see, R.E. Clements,
Isaiah 1–39 (1980/1994) 165: "The imagery of a calm and pleasant summer evening
[. . .]", and J. Høgenhaven, *Gott und Volk bei Jesaja* (1988) 133: "Das folgende Bild
ist dem Rhytmus der Natur und des Ackerbaus entnommen: Wie der Sommer mit
seiner Wärme und seinen Tauwolken verhält sich Jahwe ruhig abwartend [. . .]".
[54] Cf. S. Talmon, "צח", *ThWAT* 6 (1989) 985: "Es handelt sich um einen
Prophetenspruch, in dem Gottes gesammelte 'Ruhe' (Wildberger, Kaiser) dem festen
und friedlichen Ablauf des landwirtschaftlichen Jahres bildlich gleichgesetzt wird."

line. As YHWH's way of dwelling is likened with "glowing heat" and "a cloud of dew", the motifs of v. 4 focus the attention on YHWH and his attitude. The textual features together with the motifs of v. 4 serve to produce a cohesive message of importance to the audience.

Lack of activity: YHWH's quietness as a pattern for Judah
There are three interrelated suggestions of how to understand YHWH's quietness in this verse. First, YHWH's quietness is seen as a proof of his superiority: YHWH cannot be distracted or dissuaded by any human being, as he is above the pressures that drive earthly powers.[55] Without regard to human plans he will effectuate his fateful plans.[56] Second, YHWH can be seen as stating an example for the audience and the whole world: as long as YHWH is quiet, they should copy his behaviour and not enter into coalitions with one another.[57] A third solution is that YHWH will state an example for Judah in particular. She shall be quiet because YHWH will *act on behalf of her*.[58]

---

[55] Cf. B.S. Childs, *Isaiah and the Assyrian Crisis* (1967) 45: "[. . .] Yahweh's unruffled self-composure which arises from his sense of absolute sovereignty over the whole world", and W. Eichrodt, *Der Herr der Geschichte* (1967) 61: "[. . .] unberührt von dem irdischen Getriebe [. . .]". See also H. Wildberger, *Jesaja 13–27* (1978) 691: "[. . .] Ausdruck seiner unanfechtbaren Überlegenheit über das Treiben der irdischen Mächte."

[56] For this interpretation, see J. Fischer, *Das Buch Isaias* (1937) 138, J. Ziegler, *Isaias* (1948) 62, P. Reymond, *L'eau, sa vie, et sa signification dans l'Ancien Testament* (1958) 30–31, A.S. Herbert, *The Book of the Prophet Isaiah* (1973) 119, B. Otzen, "טל", *ThWAT* 3 (1982) 349, J.N. Oswalt, *The Book of Isaiah* (1986) 362, H. Ringgren, "נבט", *ThWAT* 5 (1986) 139. Cf. also W. Brueggemann, *Isaiah 1–39* (1998) 153–154: "Yahweh will not be hurried or provoked or pressed to any schedule of combat other than Yahweh's own", and A. Laato, *"About Zion I will not be silent"* (1998) 72: "That Yhwh is quiet indicates that the human forces attempt to do something which will not be successful." For a similar view, see B.S. Childs, *Isaiah* (2001) 138: "Far above the fever of busy diplomatic intrigue, God views the whole world in calm rest from his heavenly dwelling before he acts."

[57] Cf. K. Marti, *Das Buch Jesaja* (1900) 149, H. Donner, *Israel unter den Völkern* (1964) 125, G. Friman, *Profeten Jesaja* (1917) 26, and L.A. Snijders, *Jesaja deel 1* (1969) 195, R.E. Clements, *Isaiah 1–39* (1980/1994) 165: "The message must be understood as a clear warning to the king not to listen to, or join with, the plans of the Ethiopian ambassadors." See also J.H. Hayes and S.A. Irvine *Isaiah, The Eight-century Prophet* (1987) 256, who argue that "Yahweh will take the same posture in this situation that Isaiah recommended to Ahaz in the days of the earlier coalition—unsupportive of the revolt (see Isa 7:3–9) [. . .] The present plan for revolt is to Yahweh only a flash in the pan, insubstantial and passing, like blazing heat in the light of day and dew in the summertime. Given a little time, they both disappear, the heat with the coming of evening and the dew in the light of the sun."

[58] Cf. E.J. Kissane, *The Book of Isaiah I* (1960) 199, E.J. Young, *The Book of Isaiah*

Of these three solutions I find the second the most convincing one. Verse 4 puts the following message across to the audience: just as YHWH is quiet, so should Judah be neutral in her foreign politics. This is not because YHWH will act on Judah's behalf, but simply because YHWH states an example for Judah. This idea of not taking any action toward alliances is known also from other texts (see Isa 7:4–9; 28:16; 30:15). As the similes applied to describe YHWH's quietness create a picture of YHWH being quiet in a threatening and tense way, the comparison between YHWH's calmness with "glowing heat", and "a cloud of dew" gives associations to more than simply being at rest. YHWH is not relaxed or sleepy, rather he is awake watching the earth intensely.[59] If Judah wants help from YHWH, she should take notice of his quietness and follow YHWH's example.

Confusion: Who will be judged?
Phonetically speaking, the longer words of v. 4aβ functions to underline the quietness of YHWH. Similarly, the shorter staccato words of the three remaining lines of v. 4 serve to contrast v. 4aβ by putting across an atmosphere of urgency and uneasiness. This tense atmosphere created by the text's design is underlined by the negative associations evoked by the motifs of v. 4 as YHWH's quietness and gazing are compared with "glowing heat" and "a cloud of dew". The similes function as warnings about a coming danger.[60] Still, it is not revealed to the audience to whom this danger will appear, and this is what causes the confusion.

(1965/1978) 477, G.B. Gray, *A Critical and Exegetical Commentary on The Book of Isaiah* (1962) 315: "[. . .] in quietness lies their deliverance (7:4–9; 28:16; 30:15)". See also F. Huber, *Jahwe, Juda und die anderen Völker beim Propheten Jesaja* (1976) 132, who states that Judah is to be calm because YHWH will act on behalf of her. The same is argued by S.H. Widyapranawa, *The Lord is Saviour* (1990) 106: "But for the moment Judah should remain quiet and put all their trust in the LORD (cf. 30:15) [. . .]".

[59] Not all scholars interpret these pictures as creating a tense atmosphere, cf. Kissane who sees the heat of the summer's day and the heavy dews of the night as promoting the growth and maturing of the grape, and "[. . .] similarly Jahweh promotes the success of Assyria's conquest of Israel." E.J. Kissane, *The Book of Isaiah I* (1960) 199.

[60] That the message of the similes is that of warning is also perceived by C.R. Seitz, *Isaiah 1–39* (1993) 148: "God's judgement is to fall 'like a cloud of dew in the heat of harvest' [. . .]".

Concentration: YHWH is the main character in v. 4
The focus in this verse is on YHWH and what he says from his
dwelling place. From the text's design, this is clearly seen in the
poetic techniques of direct speech, and the naming of only one character: YHWH. Also from the motifs, YHWH is in focus as "YHWH's
dwelling place" is central, and further how YHWH's attitude is from
his dwelling. Although מכון is not more closely referred to, it most
likely refers to YHWH's heavenly dwelling. The function of not locat-
ing YHWH's dwelling place is to create a distance between YHWH
and his people. However, the poetic technique of direct speech functions to let YHWH come closer to his people. Further, as the prophet
("me") functions as a mediator between YHWH and Judah, the gap
between the deity and the people is diminished also by the use of
this technique. As YHWH is the only character who is mentioned
by name in this verse, this serves to let the audience concentrate
their attention on YHWH and what he says.

Summing up the rhetoric in the text's design and motifs
Having made observations about both textual design and motifs of
Isa 18:4, the following rhetorical features have been observed: First,
cohesion is made by the devices of alliteration and parallel lines, and
by the focus on YHWH and what he says. Second, from the textual
design it is clear that YHWH's *lack of activity* is underlined by the
way v. 4aβ is formed—the three long words of this line stand in
contrast to the many short words of the remaining of v. 4. All the
motifs of v. 4 deal with how YHWH's lack of activity is to be understood. Third, a sense of *confusion* is made as it is not yet revealed to
the audience who will be judged (cf. the הוי of v. 1). Fourth, as
YHWH is the only character who is referred to by name, and as
all of v. 4 in one or the other way refer to what YHWH says, this
functions to let the audience *concentrate* on YHWH and the message
from him. Judah should be quiet as YHWH is quiet, and not make
proposals about going into a coalition with Cush (vv. 1–2). However,
as YHWH's quietness is not referred to as a relaxed one, the text
reveals that YHWH is strongly against the actions of Judah that he
observes from his heavenly dwelling. Textual design and motifs work
together in making clear YHWH's protesting against Judah's attempt
of entering into an alliance with Cush.

CHAPTER FIVE

STROPHE IV: 18:5

5.1. Text and translation

5.1.1. *Textual criticism*

Text	Verse
כי־לפני קציר כתם־פרח	v. 5aα
ובסר גמל יהיה נצה	v. 5aβ
וכרת הזלזלים במזמרות	v. 5bα
ואת־הנטישות הסיר התז	v. 5bβ

Verse	Text

v. 5aα For, at harvest time, when the bud has been completed

v. 5aβ and [the] sour grape[s][1] [are] ripen,[2] [and] blossom has happened,

v. 5bα then he will cut off the quivering tendrils with pruning knives,

v. 5bβ and he will turn aside [and] he will strike away the twigs.[3]

5.1.2. *Translation*

The translation of כי־לפני קציר

The expression כי־לפני קציר (in v. 5aα) is here translated "for, at harvest time [. . .]". By rendering the phrase this way, this means

---

[1] MT has ובסר, "sour grape[s]", masculine singular absolute, while 1Q Isaᵃ has ובסור, which is a qaṭūl-form of the same root. I see no reason for rejecting MT's ובסר.

[2] Where MT has גמל, "ripen", qal active participle masculine singular absolute, 1Q Isaᵃ has גמול, "being ripened", which is qal passive participle. I see no reason why MT's גמל should be rejected.

[3] MT has the noun הנטישות, "twigs" in v. 5bβ, feminine plural absolute, while some Rabbinic witnesses read הנטיעות instead of MT's הנטישות. For details, cf. the textual critical apparatus in *The Hebrew University Bible* (1995). הנטיעות means "the plants" (of the root נטע, this form found only in Ps 144:12 where it is used figuratively of vigorous sons), whereas MT's הנטישות means "the twigs" (of the root נטש). However, as long as MT is linguistically sound and valid, there is no reason why MT should be rejected. For a discussion of the translation of this word, see 5.1.2.

that לפני is not temporarily understood in this text in the meaning "*before* the harvest". A similar understanding of לפני is also seen in H. Wildberger's commentary. According to Wildberger, לפני should not be taken in the sense of "*prae-*", in a temporal meaning. Rather, he argues, it has the meaning "in the sight of, in the presence of" in Isa 18:5.[4]

The translation of כתם־פרח
When the preposition כ is followed by an infinitive construct, this indicates a temporal use of the preposition.[5] Therefore, the preposition כ is here rendered "when".

The translation of בסר נמל
The translation of בסר is not difficult as the conventional rendering of this word is "sour grape". What is interesting, though, is that the noun בסר, "grape", in singular, is regarded having a plural meaning, "grapes".[6] In order to distinguish between the noun's strict grammatical form on the one hand, and its function on the other hand, it is written "grape[s]" in the translation above. The translation of נמל is in Isa 18:5 "ripen". The phrase בסר נמל means sour grapes that are ripen.[7]

The translation of יהיה נצה
In Job 15:33 and Gen 40:10, נצה means "blooming, in full blossom". This is also the case in Isa 18:5.[8] Here, יהיה נצה can thus be translated "blossom has happened". For a different rendering, see F. Wutz who makes an unnecessary emendation and reads יהוה נצה, "throws off the blooms".[9]

---

[4] Cf. H. Wildberger, *Jesaja 13–27* (1978) 681: "לפני ist nicht als 'prae' im zeitlichen Sinn zu verstehen, sondern hat die Bedeutung 'angesichts von' [. . .]".

[5] Cf. C.H.J. van der Merwe & al., *A Biblical Hebrew Reference Grammar* (1999/2002) 284: "כ + infinitive construct is used to indicate that an event referred to in the main clause following the temporal clause with the כ + infinitive construct, *immediately follows it in time.*" (His italics).

[6] Cf. D.J.A. Clines, *DCH* 2 (1995) 234.

[7] Cf. A.A. Macintosh, *Isaiah xxi A palimpsest* (1980) 47: "In Isa. xviii 5 it [נמל] denotes grapes that are ripe."

[8] Cf. D.J.A. Clines, *DCH* 5 (2001) 738.

[9] Cf. F. Wutz, "Abweichende Vokalisationsüberlieferung im hebr. Text", *BZ* 21 (1933) 20.

The translation of הזלזלים

זלזלים is a *hapax legomenon*, most likely related to זלל III. In the qal the verb means "be light, worthless", in the niphal it means "quake", "shake" "shake, quake."[10] According to H. Wildberger, הזלזלים in v. 5bα is most likely used about shoots of the vine that grow wild, without any fruit growing on them.[11] Cf. the Greek rendering τὰ βοτρύδια τὰ μικρά, "the very small clusters". In this research, הזלזלים is rendered "the quivering tendrils". The tendril of a vine is a "slender, thread-like organ or appendage of a plant, often spiral in form, which stretches out and attaches itself to some other body so as to support the plant."[12] The tendrils do not bear fruit, but with its tendrils, the vine clings to other trees in order to climb.[13]

The translation of הנטישות

הנטישות is rendered "twigs" in this research. As will be suggested later, הנטישות in Isa 18:5 seems to play on the various meanings that can be derived from נטש: "forsake", "cast off", "cast away", "reject", "leave", "spread out". In Jer 5:10, הנטישות are said to be cut off the vine, and the term is used in a context of judgement over Israel/Judah. In Jer 48:32, the same word is applied in a context of doom over Moab. Although the text of Isa 18 not explicitly states this, I find it likely that הנטישות can bear fruit.[14] The function of the two words הזלזלים and הנטישות in Isa 18:5 will be suggested in 5.4.

The translation of התז

התז in v. 5bβ is a *hapax legomenon* that most likely derives from the root תזז. In Isa 18:5 it occurs in hiphil perfect 3rd person masculine singular. In this work, התז is rendered "he will strike away".[15]

---

[10] Cf. D.J.A. Clines, *DCH* 3 (1996) 114–115. In Koehler-Baumgartner, *HALAT* (1967) 261, this meaning is found under זלל II: "beben, wanken".

[11] Cf. H. Wildberger, *Jesaja 13–27* (1978) 692; cf. also J.H. Hayes & S.A. Irvine, *Isaiah* (1987) 256, who argue that it refers to "[. . .] unwanted growth on grape vines."

[12] J. Coulson & al. (eds.), *The New Oxford Illustrated Dictionary* (1978) 1726.

[13] See K. Nielsen, *There is Hope for a Tree* (1989) 77, footnote 13, for the information that trees of various types can be planted together. At the disputation, the first opponent, Prof. Kirsten Nielsen, argued that הזלזלים and הנטישות in Isa 18:5 should not both be rendered "tendrils"—as was done by this reader at that time.

[14] This is rejected by H. Wildberger, *Jesaja 13–27* (1978) 692, who regards the two terms in v. 5, הזלזלים and הנטישות, as not referring to woody vines, but rather to green sprouts that could simply be torn off with one's bare hand.

[15] For this rendering, cf. *BDB* (1979) 1064. The understanding of התז as a tearing away of shoots is also suggested by Koehler-Baumgartner, *HALAT* (1990) 1580, as the hiphil התז is translated: "(Ranken) abreissen".

5.2. Textual design

5.2.1. *Syntactic observations*

As mentioned in the analysis of v. 4, there is a syntactic parallel between v. 4 and v. 5 that should be commented on. The particle conjunction כִּי opens both v. 4 and v. 5, and in both verses this particle conjunction כִּי is used to introduce YHWH's *acting*—though in two different ways. In v. 4 YHWH acts by speaking, and in v. 5 YHWH acts by doing:

YHWH has *spoken* "to me"	כִּי ... v. 4
YHWH (he) will *work* in the vineyard	כִּי ... v. 5

In v. 4, the particle conjunction כִּי introduces what YHWH has said "to me", whereas in v. 5 the particle כִּי introduces what YHWH is going to do. Whereas v. 4 refers to what YHWH has told "me" in the past, the focus in v. 5 is on what will happen in the future. From this, we see that the resemblance between the use of כִּי from v. 4 to v. 5 lies in that they both open up for a description of YHWH's acting either by speaking or by doing.

Reappearance of number and status
Concerning the nouns that are present in v. 5, the two first and the two last lines of v. 5 reveal a certain degree of resemblance. There is a full identification between the nouns when it comes to number and status between v. 5aα and 5aβ as well as 5bα and 5bβ, respectively, whereas there are divergences in gender between the same two and two lines. Let us briefly clarify what is similar and what is not in v. 5 when it comes to the nouns.

There are four nouns in the first half of v. 5 (5aα–5aβ). In v. 5aα the nouns קָצִיר, "harvest", and פֶּרַח "bud", both appear in masculine singular absolute. In v. 5aβ, the noun בֹּסֶר, "sour grape", also appears in masculine singular absolute, whereas the second noun in 5aβ, נִצָּה, "blossom", appears in feminine singular absolute. From this, it is evident that there is a reappearance of number and status in v. 5aα–5aβ. All four nouns appear in the same number and status, and three of four nouns appear in the same gender (masculine), and one noun appears in feminine.

When it comes to the two last lines of v. 5 (5bα–5bβ), three nouns occur altogether. V. 5bα contains two nouns, where the first noun,

הזלזלים, "quivering tendrils", appears in masculine plural absolute, and the next noun במזמרות, "pruning knives" appears in feminine plural absolute. The one noun that occurs in v. 5bβ, הנטישות, "twigs", appears in feminine plural absolute. When it comes to the three nouns in v. 5bα and 5bβ, the pattern reappearance is the following: All three nouns appear in the same number and status (plural absolute), but the first noun in v. 5bα appears in masculine whereas the two other appear in feminine.

5.2.2. *Semantic observations*

Semantically, all lines of v. 5 describe what happens in the vine-yard. Yet there is one observation in terms of semantics that catches the interest in particular: namely the verbs of v. 5. The verbs that occur in this verse are—in one or the other way—all related to the vine (the bud has been *completed*, the sour grapes *ripen*, blossom has *happened*, and the tendrils and twigs will be *cut off/turned aside/stroke away*). In the two first lines of v. 5, the three verb forms have to do with the cultivation and the growth of the vine, whereas in the two last lines of v. 5, the three verbs that frame these two lines are reductive in the sense that they describe the act of destroying parts of the vine (כרת, "cut off", הסיר, "turn aside", and התז, "strike away"). This pattern shows that the verbs in v. 5aα and 5bβ are all applied to describe the vine's growth, whereas the verbs in v. 5bα and 5bβ all express the opposite action, namely the tearing down of parts of the vine.

Play with words
MT uses the noun הנטישות, "twigs", deliberately in order to play on the various meanings that can be derived from נטש: "forsake", "cast off", "cast away", "reject", "leave", "spread out".[16] In my opinion, MT's use of this word deliberately plays on what is said about the destruction of parts of the vine in v. 5bα and 5bβ.

In addition, there is another play with words in Isa 18, but then between the word הזלזלים in v. 5bα, and the word צלצל in v. 1a. This is also observed by R.E. Clements, who states that "[t]he word for shoots (Heb. *zalzallîm*) introduces an intentional homophony upon

---

[16] Cf. Koehler-Baumgartner, *HALAT* (1983) 657, "hinstrecken, aufgeben, hinwerfen".

the word for "whirring insects/ships" (Heb. *ṣilṣal*) in v. 1."[17] How these two plays with words function will be suggested in 5.4.1.

5.2.3. *Poetic technique*

Direct speech?

As mentioned in the analysis of v. 4, the text does not reveal at which point the message from YHWH ends, and when the virtual quotation flow together with the words of "me". The confusion is created in that verse 4 refers to YHWH in 1st person singular, whereas verse 5 refers to "he" (3rd person masculine singular). By applying the poetic technique of direct speech in v. 4, and continuing in v. 5 with simply referring to an unnamed "he", the audience most likely perceives that the direct speech from YHWH ends by verse 4. Verse 5 is a continuation of the message from YHWH (begun in v. 4) delivered to the audience through "me".[18] Following the majority of scholars, I delimit the divine speech to v. 4 as this is the only verse in Isa 18 that clearly refers to YHWH in the 1st person singular.[19] What is said in v. 5 is a continuation of the speech in v. 4, though in a different form.[20]

Unnamed character

In v. 5 only one character is mentioned: "he". Whether this 3rd person masculine singular refers to YHWH is not explicitly said in v. 5.[21] K. Marti suggests that vv. 5–6 originally followed 17:11, and

---

[17] R.E. Clements, *Isaiah 1–39* (1980/1994) 165.

[18] Cf. L.J. de Regt, *Participants in Old Testament Texts* (1999) 96.

[19] See B. Duhm, *Das Buch Jesaia* (1892) 115, O. Procksch, *Jesaia I* (1930) 241, J. Fischer, *Das Buch Isaias* (1937) 138, Aa. Bentzen, *Jesaja* (1944) 142, G. Fohrer, *Das Buch Jesaja Kapitel 1–23* (1960/1966) 225, F. Huber, *Jahwe, Juda und die anderen Völker beim Propheten Jesaja* (1976) 131 footnote 194, J.H. Hayes & S.A. Irvine, *Isaiah* (1987) 256, J. Blenkinsopp, *Isaiah 1–39* (2000) 311. One scholar does not determine where YHWH's speech ends and the words of "me" take over, cf. E.J. Young, *The Book of Isaiah* (1965/1978) 477.

[20] For the same interpretation, see A. Dillmann, *Der Prophet Jesaia* (1890) 169, F. Feldmann, *Das Buch Isaias* (1925) 220, G.B. Gray, *A Critical and Exegetical Commentary on The Book of Isaiah* (1962) 315, and H. Wildberger, *Jesaja 13–27* (1978) 682: "Aber 5f. ist als Fortsetzung von 4 unentbehrlich [. . .]". See also C.R. Seitz, *Isaiah 1–39* (1993) 148.

[21] Cf. J.H. Hayes & S.A. Irvine, *Isaiah* (1987) 256: "The identity of the "he" (or "one") in verse 5*b* is left unclarified. Is it Yahweh? The Assyrian ruler? Perhaps Isaiah deliberately left the matter ambiguous."

that the words would not be YHWH's, and the indefinite construction of affirmatives to the three verbs in v. 5 would be appropriate enough.[22] In my view, however, verses 5 and 6 are further explanations of what YHWH has told "me" (in v. 4), and are thus closely related to what YHWH has said in v. 4. Therefore, the most plausible solution to who is meant by "he" in v. 5, is that this unnamed character refers to YHWH.[23] This is likely of two reasons: First, the immediately preceding strophe of v. 5 (v. 4), proposes to contain a message from YHWH, and as the character "he" is not presented by a name, the audience most likely perceives him in v. 5 to be the same as "I" in v. 4.[24] Second, as will be evident in 5.3., portraying YHWH as a vinedresser is not unfamiliar from other Old Testament texts (see for instance Isa 5:7).

Summing up the features in the text's design
The features commented upon above can be summarised as follows: First, the syntactic observations show that the nouns in the first two lines of v. 5 and in the two last lines of v. 5, respectively, appear in the same number and status. Further, it has been observed that there is a resemblance between the use of כִּי from v. 4 to v. 5 in that they both open up for a description of YHWH's acting either by speaking or by doing. Second, semantically, all verbs occurring in v. 5 have in one or the other way a relation to the vine. In addition, MT's choice of the word for twigs, הַנְּטִישׁוֹת, plays on the various negative meanings that can be derived from the root נטשׁ. Third, from the poetic techniques observed in v. 5, it is evident that the direct speech that started in v. 4 is taken further in v. 5—though in a different form. The one unnamed character mentioned in this verse most likely refers to YHWH.

---

[22] Cf. K. Marti, *Das Buch Jesaja* (1900) 149–152.

[23] For the same opinion, cf. F. Feldmann, *Das Buch Isaias* (1925) 220, and J. Fischer, *Das Buch Isaias* (1937) 138, L.A. Snijders, *Jesaja deel 1* (1969) 195–196. O. Procksch, *Jesaia I* (1930) 241, on the other hand, does not think that "he" refers to YHWH: "Subject ist nicht Jahve, wie man fälschlich annimmt, sondern der Assyrer, der den Weinberg mit der Hippe (cf. 2, 4 מִזְמֵרָה) schneitelt [...]". Subsequently, Procksch renders "man".

[24] According to L.J. de Regt, *Participants in Old Testament Texts* (1999) 23: "In poetry, the start of a new paragraph, a strophe, can be indicated by a change of person while referring to the same participant. As an organising principle, then, such a change of grammatical person to mark the next strophe seems to be a usual pattern in poetry, rather than a full reference with a proper name."

5.3. MOTIFS

An awareness of the motifs "vine" and "vineyard" are essential to the understanding of the metaphorical speech in Isa 18:5 of tendrils and twigs that are cut off (for the interpretation of this metaphorical speech, see 5.4.). Although they are not explicitly mentioned in v. 5, the intertwined motifs "vine" and "vineyard" need to be addressed *before* I can approach the motifs that are explicitly mentioned in Isa 18:5.

In the Old Testament, there are a large number of terms connected with the cultivation of the vine, appearing hundreds of times.[25] The vineyard motif is often found in the book of Isaiah, whereas the vine motif is found in the books of Jeremiah and Hosea, and in the Psalms.

5.3.1. *Vine*

Literally, "[t]he vine is a fast-growing climbing shrub with long tendrils [. . .] The minute, greenish, clustered flowers are followed by berries. The fruit, grapes, may be consumed fresh or dried into raisins and currants. Its juice may be produced into wine or vinegar. The leaves are edible and the remainder of the plant has been used for fodder and tannin."[26] In ancient Israel most vines were cultivated in vineyards, but sometimes grapevines were mixed with other fruit-trees (Cant 6:11). Other trees are occasionally described the same way as the vine (cf. Jer 11:16; Hos 9:10; 14:6–8). Vine is the first cultivated plant mentioned in the Old Testament, cf. Gen 9:20: "Noah, a man of the soil, proceeded to plant a vineyard" (כרם).[27] A large number of place-names connected with viticulture and wine production together with the vine's significance in religious ritual and

---

[25] M. Zohary, *Plants of the Bible* (1982) 54: "Innumerable words in the Bible are associated with planting, pruning, vintage and wine production, and various terms designate the parts of the plant and its fruit varieties."

[26] I. Jacob & W. Jacob, "Flora", *ABD* 2 (1992) 810.

[27] Other terms for vine are for instance: נפן, "vine" (Deut 8:8; Ps 78:47), שׂרק, "choice species of vine" (Isa 5:2; Jer 2:21). "The grapevine is the only fruit-bearing plant mentioned in the OT having different names for the plant, *gepen*, and the fruit, *'ēnāb* (Deut 32:14; pl. *'ănābîm*, Gen 40:10). It is also the only one mentioned in the OT for which the different parts are enumerated." Cf. O. Borowski, *Agriculture in Iron Age Israel* (1987) 103.

the law codes, testify to the importance of the vine in ancient Israelite life.[28]

In addition to its literal meaning, vine is used many times in the Old Testament metaphorically about YHWH's people, their destruction, and restoration (Isa 5:1–7; Jer 2:21 6:9; Ezek 15:6–8; 17:6–8; Hos 10:1; 14:8; Pss 80:9–13 and 44:3).[29] Israel is pictured as God's flourishing grain and blossoming vine (Hos 14:8 [ET: 14:7]). Besides a collective use of the vine motif as YHWH's people (cf. Jer 2:21; Ps 80:9–16), the motif of trees as individuals is also applied (cf. Job 15:33; Pss 1:3; 92:13–16; Jer 17:7–8; Esek 17:1–10; 19:10–14). Positively, the vine, together with the fig, is a sign of peace and prosperity (1 Kgs 5:5 [ET: 4:25]; Mic 4:4). In ancient Israel, the vine was regarded a national emblem.[30] The planting of vineyards is a sign of stability and permanent settlement (Isa 37:30 = 2 Kgs 19:29; 36:17; 65:21; Jer 31:5; 32:15; 35:7, 9; Ezek 28:26; Hos 2:17 [ET: 2:15]; Amos 9:14; Ps 107:37).[31] Negatively, the vine and its fruit can be used to describe the devastation of Israel (Joel 1:7, 12).

Although the motif "vine" is not explicitly mentioned in Isa 18:5, the reference to several parts of the vine—and stages of its growth ("blossom", "bud", "sour grapes", "tendrils" and "twigs")—makes the audience aware that the scene is the vineyard in v. 5, and that the plant described here is the vine. What the text literally says is this: First, the tendrils will be cut off the vine when the plant is still in the process of growing. Second, the twigs (presumably with sour grapes on them) will be cast away to the birds of prey and the wild beasts (v. 6). What this means in a non-literal way will be suggested in 5.4.

---

[28] For examples of place-names related to viticulture and wine production, see O. Borowski, *Agriculture in Iron Age Israel* (1987) 103, footnote 3.

[29] Cf. the earlier cited C.E. Walsh, *The Fruit of the Vine* (2000) 2: "[. . .] images of vines, vineyards, and grape clusters throughout the Bible are used to convey the nature of relationships between Yahweh and his people [. . .]." See also O. Borowski, *Agriculture in Iron Age Israel* (1987) 109: "The vine is used many times by the prophets as a symbol for the people of Israel, their destruction, and restoration (Jer 2:21; 6:9; Ezek 15:6; 17:6–8; Hos 10:1; 14:8; and others)."

[30] M. Zohary, *Plants of the Bible* (1982) 54: "It appeared on mosaic floors, murals, and portals of synagogues, on pottery, furniture, tombs and coins; even in exile, the Israelites still cherished the grapes of Judah, chiseling their shapes on tombstones in foreign lands."

[31] Planting a vineyard and enjoying its fruit were so important that a man could not participate in war before he enjoyed the fruit of his vineyard, cf. the law in Deut 20:6. The same view is reflected in Deut 28:30.

5.3.2. *Vineyard*

The second motif we need to present in order to sketch the background for the metaphorical speech of Isa 18:5 is "vineyard", כרם.[32]

There are two main metaphorical usages of the vineyard motif in the Old Testament: (i) erotic (found mainly in Canticum) and (ii) religious. In the majority of cases, the motif "vineyard" is collectively applied about Israel/Judah, i.e. the vineyard is the people of YHWH (cf. Isa 3:14; 5:7; 18:5; Jer 12:10–12; Ps 80:8–9).[33] In only a few cases, the motif is applied to a nation other than Judah (Isa 16:8—repeated in Jer 48:32–33—and Isa 24:13).

Alongside with its literal meaning, both individuals and collectives can be portrayed as vineyards in the Old Testament.[34] There seems to be a distinction between the vineyard as the nation and the vineyard as the chosen possession of YHWH. The latter image seems to be the basic one, and is often limited to the remnant (2 Kgs 19:30; Isa 27:2–6; 37:31; Jer 6:9). The metaphorical use of the vineyard emphasises YHWH's election of his people, and the privileges that go with this election, more than designating the nation as such. Isa 5:7 is clear about the owner's care for his pleasant plant: "the man of Judah is the garden of his delight."[35] In Ps 80:8–9, the psalmist describes the exodus in the language of a vineyard.[36] The

---

[32] For a survey of how this term is applied throughout the Old Testament, see H.-P. Müller, "כרם", *ThWAT* 4 (1984) 334–340.

[33] Cf. H. Fisch, "The Analogy of Nature, A Note on the Structure of Old Testament Imagery", *JThS.NS* 6 (1955) 161–173, 164: "There is, for instance, the image of Israel as God's vineyard [...] which clearly has a more than functional purpose."

[34] It has long been recognised that the Old Testament applies vegetation metaphors as images for people. In earlier scholarship, see for instance E. König, *Stilistik, Rhetorik, Poetik in Bezug auf die biblische Litteratur* (1900) 100, *et passim*. The only recent comprehensive analysis of the Old Testament figurative field appears to be P. von Gemünden, *Vegetationsmeaphorik im Neuen Testament* (1993). Another valuable contribution to Old Testament garden imagery and related topics is T. Stordalen, *Echoes of Eden* (2000). What is striking, though, is that Stordalen only occasionally includes Isa 18:5 when he discusses the vineyard motif. Cf. the exclusion of Isa 18:5 when he lists texts that have to do with the idea of a nation as a fruit tree/fruit garden of YHWH, *ibid.* p. 73.

[35] I interpret "house of Israel" and "man of Judah" (Isa 5:7) as a synonymous parallelism, rather than seeing the first as a reference to the northern ten tribes. For a similar view, cf. K. Snodgrass, *The Parable of the Wicked Tenants* (1983) 76.

[36] In some texts (cf. Ps 80), the tree motif and the vineyard motif are combined. Although related, I will keep strictly to the vineyard motif, and not discuss how the tree motif is used throughout the Old Testament. Cf. T. Stordalen, *Echoes of Eden* (2000) 180.

growth of the vine accentuates the blessing of YHWH onto his people (cf. Gen 49:11–12, 22). The bad fruit is not the responsibility of the vinedresser who took care of the vineyard (Ezek 17:8–10). As a result of bearing bad grapes, some Old Testament texts describe a destruction of the vine or the vineyard. Hosea describes the Israelites' worship of idols as leading to the rotten fruit of the vineyard (10:1). Also other texts from Hosea make use of vineyard imagery, see Hos 2:17 [ET: 2:15]; 9:10, 16; 14:8–9 [ET: 14:7–8]. In addition to the many shorter texts that apply the vineyard motif (Isa 3:14–15; 17:6; 18:5; 24:13; Jer 8:13; 12:10–12; Hos 10:1; Joel 1:7 etc.), there are two extended texts in the Old Testament that apply the vineyard motif metaphorically about Israel/Judah: Isa 5:1–7 and 27:2–6.[37] These two extended passages have been thoroughly studied by others.[38] From these studies, however, it seems that the Old Testament metaphorical usage of the vineyard motif is *similar* from the longer to the shorter texts. Scholars have long recognised a relationship between Isa 5:1–7 and Isa 27:2–6. Where Isa 5:1–7 is negative about the people's destiny, Isa 27:2–6 is positive, and announces YHWH's safeguarding of Israel.[39] Most scholars date this text to the post-exilic period and understand it as an announcement of the eschatological restoration of Israel.[40] As the old vineyard song (Isa 5:1–7) was not adequate for a new situation, it was reinterpreted and transformed from one of judgement to one of salvation.[41] Before concluding this excursus, a few words about how Isa 18:5 relate to Isa 5:1–7 will be suggested.

What is said about the vineyard in Isa 18:5 is scarce, and an important intertext seems to be Isa 5:1–7.[42] The song about the

---

[37] Verse 6 is here included in the redactional unit, cf. K. Nielsen, *There is Hope for a Tree* (1985) 117, and T. Stordalen, *Echoes of Eden* (2000) 178, footnote 119.

[38] Cf. A.J. Bjørndalen, *Untersuchungen zur allegorischen Rede der Propheten Amos und Jesaja* (1986) 247–343, (Isa 5:1–7) and K. Nielsen, *There is Hope for a Tree* (1989) 87–123, both with references to earlier literature. Cf. in addition the recent contribution from T. Stordalen, *Echoes of Eden* (2000) 178–180.

[39] Cf. H. Wildberger, *Jesaja 13–27* (1978) 1008–1009.

[40] Cf. M.A. Sweeney, *Isaiah 1–39* (1996) 345–353, R.E. Clements, *Isaiah 1–39* (1980/1994) 163–166, G. Fohrer, *Das Buch Jesaja* (1962/1967) 34–36, O. Kaiser, *Der Prophet Jesaja* (1983) 179–181. Cf. H. Wildberger, *Jesaja 13–27* (1978) 1008–1012, who argues that the eschatological perspective is not original.

[41] Cf. R.P. Carroll, *When Prophecy Failed* (1979) 148.

[42] K. Nielsen's elementary definition of the term "intertext" is sufficient for how the word is used in the present study: "The intertext is defined as another text which, by entering into dialogue with the text before us, contributes to its understanding."

vineyard[43]—as it is often called—in Isa 5:1–7 can be interpreted on
at least three levels.[44] Due to the mixed character of the text, the
history of research of Isa 5:1–7 shows a variety of interpretations of
the text.[45] What starts as a song about the vineyard (v. 1) ends by
not referring to a literal vineyard, but to the people of YHWH (v. 7).
In this verse it is revealed that the vineyard is being used as a
metaphor for the people of YHWH.[46] The identifying of YHWH's
people as the vineyard and YHWH as the vinedresser is of special
interest for the present interpretation of Isa 18:5. There are some

---

K. Nielsen, "Intertextuality and Hebrew Bible", *International Organization for the Study
of the Old Testament: Congress Volume 1998* (2000) 23. In this article, Nielsen shows
the practical application of the concept of intertextuality. Her main text is 1 Kgs
21 about Naboth's vineyard, and she uses Isa 5:1–7, selected texts from Canticum,
Hos 1–2, and Acts 6–7 as intertexts in order to illuminate the understanding of
1 Kgs 21.

[43] The meaning of a motif arises from the interplay between the message and
the active audience. This interplay is accentuated in C.H. Dodd's definition of parable: "At its simplest the parable is a metaphor or simile drawn from nature or common life, *arresting the hearer* by its vividness or strangeness, and leaving the mind in
sufficient doubt about its precise application to tease it into active thought." C.H.
Dodd, *The Parables of the Kingdom* (1935/1961) 16. (Italics mine).

[44] (i) The owner of the vineyard—the friend—the vineyard, (ii) the bridegroom—
the best man—the bride, (iii) YHWH—the prophet—Israel. For a thorough analysis
of this text, see A.J. Bjørndalen, *Untersuchungen zur allegorischen Rede der Propheten Amos
und Jesaja* (1986) 247–343.

[45] The following listing shows that the text has been understood in a variety of
ways: (1) an uncle's song, (2) a satirical polemic against Palestinian fertility cults,
(3) the prophet's song concerning his own vineyard, (4) the prophet's song expressing sympathy for his friend, God, (5) a drinking song, (6) a bride's love song, (7)
a groom's love song, (8) a song of the friend of the bridegroom, (9) a lawsuit or
accusation, (10) a fable, (11) an allegory, (12) a parable. In my view, the text is
best understood as a parable, cf. some selected studies: W. Schottroff, "Das
Weinberglied Jesajas (Jes 5:1–7). Ein Beitrag zur Geschichte der Parabel", *ZAW* 82
(1970) 68–91, and J.T. Willis, "The Genre of Isaiah 5:1–7", *JBL* 96 (1977) 337–362.
Willis' analysis of the text as a parable is taken further by G.A. Yee, "A Form-
Critical Study of Isaiah 5:1–7 as a Song and a Juridical Parable", *CBQ* 43 (1981)
30–40. Yee claims that Isaiah sang a juridical parable at a wedding feast as a foil
to ensnare the lighthearted listeners into self-judgement. Her article is commented
on by G.T Sheppard, "More on Isaiah 5:1–7 as a Juridical Parable", *CBQ* 44 (1982)
45–47 who—although in agreement in the major lines of her analysis—points at
some difficulties in Yee's proposals. Yee's interpretation is relevant for how Isa 18
with its vineyard imagery is interpreted by this reader, see 5.4.

[46] Cf. G. von Rad, *Theologie des Alten Testaments. Band II* (1962) 191: "Viel breiter
und noch kühner in seiner bildhaften Verkleidung lädt in dieser Hinsicht das
Weinberglied aus. Hier erscheint Jahwe als der unentwegte Liebhaber, der seinen
'Weinberg'—'Weinberg' ist das Deckwort für 'Geliebte'—mit größter Hingabe umsorgt
(Jes. 5 1–7)."

obvious differences between Isa 5:1–7 and Isa 18:5: (i) Isa 5:1–7 is more detailed about the vine and vineyard than what is the case for 18:5. (ii) The two texts are found in different literary contexts. (iii) There is no juridical language in 18:5 as it is in 5:1–7. (iv) Isa 18:5 does not have an explanation to what the parable means as is present in Isa 5. However, the similarities between Isa 5:1–7 and 18:5 are as follows: (i) In both texts, YHWH is the labourer. (ii) Likewise, the vines are said to bear fruit both in Isa 5:1–7 and Isa 18:5. (iii) Though in different ways, both texts describe the fruit to be bad (in 18:5 this is not said explicitly, but one can assume this from the way the pruning is done). (iv) Both texts foretell that the vineyard will be made into a wasteland (5:6; 18:5–6). If the metaphorical speech of Isa 5:1–7 was conventional for pre-exilic and exilic Israel/Judah, the audience of Isa 18 would probably be struck by the metaphorical speech of 18:5.

So far in this chapter, we have seen how the motifs "vine" and "vineyard" are applied throughout the Old Testament. It is now time for looking at the motifs that are explicitly referred to in Isa 18:5.

5.3.3. *Sour grapes*

The first motif explicitly mentioned in 18:5 to be discussed here is בֹּסֶר, "sour grapes" or "unripe grapes".[47] Besides the word בֹּסֶר, other terms for grapes applied in the Old Testament are: עֵנָב, "grape", (Num 13:23), and אֶשְׁכּוֹל, "grape-cluster" (Num 13:23). In its literal meaning, בֹּסֶר refers to a fully formed, but immature and sour grape that grows on the twigs of a vine, cf. the use of the term in Jer 31:29 and Ezek 18:2.

How is the term בֹּסֶר applied throughout the Old Testament? Besides Isa 18:5, the noun בֹּסֶר is found only a few other places in the Old Testament (in Jer 31:29, 30; Ezek 18:2, and in Job 15:33).[48] According to the small number of Old Testament references, the following brief presentation will include text references to various other terms used about grapes of a vine.

On the one side, Old Testament texts apply the motif "grapes" in order to describe abundance and pleasure (Judg 9:27; Amos 9:13).

---

[47] Cf. Koehler-Baumgartner, *HALAT* (1967) 135: "unreife Früchte", and D.J.A. Clines, *DCH* 2 (1995) 234: "unripe grapes".
[48] Cf. G. Lisowsky, *Konkordanz* (1981) 269.

Grapes can also be referred to as pleasant to the eyes (see Cant 7:12 [7:13]). In ancient Israel, grapes were grown in vineyards for wine production.[49] Grapes elicit a picture of a successful agriculture, cf. the cluster of grapes brought back by the spies as evidence of the promised land's fertility (Num 13:23). Ps 107:37–38 and Isa 65:8 associate wine and vineyards with blessing. Grapes and Israel are connected in Hos 9:10: "When I found Israel, it was like finding grapes in the desert [. . .]." The act of treading grapes in a wine-press can be used either in divine blessing (Amos 9:13) or judge-ment (Isa 63:3; Lam 1:15; Joel 3:13 [4:13]). This leads to the negative way in which בסר is applied in the Old Testament. On the other side, namely, sour grapes are used in order to illustrate sin and its unpleasant effects (cf. Jer 31:29–30 and Ezek 18:2). In Isa 5:1–7, Israel is seen as a vineyard expected to produce good fruit. Instead, however, it yields wild grapes. After the vinedresser has provided what is needed, the grapes are responsible for their own growth (Isa 5:2, 4). The failure of grape crops is linked to the people's disobe-dience to YHWH's law: "The failure of a grape crop to reach matu-rity signals disaster in the land. Accordingly, oracles of judgement in the Old Testament sometimes include the prediction that dis-obedient people will be deprived of the pleasure and sustenance of grapes (Deut 28:39; Is 18:5; Mic 6:15)."[50]

The information about בסר is scarce in Isa 18:5. What is said is this simply that at harvest time, when the bud has been completed and the sour grapes are ripen, and the blossom has happened, then he will cut off the quivering tendrils with pruning knives, and he will turn aside and strike away the twigs. Literally, the tendrils and twigs of the vine will be cut off.[51] Non-literally, בסר in Isa 18:5 is linked to a negative understanding of unripe grapes in that they are cut off the vine before they reach the stage of maturity. The act that is described thoroughly by three verbs (in v. 5bα and 5bβ) clearly implies something negative. The conventional reading of this verse is to understand the cutting off of grapes, tendrils and twigs as metaphorical speech about a nation that is judged. The function of the motif will be advocated in 5.4.

---

[49] Cf. "Grapes", L. Ryken & J.C. Wilhoit & al. (eds.), *DicBI* (1998) 348.

[50] Cf. *ibid.* 348.

[51] It is not explicitly stated in v. 5bβ whether or not the twigs have בסר on them. Most likely, however, the twigs carry sour grapes, as the term בסר is mentioned in v. 5aβ.

5.3.4. *Tendrils and twigs*

As mentioned under 5.1., two words to designate parts of the vine appear in 18:5: הזלזלים and הנטישות. As already said, הזלזלים is a *hapax legomenon* that is given the rendering "quivering tendrils". Most likely, הזלזלים is derived from the verb זלל III, "to be light, worthless" (qal), "shake, quake" (niphal).[52] The other term occurring in v. 5, הנטישות, "twigs", derives from the verb נטש, "spread out".[53] הנטישות is therefore rendered "twigs" of a vine understood as spread out. At a literal level, tendrils and twigs of vines are linked to the main stock that nurtures and anchors it. Besides their literal meaning, the two terms in v. 5 have a clear non-literal (metaphorical) meaning. Before this meaning is suggested, a brief survey of the Old Testament usage of twigs will take place.[54]

Positively, the twigs and branches of trees and vines stand for abundance, strength and prosperity (cf. Gen 49:22; Ezek 19:10; 31:3, 6). Also in contexts of restoration the branches play a central role (Isa 4:2; 11:1; Jer 23:5; 33:15; Zech 3:8, 6:12). Negatively, branches are applied in contexts of judgement (Job 15:32; 18:16; Dan 4:14; Isa 9:14; 17:6; Jer 5:10–13; 11:16; Ezek 15; 17:5–6; Hos 10:1; Mal 3:19 [ET: 4:1]).

In what way is הזלזלים and הנטישות applied in Isa 18:5? Literally, the tendrils of the vine referred to in v. 5 are cut off, and the twigs are turned aside and stroke away. Non-literally, this treatment of the tendrils and twigs has a distinct metaphorical meaning. In Isa 18:5, the term הנטישות, "twigs", seems to play on the meanings of נטש: "forsake", "cast off", "cast away", "reject", "leave", "spread out". This negative association to twigs, and also the play on the meanings of the verb נטש accord with what is present in some texts in Jeremiah. In Jer 5:10–13 the people of YHWH are compared to

---

[52] Cf. the earlier mentioned suggestion from D.J.A. Clines, *DCH* 3 (1996) 114–115. In Koehler-Baumgartner, *HALAT* (1967) 261, this meaning is found under זלל II: "beben, wanken".

[53] The various meanings of the verb נטש derive from a fundamental notion of separation, cf. J.[R.] Lundbom, "נטש", *ThWAT* 5 (1986) 436.

[54] As the term הזלזלים, "tendrils" is applied only in Isa 18:5 in the Old Testament, the following short section will concentrate on treating the term הנטישות, "twigs", and related terms, for instance ענף, "branch" (cf. Ezek 19:10). As "twigs" and "branches" seem to more or less comprise the same set of associations in the Old Testament, they will not be distinguished here.

alien vine twigs (נטישותיה) and no longer belonging to YHWH (cf.
Jer 2:21), therefore they must be destroyed. However, it must be
added that Jer 5:10 does communicate that there is hope for the
vineyards: "Go through her vineyards and ravage them, but do not
destroy them completely". Further, in Jer 15:6, the verb נטש is applied
in a context where YHWH's people forsakes YHWH: "You have
rejected me," declares YHWH. And in Jer 23:33, the verb נטש is
applied in a context of doom over YHWH's people. When the people asks: "What is the burden of YHWH?" Jeremiah replies: "You
are the burden, and I will cast you off" (ונטשתי).[55] For the suggestion to how the cutting down of twigs function in Isa 18:5, see 5.4.

5.3.5. *Harvest*

Although the term קציר, "harvest" is used in both v. 4 and 5, one
gets the impression that v. 4 refers to harvest in general, whereas
v. 5 refers to the specific grape harvest, בציר, "vintage". Despite this
apparent variation from v. 4 to v. 5 in what "harvest" might refer
to, the analysis of the motif "harvest" in Isa 18 is pursued only
here.[56]

In the Old Testament, there are approximately fifty references to
reaping and harvest (cf. the references where the terms קציר, "harvest" and בציר, "vintage" occur).[57] From the Old Testament texts,
it is evident that harvest is a time for rejoicing (Judg 9:27), and
merry-making (Isa 16:9–10). The harvesters (Jer 6:9 sing.; 49:9;
Obad 5) cut off the clusters of ripe grape (Num 13:23; Cant 7:8)
with a knife, probably the same as used for pruning. If the harvest
for one or the other reason fails, the living conditions are insecure,
and harvest is a period of sadness and uncertainty for the future (cf.
Jer 12:13). In addition to the annual importance, harvest is the image
of abundance (Gen 26:12; Ezek 36:30) and reward for labour (Prov
20:4). Harvest of various crops is prominent to such an extent in
the Old Testament world that specific harvests seem to be used as

---

[55] From these texts it is clear that Israel abandons YHWH out of negligence,
whereas YHWH abandons Israel only with good reason, cf. J.[R.] Lundbom, "נטש",
ThWAT 5 (1986) 441.

[56] For general information about harvesting in ancient Israel, cf. O. Borowski,
Agriculture in Iron Age Israel (1987) 57–69. For grape harvest in particular, see C.E.
Walsh, *The Friut of the Vine* (2000) 167–207.

[57] Cf. J. Hausmann, "קצר I", *ThWAT* 7 (1993) 107.

dating devices (Gen 30:14, Ruth 1:22; 2 Sam 21:19, Isa 24:13). The three main festivals were originally harvest festivals. In harvests referred to, the ethical implications are seen in several texts. Both Leviticus and Deuteronomy contain commands that farmers should leave parts of the crops for the poor and the sojourner (cf. Lev 19:9–10; 23:22; Deut 24:19). Harvest is thus an indication of the people's obedience to the covenant with YHWH. The same relationship between harvest and covenant obligations is found in the prophetic judgements towards Israel/Judah. The failed harvest is a sign of YHWH's judgement against the people's failure, cf. Mic 7:1 (and also Isa 17:11; 18:5; 32:10, Jer 8:20 and 12:13).

Usually in the Old Testament, grape harvesting is referred to as בציר ("vintage", cf. Lev 26:5; Isa 24:13; 32:10; Mic 7:1). In Isa 18:5, however, the term קציר, "harvest" is applied, a term most often applied about cereal harvesting (cf. Gen 30:14; Judg 15:1; Ruth 1:22; 1 Sam 6:13; Isa 17:5; 23:3). It is difficult to say whether or not the two occurrences of קציר (vv. 4 and 5) refer to the same situation. There are two options: (i) both v. 4 and v. 5 refer to the time of cereal harvesting, or (ii) v. 4 refer to the time of cereal harvesting whereas v. 5 refers to the time of grape harvesting.[58] The second option is the most complicated to defend as one here has to treat קציר in v. 5 as "vintage", being aware that the word קציר simply means "harvest". Most likely, then, v. 4 and 5 both refer to the "harvest time", i.e. the time when the grain is harvested. According to H. Wildberger, at this time of the year (during the month of May), the vinedresser goes through the vineyard to prune for the second time.[59] It is at this time the not matured grapes as referred to in v. 5 are cut off. What this metaphorical speech most likely means will be advocated in 5.4.

5.3.6. *Pruning knives*

Another motif of Isa 18:5 is מזמרות, "pruning knives", here occurring in the feminine plural absolute.[60] The literal meaning of מזמרה is a knife similar to a sickle. However, compared with the sickle, the

---

[58] For the second option, see J. Blenkinsopp, *Isaiah 1–39* (2000) 311.
[59] Cf. H. Wildberger, *Jesaja 13–27* (1978) 692.
[60] For the rendering "pruning knives", cf. Koehler-Baumgartner, *HALAT* (1974) 536, and D.J.A. Clines, *DCH* 5 (2001) 210.

cutting edge is thicker and the curved knife is shorter on the pruning knife.[61] Non-literally, pruning knives are applied either in contexts of blessing or doom.

On the one hand, the pruning knife is "[. . .], a tool which is regarded in the Old Testament as a symbol of peace [. . .]".[62] Pruning is regarded part of good farming practises, a tool in the task of cultivation (Isa 5:6). In order to train the vine for maximum yield, the vinedresser prunes (זמר) excessive twigs or branches (Num 13:23), and pruning is therefore performed before the vines become dormant.[63] Pruning was forbidden during the Sabbatical Year (Lev 25:3–4), and grapes harvested from an unpruned vine were forbidden for consumption (Lev 25:5, 11). The same rule was applied during the Jubilee.[64] Besides Isa 18:5, the noun מזמרה is found in three texts in Isaiah, Micah, and Joel in the meaning "pruning knives".[65] Two of these texts express the same idea:

> Isa 2:4: He will judge between the nations and will settle disputes for many peoples. They will beat their swords into plowshares and their spears into pruning knives. Nation will not take up sword against nation, nor will they train for war anymore. (Cf. also Mic 4:3).

From the texts referred to so far, it is evident that pruning is associated with life, prosperity and peace. On the other hand, the act of pruning—and also the refusal to prune—is associated with the negative, cf. Isa 5:6 where it is said that YHWH will not prune the vineyard that has yielded bad fruit. In this context, the refusal to prune is an act of judgement. Further, in Joel 4:10 [ET: 3:10] the positive idea seen in Isa 4:2 and Mic 4:3 is articulated in an opposite way: "Beat your plowshares into swords and your pruning knives into spears. Let the weak say, 'I am a mighty man!'"

How is the term מזמרה best understood in Isa 18:5? At a literal level, v. 5 describes how the tendrils and twigs of a vine are cut off, turned aside and stroke away. From this, one can ask whether the

---

[61] Cf. O. Borowski, *Agriculture in Iron Age Israel* (1987) 109, with references. See also "Pruning", L. Ryken & J.C. Wilhoit & al. (eds.), *DicBI* (1998) 683: "These were small, sickle-shaped knives forged at spearpoint and attached to a short handle".

[62] O. Borowski, *idem* 109.

[63] In the Gezer Tablet, the term זמר is applied about grape harvesting rather than the term בציר—which is the more common term for grape harvest in the Old Testament. Cf. O. Borowski, *Agriculture in Iron Age Israel* (1987) 109.

[64] See *ibid.* 110.

[65] Cf. G. Lisowsky, *Konkordanz* (1981) 775.

pruning knives (in v. 5) are used in order to destruct instead of cultivating, as tendrils not need to be pruned as they serve the function of letting the vine climb. However, the pruning of the twigs can
be perceived as an act of cultivating, as pruning is necessary to the
fruit bearing twigs if the vinedresser wishes much fruit on the vine.
What this implies will be advocated in 5.4.

Summing up the features in the text's motifs
From the observations above, it has first been showed that the Old
Testament motifs "vine" and "vineyard" are important for the understanding of Isa 18:5 as three motifs in this verse belong to the sphere
of vintage. In short, the religious usage of the vineyard motif imply
either (i) salvation and blessing, or (ii) judgement and devastation.
Second, we have seen that "sour grapes" in v. 5 are mentioned as
belonging to a vine that grows in a vineyard. Third, it has been
observed that the two words "tendrils" and "twigs" in v. 5 are referred
to in a way that evokes negative associations (cf. the various meanings of נטש). Further, the three verbs that are applied to describe
the pruning of the vine makes the cutting down of tendrils and twigs
be perceived more destructive than what is expected by a normal
pruning. Fourth, the harvest motif is used in (v. 4 and) v. 5 in order
to refer to the time of pruning. Fifth, the motif "pruning knives" is
applied in a way that evokes negative associations as the knives seem
to be used in order to destruct more than to cultivate (cf. the cutting down of tendrils that help the plant to climb). From this is it
clear that Isa 18:5 plays on a common well of associations by mentioning how the tendrils and the twigs of a vine will be cut down
and hewn away. The meaning of this metaphorical speech will be
advocated in 5.4.

5.4. RHETORICAL ANALYSIS

From what have been observed about the textual design and motifs
of v. 5, the theme of this verse is *the destruction of (parts of) the vineyard.* Verse 5 portrays an unnamed character, "he", who cuts off the
tendrils, and turns aside and strikes away twigs of the vine. In order
to describe the actions that happen in this specific vineyard, the text
makes use of three verbs: כרת, סור, and חזז. At the end of the following section, it will be considered how these three verbs function
in this verse in order to underline the theme of v. 5.

This theme occurs frequently in the prophetic literature (e.g. Isa 16:8; 18:5; Jer 5:10, 17; 12:10; Hos 2:12; Amos 4:9). When a vineyard is destroyed, it is often described as being transformed into wasteland, wilderness or uncultured vegetation (cf. Isa 5:6; Hos 2:12). Isa 5:1–7 ends with the vinedresser's destruction of the vineyard (vv. 3–7). This contrasts the positive images of a vineyard that produces fruit in right time (cf. Isa 5:2). In Jer 6:9, the vineyard imagery functions as a warning to Jerusalem before she is to be judged. The vine that is being plucked clean foretells how the city will be totally destructed. Micah varies the motif of the destruction of the vineyard, giving a picture of Samaria that is destructed so thoroughly that vineyards could be planted in the empty spaces that remain (cf. Mic 1:6). In Zephaniah, one of the judgement speeches says that vineyards will be planted and perhaps even produce fruit. However, even after all the labour, the people of YHWH—because of their sin— will not enjoy the fruit (Zeph 1:13). In Deuteronomy, the vineyard motif is used not only with an emphasis on judgement, but also with an accentuation on the organic connection between the sins of YHWH's people and those of the city of Sodom (Deut 32:32). Another facet of the destruction of the vineyard theme is seen in Isa 16:10. Usually, the harvest season is associated with happiness and joy, but in this text, the opposite is described as people cry when judgement arouses (see also Amos 5:17). The causes for ruin vary according to the overall scope of the texts. Two main answers can be found: (i) the addressee is reproached (Isa 3:14; Jer 12:10–12), or (ii) YHWH punishes his people (Isa 5:5–7; 17:6; Jer 8:13), or sometimes foreign peoples (Isa 16:6–14; 24:13). In some of the texts, there is an extended theological motivation for the destruction. In Isa 3:14–15 and Jer 2:10–12 leaders are criticised for not having followed YHWH's law and ethical standards. In Isa 5:1–7 and Jer 8:13 the vineyards— metaphorically understood—are accused for religious and ethical transgression (a similar situation is a possibility in Isa 27:2–6). All these texts illustrate the use of the vineyard motif in contexts of judgement.[66] In most of the texts referred to above, Israel/Judah

---

[66] Destruction of a nation can elsewhere in the Old Testament be characterised as threshing a field, i.e. destroying each individual straw or plant (cf. Isa 21:10; Amos 1:3; Mic 4:12). For further references, see T. Stordalen, *Echoes of Eden* (2000) 87–88.

(and not a foreign nation) is compared with the vine or vineyard/is
the vineyard, and subsequently, the people of YHWH is to be judged
(except Isa 16:10 where Moab is judged). Deut 28 touches upon the
vineyard motif in two places: vv. 30 and 39. According to Deut
28:30, those who break the law of YHWH will "[...] plant a vineyard, but [...] will not even begin to enjoy its fruit." V. 39 repeats
the same thought: "You will plant vineyards and cultivate them but
you will not drink the wine or gather the grapes, because worms
will eat them." As YHWH's anger and judgement is represented
by the destroyed vineyard, the opposite—YHWH's blessing and
restoration—is represented through the image of the fertile vineyard.

This brief Old Testament survey of the well-known theme *the
destruction of the vineyard* have several implications for how this theme
is understood in Isa 18:5. First, as already suggested, it is likely that
the character "he" in v. 5 refers to YHWH.[67] Second, most scholars hold that the metaphorical language in 18:5 in one or the other
way is linked to political alliances.

5.4.1. *Rhetorical features in the text's design*

*Syntactic observations: Repetition of the particle כִּי, and reappearance of
number and status*
It has been observed that the particle conjunction כִּי opens both v. 4
and v. 5. What function does the use of the conjunction כִּי have in
these two verses? First, the use of the particle conjunction in both
verses serves to bind verses 4 and 5 together.[68] As v. 4 describes
what YHWH *has* said, and as v. 5 says what YHWH *will* do in the
future, this use of כִּי ties together two descriptions of YHWH's actions.
Second, the use of the same particle conjunction כִּי in two verses
serves to relate the distant YHWH (in v. 4) with what happens on
the earth (in v. 5). In v. 4, YHWH mediates himself through "me",

---

[67] Cf. J. Hausmann, "קָצִיר I", *ThWAT* 7 (1993) 109: "Der allein konkrete Gebrauch
ist in Jes 18:4f verlassen, denn die Rede von der Ernte [...] dient nun zur
Verdeutlichung der Absicht JHWHs, sich zum Geschehen auf der Erde wartend in
Distanz zu verhalten, wenn es zum Getümmelt kommt, um dann unvermutet einzu-
greifen." Other texts referring to YHWH as destroying vine and vineyards are Isa
5:5–6; Ps 80:13–16.
[68] C.H.J. van der Merwe, "Old Hebrew Particles and the Interpretation of Old
Testament Texts", *JSOT* 60 (1993) 27–44.

whereas in v. 5 YHWH is depicted as being on the earth working in the vineyard. Third, the two כי's of vv. 4 and 5 introduces portrayals of YHWH with anthropological features (first having *spoken* "to me", and then being at *work* in an earthly vineyard).

In v. 5 we have also observed that the nouns that are present in v. 5aα–5aβ and 5bα–5bβ, respectively, appear in the same number and status. This reappearance of number and status (and also to a certain extent gender) functions cohesively as it ties the two first and two last lines of v. 5 together. The shift in gender serves to create an amount of variation.

Semantic observations: Contrasting verbs and play with words
Semantically speaking, the way the verbs are applied in v. 5 is striking. In the two first lines of v. 5 (5aα and 5aβ), the verbs that are applied are all related to the growth of the vine. This stands in sharp contrast to the verbs in the two last lines of v. 5 (5bα and 5bβ). In the latter part of v. 5, the three verbs are applied in order to describe the tearing down of the tendrils and twigs and function to express how parts of the vine and vineyard is destructed. All in all, the three first verbs of v. 5 (found in 5aα and 5aβ) function to create a feeling of optimism and hope for the vineyard that is almost ready to be harvested, whereas the last three verbs (found in v. 5bα and 5bβ) serve to proclaim the opposite, namely an utterly devastating situation for the nearly mature grapes. The function of this negative turn in v. 5 is closely related to how the motifs of v. 5 are applied, and this will be further suggested under 5.4.2.

There have been observed two instances of play with words in v. 5. The first is found in the noun הנטישׁות, "twigs", that deliberately plays on the meanings of the verb נטשׁ: "forsake", "cast off", "cast away", "reject", "leave", "spread out". By deliberately playing on the various meanings that can be derived from נטשׁ underlines the importance of the destruction of parts of the vine that is described in v. 5bα and 5bβ. Another word play goes beyond v. 5 as it has to do with הזלזלים in this verse and צלצל in v. 1. צלל I means "tingle" or "quiver".[69] The resemblance between these two words

---

[69] For the same observation, see J.H. Hayes & S.A. Irvine, *Isaiah* (1987) 256: "As so frequently, Isaiah engages in wordplay. Ethiopia is described as the land of *ṣilṣal* wings (= sail boats) and the unwanted growth on the grape vines, which will be

produces on the one hand a relationship between vv. 1 and 5. On the other hand, however, this use of two words that do not mean the same, but still point towards the same set of associations (something that moves in terms of buzzing or quivering) creates contrast between v. 1 and 5. In v. 1 it is said that the "land of צלצל buzzing of wings" has inhabitants that are strong and feared. The picture created in v. 5 is that of הזלזלים, quivering tendrils of a vine that will be cut off. By applying two words that can both be related to something that vibrates, the text creates a contrast between the strong Cushites and the weak Judeans (understood as the tendrils of a vine). In verse 1, צלצל evokes positive associations, whereas in v. 5, הזלזלים creates a negative atmosphere.

Poetic technique: Direct speech and unnamed character
From the observations about the text's design, it has been proposed that the direct speech ends by v. 4, and that "me" takes over from v. 5 on. What is clear, however, is that "me" still makes use of the authority from YHWH as he refers to what YHWH is going to effectuate. In verse 5, "me" says what YHWH will do by describing YHWH in action in the vineyard. "Me" presents now with his own words what he has received from YHWH in an audition (v. 4), and YHWH is referred to in 3rd person masculine singular. This functions to let the audience together with "me" witness what might happen—before it actually happens. This shift of perspective from direct speech from the distant YHWH to seeing—with one's inner eye—YHWH at work on earth functions to make the destruction of parts of the vineyard seem vivid and dramatic.[70]

---

pruned away, is the *zalzallim.*" This play with words between vv. 1 and 5 is also observed by R.E. Clements, who states that "[t]he word for shoots (Heb. *zalzallîm*) introduces an intentional homophony upon the word for "whirring insects/ships" (Heb. *ṣilṣal*) in v. 1", cf. R.E. Clements, *Isaiah 1–39* (1980/1994) 165.

[70] As the second opponent, Professor Karl William Weyde reminded me of at the disputation, it should be noted that historical critical studies in general, and form critical studies in particular, would not refer to the relationship between vv. 4 and 5 as merely a "shift of perspective", as is done in the present research. What is here described in strict literary terms as a "shift of perspective" between vv. 4 and 5, will by form critics belong to the discussion about the relationship between "Gottesrede" and "profetischen Rede". See for instance H.W. Wolff's reflections on how difficult it can be to make sharp a distinction between divine and prophetic accounts, H.W. Wolff, *Dodekapropheton 1. Hosea* (1961) 70–86.

The unnamed character of v. 5 is—as already argued for—YHWH.
However, how does it function when the distant YHWH (v. 4) suddenly performs damaging actions in the vineyard? The character—
although unnamed—is focused at by the three harsh verbs that all
are in 3rd person masculine singular (כרת, סור and חזז). By focusing
on "he", this serves to put what "he" is doing in the centre of attention. Further, by applying three verbs that all have YHWH as the
subject serves to focus on the activity performed in the vineyard.

Summing up the rhetorical features in the text's design
From what has been said about the design of v. 5, the following
rhetorical features have been observed: First, *cohesion* is made both
by the device of alliteration, and by the reappearance of number
and state between the nouns in v. 5. Further, the use of the particle
conjunction כי functions to tie v. 4 and 5 together. Second, *activity*
is attended to as the three verbs that are applied in the latter half
of v. 5 all describe what YHWH is doing in the vineyard. Third,
concentration on what YHWH is doing in the vineyard is created as
the three verbs in vv. 5bα and 5bβ all have YHWH as the subject.

5.4.2. *Rhetorical features in the text's motifs*

Sour grapes: Metaphorical speech about Judah
How does the reference to the motif "sour grapes" function in v. 5?
As the growth of the grapes from bud, blossom, and to sour grapes
is referred to in v. 5aα and 5aβ, it is not out of the context to pre-
suppose that the twigs that are turned aside and stroke away (v. 5bβ)
accommodate sour grapes. In v. 5, the phase of maturity is not
described as the twigs are turned aside and stroke away before this
stage in the process of growth is attained. However, by applying the
motif "sour grapes" in v. 5, this functions as a part in the process
of building the metaphor of the verse: "YHWH's people is the vineyard" (cf. Isa 5:1–7).

Tendrils and twigs: Metaphorical speech about Judah
In Isa 18:5 the two terms "tendrils" הזלזלים and הנטישות, "twigs",
both play with words. הזלזלים plays on the meaning of צלצל in
v. 1, and contrasts the (mighty) Cushites (v. 1) and the weak, quivering tendrils (Judah) in v. 5. The other term, הנטישות, "twigs", play
on the various meanings of the verb נטש—from which the noun is

derived: "forsake", "cast off", "cast away", "reject", "leave", "spread out". All the negative associations to נטשׁ function to give הנטישׁות in v. 5 a negative back cloth. Together, the two terms tendrils and twigs in v. 5 accommodate negative associations that build up under the metaphorical speech of judgement in v. 5. As vine and vineyard conventionally are applied as metaphors for YHWH's people in the Old Testament, it is clear that the cutting off of tendrils and twigs in v. 5 can be understood as a metaphorical speech of a judgement that will hit Judah if she follows her path of seeking human help instead of divine help.

Harvest: Metaphorical speech about a judgement towards Judah
How do the two occurrences of this same word, קציר, in v. 4 and 5 function? As the same word occurs twice, קציר functions as a word that binds verses 4 and 5 together. The agricultural speech of v. 5 is also found in the immediate literary context of Isa 18, namely in Isa 17:10b–11. 18:5aα–aβ describes the growth of the grapes from blossom to sour berries almost ready to be harvested. After a description of the natural growth of grapes, one expects that the grapes would be harvested in due time, but the opposite is described in the latter part of v. 5. Surprisingly, the grapes will be cut off, turned aside, and stroke away by "him" just before they were ready to be harvested. YHWH's far too early "harvest" in the vineyard is not expected, and creates an atmosphere of fear and danger. As pointed at under 5.4.1., the application of three verbs for growth and the three verbs for tearing down in v. 5 creates a striking effect. In order to understand YHWH's work in the vineyard, it is necessary to look at how the three verbs found in 5bα and 5bβ function.

The verb כרת occurs 288 times in the Old Testament, and of these are 134 times in the qal, 73 times in the niphal, 78 in the hiphil, twice in the pual, and once in the hophal.[71] Eighteen of the 288 occurrences of the verb כרת are found in the book of Isaiah. The basic meaning of כרת is "cut".[72] Nevertheless, in the Old Testament, the verb is applied in the following three ways. First, in the meaning of "cutting off/chopping off": branches (Num 13:23), grapes (Num 13:24), limb (Judg 9:49), the corner of a garment

[71] The nouns occur seven times, see G.F. Hasel, "כרת", *ThWAT* 4 (1984) 358.
[72] Cf. W. Gesenius, *Handwörterbuch* (1962) 364.

(2 Sam 10:4, par. 1 Chr 19:4), or parts of the body (head: 1 Sam
17:51; 31:9; 2 Sam 20:22; hands: 1 Sam 5:4, the foreskin: Exod
4:25, testicles: Lev 22:24, or the male member of the community:
Deut 23:2 [ET: 23:1]). Second, in the meaning of "breaking down":
asherahs (Exod 34:13; Judg 6:25, 26, 30; 2 Kgs 18:4; 23:14), or
abominable images (1 Kgs 15:13, par. 2 Chr 15:16). Third, in the
meaning of "felling trees": cedars and cypresses (Isa 37:24; 44:14;
Ezek 31:12), or forests (Jer 46:23). In addition, כרת is also applied
in formula-like phrases such as the covenant texts.[73] Central to the
understanding of כרת in Isa 18:5 is the use of this verb in the
prophetic literature in general, and the book of Isaiah in particular.
Common for the occurrences of the verb כרת in the prophetic books,
is the negative use of the verb often applied in contexts where it is
said that YHWH comes to judge the world (YHWH cuts off everything that lives, Zeph 1:3). In Isa 9:13 [ET: 9:14] it is said that
Israel's "head and tail" will be cut off, and in another text it is said
that the judgement will strike all Judah (Jer 44:7, 8, 11). YHWH's
eschatological extermination will destroy horses (Mic 5:9 [ET: 5:10]),
cities (Mic 5:10 [ET: 5:11]), sorceries (Mic 5:11 [ET: 5:12]; cf. Jer
27:9), bows (Zech 9:10), idols and asherahs (Mic 5:12 [ET: 5:13]).
In other words, from the prophetic texts it seems that YHWH will
destroy all that gives the people a false sense of security.[74]

From this brief survey of how the verb כרת is commonly applied
in the Old Testament, it is evident that Isa 18:5 falls into the line
of a negative use of the verb. In Isa 18:5, the verb כרת, "cut off",
appears in perfect consecutive 3rd person masculine singular. Literally,
the verb is here applied about quivering tendrils that will be cut off
by "him". Non-literally, however, this cutting off of vine tendrils
describes that Judah will experience a judgement, effectuated by
YHWH.[75]

The second verb that is used in 18:5 about the destruction of
parts of the vine is derived from סור. In the Old Testament, the
verb סור is attested 158 times in qal, whereas it occurs 133 times in

---

[73] For a survey of how the root כרת—with its derivatives—is applied in the Old
Testament, cf. G.F. Hasel, "כרת", *ThWAT* 4 (1984) 355–367.

[74] For the similar view, cf. *ibid.* 360: "[. . .] alles was falsche Sicherheit gibt, aus-
gerottet/zerbrochen werden [. . .]".

[75] Cf. the motif analysis above that has showed the likelihood of tendrils and
twigs of a vine functioning as metaphors for Judah in this text.

the hiphil. Although it is distributed quite evenly, the verb סור has a concentration in Samuel, Kings, Chronicles, and Isaiah.[76] סור in qal means "turn aside, depart from, deviate (from the path)".[77] In the hiphil (הסיר), it means to turn aside in the sense of eliminating or removing.[78] In the hiphil, סור is usually applied with the preposition מן, and both material (2 Sam 7:15; 2 Chr 14:2 [ET: 14:3]; Ezek 26:16) and immaterial (1 Sam 17:26; Job 27:2; 34:5; Isa 27:9) things can be removed. The antonym to סור is "go straight ahead", and the common expression, "turn aside neither to the right nor to the left", occurs no less than 10 times in the Old Testament. According to L.A. Snijders, there are six ways in which סור is figuratively applied, cf. the following listing: (i) Deviation from the right path, (ii) deviation from the commandments, (iii) deviation from YHWH, (iv) deviation from the way of the Father, (v) YHWH turns aside from individuals, and (vi) turning aside from evil.[79]

From this brief Old Testament survey of the usage of סור, it is clear that in Isa 18:5, סור is (literally) applied about the removing of twigs of a vine. That YHWH is the agent in the vineyard is here suggested on the basis of the forms of the verbs as all three verbs appear in 3rd person masculine singular. (סור appears in hiphil perfect, 3rd person masculine singular). "He" in v. 5 is therefore regarded the same character as the one who reveals himself as YHWH in v. 4. Non-literally, however, this verb (together with כרת and חזז) appears in a metaphorical speech about how YHWH is going to judge Judah by means of turning aside from her plans.

The third verb that is applied in Isa 18:5 about the destruction of parts of the vine is חזז. This verb appears only once in the Old Testament, and has most likely the meaning "strike away".[80] Similar to סור, the verb חזז also appears in hiphil perfect, 3rd person masculine singular in 18:5. Like the two other negatively applied verbs in v. 5, also חזז literally describes a destruction of parts of a vine. Non-literally, however, it refers to YHWH's judgement over Judah.

---

[76] See L.A. Snijders, "סור", *ThWAT* 5 (1986) 803.
[77] See A. Hurvitz, "Wisdom Vocabulary in the Hebrew Psalter: A Contribution to the Study of 'Wisdom Psalms'", *VT* 38 (1988) 47.
[78] See L.A. Snijders, "סור", *ThWAT* 5 (1986) 804–805.
[79] Cf. *ibid.* 806–809.
[80] Cf. G. Lisowsky, *Konkordanz* (1981) 1516. See also Koehler-Baumgartner, *HALAT* (1990) 1580.

In sum, from these three verbs applied in v. 5 about the (literal) destruction of parts of the vine, it is clear that they all—non-literally speaking—describe an act of doom. By applying three verbs in order to describe the cutting down of the tendrils and twigs, the judging activity is underscored. It could seem as if any expectations about a hope for the future were left out. Nevertheless, in this case too, there is "hope for the tree", cf. Job 14:7 (in Isa 18:5—the vine). The well-known idea from other Old Testament texts that a purified remnant will not experience the tearing down (cf. Isa 6:13; 11:1, 11; Ezek 6:8; 14:22; Amos 9:11; Mic 2:12; Zech 13:8–9; 14:2), is present also in Isa 18:5, as only parts of the vine are cut down (tendrils and twigs), not the entire vine with its roots.

Pruning knives: The pruning of the vine is destructive
The first half of v. 5b (5bα) mentions pruning knives as the instrument by which YHWH will cut off the quivering tendrils and the twigs. What function do the knives have in v. 5? If Isa 18:5 describes a conventional procedure in the cultivation of vineyards, could not the pruning in v. 5 then be positively understood? It is my contention that what is here described is not the normal procedure of the cultivating of a vine. First, the cutting down of tendrils together with the twigs underlines this negative message. Second, by focusing on what is removed from the vine (vv. 5–6), and not on what is still there, a negative message is brought forward. This negative understanding of the pruning in v. 5 is also emphasised by most scholars (see 5.4.2.). From the motif analysis above (cf. 5.3.4.), we have seen that pruning knives are used either in contexts of blessing or judgement. As the hewing away of the twigs is described by two verbs with negative meaning in this context, the act of pruning seems not to be done in order to cultivate, but rather in order to destruct. Non-literally, therefore, it is my contention that מזמרה is applied in a negative way in v. 5, more closely to express an act of judgement: "Sometimes God's pruning is a picture of judgement against evil."[81] Although texts like Deut 32:41 and Ezek 21:8–17 do not apply the term "pruning knives", they are related to Isa 18:5 in that they depict God as lifting a tool (his sword) in judgement. In Jer 12:10–13, the imagery of harvest and destruction is tied together.

---

[81] Cf. "Farming", L. Ryken & J.C. Wilhoit & al. (eds.), *DicBI* (1998) 271.

In v. 12, YHWH is portrayed as the destroyer, swinging the sword (חרב) so that no one is secure. Although the term sword is not applied in Isa 18:5, the image of YHWH using a tool that cuts down is present in both texts. In addition, both texts connect vineyard and YHWH's destructive acts, cf. also Jer 12:10–11.

Summing up the rhetorical features in the text's motifs
From what has been said above, it is clear that the motifs of v. 5 all function to draw attention to what is said here. The motifs "sour grapes", "tendrils" and "twigs" on the one hand, function to build the metaphorical speech about Judah as YHWH's vine(yard). On the other hand, the motifs "harvest" and "pruning knives" serve to tear down as the twigs are said to be stroke away before the grapes have reached the stage of maturity and are ready to be harvested. This metaphorical speech about parts of a vine that will be destroyed pronounces a message of doom towards Judah. This reading of Isa 18:5 is based on the fact that in the Old Testament, the metaphorical speech about the vine/vineyard conventionally is applied about the relationship between YHWH and his people.

5.4.3. *How do textual design and motifs together create the strophe's rhetoric?*

Through observations about the textual design and the motifs of v. 5, the rhetoric of entrapment that started in v. 1 has been resolved by v. 5. This is seen the following ways.

Cohesion: V. 5 contains a consistent message
Observations of both textual design and motifs of Isa 18:5 have revealed cohesive features. First, from the text's design it has been showed that v. 5 contains a reappearance of number and status. This functions to bind the various lines of v. 5 together. Second, the choice of motifs (sour grapes, tendrils, twigs, and pruning knives) shows another cohesive feature of v. 5 as these motifs are all taken from the agricultural sphere of viticulture. All the motifs of v. 5 underline the message of destruction of parts of the vine.

Concentration: YHWH destroys parts of the vineyard
From both textual design and motifs, we have seen that the focus in v. 5 is on YHWH and what he does in the vineyard. As all motifs are taken from the agricultural sphere of viticulture, this functions to concentrate on what will happen in the vineyard. From the

observations about the poetic technique of v. 5 we have seen that
the only character mentioned in this verse is "he", and that this 3rd
person masculine singular most likely refers to YHWH (see 5.2.4).
By this technique of changing from "I" (v. 4) to "he" (v. 5), the text
now puts "he" on the scene, and this creates a focus on what YHWH
does. From being described as watching the earth from a distance
(v. 4), YHWH now works on the ground destroying parts of a vineyard (v. 5), and this gives a strong concentration on YHWH. In the
Old Testament, metaphors and similes are widely used for describing the divine.[82] Although texts in the Old Testament speaks about
YHWH as a man, cf. Isa 42:13 (אִישׁ, "man") and 54:5 (בַּעַל, "husband"), the Old Testament affirms time and again that YHWH is
not a man, cf. Num 23:19 (לֹא אִישׁ אֵל); Hos 11:9 (כִּי אֵל אָנֹכִי וְלֹא־אִישׁ),
cf. also Prov 5:21; Job 12:14, and 32:13. Especially the later books
of the Old Testament express the incomparability of YHWH (cf. Isa
40:25; 46:9). However, the book of Isaiah contains an extensive number of descriptions of YHWH in various kinds of metaphors and
similes, one of these to be found in Isa 18:5 where YHWH is referred
to as working in a vineyard. The way that YHWH is spoken about—
as a vinedresser—functions to create a realistic picture of what is
done in the vineyard. The anthropomorphism functions to express
YHWH's dominion and authority. The deity is no longer distant in
his fixed place looking down on the earth (v. 4). At a first glance
"he" seems to be described as acting like people do during the harvest season, but soon the audience understands that "he" acts somewhat unexpected when he cuts off the twigs with fruit that are soon
ready to be harvested. The calmness of YHWH referred to in v. 4
has suddenly turned into the opposite state of mind (v. 5). This shift
in behaviour functions to create a picture of YHWH as frightening
and unpredictable. What kind of deity is YHWH who is calm in
one moment and bursts out in fury the next moment? The scene
from the vineyard creates anxiousness among the audience, and this
is the intention of applying a rhetoric of entrapment. In the moment
when Judah feels secure and safe in seeking human help for her
political challenges (vv. 1–2), she is harshly doomed (v. 5). Through
a metaphorical speech about tendrils and twigs that are struck down,
Judah suddenly understands that the judgement is not going to hit
somebody else, but herself.

---

[82] For numerous examples of this, cf. M.C.A. Korpel, *A Rift in the Clouds* (1990).

Activity: YHWH's destruction of parts of the vineyard is underlined
The images used to describe the harvest scene are strong, colourful
and visual. "Me" draws a picture of what it looks like at harvest
time when the blossom is over and the bud has become a ripe grape.
From verse 3 on, the atmosphere has been tense. "All" are called
to attention (v. 3), YHWH's gazing and quietness is likened with
weather types that connotes tenseness (v. 4), and now (v. 5), the dramatic action takes place. The verbs used to describe YHWH's actions
in the vineyard are, as already pointed at, three negative and harsh
verbs: כרת "cut off", הסיר "turn aside", and התו "strike away". The
framing of the strophe by these verbs functions to create an atmosphere of fear. From this, it is clear that both textual design and
motifs reveal an atmosphere of activity in v. 5. Semantically, all lines
of v. 5 describe what *happens* in the vineyard, and the sense of activity culminates when YHWH destroys parts of the vineyard. Also
from the motifs, it is clear that the growth of the vine (described in
v. 5aα and 5aβ) on the one hand, contrasts the tearing down of
parts of the vineyard on the other hand (v. 5bα and 5bβ). The activity of building up and of striking down, function to underline the
message of the text.

Confusion resolved: Judah is judged
To the analysis of 18:1–4, it has been stated that the use of הוי in
v. 1 keeps the audience in a state of confusion as long as the text—
until now—has not revealed who will be judged. This way of confusing the audience has in this book been called a rhetoric of
entrapment. However, at this stage in the speech the confusion is
resolved. The majority of scholars agree that the metaphorical speech
about a vineyard that will be partly destroyed (v. 5) prophesies judgement over a specific nation. However, as presented in the introductory chapter of this book, there are four main solutions to *who*
the metaphorical speech of v. 5 is meant to hit.

Most scholars understand the partly destruction of the vineyard
(v. 5) as a judgement over Assyria.[83] One example is E.J. Kissane,

---

[83] Cf. J. Høgenhaven, *Gott und Volk bei Jesaja* (1988) 133: "Die meisten Ausleger
beziehen die Katastrophe auf die Assyrer." The following is a selected chronological
listing of examples of commentators who suggest Assyria to be judged in Isa 18:5–6:
R. Lowth, *Isaiah* (1795) 149–150, W. Gesenius, *Philologisch-kritischer und historischer
Commentar über den Jesaia* (1821) 586–587, A. Knobel, *Der Prophet Jesaia* (1843) 125,
F. Delitzsch, *Commentar über das Buch Jesaia* (1889) 241–242, A. Dillmann, *Der Prophet*

who suggests that the vine referred to in v. 5 is a "[. . .] comparison of Assyria to a flourishing vine whose growth is fostered by
Jahweh."[84] Further, Kissane interprets Isa 18 as YHWH's way of
comforting the Judean people.[85] Assyria's object is to destroy Israel
(Isa 10:7), and YHWH will let Assyria's plans grow until just before
they are effectuated (Isa 10:24–25; 33:10–12, Job 15:33), then YHWH
will intervene and ruthlessly stop her actions against Israel: Assyria
is "[. . .] sent out to carry His will, and His purpose—the chastise-
ment of Israel—must first be realised before He intervenes to over-
throw Assyria and deliver His people."[86] Vv. 5–6 should then,
according to Kissane, be seen as YHWH's intervention and judgement over Assyria. "Jahweh will wait until the appointed time, and
then strike down Assyria".[87] A more recent example of the same
opinion comes from J.N. Oswalt. Oswalt concludes on the grounds
of historical information that Assyria is the one to be judged in 18:5:
"The historical circumstance which comes quickly to mind is that
of Sennacherib's attack upon Judah".[88]

A smaller group of commentators—and not the majority, as B.S.
Childs claims[89]—proposes the remote nation Cush to be doomed by
YHWH.[90] Some scholars in this group define the term Cush as Egypt

---

Jesaia (1890) 169–170, C. von Orelli, *Die Propheten Jesaja und Jeremia* (1891) 73,
E. Michelsen, *Profeten Esaias* (s.a.) 69, B. Duhm, *Das Buch Jesaia* (1892) 114–116,
F. Buhl, *Jesaja* (1894) 286–288, T.K. Cheyne, *Einleitung in das Buch Jesaja* (1897)
96–97 (cf. also T.K. Cheyne, *The Book of the Prophet Isaiah* (1899) 191), E. Brandes,
Jesaja (1902) 46, F. Wilke, *Jesaja und Assur* (1905) 87–88, W. Staerk, *Das assyriche
Weltreich* (1908) 122 and 220, G. Friman, *Profeten Jesaja* (1917) 26, F. Feldmann, *Das
Buch Isaias* (1925) 217 and 220, E. König, *Das Buch Jesaja* (1926) 199–200, J. Fischer,
Das Buch Isaias (1937) 138–139, Aa. Bentzen, *Jesaja* (1944) 142, J. Ziegler, *Isaias*
(1948) 62, I.W. Slotki, *Isaiah* (1949) 86, A. Parmelee, *All the Birds of the Bible* (1959)
127, G.B. Gray, *A Critical and Exegetical Commentary on the Book of Isaiah* (1962) 315,
H. Donner, *Israel unter den Völkern* (1964) 126, B.S. Childs, *Isaiah and the Assyrian Crisis*
(1967) 45, E.J. Young, *The book of Isaiah* (1965/1978) 477–478, H. Eising, *Das Buch
Jesaja* (1970) 138, A.S. Herbert, *The Book of the Prophet Isaiah* (1973) 119, J. Jensen,
Isaiah 1–39 (1984) 165, H.M. Wolf, *Interpreting Isaiah* (1985) 122, S.H. Widyapranawa,
The Lord is Saviour (1990) 106, and J. Blenkinsopp, *Isaiah 1–39* (2000) 311.
    [84] E.J. Kissane, *The Book of Isaiah* (1960) 199. See also J.[R.] Lundbom, "נשא",
ThWAT 5 (1986) 441.
    [85] E.J. Kissane, *The Book of Isaiah* (1960) 197–200.
    [86] *Ibid*. 199.
    [87] *Ibid*. 199.
    [88] J.N. Oswalt, *The Book of Isaiah* (1986) 362.
    [89] B.S. Childs, *Isaiah* (2001) 136.
    [90] Cf. G. Fohrer, *Das Buch Jesaja* (1960/1966) 223–224, H.W. Hoffmann, *Die
Intention der Verkündigung Jesajas* (1974) 72–73, O. Kaiser, *Der Prophet Jesaja* (1983)

and Cush, whereas others do not include Egypt when they refer to the Hebrew term Cush. N.K. Gottwald is an example of a scholar who interprets the tendrils and twigs of v. 5 as referring to "[...] the Egyptian aspirations in Asia, which are to be cut short".[91] He points to the dialectic of Isaiah's message when he on the one hand opposes Ahaz' pro-Assyrian policy and on the other hand warns an anti-Assyrian power that "[...] it would soon suffer a shattering set-back."[92] L.A. Snijders is another scholar who suggests that verse 5 is directed towards Cush: "[...] de kusitische wijnranken afsnijden."[93] H. Wildberger takes the same position and regards the imagery to point at the Cushites: "Die abgerissenen Ranken der Reben sind die in der Schlacht gefallenen Äthioper [...]".[94] L. Alonso Schökel follows the same line and suggests the text to describe YHWH's "[...] action against Nubia."[95] According to S. Talmon, the entity judged in 18:5 cannot be unequivocally identified, nevertheless, he regards Isa 18 an oracle against a foreign nation by stating that the "[...] punishment will come over אֶרֶץ צִלְצַל כְּנָפָיִם (Isa 18:1) with as much certainty as the seasons follow one upon the other."[96] A recent example within this group is U. Becker, who suggests that the text, although addressing Judah, is directed to Cush: "Der Weheruf wendet sich [...] *gegen Kusch*."[97] Another recent interpreter, W. Brueggemann, suggests—with reservation—that the judgement will strike "Ethiopia": "We may assume, in context, that the campaign concerns Ethiopia,

---

78–79, R.E. Clements, *Isaiah 1–39* (1980/1994) 165 (Ethiopia and Egypt), K. Jeppesen, *Jesajas Bog fortolket* (1988) 125 (Nubien/Kush), C.R. Seitz, *Isaiah 1–39* (1993) 148, ("the spreading branches of Ethiopia"), A. Laato, *"About Zion I will not be silent"* (1998) 72, ("[...] it calls down doom on Ethiopia"), H. Hagelia, *Coram Deo* (2001) 184–185. Although Hagelia's main focus is on 18:7, he has given the analysis of Isa 18:1–7 the headline "Message against Ethiopia", and this suggests that he interprets the text to contain a doom over Cush. See also H.T. Aubin, *The Rescue of Jerusalem* (2003) 172: "[...] if the Kushites engage the enemy, their corpses will be left to the "birds of prey and to the wild animals"."

[91] N.K. Gottwald, *All the Kingdoms of the Earth* (1964) 163.

[92] *Ibid.* 163.

[93] L.A. Snijders, *Jesaja deel 1* (1969) 196.

[94] Cf. H. Wildberger, *Jesaja 13–27* (1978) 693.

[95] L. Alonso Schökel, *A Manual of Hebrew Poetics* (1988) 183–184.

[96] S. Talmon, "Prophetic Rhetoric and Agricultural Metaphora", *Storia e tradizioni di Israele* (1991) 267–279, 272.

[97] U. Becker, *Jesaja—von der Botschaft zum Buch* (1997) 276. (His italics). Becker does not explicitly state that Isa 18:5–6 should be interpreted as a judgement against Cush, but as long as his discussion of Isa 18 several times contains the expression "gegen Kusch", I consider his contribution to belong to this group.

but nothing is said of that."[98] Further, however, Brueggemann's reservation has diminished as he interprets v. 6 about the twigs that are hewn away the following way: "The Ethiopians are "fodder" to help all the creatures to live".[99] The main point of Isa 18 is according to Brueggemann that of showing YHWH's might. He concludes that "[. . .] the main body of the oracle is not interested in any particular enemy but voices the sovereign power and will of Yahweh in general terms."[100]

A third group of scholars—to which I belong—sees the judgement in Isa 18:5–6 as directed against the Judeans.[101] Although it seems to be a rather recent suggestion that Judah/Israel is referred to in Isa 18:5, this point of view had a supporter already with K. Marti.[102] Marti suggests the judgement described in vv. 5–6 to hit the "Ephraimäer" because they put their trust in "Syrien". The coalition with "Syrien" does not bring anything but disappointment, according to Marti. Although Marti's conclusion—in my view—seems to be sound, he does not argue thoroughly in favour of his stance, he simply states what he regards as the text's meaning. A recent example of a scholar belonging to this group is M.A. Sweeney. By demonstrating that the overarching structure of the unit extends from 17:1 to 18:7, he suggests that YHWH's actions in the vineyard (18:5) most probably refer to "[. . .] YHWH's punishment of Israel [. . .]."[103]

---

[98] W. Brueggemann, *Isaiah 1–39* (1998) 153.

[99] *Ibid.* 154.

[100] *Ibid.* 154.

[101] Few scholars seem to maintain this view, cf. K. Marti, *Das Buch Jesaja* (1900) 150, O. Procksch, *Jesaia I* (1930) 241, J. Høgenhaven, *Gott und Volk bei Jesaja* (1988) 132–134, M.A. Sweeney, *Isaiah 1–39* (1996) 257, and B.S. Childs, *Isaiah* (2001) 138. When it comes to O. Procksch, it is not clear who are judged, the Judeans or the Assyrians. According to O. Procksch, *Jesaia I* (1930) 241, the vine is a metaphor for "des judäischen Landes", whereas one page later, [. . .], *ibid.* 242 he states: "Mit ist der Assyrer gemeint [. . .]", and further: "[. . .] Das assyrische Heer [. . .], wird von Jahve in geheimnisvoller Weise erschlagen [. . .]". J. Høgenhaven, *Gott und Volk bei Jesaja* (1988) 134, holds that the Jerusalem court is the addressee of Isa 18:1–6: "Als eigentlicher Adressat ist das Jerusalemer Hof anzusehen [. . .]". However, it is not clear from Høgenhaven's brief analysis whether or not the addressee is seen to be judged in this text.

[102] K. Marti, *Das Buch Jesaja* (1900) 150.

[103] M.A. Sweeney, *Isaiah 1–39* (1996) 257. In an earlier work, Sweeney has another solution to who is judged in Isa 18: "[. . .] chapter 18 simply directs Ethiopia's (and the world's, cf. v. 3) attention to YHWH's responsibility for defeating Assyria [. . .]", cf. M.A. Sweeney, *Isaiah 1–4* (1988) 48.

He does however not argue *why* he sees the Judeans to be the most probable receivers of YHWH's judgement.[104] Following Sweeney, B.S. Childs is another interpreter who have recently suggested that Judah/Israel is the nation that is judged in 18:5.[105] However, as none of these scholars come forth with arguments for why the most likely to be judged is Israel/Judah, this is what is suggested in the present research.

The fourth and last group of scholars hesitates to suggest any addressee at all for YHWH's judgement as described in 18:5. This seems as the most secure and "objective" (if that is an aim) interpretation as long as the text is indefinite about who is to be judged. Still, despite their hesitance, the two scholars referred to here cannot avoid interpreting what the cutting and destroying of ripe grapes referred to in 18:5–6 might mean. In the end, they both have suggestions to this problem, either in a concrete or in a more abstract manner. W. Eichrodt suggests the vine tendrils and twigs not to be any nation in particular, he rather perceives the metaphor in a more abstract way: "Jesaja weiß sich jezt an einen Wendepunkt gestellt, da alle menschlichen Anstrengungen zur Erreichung irdischer Ziele vom Weltherrn vereitelt werden, der im Begriff steht, sein eigenes Werk zu vollenden."[106] A recent example is P.D. Miscall who makes a point of the fact that "[t]he poet does not specify the objects of the Lord's activity [. . .]". Despite this, in the very same sentence, Miscall interprets YHWH's actions this way: "[. . .] the Lord cuts and hews all in his way [. . .], including Judah and Zion."[107] It is difficult to discuss Miscall's views since he is this brief about how to understand the cutting down and throwing away of branches (v.5). On the one hand Miscall points to the fact that the text does not reveal who the judgement is meant to hit, but on the other hand he concludes—withouth any discussion—that all the branches means "all [. . .], including Judah and Zion." Common for these four

---

[104] M.A. Sweeney, *Isaiah 1–39* (1996) 257. However, like Marti and Høgenhaven, he does not give any argument for stating this, except the following sentence: "In the context of 17:1–18:7, this trimming of the shoots must be understood as YHWH's punishment of Israel (cf. 17:4–6, 10b–11; 18:2b)." M.A. Sweeney, *Isaiah 1–39* (1996) 257.

[105] B.S. Childs, *Isaiah* (2001) 138: "In the context of the chapter the imagery can only mean that of judgement against Judah, not Ethiopia."

[106] Cf. W. Eichrodt, *Der Herr der Geschichte* (1967) 62–63.

[107] Cf. P.D. Miscall, *Isaiah* (1993) 56.

suggestions to who the metaphorical speech of v. 5 is meant to hit,
is the lack of arguments put forth for each solution.[108]

As has already been hinted at, this study regards Isa 18 to be
dressed in a rhetoric of entrapment. By this I mean that the audience
of this speech was ensnared to believe that the opening הוי of 18:1
was meant for Cush.[109] However, as the speech continued, it gradually was revealed for them that the ones who were going to be
judged were themselves (v. 5). To this interpretation, one can object
that the text does not reveal who will be judged. What is clear from
the text is that YHWH will wait for some time, and then effectuate
the catastrophe. If one reads v. 5 at a literal level only, the text
gives no answer to the question about what the catastrophe implies.
However, if one understands the partly destruction of the vineyard
as metaphorical speech about a judgement over a nation, some interpretations seem more likely than others. The confusion is resolved
when the audience hears about vine tendrils that will be cut down
and twigs that will be hewn away. From what has been said about
how vine and vineyard imagery is applied throughout the Old
Testament, it is obvious that Judah would feel struck by what is said
in Isa 18:5. This has been argued for under 5.3. The prophet pronounces doom over Judah because she wants to enter into a political alliance with Cush instead of trusting YHWH. The word play
between צלצל in v. 1 and הזלזלים in v. 5 is striking by means of
rhetorical effect. As earlier said, a tendril is a threadlike organ or
appendage of a plant, which stretches out and attaches itself to some
other body so as to support the plant. When the Judeans metaphorically are spoken about in terms of a vine—with tendrils—(v. 5) this

---

[108] In determining who might be meant by the metaphorical speech in v. 5, cf.
Aa. Bentzen, *Jesaja* (1944) 142, who uses the criteria of "likely" and "not likely".

[109] Why is a message to Judah placed together with messages directed towards
other nations? I advocate in this work that the audience is entrapped to believe
that this message is not relevant for themselves, but for somebody else—as long as
the context in which Isa 18 is found is Isa 13–23. In addition, E.K. Holt's work
on the book of Jeremiah is interesting at this point as she has suggested that
Israel/Judah is addressed as a people that has become unfamiliar to YHWH, and
therefore has to accept that YHWH speaks to them in some of the same way as
foreign nations are spoken to, cf. E.K. Holt, "The meaning of an *inclusio*: A
Theological Interpretation of the Book of Jeremiah MT", *SJOT* 17 (2003) 183–205.
This view of E.K. Holt (on the book of Jeremiah) can also be applied on the relationship between Judah and YHWH as described in Isa 18.

underlines the text's ridiculing of the Judeans' diplomatic activity in
order to attach themselves to the Cushites as alliance partners.[110] Isa
18 functions thus as a speech of judgement over Judah (and perhaps others) who enter into coalitions. By applying the common Old
Testament metaphor "Israel/Judah is the vine/vineyard", the text
forces the audience to realise that the judgement will strike themselves, and not somebody else.

Summing up the rhetoric in the text's design and motifs
The theme of the verse is the destruction of parts of the vineyard.
The rhetoric of entrapment that started in v. 1 has by v. 5 reached
its clarification. This solution is seen the following ways: First, the
clarification can only be grasped if what is said in v. 5 hangs together.
Both from the textual design (reappearance of number and status)
and the motifs (all of v. 5 is taken from the sphere of viticulture),
we have seen that *cohesion* is created. Second, both textual design
and motifs of v. 5 show that the focus in this verse is on YHWH
and what he does in the vineyard. This *concentration* on YHWH and
what he does functions to put the theme of the destruction of parts
of the vineyard in the centre. Third, an atmosphere of *activity* is created in v. 5. Semantically, all lines of v. 5 describe what happens
in the vineyard, and the sense of activity culminates in that YHWH
tear down parts of the vineyard. Also from the motifs, the building
up (v. 5aα–5aβ) and the striking down (v. 5bα–5bβ) of the tendrils
and twigs function to create a strong sense of activity. Fourth, the
feeling of *confusion* that has been created from v. 1 on is finally solved
in v. 5. To the analysis of 18:1–4, it has been stated that the use
of הוי in v. 1 keeps the audience in a state of confusion about who
will be judged as this is not explicitly stated. However, the way the
rhetoric of Isa 18 works functions in such a way that it entraps the
audience to believe that somebody else is judged until the message
of v. 5 is pronounced. In v. 5, namely, the audience find *themselves*
as the ones who are judged—and not the Cushites or anybody else.
This is clearly seen from the motifs that are applied in v. 5. The
metaphorical speech about the pruning of the vine (in Isa 18:5) is
applied in accordance with a conventional Old Testament usage of

---

[110] This observation that builds up under my thesis was kindly communicated to
me at the disputation by my first opponent, Professor Kirsten Nielsen.

this motif (see 5.3.), and here the reference to a destruction of parts of the vineyard clearly functions to announce a judgement over Judah.[111] "The vine here is the people and the farmer Yahweh."[112] However, v. 5 does not say that the entire vine is cut down. In that there is something left of the vine after YHWH has cut off the tendrils and twigs, the possibility that the vine might blossom again next season is present.[113]

---

[111] For others suggestions to who the vine in v. 5 refers to, see above.

[112] F.E. Deist, *The Material Culture of the Bible* (2000/2002) 150, who briefly interprets Isa 18:5.

[113] I agree with the first opponent at the disputation, Professor Kirsten Nielsen, who suggested along these lines to read Isa 18 in connection with Isa 5 and Isa 27. Isa 18—as being found between these two texts—shows that there *is* hope for the vineyard.

CHAPTER SIX

STROPHE V: 18:6

This chapter includes a section called *contextual analysis* (see 6.5.), where the relations between the first (vv. 1–2) and second (vv. 3–6) stanza of Isa 18 will be attended to.

6.1. Text and translation

6.1.1. *Textual criticism*

	Text	Verse
	יעזבו יחדו לעיט הרים	v. 6aα
	ולבהמת הארץ	v. 6aβ
	וקץ עליו העיט	v. 6bα
	וכל־בהמת הארץ עליו תחרף	v. 6bβ

Verse	Text
v. 6aα	They will together be left[1] to the bird of prey of the mountains,
v. 6aβ	and to the beast of the earth.[2]
v. 6bα	The bird of prey shall summer upon him,
v. 6bβ	and every beast of the earth[3] shall winter upon him.

---

[1] 1Q Isaᵃ has ועזבו, qal perfect consecutive 3rd person plural, while MT has niphal imperfect 3rd person masculine plural, יעזבו, "they will be left". I see no reason to reject MT's יעזבו, cf. *versiones*.

[2] 1Q Isaᵃ has the expression ולבהמות ארץ in plural to בהמה, and without the definite article to ארץ, while MT has singular with definite article ולבהמת הארץ. The expression of 1Q Isaᵃ is more evident than that of the MT, however, MT is *lectio difficilior*, and I see no reason to reject MT. In Hebrew, singular often designates the whole group and can therefore be rendered plural, cf. *BDB* (1979) 96–97 (3), which has rendered the singular expression in 18:6 "wild beasts", plural.

[3] Cf. the immediate preceding note. כל followed by singular can, according to *BDB* (1979) 481 (1b), be understood collectively, whether with or without the article. For the same understanding, see D.J.A. Clines, *DCH* 2 (1995) 99: "every beast".

6.1.2. *Translation*

In Isa 18:6, summer and winter are referred to by two verbs: וקץ
and חרף. As קיץ and חרף most commonly are applied as nouns in
the Old Testament ("summer" and "winter"), some comments are
needed at this point.

The translation of וקץ עליו העיט

The expression וקץ עליו העיט (v. 6bα) has been given the rendering
"the bird of prey shall *summer* upon him". The way קיץ is applied
in this verse is uncommon as it is here applied as a verb, "to (spend
the) summer".

Most commonly, קיץ in the Old Testament is referred to as a
noun. The noun has two meanings, (i) the season "summer", or (ii)
a fruit, more closely a "summer-fruit" (cf. 2 Sam 16:1; Pss 32:4;
74:17; Isa 28:4; Jer 8:20; Amos 8:1–2; Mic 7:1). Altogether, this
noun occurs twenty times in the Old Testament.[4] Applied as a noun,
קיץ is used in the Old Testament either positively in contexts of
blessings, or negatively in contexts of judgement.[5]

In Isa 18:6, קיץ appears in qal waw consecutive perfect 3rd person masculine singular.[6] This denominative verb occurs only in Isa
18:6.[7] The season summer, קיץ, is in 18:6 applied as a verb, and
therefore given the rendering "shall summer upon him".

The translation of וכל־בהמת הארץ עליו תחרף

Further, the expression וכל־בהמת הארץ עליו תחרף (in v. 6bβ) is rendered: "and every beast of the earth shall *winter* upon him." In the

---

[4] Cf. J. Hausmann, "קיץ", *ThWAT* 7 (1993) 26–29: Gen 8:22; 2 Sam 16:1, 2;
Pss 32:4; 74:17; Prov 6:8; 10:5; 26:1; 30:25; Jes 16:9; 28:4; Jer 8:20; 40:10, 12;
48:32; Amos 3:15; 8:1, 2; Mic 7:1; Zech 14:8.
[5] Cf. *ibid.* 28: "In Jer 40, 10.12 wird *qajiṣ* zum Symbol neuer Hoffnung, da neue,
reichliche Ernte angesagt ist". Further, in a negative context, קיץ can be applied
the following way, *ibid.*, 28: "Nach Jes 28,4 werden die Früchte gleich von der
Pflanze weggegessen—analog, und d.h. vernichtend, wird es auch Samaria ergehen.
Mi 7,1ff. klagen über die Verdorbenheit des Völkes: Von den Frommen ist genauso
wenig zu sehen wie von den Früchten auf dem Felde nach vollzogener Ernte." For
another negative usage of קיץ, see also Amos 8:1–2. In this text, קיץ seems to play
on the word קץ, "end".
[6] For this rendering, see G. Lisowsky, *Konkordanz* (1981) 1258: "übersommern",
and Koehler-Baumgartner, *HALAT* (1983) 1026: "übersommern". Surprisingly,
J. Hausmann, "קיץ", *ThWAT* 7 (1993) 26–29, does not even mention Isa 18:6 and
the way the denominative verb קיץ is applied here.
[7] Cf. G. Lisowsky, *Konkordanz* (1981) 1258.

Old Testament there are two roots חרף. From one derives the meaning "fall", "winter", and from the other derives "disgrace", "shame".[8] Important for Isa 18:6 is חרף I, "fall", "winter".

The Old Testament occurrences of חרף I include the verb in Lev 19:20 (niphal) and Isa 18:6 (qal), and the noun in Gen 8:22; Job 29:4; Ps 74:17; Prov 20:4; Jer 36:22; Amos 3:15; Zech 14:8. Literally, חרף is characterised by cold (Gen 8:22), and refers to the winter period from December through January (cf. Prov 20:4).[9]

In Isa 18:6, the qal of חרף is a denominative verb from (the noun) חרף, meaning "spend the winter".[10] In v. 6 חרף occurs in qal imperfect 3rd person feminine singular. As was the case for קיץ, this denominative verb, too, occurs only in Isa 18:6.[11] The season winter is in 18:6 applied as a verb, חרף, and therefore given the rendering "shall winter upon him".[12] As already touched upon, חרף and קיץ is a word-pair in the Old Testament, and together they designate the whole year.[13]

6.2. TEXTUAL DESIGN

6.2.1. *Syntactic observations*

Gender-matched parallelism

Verse 6aα–aβ conveys a gender-matched parallelism which is patterned m.-m.//f.-f. by the following nouns: עיט bird of prey (masculine), הרים mountains (masculine) in v. 6aα, and בהמת beast (feminine),

---

[8] For an attempt to sketch the philological history of the roots, see E. Kutsch, "חרף I", *ThWAT* 3 (1982) 217–219.

[9] Cf. E. Kutsch, "חרף I", *ThWAT* 3 (1982) 219.

[10] For this rendering, see Koehler-Baumgartner, *HALAT* (1967) 341: "überwintern", E. Kutsch, "חרף I", *ThWAT* 3 (1982) 220: "überwintern", W. Gesenius, *Handwörterbuch* (1995) 399, "überwintern", and D.J.A. Clines, *DCH* 3 (1996) 320: "spend winter". In Clines' dictionary, this meaning of חרף is referred to as חרף II.

[11] Cf. G. Lisowsky, *Konkordanz* (1981) 532.

[12] Cf. W. Brueggemann, *Isaiah 1–39* (1998) 154: "It is of interest that 'summer' and 'winter' are here employed as verbs, so that the seasons themselves, as agents of the creator, work the will of the creator."

[13] Cf. E. Kutsch, "חרף I", *ThWAT* 3 (1982) 219. J. Hausmann, "קיץ", *ThWAT* 7 (1993) 27, though speaking about the texts Gen 8:22; Ps 74:17; Amos 3:15, and Zech 14:8, regards חרף and קיץ as two seasons of the year: "Die Kombination macht deutlich, daß *qajiṣ* in diesen Texten als Bezeichnung einer Jahreszeit zu verstehen ist [. . .]".

אֶרֶץ earth (feminine) in v. 6aβ.[14] Evidently, we do not have to do with the same noun occurring in two different genders, however, the pairing of masculine with feminine nouns can be classified as what A. Berlin calls an "[. . .] incidental morphologic parallelism [. . .]".[15] According to Berlin, such a contrast in gender does not qualify for a "real contrast", which in her opinion would be "[. . .] when the same noun (or same root) appears in two different genders."[16]

Further, there is a gender-matched parallelism between the two last lines of v. 6. In v. 6bα, the masculine noun עַיִט appears, and this noun corresponds to the feminine noun בהמת in v. 6bβ. The gender-matched parallelism between the two last lines of v. 6 would have been just as complete here as we have seen in v. 6aα–6aβ, were it not for the occurrence of gapping in this part of the verse.

As mentioned above, there are also relations between the first and the third lines of v. 6, and between the second and the fourth. From v. 6aα to v. 6bα, the noun עַיִט, "bird of prey" (masculine, singular) is repeated. The reappearance of the noun הרים, "mountains" (masculine plural) is however omitted in v. 6bα (see below, under gapping). From v. 6aβ to 6bβ the nouns בהמת, "beast" (feminine, singular) and הָאָרֶץ, "earth" (feminine, singular) are repeated. The function of this reappearance of class, gender and number between the lines 6aα and 6bα on the one hand, and between 6aβ and 6bβ on the other hand, will be suggested in 6.4.1.

Gapping

From v. 6bα to v. 6bβ there is an instance of gapping as the noun הרים, "mountains", does not occur in v. 6bα where one would expect its presence (cf. the gender-matched parallelism between "bird of prey"//"mountains" and "beasts"//"earth" from v. 6aα to 6aβ). In v. 6bα "bird of prey" is mentioned, and not "mountains", whereas in v. 6bβ both "beast" and "earth" are mentioned. Still, this somewhat incomplete gender-matched parallelism might have a function. This will be advocated in 6.4.1.

---

[14] As mentioned above, the word עַיִט, "bird of prey", and בהמת, "beast", are both grammatically singular. However, as singular in this case seems to have a collective meaning designating the whole group, these words can also be rendered plural. Cf. *BDB* (1979) 96–97 (3), which has rendered the singular expression of MT "wild beasts", plural.

[15] A. Berlin, *The Dynamics of Biblical Parallelism* (1985) 41.

[16] *Ibid.* 41.

6.2.2. *Semantic observations*

Internal parallelism

Semantically, verse 6 is designed in a way where the first and the third lines are parallel, and the second and the fourth lines are parallel. In v. 6aα it is said: "they will all be left to the bird of prey of the mountains", whereas v. 6bα says that "the bird of prey shall summer upon him". Although the two lines express the same idea of annihilation of the tendrils and twigs (v. 5), it is clear that v. 6bα develops the thought that is first introduced in v. 6aα. In v. 6bα the leaving of "they" (the tendrils and twigs) is extended into "summer upon him". Further, the same kind of development or extension is seen from v. 6aβ to 6bβ. First, it is said that they will all be left "to the beast of the earth" (v. 6aβ). This is in v. 6bβ further developed into: "and every beast of the earth shall winter upon him".[17] How these semantically extensions function will be explained in 6.4.1.

Word-pairs

In this verse, three word pairs occur: bird//beast, mountain//earth, and summer//winter. Most commonly, word-pairs appear with one member of the pair occurring in the first line, and the other member of the pair in the parallel line.[18] What is striking, though, is that what is here referred to as word-pairs occur from the first to the second line of v. 6, and from the third to the fourth line of v. 6— and not between the semantically parallel lines of v. 6 (which are the first and third, and the second and third lines, respectively, see *internal parallelism* above). However, from the two and two semantically parallel lines (v. 6aα–6bα and 6aβ–6bβ), there is an identical repetition of words as the words bird of prey and beast are paralleled by themselves.[19] What will be presented here, however, are

---

[17] As referred to earlier in this work, this development between two parallel lines corresponds with Kugel's idea about a kind of progression between the two lines A and B: "And this, it is suggested, corresponds to the expectations the ancient Hebrew listener, or reader, brought to every text: his ear was attuned to hearing "A is so, and *what's more*, B is so." Cf. J.L. Kugel, *The Idea of Biblical Poetry. Parallelism and Its History* (1981/1998) 8 and 23, (Kugel's italics).

[18] Cf. W.G.E. Watson, *Classical Hebrew Poetry* (1984/1986) 128.

[19] This phenomenon is described by A. Berlin, *The Dynamics of Biblical Parallelism* (1985) 71: "[. . .] a word may be paralleled by itself or by a parallel word—i.e., a word that is in some sense equivalent".

word-pairs that occur between the two first and the two last lines
of v. 6—i.e. lines that are *not* semantically parallel (bird//beast,
mountain//earth, and summer//winter). It is evident that the word
pair bird//beast occurs twice in v. 6. The constituents of the word-
pair bird//beast belong to the same grammatical class (nouns), but
have different gender (bird: masculine, beast: feminine). The word-
pair bird//beast (in these texts the corresponding term for bird, עוֹף
is applied) occurs several times throughout the Old Testament, cf.
Jer 7:33; 15:3; 16:4; Dan 2:38 (see 6.3. in this study).[20]

The second word-pair of v. 6 is made up by the nouns mountain//
earth. Also in this word-pair, the gender is not the same in the two
nouns. Other instances in the Old Testament where mountain and
earth are applied in one or the other kind of parallel lines are: Pss
18:8; 72:16; 97:5; 104:13; Isa 40:12; Ezek 7:7; Jonah 2:7; Nah 1:5.
As already mentioned above, there is a relation between the two
word-pairs bird//beast and mountain//earth. It is obvious from this
that the word-pairs bird//beast and mountain//earth are related.
As the word "bird" evokes associations to flying, and as "mountains"
are tall and can be reached by birds, the words bird and mountain
are related. Likewise, "beast" and "earth" correspond as beasts belong
on the ground.

The third word-pair of v. 6, summer//winter, consist of two verbs,
וְקָץ in v. 6bα, and תֶּחֱרַף in v. 6bβ. Although the verbs are both in
3rd person singular, וְקָץ is in masculine, while תֶּחֱרַף is in feminine.
They also appear in two different forms: perfect and imperfect, respectively. This word-pair of the denominative verbs קַיִץ and חֹרֶף does
not appear in the Old Testament apart from in Isa 18:6. However,
there are examples where the nouns קַיִץ and חֹרֶף appear in combination (cf. Gen 8:22; Ps 74:17; Amos 3:15; Zech 14:8).

6.2.3. *Poetic technique*

No human characters
In this verse, no human are referred to. However, the absence of
human characters is filled with repetitive references to bird of the
mountains and beast of the earth. How this reference to bird and
animal function in v. 6 will be suggested in 6.4.

---

[20] This word-pair and its variants are set out in tabular form by H. Weippert,
Die Prosareden des Jeremiabuches (1973) 185.

Summing up the features in the text's design

The features commented upon above can be summarised as follows: First, there are several syntactic patterns observable in v. 6. This verse is designed in a way where the two first and the two last lines show gender-matched parallelisms, and there is an instance of gapping in v. 6. Between the first and the third, and the second and the fourth lines of v. 6, there is the syntactic instance of reappearance of class, gender, and number. The syntactic observations above also showed that this verse is framed by the grammatical mood imperfect. Second, it has been observed that there is a semantic resemblance between the first and the third lines of v. 6, and between the second and the fourth lines. Three word-pairs present in v. 6 have also been presented. Third, of poetic techniques applied in this verse is the most striking the omission of human characters in v. 6. Unlike all other verses of Isa 18, v. 6 does not mention any human beings, but instead repeats that birds and animals are over the tendrils and twigs.

6.3. MOTIFS

6.3.1. *Bird*

The word עיט, "bird of prey", is mentioned twice in Isa 18:6.[21] In the Old Testament, the combination of the terms for "bird" and "beast" occur together approximately 35 times.[22] However, in order to grasp the usage of these two motifs in Isa 18:6 they will be treated separately.

In the Old Testament, when birds are mentioned they seem to stand for either the positive or the negative.[23] On the one hand,

---

[21] In v. 6aα עיט, "bird", appears in masculine singular construct, and in v. 6bα it appears in singular absolute.

[22] Cf. M.L. Barré, "Of Lions and Birds: A Note on Isaiah 31:4–5", *Among the Prophets* (1993) 56. As the term for "bird of prey" applied in 18:6 (עיט) is not frequently used about birds in the Old Testament, this motif analysis will survey a variety of Old Testament terms that designate birds. In combination with the term "beast", עוף is the more common term used in the Old Testament (see Deut 28:26 for an example). However, it is the same phenomenon of devouring that is described in Isa 18:6, cf. J.A. Rimbach, "Animal Imagery in the Old Testament" (1972) 49.

[23] For surveys of how terms for "birds" are applied throughout the Old Testament, cf. J.A. Rimbach, "Animal Imagery in the Old Testament" (1972) 46–75, E. Firmage, "Zoology", *ABD* 6 (1992) 1109–1167, and "Birds", L. Ryken & J.C. Wilhoit et al.

birds are referred to in positive contexts: (i) birds are used as navi-
gators (Gen 8:7–12), (ii) birds are beautiful (1 Kgs 10:22; 2 Chr 9:21;
Ps 68:14 [ET: 68:13]; Cant 5:11), (iii) birds represent food, easily
kept alive and fresh (Deut 22:6; 1 Kgs 5:3 [ET: 4:23]; Neh 5:18),
(iv) birds are acceptable as sacrifice to God (Gen 15:9; Lev 12:6, 8;
15:14; Num 6:10), (v) the purity of birds stand for safety (Lev 14:52–53;
cf. Lev 16:22; Ps 55:7 [ET: 55:6]), (vi) the soul can be associated
with a bird (Ps 11:1), (vii) birds are referred to as pious as they trust
the divine providence (Ps 147:9; Job 38:41, birds can also be used
to provision food for humans, see 1 Kgs 17:4), and (viii) birds' nests
are paralleled with human houses (Ps 84:4 [ET: 84:3]).[24] On the
other hand, birds are referred to in negative contexts: (i) birds are
victims for quarry (1 Sam 26:20; Job 18:8–9; Prov 1:17; 7:23; Ps
91:3; 124:7; see also Dan 2:38), (ii) birds that frequent ruins and eat
corpses are linked with the realm of the dead (for the former, see
Isa 13:20–23; 34:11–14; Zeph 2:13–15; for the latter, see 1 Sam
17:44; 2 Sam 21:10; Deut 28:26; Job 39:30; Jer 7:33), (iii) birds of
prey are agents of divine punishment (Jer 12:9; Hos 8:1; Prov 30:17),
and (iv) birds are applied as moral examples for humans (Prov 26:2;
Jer 8:7; 17:11; Lam 4:3; Hos 7:11).

How is the motif "birds" applied in Isa 18:6? Isa 18:6 alludes to
Old Testament texts where birds (together with animals) are depicted
as consuming what is left on the battle-ground. In Deut 28:26 the
birds of the air and the beasts of the earth will eat נבלתך, "your
dead boby", i.e. the people of YHWH if they do not live according to YHWH's will (cf. Deut 28:15). Jer 7:33 alludes to the same
tradition of imagining the unfaithful people to be eaten of birds of
heaven (and animals of the earth).[25] The same is the case for Jer
15:3. This text is harsh towards the people of Jerusalem, and the
judgement is extended to include two more ways of exterminating
the people:

(eds.), *DicBI* (1998) 92–95. For an attempt to identify birds mentioned in the Old
Testament, see G.R. Driver, "Birds in the Old Testament", *PEQ* (1954–1955)
129–140.

[24] Related to what is said about birds in the Old Testament, is how wings are
used. Positively, wings stand for divine protection (Pss 17:8; 36:8 [ET: 36:7]; 57:1;
61:5 [ET: 61:4]; 63:8 [ET: 63:7]; 91:4; Ruth 2:12), strength (Isa 40:31), swiftness
(2 Sam 1:23), and even healing (Mal 3:20 [ET: 4:2]).

[25] "The specific horror of this threat/curse [of being devoured by beasts and
birds] is lack of burial [. . .]", cf. J.A. Rimbach, "Animal Imagery in the Old
Testament" (1972) 47.

I will appoint over them four kinds of destroyers, says YHWH: the sword to slay, the dogs to tear, and the birds of the air and the beasts of the earth to devour and destroy.

In Jer 19:7 the plans of Jerusalem and Judah will be made void, and YHWH "will cause their people to fall by the sword before their enemies, and by the hand of those who seek their life. I will give their dead bodies for food to the birds of the air and to the beasts of the earth." None of these texts leave doubts about who is to be devoured by birds and animals. It is said straight out that it is the people of YHWH who are meant to be consumed in such a way. In Isa 18:6, however, the metaphorical speech is not straight-forwardly explained. In 1 Sam 17:44, 46–47, it is evident that both David and Goliath threaten each other by saying that the birds of the air and the animals of the earth will consume the looser's dead body. In this text, the metaphorical speech is applied not just on the people of YHWH, but also on a representative for the Philistines.

From what has been said about Isa 18:5 (see chapter 5 in this book), the metaphorical speech of vv. 5 and 6 is apparently applied about the people of YHWH. M.L. Barré is right when he lists Isa 18:6 among the negative references of "birds" (and "beasts"): "[. . .] in the majority of cases (19x) it [the image of birds and beasts] appears in a negative context, concerned with human bodies (usu-ally of God's people) given to the birds and beasts as prey."[26] Within this group, five texts show similarities with Isa 18:6 in that the prepo-sition על is used in order to describe how the beasts and birds will act upon the prey (2 Sam 21:10, Isa 31:4–5, Jer 12:9, Ezek 31:13; 32:4).[27]

6.3.2. Beast

Another central motif of v. 6 is the feminine noun בהמה, "beast", "cattle", "domestic animal", "game".[28] בהמה occurs 188 times in the Old Testament, and of these, the book of Isaiah contains five.[29] בהמה

[26] See M.L. Barré, "Of Lions and Birds: A Note on Isaiah 31:4–5", *Among the Prophets* (1993) 56.

[27] See *ibid.* 56.

[28] For suggestions to the translation of בהמה, cf. J.G. Botterweck, "בהמה", *ThWAT* 1 (1973) 524, W. Gesenius, *Handwörterbuch* (1987) 127–128, and D.J.A. Clines, *DCH* 2 (1995) 98–100.

[29] For details, cf. the statistics in J.G. Botterweck, "בהמה", *ThWAT* 1 (1973) 524.

can mean horse or mule (Neh 2:12, 14), it can refer to cattle (Isa 46:1, "beast of burden"). In Isa 30:6 בהמה refers to asses and camels which carry riches and treasures.

In the Old Testament, בהמה is applied in stereotyped phrases, such as: (i) "the beasts of the earth"/"the beasts that are on the earth" (Lev 11:2; Deut 28:26; Isa 18:6; Jer 7:33; 15:3; 16:4; 19:7; 34:20; Job 35:11), (ii) "the beasts of the field" (Exod 9:19; 1 Sam 17:44; Joel 1:20; 2:22; Ps 8:8 [ET: 8:7]), (iii) "the beasts of the forest" (Mic 5:7 [ET: 5:8]), (iv) "man-beast"/"from man (even) to beast" (20 times in Exodus and Numbers, 24 times in the Prophets, and 3 times in the Psalms).

Positively, (i) the firstborn of בהמה is holy and belongs to YHWH (Exod 13:2, 12, 15; Lev 27:9–10; 27:26–27; Num 3:13; 8:17; 18:15; Ps 50:10), (ii) בהמה followed the Israelite army in the campaign against Mesha of Moab (2 Kgs 3:17), further, (iii) there is an intimate association of animals with the family (Gen 34:23; 36:6; Exod 20:10;[30] Deut 5:14; Lev 25:2–7; see also Prov 12:10), and (iv) many Old Testament texts express a connection between human beings and beasts in calamity and fate (see for instance Exod 8:13; 9:9–10, 19, 22, 25; Num 31:26, 47; Jer 21:6; 50:3; 51:62; Ezek 14:13, 17, 19, 21; Jonah 3:7; Zeph 1:3; Hag 1:11; Zech 8:10; Ps 135:8; see also the more positive texts such as Jer 31:27; Ezek 36:11; Zech 2:8 [ET: 2:4]). (v) There is a law for restitution for an animal which is hurt, driven away or dead (Exod 22:9–10 [ET: 22:10–11]; see also Lev 24:18, 21), (vi) בהמה is included in lists of possessions of wealth (Ezra 1:4, 6; 2 Chr 32:28–29), (vii) בהמה enjoy special divine care (Deut 11:15; Ps 107:38; 147:9), (viii) בהמה together with all creation are to praise God (Ps 148:10), and (ix) animals can teach human beings about God (Job 12:7–8), and humans are not given any advantage over the בהמה (Eccl 3:18–19, 21). Negatively, (i) בהמה is described as a "dumb" animal (Ps 49:13, 21 [ET: 49:12, 20]; 73:22; Job 18:3; 35:11) (ii) בהמה is used in connection with "serpent" to denote a wild and dangerous animal (Deut 32:24), (iii) animals are agents for the divine, sent to punish YHWH's people (Lev 26:22; Jer 7:33; 15:3; 16:4; 19:7; 34:20), (iv) references to animals in curse formulas announce that YHWH's people will be oppressed by enemies and suffer a humiliating death (Deut 28:26), (v) in cultic

---

[30] Note that בהמה is placed after maidservant and before sojourner.

regulations, having sexual relations with a בהמה is strongly prohib-
ited (Exod 22:18 [ET: 22:19]; Lev 20:15–16; Deut 27:21), and also
hybridisation is forbidden (Lev 19:19; see also Deut 22:9–11), (vi)
the law against making images forbids the manufacture of any like-
ness of human beings, bests, and heavenly bodies (Deut 4:16–18;
Ezek 8:7–12).[31]

In Isa 18:6, בהמה appears twice (in v. 6aβ and 6bβ), both times
in singular construct.[32] In v. 6, it belongs to the stereotyped phrases
mentioned above ("the beasts of the earth"/"the beasts that are on
the earth"). What seems clear from what has already been said about
Isa 18 is that בהמה in verse 6 is applied in a negative context. In
terms of imagery, Hos 2:14 is close to Isa 18:5–6 as the vines are
to be consumed by the beasts. From the analysis of v. 5 we have
seen that most scholars interpret the metaphorical speech taken from
the area of viticulture as referring to either Assyria or Cush.[33] Very
few scholars suggest that it is the people of YHWH who are hit by
the metaphorical speech of vv. 5–6. In my view, however, Isa 18:6
develops the metaphorical speech from v. 5 and explains how the
people of YHWH will be judged and annihilated. How this metaphorical speech of v. 6 functions in its context will be suggested in 6.4.

Summing up the features in the text's motifs
From the observations above, we have seen that Isa 18:6 makes use
of two motifs ("bird" and "beast") that are frequently used in the
Old Testament. Although these two motifs are often positively applied
in the Old Testament corpus, it has been advocated above that
"bird" and "beast" are negatively applied in Isa 18:6. This seems
clear as the bird and beast are not only depicted as devouring the
tendrils and twigs, but to "summer" and "winter" upon them. In
accordance with other Old Testament texts, it has been showed that

---

[31] For various interpretations of Ezek 8:7–12, cf. the brief survey in J.G. Botterweck,
"בהמה", *ThWAT* 1 (1973) 529.

[32] For suggestions to what the plural בהמות of 1Q Isaᵃ might refer to, cf. *ibid.*
533–536, and W. Herrmann, "Eine notwendige Erinnerung", *ZAW* 104 (1992)
262–264.

[33] For a similar interpretation of Isa 18:6, see J.G. Botterweck, "בהמה", *ThWAT*
1 (1973) 528: "Nach Jes 18, 6 werden die Assyrer "den Raubvögeln des Gebirges"
עיט הרים zum Übersommern und den Tieren der Erde zum Überwintern überlassen
[...]". For a survey of the various solutions to the interpretation of the metaphorical speech of Isa 18:5, see 5.4 in this book.

these two motifs of Isa 18:6 are applied in a context of judgement.
A more detailed suggestion of how these motifs function in the context of doom in v. 6 will be dealt with in 6.4.

6.4. RHETORICAL ANALYSIS

From the analysis of the verse's textual design and motifs, it is evident that the theme of Isa 18:6 is that of judgement of Judah. This
is clearly seen from the analysis of v. 5 as the judgement that is
already pronounced over YHWH's people as referred to in v. 5 is
extended and underscored by what is said in v. 6. To describe a
judgement of YHWH's people, Isa 18:6 makes use of the motifs
"bird" and "beast", and applies these in a negative way in this verse.
The theme of destruction is also known from other Old Testament
texts (cf. Hos 4:1–10; 5:9; 12:1–3). The Old Testament uses several
different terms (both nouns and verbs) to express the idea of judgement.[34] However, in Isa 18:5–6 no such terms are applied as it is
here the actual *act* of destruction that is described. In the Old
Testament, God is regarded as the judge of the whole world, and
it is in the last instance God who judges both the nations and
Israel/Judah.[35] From the context of Isa 18:5–6, it has been argued
that "he" most likely refers to YHWH in v. 5, and as v. 6 extends
the act of judgement described in v. 5 it is likely that YHWH is in
charge of the events referred to here, too.

6.4.1. *Rhetorical features in the text's design*

Syntactic observations: Gender-matched parallelism and gapping
Isa 18:6 shows several syntactic patterns. The gender-matched parallelism created by the nouns "bird of prey" (masculine) and "mountains" (masculine) on the one hand, and "beast" (feminine) and
"earth" (feminine) on the other hand, functions to produce elevated
language as the two genders balance each other and make a pattern.
Further, there are three other effects of this gender-matched parallelism. First, by means of contents, the gender-matched parallelism

---

[34] Cf. T.L.J. Mafico, "Judge, Judging", *ABD* 3 (1992) 1104–1106.
[35] Cf. *ibid.* 1106.

envisages two types of creatures that will be given something.[36] What function does the references to these two groups of creatures serve? A *contrast* is made between the birds and animals as living creatures on the one hand, and the tendrils and twigs as dead because they have been removed from the stock, on the other hand. Second, the four words in the gender-matched parallelism contrast each other by means of territory: עיט "bird of prey" (m), הרים "mountains" (m), בהמת "beast" (f), ארץ "earth" (f). "Bird" and "mountains" both belong to the area *above* the ground, and "beast" and "earth" both belong *on* the ground, and this makes a contrast between what is above and what is on the ground. This functions to create a *totality* of space as the tendrils and twigs are reported to be surrounded by devourers. Third, there is a reappearance of class, gender, and number in this verse. The echoing of the nouns עיט "bird of prey" on the one hand, and of בהמת "beast" and הארץ "earth" on the other hand function to make the message *cohere*. Evidently, the repetition strengthens and underlines the dramatic message about the vine tendrils and twigs that are given to these creatures. These three points show that the gender-matched parallelism in this strophe indeed has poetic significance, and that the juxtaposition of genders is not an aimless happening of no importance.

Another syntactic observation from v. 6 is that there is an instance of gapping in this verse. Where one would expect its presence, the noun "mountain" does not (re-)occur in v. 6bα. At a first glance, this instance of gapping seems only to make the parallelism incomplete. However, something more might be the idea here. As the noun "mountain" is lacking in v. 6bα, the focus is on what is actually mentioned in this line: "bird of prey" and "summer". Subsequently, the "summering" upon the tendrils and twigs from the bird's side is the central in v. 6ba, and if the bird were referred to together with "mountain" this could have been perceived as if the bird was still above the tendrils and twigs in the sky somewhere. However, by leaving out the expected noun "mountain", this gapping creates a *closeness* between "bird" on the one hand, and tendrils and twigs on the other hand, and brings the bird down to the ground.

---

[36] What will be left to these creatures? The only verb in this gender-matched parallelism, עזב, "leave", "forsake", "loose", niphal imperfect, 3rd person masculine plural, most likely refers to הזלזלים "the quivering tendrils", and הנטישות, "twigs" (in verse 5).

Semantic observations: Internal parallelism and word-play

Semantically, v. 6 is designed in a way where the first and the third lines on the one hand, and the second and the fourth lines on the other hand are parallel. However, although two and two lines are semantically parallel, it has been observed that when a line is paralleled by another line in v. 6, it is developed. This development functions to strengthen the message of judgement. As the audience presumably interpreted the tendrils and twigs of the vine as referred to in v. 5 to mean themselves, v. 6 this development functions to strengthen the message of judgement as v. 6 contains an even harsher message of devastation and annihilation than what was said in v. 5.

Further, although the two first and the two last lines are not semantically parallel, there are relations between them, and this is clearly seen from the perspective of word-pairs. It has been observed that three word-pairs occur between the two first and the two last lines of v. 6 (bird//beast, mountain//earth, and summer//winter). On the one hand, the word-pairs bird//beast, mountain//earth, and summer//winter create a feeling of contrast as they refer to contrasting elements or parts of the known world. On the other hand, however, as the words bird and beast are repeated from A to A' and from B to B' this creates equivalence between the lines of v. 6. Thus, the word-pairs add to the effect of the parallelism. Cf. A. Berlin, who states along the same lines that "[i]t is not word pairs that create parallelism. It is parallelism that activates word pairs".[37] Further, these word-pairs function to create cohesion as they bind together the lines of v. 6 that are not semantically parallel.

Poetic technique: No human characters

As no human characters are mentioned in v. 6, this functions to create a horrifying scene of death at the same time as it focuses on the creatures of heaven and earth that are on the scene, and that will devour the tendrils and twigs. The rhetorical function of reporting this vision is to make the audience believe that the judgement will be effectuated, and that it will be devastating. Further, the idea behind reporting such a harsh judgement is to make the audience distressed, and to prevent them from taking any actions towards political alliances with neither Cush nor any other nation.

---

[37] A. Berlin, *The Dynamics of Biblical Parallelism* (1985) 79.

Summing up the rhetorical features in the text's design
Through observations about the textual design of Isa 18:6, we have
seen that the rhetoric of entrapment that started in v. 1 has been
resolved by v. 5. Verse 6 extends this resolving as the judging tone
from v. 5 is further developed here in a way that makes the doom
even more harsh than what was pronounced in v. 5. The devastating judgement in v. 6 is pronounced in the following ways: First,
cohesion between words and lines are created through the various
forms of resemblance that occurs in this verse. Second, an atmosphere of devastating *activity* is created through the denominative verbs
"summer" and "winter", and through the reference to bird and beast
that will devour the tendrils and twigs that have been cut off the
vine (v. 5). Third, *concentration* on the coming judgement is created
through the focus on non-human creatures and on their devouring
of the tendrils and twigs. Fourth, the *confusion* that has held the audience awake through the whole speech is resolved by vv. 5–6. Likening
the people of YHWH with a vineyard (v. 5) is a well known and
frequently used metaphor in the Old Testament (see 5.3. in this
book), and when the tendrils and twigs of the vine are given to the
birds and beasts this is most likely understood by the audience as
having to do with their relationship with YHWH.

6.4.2. *Rhetorical features in the text's motifs*

Bird and beast: Divine agents in the judgement of Judah
There are two ways in which v. 6 has been interpreted. One group
of scholars read both v. 5 and v. 6 metaphorically, and see v. 6 as
continuing to describe what destiny the tendrils and twigs of the vine
are given.[38] The other group of scholars claim (explicitly or implicitly)

---

[38] F. Delitzsch, *Commentar über das Buch Jesaia* (1889) 241–242 (Assyria), F. Buhl,
Jesaja (1894) 286–288 (Assyria), J. Ziegler, *Isaias* (1948) 62 (Assyria), G. Fohrer, *Das
Buch Jesaja Kapitel 1–23* (1960/1966) 223–224 (Egypt), O. Kaiser, *Der Prophet Jesaja*
(1983) 78–79 (Ethiopia), S.H. Widyapranawa, *The Lord is Saviour* (1990) 106 (Assyria),
C.R. Seitz, *Isaiah 1–39* (1993) 148–149 ("the spreading branches of Ethiopia"),
W. Brueggemann, *Isaiah 1–39* (1998) 154: "The shoots and branches are twice eliminated—first by Yahweh's own forceful verbs of harvest, and then by animals that
devour until nothing is left [. . .] The Ethiopians are "fodder" to help all the creatures to live." Within this group, some scholars abstracts the metaphorical speech
of v. 6 to mean plans. The tendrils and twigs that are ruthlessly cut off (v. 5) are
together with the slain on the mountain side (v. 6) regarded as a description of

that the metaphorical language of vine tendrils and twigs in v. 5 is
dropped in v. 6. This group of scholars interpret v. 6 as a concrete
description of how human bodies lie dead on the ground, and of
how these corpses are to be devoured by birds and beasts.[39]

Is it possible—and of interest for the understanding of Isa 18:6—
to suggest *who* the bird and beast might refer to in Isa 18:6? What
seems clear is that the bird of prey is applied in a negative way in
this verse. There seem to be two possibilities to who the bird of prey
can be. First, the bird of prey can refer to an enemy of Judah. From
another text in the book of Isaiah, Isa 46:11, the Persian ruler Cyrus
is referred to as a bird of prey, עִיט. Could this indicate that the
bird of prey referred to in 18:6 might hint towards a foreign leader?
Second, the bird of prey can refer to YHWH. In Isa 31:4–5 the
bird of prey is understood as representing YHWH himself who swoops
down over his prey.[40] In my view, it is not vital to the understanding of v. 6 to find out who the bird of prey might be. Rather, what
seems to be the point is that Isa 18:6 applies the metaphorical speech
about the bird of prey negatively, in a context of doom over Judah
(cf. the analysis of v. 5). Whether it is YHWH himself who is meant

---

how a nations *plans* are destroyed. Cf. E.J. Kissane, *The Book of Isaiah* (1960) 199.
For his interpretation, Kissane refers to Isa 14:19, 24–27; 34:1ff.; Ezek 34:17ff. For
a similar interpretation of Isa 18:6, see also W. Eichrodt, *Der Herr der Geschichte*
(1967) 62–63.

[39] Cf. W. Gesenius, *Philologisch-kritischer und historischer Commentar über den Jesaia*
(1821) 591 (Assyria), A. Dillmann, *Der Prophet Jesaia* (1890) 170 (Assyria), G. Friman,
Profeten Jesaja (1917) 26 (Assyria), F. Feldmann, *Das Buch Isaias* (1925) 220 (Assyria),
O. Procksch, *Jesaia I* (1930) 241–242 (Cush or Assyria), Aa. Bentzen, *Jesaja* (1944)
142 (Assyria), E.J. Kissane, *The Book of Isaiah* (1960) 199–200 (Assyria), G.B. Gray,
A Critical and Exegetical Commentary on The Book of Isaiah (1962) 315 (Assyria), N.K.
Gottwald, *All the Kingdoms of the Earth* (1964) 163 ("the Egyptian aspirations in Asia"),
E.J. Young, *The Book of Isaiah* (1965/1978) 478 (Assyria), B.S. Childs, *Isaiah and the
Assyrian Crisis* (1967) 45 (judgement over Assyria), H. Eising, *Das Buch Jesaja* (1970)
138 (Assyria), A.S. Herbert, *The Book of the Prophet Isaiah* (1973) 119 (Assyria or
Egypt), H.W. Hoffmann, *Die Intention der Verkündigung Jesajas* (1974) 72–73 (Egypt/
Ethiopia), R.E. Clements, *Isaiah 1–39* (1980/1994) 165 (Ethiopia and Egypt),
J. Jensen, *Isaiah 1–39* (1984) 165 (Ethiopia), H.M. Wolf, *Interpreting Isaiah* (1985) 122
(Assyria), J.H. Hayes & S.A. Irvine, *Isaiah* (1987) 256 ("The supporters of the pre-
sent revolt"), K. Jeppesen, *Jesajas Bog fortolket* (1988) 125 (Nubien/Kush).

[40] For this interpretation, cf. the understanding of Isa 31:4–5 from M.L. Barré,
"Of Lions and Birds: A Note on Isaiah 31:4–5", *Among the Prophets* (1993) 58. Barré
lists other Old Testament texts where YHWH is pictured as winged (in all the listed
texts the image is applied positively): Exod 19:4; Deut 32:11; Pss 17:8; 36:8 [ET:
36:7]; 57:2 [ET: 57:1]; 61:5 [61:4]; 63:8 [63:7]; 91:4; Ruth 2:12.

by the reference to a bird of prey, or it is an agent sent by YHWH
to punish Judah is not said in Isa 18:6. In both cases, however,
YHWH would be the one responsible for the events. However, what
is clear is that YHWH who acts in a devastating way (as referred
to in v. 5) is also the one who extends the punishment over Judah
by letting birds and beasts summer and winter over the tendrils and
twigs (v. 6).[41]

Summing up the rhetorical features in the text's motifs
The two motifs of v. 6 that have been discussed above are "bird"
and "beast". From what has been observed, the motifs of Isa 18:6
are negatively applied. The tendrils and twigs are not merely being
cut off the vine (v. 5), they are also devoured by birds and beasts
(v. 6), and this twofold act of judgement clearly pronounces a harsh
doom over the people of YHWH.[42] Although it is not clear from
the text whether or not "bird" and "beast" refer to an enemy, a
power, or YHWH, it is evident that the "bird" and "beast" are
applied as YHWH's agents in his punishment of Judah.

6.4.3. *How do textual design and motifs together create the strophe's rhetoric?*

Cohesion: Gender-matched parallelism, word-pairs, and repetition of motifs
Semantically, the first, and the third, as well as the second and the
fourth lines are parallel. From the text's design we have seen that
the gender-matched parallelism together with word-pairs function to
create cohesion as they bind together the lines of v. 6. The two
motifs of v. 6 ("bird" and "beast") are mentioned twice each, and
this repetition also functions to bind the four lines of the verse
together.

---

[41] If one suggests that the Persian ruler is the one who is referred to by the bird
of prey in Isa 18:6, also he is sent by YHWH, and does not act on behalf of himself, cf. J.J. Ferrie Jr., "Singing in the Rain: A Meteorological Image in Isaiah
42:10–12", *Imagery and Imagination in Biblical Literature* (2001) 104: "But Cyrus is merely
Yahweh's agent (41:2–3), the "bird of prey" he has called from the east (46:11)." (My
italics).

[42] Cf. W. Brueggemann, *Isaiah 1–39* (1998) 154: "The shoots and branches are
twice eliminated—first by Yahweh's own forceful verbs of harvest, and then by animals that devour until nothing is left." (My italics).

Activity: "Bird" and "beast" devour the tendrils and twigs
Both from the text's design and motifs, we have seen that an atmosphere of activity is created. The only characters that are referred to
in this verse are the bird and the beast, and as they are repeatedly
said to be given the tendrils and twigs, and to "summer" and
"winter" upon them, this creates an atmosphere of activity over time.
However, this activity is not said to last forever, as "summer" and
"winter" designates one year, and not years to come. In this expression lies the notion that even though the judgement is harsh, it is
not going to last for ever.

Concentration: The destruction is harsh
From both textual design and motifs we have observed that there is
a concentration in v. 6 on non-human characters. The creatures
"bird" and "beast" are mentioned twice each, and they are depicted
as devouring the tendrils and twigs of the vine (v. 5). In v. 6 the
concentration is on what is removed from the vine. An aspect of
totality is seen in three ways. First, when v. 6 opens by: יעזבו יחדו
"they will together be left", this expresses the numerical aspect of
the prey. The bird and beast are to be given all that is left from
the cutting down of the tendrils and twigs (v. 5). Second, totality is
also expressed through the fact that birds and beasts cover heaven
and earth. From above, and from the ground, the tendrils and twigs
will be consumed. Third, the totality is expressed by describing the
period of time of which the prey will be devoured. The time perspective of the destruction is not restricted to day and night, the
bird and beast are to "summer" and "winter" upon the tendrils and
twigs, i.e. the whole year is covered. These three ways of expressing totality functions to concentrate on a situation of judgement.
However, even though the judgement is severe, the text opens the
possibility that there is still some left—as the vine itself with roots
is not cut down. This means that there is hope for the vine to blossom again next season.[43] For the relationship between destruction
and restoration also in other texts in the Old Testament, cf. for
instance Isa 5:1–7; 27:2–6; 31:4–5; Jer 5:10–13; Hos 11:6–7.

---

[43] That there might be hope for the vine for next season, was suggested to me
by the first opponent of the disputation, Professor Kirsten Nielsen. At that time I
perceived that the judgement was more harsh than the text in fact describes.

Confusion resolved: The people of YHWH is judged
As said earlier, the way Isa 18 is designed entraps the audience to first believe that somebody other than themselves are judged. However, by vv. 5 and 6 the confusion is resolved as the answer is given to who is the object of YHWH's doom. This verse concludes with the declaration that nothing will be left, and that the bird and beast will "summer" and "winter" upon tendrils and twigs. The metaphorical speech in v. 5 of a vine that will be cut down and hewn away continues by the reference in v. 6 to tendrils and twigs that are given to the bird and beast. For the audience of Isa 18, this metaphorical speech taken from the sphere of viticulture most likely struck them harshly as they knew that Israel/Judah often were spoken of as a vine, and YHWH as a vinedresser (for Old Testament references to such imagery, see 5.3. in this research). The message that comes across to the audience is that a harsh judgement will be effectuated towards Judah if she seeks help by humans instead of by her God.

Summing up the rhetoric in the text's design and motifs
Through the analysis of textual design and motifs of Isa 18:6 it has been showed that this verse consists of four lines where the first and the third and the second and the fourth are semantically parallel. Further, this strophe shows a deliberate rhetoric. This is seen the following ways: First, as a deliberate rhetoric can only be efficient if what is said makes sense, there have been observed several cohesive features of v. 6. Both by the use of gender-matched parallelism and word-pairs on the one hand, and by repeating the two motifs "bird" and "beast" on the other hand, this functions to give a *coherent* message to the audience. Second, both textual design and motifs of v. 6 create an atmosphere of *activity*. The characters that are mentioned in this verse are "bird" and "beast", and as they are referred to as devouring the tendrils and twigs, this functions to focus on the activity. Third, both observations about textual design and motifs have showed that this verse *concentrates* on describing a destruction. Fourth, the feeling of *confusion* that the audience might have in the beginning of the message of Isa 18 is now resolved as v. 6 (together with v. 5) have made it clear that the strong metaphorical speech of tendrils and twigs that are cut down most likely is meant to hit the Judeans themselves, and not a foreign nation.

6.5. Contextual analysis

Are there any connections at all by means of textual design, motifs or rhetorical drive between the two first stanzas of Isa 18 (vv. 1–2 and vv. 3–6)?

6.5.1. *Textual design*

The stanza that begins by v. 3 and ends by v. 6 vary both in scene, shape, size and contents from the previous stanza (vv. 1–2). From the first to the second stanza of the text the scene has changed from the (diplomatic) travelling scene (18:1–2) to the summoning scene (v. 3) and further to the harvest scene (v. 5) and destruction scene (v. 6). According to the shape and size, the stanza that begins with v. 3 contains four strophes (vv. 3, 4, 5 and 6), and is thus unlike the foregoing stanza which contains two strophes (vv. 1–2). Let us look at some relations between these two stanzas in terms of textual design.

The choice of characters in 18:1–6 builds the message of judgement
As the analysis has showed, the characters vary from part to part in this text. Who are major, and who are minor participants throughout 18:1–6? In vv. 1–2 the major characters are the Cushites. They are introduced in terms of how they look, and where they live. In this part of the text, the minor participants are the messengers who travel from an unidentified area to the land of Cush. In vv. 3–6, however, the Cushites have disappeared from the scene, and the major participants are "all who dwell on the earth" (this does not however exclude the Cushites), YHWH, and "me." Throughout vv. 3–6 the participants vary in status. YHWH seems to be the major character from vv. 3–5, whereas "me" seems to occupy the scene in the role of a mediator (v. 4) and a spectator (vv. 5–6). This shift in reference to characters functions to confuse the audience as they only at the end of stanza II understands that this speech in the end deals with themselves (the tendrils and twigs of a vine, v. 5).

6.5.2. *Motifs*

All motifs of Isa 18:1–6 build the message of judgement
Are there relations between the motifs of vv. 1–2 and 3–6? In vv. 1–2, the motifs messengers, rivers, and Cush are applied in order

to describe diplomatic relations between Judah and Cush. In v. 3, the motifs standard, horn, and mountain widen the perspective, and are used to make all nations of the earth be aware of YHWH's presence in the following. In v. 4, the glowing heat and the cloud of dew together with YHWH's quietness in his dwelling place function to on the one hand make a pattern for Judah to be quiet, and on the other hand, this tense atmosphere prepares fro the coming judgement. That the שׁוֹפָר in 18:3 is applied in a context of judgement is clearly seen in the continuing verses, 4–6. In Isa 18:3–6 there is an association between the destructive מַזְמֵרָה ("pruning knives", v. 5) and the שׁוֹפָר ("horn", v. 3).[44] The blowing of the horn (v. 3) *together with* the cutting down of vines (v. 5) functions as a warning to Judah. The warning is harsh as it is YHWH himself who will perform the cutting of vine tendrils and twigs (v. 5). The results of YHWH's pruning knives are related to the warning by the שׁוֹפָר. The sound of the שׁוֹפָר is a warning to Judah that YHWH will use the pruning knife if she does not leave her plans about entering into a coalition with the Cushites (vv. 1–2). By the connection between horn and pruning knives, Judah is strongly encouraged to trust in YHWH instead of in the Cushites. The opening motifs of Isa 18 are explicated in order to confuse the audience to believe that the Cushites are judged in this speech. However, as the motifs unfold, it becomes clearer and clearer that the judgement is meant for the people of YHWH (vv. 5–6).

6.5.3. Rhetoric

The diplomacy of Judah (v. 2) is ridiculed (v. 4)
Are there relations in terms of rhetoric between the two first stanzas of Isa 18? When it comes to the argumentative shape of the text it is evident that the rhetoric of vv. 1–2 must be read together with vv. 3–6 in order to come to grips with the underlying message of

---

[44] It has been noticed that there is a connection between the sword and the horn in Ezek 33:3, and in Zech 9:13–14, cf. K.D. Jenner, "The Big Shofar (Isaiah 27:13): A Hapax Legomenon", *Studies in Isaiah 24–27* (2000) 175. In the latter text (Zech 9:13–14), the sound of the שׁוֹפָר will warn Judah and Israel that YHWH will use them as a sword of the hero with which he will attack Greece. In Ezek 33:3, the watchman warns the people when the sword is coming upon the land.

this chapter. The way the Cushites and their land are described (vv. 1–2) is overwhelmingly positive, and this is done in order to entice the audience into a rhetorical trap. By focusing entirely on the Cushites' *positive* reputation, the rhetor exaggerates their position as an attractive coalition partner. Both their look and their position (geographically and military) is hinted to as invincible. The command to go to Cush (v. 2b) seems to be contradicted by the indirect invitation to take model of YHWH's quietness (v. 4). In the context, YHWH's tranquility functions as a pattern for how Judah should behave herself. As pointed at in the analysis of vv. 1–2, the command to go (in v. 2b) ridicules the intense diplomatic activity from the Judean side towards finding a human alliance partner instead of waiting for help from YHWH. From this, it is evident that vv. 1–2 must be read together with v. 4 to achieve the understanding of the rhetoric of the text.

The judgement of Judah (vv. 5–6) is hinted at in v. 1
Verse 1 opens with a הוֹי to the land of Cush. However, in this work it has been advocated that the הוֹי is directed to someone else (vv. 5–6). The rhetorical function of pronouncing a judgement is to make the audience distressed, and through this prevent Judah from taking any actions towards political alliances with neither Cush nor any other nation. Even before the political and military results of an alliance are achieved (before the vine blossom has come to an end, v. 5), YHWH will stop the alliance (the tendrils and twigs will be thrown away and destructed, vv. 5–6). The calmness of YHWH (v. 4), and his way of judging Judah (vv. 5–6) functions to show Judah who she should attach herself to, and to make the people focus on the transcendent power in whom they should put their trust; YHWH. Judah is judged (vv. 5–6) because of her wish to cling to foreign peoples instead of to YHWH. If this solution turns out to be the most convincing, the text addresses its audience in an ambiguous way. The way the הוֹי of Isa 18:1 is applied seems to be different from the common usage of the term in connection with foreign nations throughout the Old Testament. The הוֹיs concerning foreign nations in other prophetic books predict downfall of Israel's enemies (cf. for instance Jer 48:1, 50:27, Zeph 2:5, Nah 3:1). This seems not to be the case with Isa 18:1 as there is no explicit judgement predicted over the nation of Cush. As we have seen, some scholars interpret 18:5 as a judgement over Cush, however, the more

common suggestion is that v. 5 pronounces doom over Assyria.[45]

It has been stated that this text is dressed in a rhetoric of entrap-ment.[46] According to R. Alter, such a rhetorical strategy often con-tains figurative language. This is clear also in this text (vv. 5–6). A typical element in a text that is clothed in a rhetoric of entrapment is a concentration of nearly synonymous words with reference to sin or destruction. As we have seen, verses 5–6 carry designations for destruction. YHWH makes use of knives in the cutting of the vine tendrils and twigs, and destructive verbs such as "cutting off", "turn-ing aside" and "striking away" are applied in the same verse (v. 5). Verse 6 continues the intensification by describing even more events: the tendrils and twigs will be left to "the bird of prey of the moun-tains and to the beast of the earth". As if this was not enough, the bird of prey and beast will be over the tendrils and twigs all year. By applying the rhetorical strategy of entrapment, the text—through an intricate way—fools the audience to judge themselves. In the beginning, they might think that the message is meant to hit other peoples, since there is one people in particular who is mentioned in the text (v. 1). However, the way the text is structured surprisingly puts the Judeans in the centre and indirectly accuses them (vv. 5–6). The rhetorical effect of such a way of addressing one's audience is achieved by applying this well-known metaphorical language. What seems to—in the first place—hit the Cushites or other foreign nations turns out to be a message to the people of YHWH, and this is the aim of the whole argument. By confusing the audience as to who is the actual receiver of this message, the text—with its rhetoric of entrapment—wants to persuade its audience to put their trust YHWH and not in foreign nations. As earlier pointed at, the two words צלצל (v. 1) and הזלזלים (v. 5) are related. In verse 1, צלצל evokes posi-tive associations, whereas in v. 5, הזלזלים creates a negative atmos-phere. The picture created in v. 5 is that of הזלזלים, quivering tendrils of a vine that will be cut off. By applying two words that can both be related to something that vibrates, the text creates a contrast

---

[45] Cf. the motif analysis of Isa 18:5.

[46] The term is taken from R. Alter, *The Art of Biblical Poetry* (1985/1990) 144. In the chapter "Prophecy and Poetry" Alter explains how prophetic poetry can be clothed as a rhetoric of entrapment: "Prophetic poetry is thus very often constructed as a *rhetoric of entrapment*, whether in the sequence of a few lines or in the larger scale of a whole prophecy." (Alter's italics).

between the strong Cushites and the weak Judeans (understood as the tendrils of a vine). The diplomatic relations between Judah and Cush will be cut off, and this comes clearly across to the audience in v. 5 where it is said that the tendrils (used by the vine to attach itself to others) will be cut off so that the vine cannot stand by itself anymore.

CHAPTER SEVEN

STROPHE VI: 18:7

Obviously, there are connections between v. 7 and v. 2 of Isa 18 as v. 7 contains a repetition of parts of what is said in v. 2.[1] In v. 2 there is a recommendation that swift messengers shall go to a people tall and smooth-skinned whose land is divided by rivers. In v. 7, this tall and smooth-skinned people comes to Mount Zion with gifts.

7.1. TEXT AND TRANSLATION

As parts of v. 7 are identical with elements in v. 2, this section will not repeat what has already been said in the analysis of vv. 1–2.

7.1.1. *Textual criticism*

Text	Verse
בעת ההיא יובל־שי ליהוה צבאות	v. 7aα
עם ממשך ומורט	v. 7aβ
ומעם נורא מן־הוא והלאה	v. 7aγ
גוי קו־קו ומבוסה	v. 7bα
אשר בזאו נהרים ארצו	v. 7bβ
אל־מקום שם־יהוה צבאות הר־ציון	v. 7bγ

Verse	Text
v. 7aα	In that time[2] gifts will be borne along[3] to YHWH Sebaoth
v. 7aβ	[from][4] a people tall and smooth-skinned,[5]

[1] There is a slight variation between v. 2 and v. 7 when it comes to the application of the words גוי and עם. In v. 2 the pattern is: גוי עם גוי, whereas in v. 7 the pattern is: עם גוי עם.

[2] While the MT has בעת 1Q Isaᵃ has בעתה. There is a slight difference between these two; MT expresses time of an event, *in that time*, and 1Q Isaᵃ expresses the present now, *at the time*, whether in opposition to past time or to future, cf. *BDB* (1979) 773–774.

[3] MT has hophal of יבל, while quotations from non-biblical Scrolls/Rabbinic literature have hiphil. I see however no reason why the MT should be changed.

[4] MT reads עם, "a people", and does not have the preposition "from". 1Q Isaᵃ read מעם "from a people", cf. the reading of LXX and the Vulgate. In view of

v. 7aγ   and from a people feared from that day and onwards,
v. 7bα   [from] a nation line upon line and down-treading,
v. 7bβ   whose land rivers cut through,[6]
v. 7bγ   to the place of the name of YHWH Sebaoth[7]—Mount Zion.

7.1.2. Translation

As parts of v. 2 reappear in v. 7, some of the challenges from v. 2 are also present in v. 7. However, the discussion pursued in chapter 2 of this book will not be repeated here. What needs to be mentioned here, however, is the general agreement that this verse is a later addition.

Is v. 7 a later addition?
As has been touched upon in the introductory chapter of this work, scholars have traditionally not considered 18:7 as "authentic" from the hands of the 8th century prophet. It has been a widespread opinion that v. 7 is added to Isa 18:1–6 at a later stage.[8] Reasons and criteria for regarding v. 7 as a later addition, however, have only occasionally been put forward by those who advocate this view. This study will not to go into a detailed discussion about the "authenticity" of v. 7 as this research studies Isa 18 in its final form. The

---

the following וּמֵעַם, "and from a people" in v. 7aγ, MT could be considered as a graphical error. One could subsequently imply a "from" in the first instance. However, as MT is sound and valid as it stands, I see no reason to reject MT.

[5] Cf. the analysis of verse 2.
[6] Cf. the analysis of verse 2.
[7] 1Q Isaᵃ does not have the word צבאות.
[8] Cf. the following selected listing: B. Duhm, *Das Buch Jesaia* (1892) 116, K. Marti, *Das Buch Jesaja* (1900) 149–150, O. Procksch, *Jesaia I* (1930) 242, Aa. Bentzen, *Jesaja* (1944) 143, R.H. Pfeiffer, *Introduction to the Old Testament* (1953) 443, E.J. Kissane, *The Book of Isaiah* (1960) 200, G. Fohrer, *Das Buch Jesaja Kapitel 1–23* (1960/1966) 220–224, G.B. Gray, *A Critical and Exegetical Commentary on the Book of Isaiah* (1962) 316, H. Donner, *Israel unter den Völkern* (1964) 123, A.S. Herbert, *The Book of the Prophet Isaiah* (1973) 119, H.W. Hoffmann, *Die Intention der Verkündigung Jesajas* (1974) 66, footnote 254, F. Huber, *Jahwe, Juda und die anderen Völker beim Propheten Jesaja* (1976) 3, R.E. Clements, *Isaiah 1–39* (1980/1994) 166, R.E. Clements, *Isaiah and the Deliverance of Jerusalem* (1980) 31, G.R. Hamborg, "Reasons for Judgement in the Oracles Against the Nations of the Prophet Isaiah", *VT* 31 (1981) 148, T.N.D. Mettinger, *The Dethronement of Sabaoth* (1982) 63, O. Kaiser, *Der Prophet Jesaja* (1983) 75, K. Jeppesen, *Jesajas Bog fortolket* (1988) 125, E. Otto, "צִיּוֹן", *ThWAT* 6 (1989) 1013, S.H. Widyapranawa, *The Lord is Saviour* (1990) 107, B.M. Zapff, *Schriftgelehrte Prophetie* (1995) 289–290, footnote 241 and 297, W. Brueggemann, *Isaiah 1–39* (1998) 154, B.U. Schipper, *Israel und Ägypten in der Königszeit* (1999) 208, footnote 59.

following gives only some hints about how other scholars argue when they regard v. 7 as a later addition. Some scholars seem to focus on the change from poetry (vv. 1–6) to prose (v. 7), while others attend to the contents of v. 7. To the latter point, one of the reasons why some scholars do not consider v. 7 as "original" is this verse's terminology "Zion", and "YHWH Sebaoth". H. Wildberger is one of those who argue that the assertion in Isa 18:7 that Mount Zion is "the place of the name of YHWH Sebaoth" shows that this verse is a later addendum.[9] As has been said earlier, this research seeks to show how Isa 18 in its final form is designed in a way that communicates a message of judgement towards Judah. Accordingly, v. 7 is throughout this work regarded as an integral part of Isa 18. However, this stance does *not* automatically imply that Isa 18 from the very beginning has had the shape it has been transmitted in, and that a modern reader finds in the *BHS*. Nevertheless, if not put there from the start, it is evident that the redactor(s) of the book of Isaiah at one point regarded v. 7 as an integral part of chapter 18 of Isaiah.[10] It is of course possible that Isa 18 experienced a process of growth *before* it reached the form it has in Codex Leningradensis. However, tracing this process of growth seems impossible due to all the factors that are hidden to the modern interpreter, and this study has chosen the final form of the text as its point of departure, and has not discussed its eventual process of growth. Although they are few, there are examples of scholars who—like me—consider v. 7 as an integral part of Isa 18.[11]

---

[9] According to H. Wildberger, *Jesaja 13–27* (1978) 695–696, Isaiah of Jerusalem did not know the Deuteronomic terminology. Subsequently, v. 7 is added to vv. 1–6 at a later stage. A few pages earlier, *ibid.*, p. 682, Wildberger argues that the "original" parts of Isa 18 are 18:1, 2a, 2bα, and 4–6a. For a similar view, see J. Jensen, *Isaiah 1–39* (1984) 164: "Verse 7 is without doubt a later addition and in all probability v 3 and v 6b are also later additions."

[10] For suggestions about Zion as one of the unifying elements between the various parts of the book of Isaiah, cf. B.G. Webb, "Zion in Transformation. A Literary Approach to Isaiah", *The Bible in Three Dimensions* (1990) 65–84, and R.E. Clements, "Zion as Symbol and Political Reality: A Central Isaianic Quest", *Studies in the Book of Isaiah* (1997) 3–17.

[11] Cf. C.R. Seitz, *Isaiah 1–39* (1993) 149, who pursues a "unitary reading", (see p. 147) of Isa 18 as a whole: "Such an interpretation is further strengthened by the final verse (v. 7), which has not misunderstood the preceding oracle [vv. 1–6] but offers a final comment consistent with it." See also B.S. Childs, *Isaiah* (2001) 139: "Verse 7 is not a scribal gloss, but integral to the editor's intention in shaping the entire passage as a testimony to God's future rule over the nations of the world."

7.2. TEXTUAL DESIGN

7.2.1. *Syntactic observations*

The nearly precise repetition of verse 2 in v. 7 draws the attention to the elements that are *not* the same from the opening to the end of Isa 18.

Gapping
In the lines 7aβ, 7aγ, and 7bα it is said from where the gifts to YHWH on Mount Zion are brought. However, only v. 7aγ contains the preposition "from". As vv. 7aβ and 7bα do not include the preposition ןמ/מ, "from", an instance of gapping is at work as this preposition is expected here.

7.2.2. *Semantic observations*

Verse 7 is set up as poetry (with six lines) in this investigation.[12] Semantically, all of v. 7 has to do with future events ("in that time") when gifts will be brought to YHWH Sebaoth on Zion from the Cushites.[13] In some or the other way, all six lines deal with the Cushites. The four lines that make up the mid-part of the strophe all describe the people (and their land) from which the gifts are borne along to YHWH, whereas the two remaining lines (vv. 7aα and 7bγ) make known *where* the gifts will be borne along—to the place of the name of YHWH Sebaoth, Mount Zion.

7.2.3. *Poetic technique*

Characters from v. 2 are reintroduced
As was the case for v. 2, also v. 7 accommodate a thorough description of the Cushites. In v. 2, the portrayal of the Cushites was done at the expense of the other group of people mentioned in the same

---

[12] It can of course be discussed whether or not v. 7 should be treated as poetry or prose. For two opposite solutions, cf. *BHS* where Isa 18:7 is printed as prose, and the American Jewish translation *Tanakh—The Holy Scriptures* (1988) 654, where the same verse is printed as poetry. For a discussion of the borders (or the lack of such) between prose and poetry in Old Testament texts, cf. the excursus in K. Holter, *Second Isaiah's Idol-Fabrication Passages* (1995) 207–212.

[13] For other semantic features of v. 7, such as word-pairs and play with words, see the analysis of vv. 1–2 in this book.

strophe, namely the messengers (מלאכים). The design is different in
v. 7 as YHWH Sebaoth is mentioned alongside with the Cushites.
The reference to YHWH Sebaoth opens and closes v. 7 (v. 7aα and
7bγ). The function of this poetic technique will be explored in 7.4.1.

7.3. MOTIFS

Together with the repetition of parts of v. 2, v. 7 contains information about gifts that will be brought to YHWH on Mount Zion
"[from] a people tall and smooth-skinned [. . .]". The present analysis of the motifs of v. 7 will not repeat what is said about the same
motifs in vv. 1–2, but rather concentrate on the motifs that are *not*
present in v. 2: "gift" and "Zion".[14]

7.3.1. *Gift*

One of the motifs that plays a significant role in v. 7 is שי, "gift".
In order to describe how it is used in this verse it is necessary to
look at its application in the Old Testament.

The comparable material is sparse since the word שי, "gift", appears
only 3 times in the Old Testament.[15] In the two occurrences in the
book of Psalms, the term is applied about gifts offered as homage
either to kings or to the divinity.[16] In Ps 68:30 [ET: 68:29], שי are
referred to as being brought to God in the temple in Jerusalem from
kings: "Because of your temple at Jerusalem kings will bring you
gifts."[17] Only a few sentences further below in the same psalm, Ps
68:32 [ET: 68:31], the following is said: "Envoys will come out of
Egypt; Cush will quickly stretch out her hands to God." Knowing

---

[14] Verse 7 contains a motif that is also present in vv. 3, 5 and 6: הר, "mountain". Although the mountain(s) that are mentioned in vv. 3, 5, and 6 seem to be
different from that one mentioned in 18:7, the analysis of v. 7 will not analyse the
motif "mountain" as such, as this will be included in the treatment of the motif
"Zion".

[15] Cf. G. Lisowsky, *Konkordanz* (1981) 1426: Isa 18:7; Pss 68:30 [68:29]; 76:12
[76:11].

[16] Cf. H. Wildberger, *Jesaja 13–27* (1978) 694–695, who also refers to Ps 72:10–11,
15; 45:13 in this connection.

[17] Although the term שי is not applied in Ps 72:10, the idea that kings will come
with gifts (here to the king of YHWH's people) is expressed: "The kings of Tarshish
and of distant shores will bring tribute to him; the kings of Sheba and Seba will
present him gifts."

the preceding context (Ps 68:30), the Cushites' stretching of hands probably means their bringing of gifts to God.[18] In another text taken from the book of Psalms (76:12 [ET: 76:11]), the same idea of gifts being brought to God from the peoples is expressed. That peoples will pay homage to YHWH is also known from Isa 45:14; 49:7; 55:3b–5, and from Zech 2:15; 6:15; 8:20–22. In an expanded form, the idea is also applied in Isa 60.

How is the motif שׁי, "gift", applied in Isa 18:7? In this verse it is said that "in that time", gifts will be brought "[from] a people tall and smooth-skinned [. . .]" to Mount Zion, the place of the name of YHWH Sebaoth. This has an equivalent in Zeph 3:10 where it is said:

> From along the rivers of Cush my worshipers, my dispersed daughter, will bring my offering.

Although Zeph 3:10 contains the term מנחה, "offering" (feminine singular construct), and not שׁי, "gift", Isa 18:7 and Zeph 3:10 are correspondent to such an extent that some comments are required.[19] Do these two texts express the same thought? In Isa 18:7 it is the nations (here represented by Cush) which come from afar with gifts to YHWH Sebaoth, whereas in Zeph 3:10 it seems as if it is the dispersed people of YHWH that comes from "along the rivers of Cush" and brings offering to YHWH. Pursuing these observations further, it is on the one hand evident that the two texts play on each other, and refer to the same area, namely Cush. On the other hand, however, Isa 18:7 clearly expresses that the people from the area of Cush will bring gifts to YHWH, whereas in Zeph 3:10 it is said that "my dispersed daughter" will bring offerings.[20] This is most

---

[18] To this text it is correctly observed by H. Wildberger, *Jesaja 13–27* (1978) 695, that when (what he calls the *motif*) "Völkerhuldigung" is employed, Cush appears on the scene. Wildberger regards Ps 68:31–33 as dependent on Isa 18:7.

[19] E.J. Kissane suggests that Isa 18:7 may have been influenced by Zeph 3:10, cf. E.J. Kissane, *The Book of Isaiah* (1960) 200. Both H. Wildberger, *Jesaja 13–27* (1978) 695, J. Blenkinsopp, *Isaiah 1–39* (2000) 311, and M.A. Sweeney, *Zephaniah. A Commentary* (2003) 16, argue that Zeph 3:10 is dependent on Isa 18:1, 7. Concerning the book of Zephania, it is striking that this short book of three chapters has as many as three occurrences of the term "Cush/Cushi" (1:1; 2:12; 3:10).

[20] For a discussion of whom the "dispersed daughter" in Zeph 3:10 most likely refers to, see E. Ben Zvi, *A Historical-Critical Study of the Book of Zephaniah* (1991) 228–230, with references.

likely to be understood as the people of YHWH, and not the Cushites.[21]
A similar mentioning of Cush in the context of the remnant of
YHWH's people who will be brought home from afar, is Isa 11:11:

> In that day YHWH will reach out his hand a second time to reclaim
> the remnant that is left of his people from Assyria, from Lower Egypt,
> from Upper Egypt, from Cush, from Elam, from Babylonia, from
> Hamath and from the islands of the sea.

From the Old Testament background that has been briefly referred
to above, it is clear that the motif שׁי, "gift" in Isa 18:7 is applied
in the sense of bringing homage to the deity. The tall and smooth-
skinned people from along the rivers of Cush are the *deliverers* of the
שׁי, whereas YHWH Sebaoth on Mount Zion is the *receiver*.[22] As the
preposition "from" is lacking in v. 7aβ and v. 7bα, it is somewhat
unclear whether the people themselves are to be understood as gifts,
or if they carry gifts with them to YHWH on Zion:[23]

בעת ההיא יובל־שׁי ליהוה צבאות עם ממשך ומורט [. . .]

However, despite this minor confusion, it is clear that the Cushites
are representatives for the nations when they bring to YHWH on
Zion. How the motif Zion is applied in Isa 18:7, is another question, and this leads to the next paragraph.

7.3.2. *Zion*

As has already been touched upon, a central motif of Isa 18:7 is
"Zion". To understand the meaning of the movement from Cush to
Zion that is referred to in v. 7, it is necessary to detect some of the
significance of the motif Zion. In the Old Testament, there is however a wide range of connotations to the motif Zion, with various

---

[21] For this understanding, cf. W. Rudolph, *Micha—Nahum—Habakuk—Zephanja*
(1975) 296, R.L. Smith, *Micah-Malachi* (1984) 141–142, P.R. House, *Zephaniah. A
Prophetic Drama* (1988) 67, J. Blenkinsopp, *Isaiah 1–39* (2000) 311, and H. Irsigler,
Zefanja (2002) 372–373. For the understanding of Zeph 3:10 as dealing with the
Cushites, and not the people of YHWH, see D.W. Baker, *Nahum, Habakkuk and
Zephaniah* (1988) 116, and perhaps also M.A. Sweeney, *Zephaniah. A Commentary* (2003)
16.
[22] See J.D.W. Watts, *Isaiah 1–33* (1985) 246, and J.H. Hayes & S.A. Irvine, *Isaiah*
(1987) 257, who claim that the gifts brought to YHWH come from the Assyrians.
[23] Cf. G.B. Gray, *A Critical and Exegetical Commentary on the Book of Isaiah* (1962)
316: "[. . .] the text of M makes the tribute consist of the people themselves!"

nuances appropriate to differing historical and theological contexts.[24] Subsequently, this entry can only deal with some of these connotations.

The word Zion occurs 152 times in the Old Testament, and its connotations varies from text to text.[25] Among the many Old Testament references to Zion are (i) "The sons of Zion" (once, Lam 4:2), (ii) the "Daughters of Zion" (once, in Cant 3:11), (iii) "the Daughter of Zion" (cf. Isa 1:8; 16:1; Jer 4:31; Mic 4:8), (iv) "the virgin Daughter of Zion" (three times: 2 Kgs 19:21; Isa 37:22; Lam 2:13),[26] (v) "Mount Zion" (cf. Pss 2:6; 43:8; 48:11; Isa 18:7; 29:8; Lam 5:18; Obad 1:21), (vi) "Zion" (cf. 1 Kgs 8:1; Pss 9:12; 48:12; 69:36; 87:2; 97:8; Isa 1:27; 10:24; 14:32; 33:20; 60:14; Jer 3:14; 50:5; Lam 1:17; Mic 3:12), or (vii) "O Zion" (Zech 2:11). From these and other texts where Zion occurs, to what does the term refer?

The Old Testament usage of the motif Zion refers to at least four meanings: (i) Literally, Zion refers to a fortress in Jerusalem probably on a ridge in the south-east section of the city during the period before David captured the city from the Jebusites (2 Sam 5:7, 9), and to (ii) the hill on which Salomon built the temple, known as the Temple Mount (Ps 78:68–69). Non-literally, (iii) Zion refers to the entire temple city of Jerusalem (as the city of YHWH, cf. Pss 132; 137:1; Lam 1:17; 2:6–8; Isa 8:18),[27] and last, (iv) Zion—like Jerusalem—is applied about the people of Israel (Isa 51:16; Zech 2:11). From this, it is evident that the Zion motif can refer to either parts of Jerusalem, the capital Jerusalem, the inhabitants of Jerusalem, or the whole country (with its inhabitants, i.e. the people of YHWH).[28]

---

[24] Cf. the immense selected listing of relevant literature to the Zion material, in E. Otto, "ציון", *ThWAT* 6 (1989) 994–1005.

[25] Cf. Koehler-Baumgartner, *HALAT* (1983) 958. For the distribution of these occurrences, see E. Otto, "ציון", *ThWAT* 6 (1989) 1007. Cf. also F. Stolz, "ציון", *THAT* 2 (1976) 544, who counts 154 occurrences of Zion in the Old Testament. For a brief overview of both the Sinai and Zion material in the Old Testament, see R.J. Clifford, *The Cosmic Mountain in Canaan and the Old Testament* (1972) 98–181.

[26] For a picturing of the city as a woman, cf. J.J. Schmitt, "The City as Woman in Isaiah 1–39", *Writing and Reading the Scroll of Isaiah* (1997) 95–119, with references.

[27] In Lamentations Zion and Jerusalem are used interchangeable.

[28] J.D. Levenson, "Zion traditions", *ABD* 6 (1992) 1098–1102, suggests a growth from the first to the fourth meaning of the term, and this is most likely the case. However, as this research is not about the growth of the Zion motif, but an analysis of a text that mentions Zion, I refrain from going into the debate about this motif's process of growth.

The significance of the motif Zion lies not in its topography, but in its theology. What theological concepts are typical for the motif Zion? The Old Testament Zion motif is tightly associated with the theology of the temple. J.D. Levenson has managed to define the term Zion in a way that includes many of its facets: "The term evokes a whole range of concepts having to do with the kingship, might, justice, and faithfulness of YHWH and the security and beatitude of those privileged to lodge in his sacred mountain in humility and faith and to witness his (re)enthronement upon it."[29] Zion is the residence of YHWH, and Zion is a cosmic centre. The Zion motif is especially evident in Psalms and Isaiah.[30] The subject of texts that mention Zion is not Zion *per se*, but YHWH. Often, the worship of the king of Zion (YHWH) is effectuated after a victory. Joy is therefore a prominent feature of the Zion tradition (Ps 48:3 [ET: 48:2]).[31] The Zion traditions express confidence in the God that fought against the chaos, and won. In the Zion theology, the chaos is no longer the waters, but rather the peoples. The privileged to dwell in Zion are secure as they trust the power of YHWH to master all assaults whether from raw nature or from the rebellious human heart. Mount Zion is in the end the place where YHWH manifests himself, and

---

[29] *Ibid.* 1099. See also R.J. Clifford, *The Cosmic Mountain in Canaan and the Old Testament* (1972) 157, who comments upon Isa 2:2–4 by stating: "With YHWH effectively ruling on his mountain, over the nations, there will be no need for men to fight."

[30] 46 of the 152 Old Testament occurrences of Zion are found in the book of Isaiah, whereas 37 are found in the Psalms. The traditionally designation "Zion traditions" are pronounced in Pss 2; 46; 48; 65; 76; 84; 87; 95–99; 110; 122; 125; 128 and 132. In the book of Isaiah the "Zion traditions" are most distinct in 8:5–10; 17:12–13; 18:1–7; 24:21–23; 25:6–12; 26:1–6; 30:27–33; 33: 5–6, 14–24; 37:33–38; 60–62; 65:17–25, and 66. Among these references, the term Zion is not always mentioned, however, the theological concepts associated with it are in abundant evidence. The term Zion evokes concepts having to do with kingship, might, justice, faithfulness of YHWH, security for those belonging to YHWH, the impregnability of the city, the idea of YHWH's victory in wars etc. It has been argued that the Zion theology in Isaiah is a later interpolation, cf. R.E. Clements, *Isaiah and the Deliverance of Jerusalem* (1980) 72–89. Cf. also E. Otto, "צִיּוֹן", *ThWAT* 6 (1989) 1007, who argues that only a few occurrences date reliably to the preexilic period. However, there are also scholars who think that the book of Isaiah has a well-developed Zion theology, cf. J.D. Levenson, *Sinai and Zion* (1985) 89–184, and J.H. Hayes & S.A. Irvine, *Isaiah* (1987) 54–56. In the present research it is presupposed that Zion was an established motif for the audience of Isa 18.

[31] For a brief discussion of what Ṣāphôn and Zion imply in this verse, see A. Robinson, "Zion and Ṣāphôn in Psalm XLVIII 3", *VT* 24 (1974) 118–123.

the place where all acceptable offerings must be brought. The city
is seen as a place for a stable lifestyle and of permanent relationships.[32] The city is a refuge for the people of YHWH who fear the
foreign peoples. The consequence of YHWH's victory at his holy
city is the futility of wars and weapons.[33] Another important feature
of the motif Zion is its connection to rivers. Like the Garden of
Eden, also Mount Zion is described as the source of life-giving waters,
and as a place of paradisiacal abundance (Gen 2:6–14; Pss 36:9 [ET:
36:8]; 46:5–6 [ET: 46:4–5]; Zech 14:8; Joel 4:18 [ET: 3:18]). In
contrast to the chaotic waters mentioned in Pss 46:3–4 [ET: 46:2–3]
and 65:7–8 [ET: 65:6–7], "[. . .] there is a river whose streams make
glad the city of God, the holy dwelling places of the Most High"
(Ps 46:5 [ET: 46:4]). This might be synonymous with "the gently
flowing waters of Shiloah [. . .]" referred to in Isa 8:6. The vision
of the new order of things in Ezek 47:1–12 describes how a spring
arises from the temple, and flows into the Dead Sea where it desalinises
it (Ezek 47:8): "This water flows toward the eastern region and goes
down into the Arabah, where it enters the Sea. When it empties
into the Sea, the water there becomes fresh." The same is envisioned in Zech 14:8 and Joel 4:18. A combination of rivers, Zion
and nations is found in Isa 66:12.

Two features of the motif are especially evident in Isa 18:7: (i)
YHWH's name is said to reside at Mount Zion, and (ii) Zion is here
mentioned in connection with rivers.

Gifts will be borne along to the place of the name of YHWH
Sebaoth—Mount Zion: אֶל־מְקוֹם שֵׁם־יהוה צְבָאוֹת הַר־צִיּוֹן. This expression needs some comments. The divine epithet צְבָאוֹת occurs 285
times throughout the Old Testament, and identifies a characteristic
of the Old Testament understanding of God.[34] The term צְבָאוֹת is
never used alone, and YHWH Sebaoth is the most frequently attested
combination.[35] The majority of occurrences are found in the prophetic
literature, mainly in Isaiah (56 of 62 occurrences in the book of
Isaiah are found in Isa 1–39) and Jeremiah (82).[36] Grammatically,

---

[32] Cf. Ps 107:4–7 which expresses the city as a place where people can settle in
contrast to the uninhabitable desert and wastelands.

[33] Cf. Ps 46:10–11 [ET: 46:9–10]; 76:4 [ET: 76:3]; Ezek 39:9–10.

[34] The various suggestions to what this epithet says about God will not be dealt
with here. For proposals, cf. H.-J. Zobel, "צְבָאוֹת", ThWAT 6 (1989) 880–881.

[35] Cf. ibid. 879.

[36] For the distribution of references to YHWH Sebaoth, cf. ibid. 878.

the term צבאות is plural with the feminine ending of the noun צבא, "army", "host" (1 Sam 17:45).[37] There is a strong linkage between the designation YHWH צבאות on the one hand, and Zion with the temple, on the other hand (cf. Isa 6:3, 5).[38] In the motif analysis above, we have already seen that YHWH צבאות is linked to Zion (cf. Pss 46:8, 12 [ET: 46:7, 11]; 48:9 [ET: 48:8]; 84:2, 4, 9, 13 [ET: 84:1, 3, 8, 12]). In Isa 8:18, YHWH Sebaoth is explicitly called "he who dwells on Mount Zion". Other texts that relate YHWH's dwelling place with Zion are for instance Pss 9:12 [ET: 9:11]; 43:3; 48:2–4 [ET: 48:1–3]; 76:3 [ET: 76:2]; 74:2; 99:2; 132:7, 13; Isa 8:18; 24:23; 33:20–21; Jer 8:19; Joel 4:17, 21 [ET: 3:17, 21]. The reference in Isa 18:7 to Mount Zion as the place where YHWH's name dwell shows a familiarity with a central Deuteronomic concept: YHWH has chosen a place to make his name dwell (Deut 12:5, 11).[39] The Isaiah Apocalypse describes that YHWH Sebaoth establishes his royal sway on Zion (Isa 24:23), and how he holds a banquet on this mountain (Isa 25:6). T.N.D. Mettinger sees this banquet in relation to the portrayal of how "[. . .] the nations will go up YHWH Sabaoth on Zion (Zech 14:16–17), bringing gifts (Isa 18:7)."[40] In Jer 3:17 there is a phrase concerning the name of YHWH that corresponds to Isa 18:7 and 60:9.[41] In all three texts the nations (or riches from them) are included in the pilgrimage to Zion. According to Mettinger, in the time of the exile, the combination YHWH and Sebaoth is no longer found. Instead, it is YHWH's *name* (שם) that occurs in conjunction with the sanctuary.[42] In Isa 18:7 YHWH's name is mentioned in connection with צבאות. What does this combination of

---

[37] Cf. Koehler-Baumgartner, *HALAT* (1983) 933–935. For various understandings of how Sebaoth is to be understood, cf. H.-J. Zobel, "צבאות", *ThWAT* 6 (1989) 879–881, 884–892.

[38] See T.N.D. Mettinger, "YHWH SABAOTH—The Heavenly King on the Cherubim Throne", *Studies in the Period of David and Solomon and Other Essays* (1982) 112.

[39] See O. Procksch, *Jesaia I* (1930) 243: "Diese Unterscheidung des "Namens" Jahves (cf. 30, 27) als wohnhaft am Kultorte von Jahve selbst erinnert an die Theologie des Deuteronomiums (Dt 12, 11. 14, 23. 16, 2.6.11. 26, 2. Jer 7, 7)." See also H. Wildberger, *Jesaja 13–27* (1978) 695, for the same point.

[40] See T.N.D. Mettinger, "YHWH SABAOTH—The Heavenly King on the Cherubim Throne", *Studies in the Period of David and Solomon and Other Essays* (1982) 112.

[41] See T.N.D. Mettinger, *The Dethronement of Sabaoth* (1982) 63.

[42] See *ibid.* 38: "In the Zion tradition, we encountered Lord Sabaoth on his cherubim throne in the *dĕbîr* of the Temple. However, if we remove to the time of the Exile the picture is radically different, since we no longer find Lord Sabaoth, but God's *šēm*, that is, his "Name", in conjunction with the sanctuary."

"YHWH Sebaoth" and "name" imply? As was mentioned in 7.1.2.,
it has been argued that the assertion in 18:7 that Mount Zion is
"the place of the name of YHWH Sebaoth" shows that this verse
is a late addendum. As has been said earlier in this book, many
scholars argue that Isa 18 most likely has experienced a process of
growth, but whether or not the combination of words in Isa 18:7
indicates that this verse is later than vv. 1–6 is a question that is
not dealt with here. The *search* for this text's process of growth is
not prioritised here as this research is occupied with showing how
Isa 18:1–7 as *an integral whole* expresses a consistent message. Evidently,
at least some redactor(s) must have regarded vv. 1–7 as suitable to
be read together as the text is transferred to us consisting of these
seven verses.

The other facet of the Zion motif that is of particular interest for
the understanding of Isa 18:7, is the connection of rivers with Zion.
The repetition of parts of v. 2 in v. 7 emphasises the rivers that are
connected to Cush. This association of rivers with Cush is also present in Gen 2:13 where one of the rivers of Eden is said to flow
around the entire land of Cush. Zeph 3:10 has the same combination, and—as we have seen—its mentioning of Cush makes it an
important communication partner for Isa 18:7. As said under the
treatment of the motif "gift", in Zeph 3:10, the "dispersed daughter"
of YHWH most likely refers to the people of YHWH living afar.
Thus, the people who approach Zion as referred to in Zeph 3:10
are not the remote Cushites—as is the case in Isa 18:7—but the dispersed ones from the people of YHWH. In Isa 18:7, then, the mentioning of rivers and Cush in connection with Zion makes an interesting
connection between Isa 18:7 and Gen 2:10–14 about the paradisiacal abundance of life-giving water that flows around Cush. An
identification of Eden and Zion is also known from Ezek 28:13–14.[43]
Along the same lines, Isa 18:7 and Gen 2:10–14 connect rivers, Zion
and Cush.[44] This serves the purpose of placing Cush as one of the
ends of the world, in a relationship with Zion.

From what has been said about the two motifs, "gift", and "Zion",
it is clear that v. 7 expresses the centripetal movement from the

---

[43] Cf. B.S. Childs, *Myth and Reality in the Old Testament* (1960) 87: "[. . .] the
prophetic description of Zion as a world-mountain receives its full significance. Zion
has become Eden."

[44] Cf. J.D. Levenson, *Sinai and Zion* (1985) 131.

nations (here represented by Cush) towards Zion.[45] The idea that nations shall come to Zion is known in three ways in the Old Testament: (i) the dispersed people of YHWH return by YHWH's power (Isa 11:11–12; Jer 31:8), (ii) the dispersed people of YHWH are transported back to Zion by the nations (Isa 60:4–9; 62:10–12; 66:12, 18–20),[46] (iii) the nations come towards Zion and receive restoration together with YHWH's people (Ps 68:32 [ET: 68:31]). In Isa 18:7, the latter meaning seems to be the most likely. Verse 7 says that the foreign Cushites will bring gifts to YHWH on Mount Zion.[47]

Summing up the features in the text's motifs
From the observations above, we have seen that Isa 18:7 contains a repetition of some of what is said in 18:2. The motif analysis of v. 7 has therefore concentrated on two motifs that are *not* mentioned in v. 2: "gift", and "Zion". The former motif is not often applied throughout the Old Testament, whereas the latter motif has a wide range of connotations attached to it. The motif "gift" is in Isa 18:7 applied in a context where it associates with the nations' pilgrimage towards Zion (here represented by Cush). In accordance with how the motif Zion is applied in the Old Testament, it has been argued that in 18:7 Zion is referred to as the place where YHWH's name dwells, and as the place where the nations will come in eschatological times. By repeating rivers (from v. 2) in connection with Zion, and by connecting Cush to Zion (v. 7), this verse seems to carry some of the same associations as the narrative about the Garden of Eden in Gen 2:10–14.

---

[45] Here, and throughout this study, "centripetal" refers to the movement of the nations towards Zion. ("Centrifugal" stands for the opposite movement, *from* Zion towards the nations). For this usage of the terms, see for instance J. Blenkinsopp, *Isaiah 1–39* (2000) 311, who applies the term "centripetal" in this meaning in his analysis of Isa 18:7.

[46] For a recent contribution to a reading of Isa 60 and its function in the book as a whole, see G.J. Polan, "Zion, the Glory of the Holy One of Israel: A Literary Analysis of Isaiah 60", *Imagery and Imagination in Biblical Literature* (2001) 50–71.

[47] That a conversion of the nations might be implicitly stated in Isa 18:7 is mentioned by H. Wildberger, *Jesaja 13–27* (1978) 695.

7.4. RHETORICAL ANALYSIS

As already mentioned in the motif analysis, the theme of *a centripetal movement of the nations to Zion* are known from several Old Testament texts: cf. Isa 2:2–4; 60:3; Jer 31:8; Mic 4:6–7, Zech 2:14–16. YHWH's name will be declared in Zion when the peoples and the kingdoms assemble to worship him, cf. Ps 102:22–23. The remnant of the people of YHWH will also come to Zion: Jer 3:14; 31:12; 50:5. Similar to 18:3, Isa 27:13 refers to trumpets that will sound when the remnant of YHWH's people will come to Zion. Could the blowing of horns referred to in Isa 18:3 be interpreted as announcing the collection of the people of YHWH, as is the case in Isa 27:13? Isa 27:13 describes the centripetal movement towards Zion, and links YHWH with the holy mountain in Jerusalem (= Zion). The standard that shall be lifted up (18:3) is elsewhere found in relation to the centripetal movement of the nations towards Zion, cf. Isa 11:10–12. Isa 62:10 applies the same term for the coming of the nations to Zion. When the people of YHWH will return to Zion, a standard will be raised, Jer 50:2.

As we have seen, tied to the motif Zion are the visions of peace. Pacifism is not what is meant, rather the limitless scope of YHWH's triumph is the basis of the visions (cf. Ps 46:10–11; 76:4 and Ezek 39:9–10). YHWH's reign over the nations together with his dominance over the world ensures that weapons will not be needed. Subsequently, the acceptance of YHWH's domination secures peace on earth. It is in this context the pilgrimage of the nations is to be understood (cf. Isa 2:2–4, paralleled in Mic 4:1–4; Isa 66:18–24; Zech 2:14–16). Connected to the centripetal movement of the nations is the bringing of gifts to YHWH on Zion. What meanings does this motif imply? First, the centripetal movement can imply that the exiles (YHWH's people) might return by their own power. Second, the exiles might be transported back to Zion by the nations. Third, the centripetal meaning of this motif can imply that the nations come to Zion and attain salvation. As we have seen, the third meaning is the most plausible in Isa 18:7. Theologically, v. 7 concludes by underlining the point that YHWH has the authority over all nations of the world.[48] Even the feared Cushites (Isa 18:2) have to submit under YHWH.[49]

---

[48] For a similar view, cf. H. Wildberger, *Jesaja 13–27* (1978) 695.
[49] This interpretation of v. 7 is also held by H. Wildberger, *ibid.* 696–697.

7.4.1. *Rhetorical features in the text's design*

Syntactic observations: Gapping
The gapping in v. 7aβ, and v. 7bα functions to make the text somewhat ambiguous when it comes to the gifts that are said to be given
to YHWH on Mount Zion. On the one hand, as the preposition
"from" in MT is only included in v. 7aγ, one could perceive v. 7aβ
and v. 7bα in the sense that the "people tall and smooth-skinned"
themselves are gifts brought to YHWH on Zion. On the other hand,
if one follows 1Q Isaᵃ, LXX and the Vulgate, and includes a preposition, the gifts are understood as something brought to YHWH at
Mount Zion *from* "a people tall and smooth-skinned". Although there
is a slight uncertainty whether the gifts are borne along from the
Cushites, or whether the Cushites themselves are to be perceived as
gifts, this ambiguity does not question the statement that the Cushites
in some or the other way are to be represented at Zion.

Semantic observations: Repetition of parts of v. 2
At a first glance it looks as if verse 7 merely repeats what has been
said about the Cushites in v. 2, and as such, this repetition seems
quite unnecessary. This seems however not to be the case. The repetition serves to *develop* the information in v. 2 by transforming the
portrayal of the Cushites as warriors and politicians (v. 2) into a portrayal of the same Cushites as submitting themselves under YHWH
on Zion. The reappearance of what E.J. Kissane calls "[. . .] the
obscure terms of the description in 2d–g [. . .]" in v. 7 is by him
seen to indicate that the writer was not able to identify the nation
referred to in the beginning of the text.[50] In my view, this is not the
case. Rather, the repetition of the detailed description of the Cushites
and their land serves to put this nation in relation with Zion and
YHWH. By explicitly referring to Cushites and rivers, and by connecting these two entities with Zion, we have already seen that Isa
18:7 and Gen 2:10–14 have some of the same associations.

Poetic technique: The reintroduction of the Cushites forms an inclusio
We have observed that the only *other* character that is mentioned in
v. 7 apart from the Cushites is YHWH Sebaoth. As the reference

---

[50] Cf. E.J. Kissane, *The Book of Isaiah* (1960) 200.

to YHWH Sebaoth opens and closes v. 7 (see v. 7aα and 7bγ), this
functions to let YHWH Sebaoth *frame* the verse. This serves to focus
on YHWH Sebaoth, and to let the Cushites submit themselves before
the deity.

Another important feature of v. 7 is the reintroduction of the
Cushites. The description of the Cushites in v. 7 seems at a first
glance to be merely an over-specification since this group has already
been thoroughly introduced in v. 2.[51] However, there are several
functions of this repetition. First, it functions to make up the boundaries of the poem, and thereby to form an *inclusio* of Isa 18 as a
whole. Second, this reintroduction and over-specification function to
form a new stanza. Third, the repetition also serves to create a contrast to the negative message of vv. 5–6, as it begins a new positive
theme (the centripetal movement of the nations towards Zion). Fourth,
the repetition of parts of v. 2 in v. 7 functions to comment upon
what is said earlier about the Cushites as it emphasises a new role
of the Cushites in the future.[52]

Summing up the rhetorical features in the text's design
Through the observations about the textual design of Isa 18:7, we
have seen that the negative message of judgement in vv. 5–6 has
now been replaced by a positive description of how the Cushites "in
that time" will bring gifts to YHWH Sebaoth on Mount Zion. This
positive message is pronounced the following ways: First, *cohesion*
between the six lines of v. 7 is created as the reference to YHWH
Sebaoth frames this verse. Second, also in this verse an *activity* is
described as the Cushites are envisioned to come forth to Zion with
gifts. Third, *concentration* on what will happen on Zion is created as
the character YHWH Sebaoth is mentioned twice. Further, as the
only characters who are mentioned are the Cushites and YHWH
Sebaoth, this concentrates the attention to what will happen when
they encounter. Fourth, the *confusion* that was resolved when the message of vv. 5–6 was given is further put an end to. As the message

---

[51] On over-specification in general, see L.J. de Regt, *Participants in Old Testament
Texts* (1999) 57–72.
[52] For a relationship between what is said in vv. 5–6 and in v. 7, see M.A.
Sweeney, *Isaiah 1–39* (1996) 257: "The presentation of this gift 'at that time' associates it with YHWH's 'trimming of the shoots' and indicates that it is the result
of the Ethiopians' witness of YHWH's punishment of Israel."

of v. 7 is spoken out, the audience can no longer be in doubt that the Judeans will be judged by YHWH (vv. 5–6), and that the Cushites will be welcomed by YHWH (v. 7).

7.4.2. *Rhetorical features in the text's motifs*

Gift: Homage to YHWH Sebaoth on Mount Zion

From what has been said about the motif שׁי, "gift" above, it is clear that this motif is applied in 18:7 in the sense of bringing homage to YHWH Sebaoth. As the tall and smooth-skinned people from along the rivers of Cush are the *deliverers* of the שׁי, and YHWH Sebaoth on Mount Zion is the *receiver*, this functions to show a connection between this remote people and YHWH.[53] As the preposition "from" is lacking in v. 7aβ and v. 7bα, it is somewhat unclear whether the people themselves are to be understood as gifts, or if they carry gifts with them to YHWH on Zion.[54] This serves to underline the atmosphere of submission of the Cushites in front of the deity. Further, the mentioning of the Cushites in relation to YHWH on Zion functions to let the Cushites *represent* the nations that will come to Zion in eschatological times (this motif is well-known from the Old Testament, see 7.3. in this book).[55]

Another important function of this reference to the Cushites as bringing gifts to YHWH is the text's arguing against the Judean wish to enter into coalitions with foreign peoples. As has been pointed at many times throughout this book, Isa 18 tries to motivate Judah not

---

[53] J. Blenkinsopp, *Isaiah 1–39* (2000) 311, questions who are the deliverers of the gift brought to YHWH on Zion: "The scholiast provides no clue as to whether he understood these Nubians to be Gentiles, proselytes, or diaspora Jews." It is my contention that the deliverers referred to in v. 7 are the same people as was described in v. 2. For this latter view, see for instance R.E. Clements, *Isaiah 1–39* (1980/1994) 166.

[54] Cf. F. Buhl, *Jesaja* (1894) 288: "[. . .] Offergaven dog næppe bestaar i Æthioperfolket selv [. . .]".

[55] Cf. E.J. Young, *The Book of Isaiah* (1965/1978) 478, H.M. Wolf, *Interpreting Isaiah* (1985) 122, A. Laato, *"About Zion I will not be silent"* (1998) 73, and R.S. Sadler, "Can a Cushite Change His Skin? An Examination of Race, Ethnicity, and Othering in the Hebrew Bible" (2001) 112. Not all will consider v. 7 as dealing with eschatological times, cf. J.H. Brangenberg, "A Reexamination of the Date, Authorship, Unity and Function of Isaiah 13–23" (1989) 304, who suggests that "[t]he Ethiopians may simply be acknowledging the power of Yahweh and offering thanks for his defeat of their chief rival [. . .]". See also J.D.W. Watts, *Isaiah 1–33* (1985) 246, and C.R. Seitz, *Isaiah 1–39* (1993) 149.

to find an ally other than YHWH. The rhetoric of the text says that
if she does not follow the prophet's advice, she will be punished.
The depiction of the Cushites as submitting themselves under YHWH
at Zion is a rhetorical device functioning to persuade the Judeans
to be quiet and not take any actions towards political alliances. Even
the attractive Cushite ally (vv. 1–2) of Judah will have to cast herself under YHWH (v. 7).[56] Judah should take notice, and rely on
YHWH who is capable of making order out of chaos (17:12–14). If
Judah will not listen to the message from YHWH, but rather to the
messengers to and from Cush, she will be judged (18:5–6).

Zion: The place of the name of YHWH Sebaoth
In accordance with how the motif Zion is applied in the Old
Testament, it has been argued above that in 18:7 Zion is referred
to as the place where YHWH's name dwells, and as the place where
the nations will come in eschatological times. The identification of
Zion as YHWH's cosmic mountain is clear in Isa 18:7. The vision
of peoples coming to Zion is common in the Old Testament, and
here Cush serves as a representative for the nations that is envisioned to approach Zion in eschatological times. That the remote
Cushites are welcomed to Zion serves to continue the harsh judgement over Judah as referred to in vv. 5–6. Those who the Judeans
look up to and wants to attach themselves to (vv. 1–2) will come to
Zion, whereas YHWH's people are metaphorically spoken about as
tendrils and twigs that will be cut off, cast away and devoured by
the birds and animals. In addition, by repeating rivers (Isa 18, v. 2
and v. 7) in connection with Zion, v. 7 seems to carry some of the
same associations as the narrative about the Garden of Eden does
in Gen 2:10–14. Both Isa 18:7 and the creation narrative serves the
purpose of placing Cush in a relationship with YHWH. Cush is
related to YHWH from the beginning to the end, from Eden to
eschatological times.

Summing up the rhetorical features in the text's motifs
The two motifs that have been discussed above are "gift" and "Zion".
From what has been observed, both motifs are positively applied in

---

[56] Cf. S.H. Widyapranawa, *The Lord is Saviour* (1990) 107.

Isa 18:7. The gifts that will be given to YHWH Sebaoth on Mount Zion are from the people of the remote nation Cush. This reference to a foreign nation who brings gifts to YHWH functions to put Isa 18:7 in relation with other Old Testament texts that portrays the centripetal movement of the nations towards Zion. Further, as Zion is the place where the name of YHWH Sebaoh dwells, this strengthens the relations between the remote nation Cush and YHWH. As the two foregoing verses (vv. 5–6) have pronounced a devastating doom over the people of YHWH, this positive speech about the including of the Cushites at Zion stands in sharp contrast to what is metaphorically said will happen to the Judeans (vv. 5–6).

7.4.3. *How do textual design and motifs together create the strophe's rhetoric?*

Cohesion: YHWH Sebaoth frames the verse
Semantically, the first and last line of v. 7 mentions YHWH Sebaoth. Further, the four lines that remain of this verse all describe the Cushites. This way of designing the verse creates a verse that coheres.

Activity: The Cushites move towards Zion
By reintroducing the motif "Cush" (known from v. 2) in v. 7, an atmosphere of activity is again created. However, the activity described in v. 7 is different from that referred to in vv. 1–2. In v. 7, the only active agents are the Cushites who are envisaged to approach Zion with gifts to YHWH Sebaoth. The receiver of the gifts, YHWH Sebaoth, is the non-active receiving part, whereas the Cushites are active as they are depicted as being in movement *from* (מן, v. 7aγ) their land *to* (ל, v. 7aα and אל, v. 7bγ) the place of the name of YHWH Sebaoth—Mount Zion.

Concentration: YHWH Sebaoth on Mount Zion is in the centre of attention
That v. 7 is designed in a way where YHWH Sebaoth frames the verse has the function of letting the deity be in the centre of attention, and not human beings or human plans—whatever they ought to be. This twofold reference to YHWH Sebaoth in v. 7 also functions to put the divinity in the centre, and not mankind. This stands in sharp contrast to the message of vv. 5–6 where the people of YHWH is the ones who are described metaphorically. That the only characters of v. 7 are YHWH Sebaoth and the Cushites functions to concentrate the attention to what is happening in their encounter.

Confusion resolved: The remote Cushites are welcomed at Mount Zion
The confusion that has kept the audience in tension for a while has
been resolved as the message of vv. 5–6 has been given. However,
when the message of v. 7 is spoken out, the audience knows that
the Cushites are welcomed at Zion—the place of the name of YHWH
Sebaoth (v. 7). The destiny of the Judeans however, depends on who
they see as their primary ally—human beings or YHWH, cf. Isa 31:
1 and 3:

> Woe to those who go down to Egypt for help, and rely on horses,
> and trust in the multitude of their chariots and in the great strength
> of their horsemen, but do not look to the Holy One of Israel, or seek
> help from YHWH. [. . .] Now the Egyptians are men and not God.
> Their horses are flesh and not spirit. When YHWH stretches out his
> hand, he who helps will stumble, he who is helped will fall, both will
> perish together.

Summing up the rhetoric in the text's design and motifs
Through the analysis of textual design and motifs of Isa 18:7 it has
been showed that this verse consists of six lines where the first and
the last both refer to YHWH Sebaoth. This strophe shows further
a deliberate rhetoric. This is seen the following ways: First, as a
deliberate rhetoric can only be efficient if what is said makes sense,
there has been observed that this verse *coheres*. Second, both textual
design and motifs of Isa 18:7 create an atmosphere of *activity*. The
human characters who are mentioned in this verse, the Cushites, are
referred to as moving towards Zion, and this functions to create a
sense of activity. Further, as the Cushites bring gifts, this activity is
also described in this verse. Third, both textual design and motifs
concentrate on YHWH Sebaoth. This divine character frames the verse,
and as the motif Zion is strongly associated with YHWH throughout the Old Testament, this serves to emphasise on YHWH. Fourth,
the *confusion* that was resolved by vv. 5–6 has made it clear that the
Judeans are judged, and that the Cushites are described in relation
to YHWH Sebaoth on Mount Zion.

7.5. CONTEXTUAL ANALYSIS

Are there any connections at all by means of textual design, motifs
or rhetorical drive between the two first stanzas (vv. 1–2 and vv. 3–6)
on the one hand, and the third stanza (v. 7), on the other hand?

7.5.1. *Textual design*

The choice of various characters in Isa 18 entraps the audience, and the rein-
troduction of the Cushites in v. 7 forms an inclusio
Concerning Isa 18's textual design, there are two elements that are
important when speaking about relations from part to part of the text.

First, as the analysis of this text has showed, the characters vary
from part to part in Isa 18. In vv. 1–2 the major characters are the
Cushites, whereas in vv. 3–6 several groups of characters are mentioned: "all" (v. 3), YHWH, "me" (v. 4), YHWH (v. 5), non-human
characters birds and beasts (v. 6). As was observed in 6.5.1., the
characters vary in status in vv. 3–6. YHWH is the major participant in this stanza, whereas "me" takes the role of a mediator
(v. 4), and a spectator (vv. 5–6). Whereas this constant shift of characters functions to confuse the audience when it comes to *who* will
be judged (only resolved in vv. 5–6), the reference to the characters
YHWH and the Cushites in v. 7 serves to extend the humiliation
of the Judeans. In v. 7 the Judeans are not mentioned explicitly,
whereas the Cushites are envisioned to approach YHWH Sebaoth
on Mount Zion. This way of choosing various characters from strophe to strophe functions to entrap the Judeans to believe that somebody other than themselves will be judged. When their belief turns
out to be incorrect (vv. 5–6), the strong emphasis on Cushites in
relation to YHWH (in v. 7) functions to contrast and also to underscore the harsh message of doom towards the Judeans.

Second, as has been dealt with earlier, the reintroduction of the
Cushites (from v. 2 to v. 7) can be seen as somewhat superfluous as
the Cushites were thoroughly portrayed in the opening lines of the
text. However, from the viewpoint of the text's design, this dupli-
cation of the detailed portrayal of the Cushites in v. 7 functions to
form an *inclusio*. As such, the repetition is not unnecessary, but rather
an elegant way of bringing together the various parts of Isa 18. As
has been mentioned before, this repetition of the description of the
Cushites and their land functions to focus on Cush, and thereby to
entrap the audience to believe that this speech is concerned with
their attractive alliance partner, and not with themselves.

7.5.2. *Motifs*

The motifs of Isa 18:7 announce an eschatological restoration for the nations
Are there any relations between the motifs of vv. 1–2, 3–6, and v. 7?
As is obvious to everyone, there are strong connections between
vv. 1–2 and v. 7 as v. 7 contains a repetition of the detailed description of the Cushites found in v. 2. As the motif Cush in v. 7 is
applied in a different context from what is the case in vv. 1–2, this
repetition functions to *develop* the motif as the Cushites are no longer
seen as attractive coalition partner, but part of the eschatological
restoration of the nations that will submit under YHWH at Zion.[57]
    Are there any connections between vv. 3–6 on the one hand, and
vv. 1–2 and 7 on the other hand? Let us look at a few examples.
An intensifying effect is created from v. 3 to v. 7 as "all" the nations
are mentioned in v. 3, whereas one specific nation (Cush) is mentioned in v. 7. As has been pointed at in the analysis of v. 3, the
motifs "mountain", "standard", and "horn" of v. 3 widen the perspective. This widening of the perspective prepares for what is explicitly referred to in v. 7 when the nations—here represented by the
Cushites—are coming to Zion.[58] Likewise, the "mountain" of v. 3
(and v. 6) prepares for the mentioning of one particular mountain—
Zion in v. 7. There is a rhetorical development from v. 3 (and
v. 6) to v. 7 as v. 3 and (v. 6) mention mountains in general, whereas
v. 7 talks about the particular Mount Zion—the place of the name
of YHWH. This development with view to usage of the motif "mountain" is powerful as it shows an inner-textual intensifying from the
general (v. 3 and 6) to the specific (v. 7). Allusion to the specific
Mount Zion is also seen in v. 4. Here, the motif "YHWH's dwelling
place" draws lines to the explicitly mentioned Mount Zion in v. 7—
the place of the name of YHWH Sebaoth. Further, the function of
the motif "horn" in 18:3 is twofold. It is a warning signal about a
judgement that is forthcoming if Judah will not repent (vv. 5–6). At
the same time, it signals (together with the standard) that the nations

---

[57] An opposite view of how the repetition of parts of v. 2 in v. 7 functions, is
pronounced by J. Jensen, *Isaiah 1–39* (1984) 165: "[. . .] this is out of harmony with
the context of the preceding verses [. . .]".

[58] This relation between v. 3 and v. 7 is also seen by and F. Buhl, *Jesaja* (1894)
288: "[. . .] Æthioperne, der nævnes som Repræsentanten for de øvrige Folkeslag
v. 3 [. . .]". See also F. Feldmann, *Das Buch Isaias* (1925) 221, and H. Wildberger,
Jesaja 13–27 (1978) 694.

will approach Jerusalem "in that time" (v. 7). As שׁופר and נס is mentioned together in Isa 18:3, this gives associations to texts such as
Isa 11:12 where the standard is lifted in order to announce the coming of the nations to Zion (cf. Isa 11:12). Along these lines the horn
and standard in 18:3 forecast the events that will come "in that
time" (v. 7). K.D. Jenner sees the sound of the horn as a warning
signal in order to announce the return of the exiles to Israel: "In
Isa 18:3 it is announced by blowing upon the shofar and raising the
standard that a present will be brought to Mount Zion."[59]

At a first glance there seems to be no connections between vv.
5–6 on the one hand, and vv. 1–2 and v. 7 on the other hand
(except the mentioning of "mountain" in v. 6 and in Zion in v. 7).
However, the metaphorical speech about Judah (vv. 5–6) that pronounces judgement is related to how the motif Cush is presented in
vv. 1–2 and 7. Judah's active search for a coalition partner (vv. 1–2)
is the *reason why* Judah is harshly punished (vv. 5–6), and this devastating doom over YHWH's people creates a contrast to v. 7 where
the motif Cush is reintroduced, but now in a different setting. Verse
2 describes a movement *to* the Cushites, whereas in v. 7 the movement goes *from* the Cushites to YHWH on Mount Zion. As already
pointed at, v. 7 develops verse 2 and transforms the portrayal of the
Cushites as warriors and politicians (v. 2) into a portrayal of the
same Cushites as bringing homage to YHWH on Zion (v. 7).[60] This
including of the Cushites at Zion represents a positive development
of the portrayal of them.

7.5.3. Rhetoric

*The eschatological restoration of the nations contrasts the harsh judgement of
Judah (vv. 5–6)*
Last, are there relations in the sense of rhetorical drive between the
three stanzas of Isa 18? The most important endeavour of this

---

[59] Cf. K.D. Jenner, "The Big Shofar (Isaiah 27:13): A Hapax Legomenon", *Studies
in Isaiah 24–27* (2000) 173.
[60] W. Brueggemann, *Isaiah 1–39* (1998) 154, does not see this developing portrayal of the Cushites as something positive, he rather perceives it as a weakening:
"The Ethiopians are no more 'swift ambassadors', but now are reduced to suppli-
ants who come to Jerusalem, not to bargain and negotiate but to submit. The image
is of representatives bringing tribute money, the losers placating the winners."
Further, Brueggemann takes v. 7 as irony, cf. p. 159: "They may be 'smooth and
tall', but now they are defeated and no longer feared near or far."

research has been to show that Isa 18 as a whole is shaped in a way that tries to pursue the Judeans *not* to seek human allies, but to rely on help from YHWH. It is not necessary to repeat what has already been said in 6.5.3. about the rhetorical drive of vv. 1–2 in relation to vv. 3–6, it should only be added some comments about how v. 7 functions in relation to these two stanzas. As already said in 6.5.3., the choice of words that give an overwhelmingly positive description of the Cushites (in vv. 1–2) functions to entrap the audience to regard Cush as an attractive coalition partner. At the same time, however, as a הוֹי is shouted over this nation, the audience is confused when it comes to who will be judged in this speech. What becomes clear later in the speech (vv. 5–6) is that this הוֹי prepares for the judgement over Judah, but at the opening of the speech, this הוֹי functions to let the audience think this is directed towards Cush. As YHWH is referred to as quiet (v. 4), this behaviour is meant to be a pattern for Judah when it comes to political allies. When v. 7 not explicitly mentions the Judeans, but refers to Cush in relation to YHWH on Mount Zion, this can function to humiliate the Judeans even more than what has already been done by the message of vv. 5–6. Even the strong and feared Cushites—that Judah put her trust in—will have to submit under YHWH one day, and this tells the audience of Isa 18 that *YHWH* should be Judah's ally, and *not* any strong and powerful nation.

CHAPTER EIGHT

CONCLUSION

From the analysis above, we have seen that the range of interpretations that have been proposed to this text have led to quite an array of views and certainly one cannot speak of agreement among scholars on many aspects of the discussion. However, it is possible to observe three viewpoints that have emerged in recent years, all of which I think are plausible: (i) An awareness of literary approaches has opened a possibility to approach this text with different questions from those of traditional historical critical methods. (ii) This has led to a situation where there is an increasing recognition that vv. 1–7 can be read as a unit. (iii) This has inaugurated an interest in the text's literary features and qualities, and not merely the text's presumed references to historical situations. However, in order to clarify the results of the *present* study, three questions will be briefly answered in the following: First, what has been analysed in this book? Second, in what way have I pursued the analysis? Third, what are the results of the present analysis?

First, this book has had the rhetoric of Isa 18 as its subject of investigation, and as such, the present work is a literary study. Let me illustrate this point by referring to how "Cush" is treated here. In the present work Cush is dealt with as a literary motif, and as such, the way the motif Cush *functions* in Isa 18 is central—at the expense of discussions about its geographical location and historical attestation. In the motif analysis to Isa 18:1–2 above, we have seen that most commentators encounter the term Cush by going into questions about the historical and geographical background of this entity—at the expense of a discussion of how Cush functions as a literary motif. This research goes the opposite way and emphasises how Cush is applied as a literary motif, and contributes in this way with a new perspective on the text. As the present analysis of Isa 18 is done from a literary, and not an historical perspective, factors outside the text (such as geography and history) have not been discussed to a certain degree. I have however not divorced the analysis completely from elements outside the text as it is clear that Isa

18 refers to relations between nations, and evidently describes a foreign nation. However, my project in this research has not been to *reconstruct* historical events the text might refer to. That would certainly demand an investigation of its own. Rather, my emphasis has been on textual design, literary motifs and themes, and on how these function to create a persuasive rhetoric.

Second, in order to pursue an analysis of the rhetoric of Isa 18, the present work has found it adequate to approach each strophe from the following four angles: text and translation, textual design, motifs, and rhetorical analysis. In addition, after each stanza I have asked whether or not there are connections between this and the foregoing stanza(s), and this procedure has been labelled contextual analysis. Under the heading *text and translation*, textual critical, translational, and/or syntactical problems have been discussed. *Textual design* has observed how each strophe is arranged phonetically, syntactically, and semantically. Further, poetic techniques have been described. Under the heading *motifs*, each strophe's central motifs have been identified. Further, the motifs' Old Testament usage in general have been presented, before their application in Isa 18 in particular have been advocated. Under the heading *rhetorical analysis*, I have started by showing what thematic perspectives each strophe carry. Further, the rhetorical features in the text's design and motifs have been described, and last, I have argued how textual design and motifs work together to create the rhetoric of the strophe. Although *textual design* and *motifs* both contribute to build the rhetoric of Isa 18, it has been suitable throughout the work to distinguish between the *description* of the various elements in the text (textual design and literary motifs) on the one hand, and how these elements *function* in order to create the rhetorical shape of the text (rhetorical analysis), on the other hand.

Third, by pursuing a literary analysis of the rhetoric of Isa 18, the results of the present work contribute to the understanding of the text as an integral unit. The message of Isa 18 is that of judgement over Judah—unless she understands the warning and changes her behaviour. To pass this message of judgement over to the audience of Isa 18, the text sometimes confuses the audience (vv. 1–2), whereas other times it delivers a message that is not to be misunderstood (v. 5). In short, the story of Isa 18 is the following: All the activity from the Judean side in order to entering into a coalition with the Cushites is in vain (vv. 1–2). What Judah should take notice of is the following: As YHWH is quiet (v. 4), so should also Judah be. If Judah does not follow YHWH's example, but rather goes on with her alliance making, the judgement will be effectuated in a way that does not even leave a remnant (vv. 5–6). This metaphoric speech strikes Judah as vine and vineyard are commonly applied metaphors in the Old Testament for YHWH's people. Verse 7 shows an eschatological restoration for the nations—here represented by Cush.

At the end of each chapter throughout this book, the text's rhetoric of entrapment has been summed up by the following four head words: *cohesion, activity, confusion,* and *concentration.* Let us now briefly go through Isa 18 and see how this rhetoric of entrapment is visible. In Isa 18 scenes are shifting from strophe to strophe, and at a first glance, the text as a whole seems not to *cohere.* The motif Cush is referred to in vv. 1–2 and 7, whereas vv. 3–6 contain scenes where Cush is not present. The question has then been whether there are any connections at all between 18:1–2 and 7 on the one hand, and vv. 3–6 on the other hand. By the way the text opens (הוֹי towards Cush), the audience is ensnared to believe that Cush will be judged. However, only positive attributes are applied to describe Cush in the following (v. 2), and the hectic diplomatic *activity* between Cush and Judah makes the audience feel *confused* about who is judged in this speech. The confusion continues in verse 3 addresses "all inhabitants of the world" and does not mention Cush with a word. In v. 4 a new scene reports YHWH's quietness, and as the speech carries on (vv. 5–6), the scene has again changed as vine tendrils and twigs are reported to be cut down and given to the birds of prey and beasts of the earth. In v. 7, the text *concentrates* again on the Cushites as they are described in positive terms as bringing gifts to YHWH on Zion. How does this cohere? The present analysis of Isa 18:1–7 has demonstrated that this text is an example of Hebrew rhetoric, and that it can be regarded as a coherent whole. From the motif analysis it has been argued that the confusion about who will be judged in this speech is resolved as the metaphorical language of v. 5 hits the Judeans, and *not* a foreign nation. As the motif "vineyard" is commonly applied in the Old Testament as a metaphor for the people of YHWH (cf. Isa 5:1–7), the metaphorical speech of cutting down vine tendrils and twigs (v. 5) functions to deliver a message of judgement over Judah because Judah seeks help by human beings instead of by YHWH (18:1–2). We have seen from the text's design that alliteration, sound patterns, play with words, chiastic patterns, *inclusio* etc., together with poetic techniques all serve a function in the over-all rhetorical strategy of pronouncing a harsh message of doom towards the Judeans (see the analysis of each strophe). Also the text's choice of motifs has a specific purpose of persuading the Judeans not to enter into coalitions with foreign nations (in this text exemplified by Cush). The message of vv. 5–6 functions to let the audience eventually grasp that the speech as a whole concerns themselves. When v. 5 is heard, and this point is understood, the various parts of Isa 18 fall into place, and makes the text *cohere*: The quietness of YHWH reported in v. 4 functions as a request to Judah to be quiet and *not* enter into alliances with other nations, but rely on YHWH (cf. Isa 14:32; 30:1–5; 31:1–3). The *confusing* opening of the speech (first הוי over Cush, and then a positive portrayal of the nation) functions as a ridiculing of the Judean leaders who *actively* want to establish an alliance with Cush. Finally, the eschatological vision of the bringing of gifts from Cush (v. 7) shows an eschatological restoration for the nations—here represented by Cush—and also that even the strong and down-treading remote nation that Judah looks to for help has to acknowledge the authority of YHWH Sebaoth at Zion. However, if Judah will not *concentrate* on the message from YHWH, but rather rely on human beings (here represented by Cush), she will be judged (18:5–6). Although the opening of Isa 18 can look like a judgement over Cush, the present analysis of the chapter as a whole has showed that the ones who are reported to be judged are the Judeans (vv. 5–6), and nobody else. However, although the judgement over Judah is harsh (vv. 5–6), the text does open for a restoration in the future. Even though both tendrils and twigs of the vine are cut down and given to the birds and beasts (vv. 5–6), the roots of the vine are still intact. And as long as the vine has its roots planted in the soil, there is always hope for a new beginning.

BIBLIOGRAPHY[1]

The following bibliography lists only works that are explicitly referred to in this book.

Biblia Sacra Iuxta Vulgatam Versionem. Vols. 1–2. Ed. by B. Fischer & al. Stuttgart: Würtembergische Bibelanstalt 1969.
Septuaginta. Ed. by A. Rahlfs. Stuttgart: Deutsche Bibelgesellschaft 1979.
Septuaginta. Vetus Testamentum Graecum. Isaias. Ed. by J. Ziegler. Göttingen: Vandenhoeck & Ruprecht 1939 (SLittG 14).
Tanakh—The Holy Scriptures. The New JPS Translation According to the Traditional Hebrew Text. Philadelphia, New York: The Jewish Publication Society 1988.
The Great Isaiah Scroll (1Q Isa^a). A New Edition. Ed. by D.W. Parry & E. Qimron. Leiden: Brill 1999 (StTDJ 32).
The Hebrew University Bible. The Book of Isaiah. Ed. by M.H. Goshen-Gottstein. Jerusalem: The Magnes Press 1995.
The Old Testament in Syriac according to the Peshitta Version. Ed. by the Peshitta Institute, Leiden: E.J. Brill 1972ff.

Adamo, D.T., *Africa and Africans in the Old Testament.* San Francisco, California: Christian University Press 1998 (ISP).
———, "Amos 9:7–8 in an African Perspective", *Orita* 24 (1992) 76–84.
———, "Ethiopia in the Bible", *AfrCSt* 8 (1992) 51–64.
———, "The African Wife of Moses: An Examination of Numbers 12:1–9", *ATJ* 18 (1989) 230–237.
———, "The Black Prophet in the Old Testament", *JARSt* 4 (1987) 1–8.
———, "The Table of Nations Reconsidered in African Perspective (Genesis 10)", *JARP* 2 (1993) 138–143.
Aharoni, Y. & Amiran, R., "Arad: A Biblical City in Southern Palestine", *Arch.* 17 (1964) 43–53.
———, "Excavations at Tel Arad. Preliminary Report on the First Season, 1962", *IEJ* 14 (1964) 131–147.
Aharoni, Y., *The Land of the Bible. A Historical Geography.* Tr. by A.F. Rainey. London: Burns & Oates 1962/1967.
Alexander, J.A., *The Prophecies of Isaiah.* New York, New York: Charles Scribner 1870.
Alfrink, B., "Der Versammlungsberg im äussersten Norden (Is. 14)", *Bib.* 14 (1933) 41–67.
Allen, L.C., "Ezekiel 24:3–14: A Rhetorical Perspective", *CBQ* 49 (1987) 404–414.
Alonso Schökel, L., *A Manual of Hebrew Poetics.* Roma: Editrice Pontificio Instituto Biblico 1988 (SubBi 11).

---

[1] The observant reader has probably noticed that the bibliographical data sometimes include two years, see for instance W.G.E. Watson, *Classical Hebrew Poetry. A Guide to its Techniques.* Sheffield: JSOT Press, 1984/1986 (JSOT.S; 26). Throughout this work, when two years are listed, this means that I have always used the most recent edition, but that I am aware of the earlier edition.

——, *Estudios de poética Hebrea*. Barcelona: Juan Flors 1963.

Alter, R., *The Art of Biblical Narrative*. London: George Allen & Unwin 1981.

——, *The Art of Biblical Poetry*. Edinburgh: T & T Clark 1985/1990.

——, "The Poetic and Wisdom Books", *The Cambridge Companion to Biblical Interpretation*. Cambridge: Cambridge University Press (1998) 226–240.

Alter, R. & Kermode, F. (eds.), *The Literary Guide to the Bible*. London: Fontana Press 1989.

Anderson, R.W., "Zephaniah ben Cushi and Cush of Benjamin", *The Pitcher is Broken. Memorial Essays for Gösta W. Ahlström* Ed. by S.W. Holloway & L.K. Handy. Sheffield: Sheffield Academic Press (1995) 45–70 (JSOT.S 190).

Aubin, H.T., *The Rescue of Jerusalem. The Alliance between Hebrews and Africans in 701 BC*. [Toronto]: Anchor Canada 2003.

Auvray, P., "Cyrus, instrument du Dieu unique. Isaie 45:1–8", *BVC* 50 (1963) 17–23.

Avishur, Y., "Addenda to the Expanded Colon in Ugaritic and Biblical Verse", *UF* 4 (1972) 1–10.

Bailey, L.R., "Isaiah 14:24–27", *Interp.* 36 (1982) 171–176.

Baker, D.W., *Nahum, Habakkuk and Zephaniah. An Introduction and Commentary*. Leicester: Inter-Varsity Press 1988 (TOTC).

Bar-Efrat, S., *Narrative Art in the Bible*. Sheffield: The Almond Press 1989 (JSOT.S 70 Bible and Literature Series 17).

Barr, J., *Comparative Philology and the Text of the Old Testament*. Oxford: Clarendon Press 1968.

——, "Etymology and the Old Testament", *Language and Meaning. Studies in Hebrew Language and Biblical Exegesis*. Ed. by A.S. van der Woude. Leiden: E.J. Brill (1974) 1–28 (OTS 19).

——, *The Semantics of Biblical Language*. Oxford: Oxford University Press 1961.

Barré, M.L., "Of Lions and Birds: A Note on Isaiah 31:4–5", *Among the Prophets. Language, Image and Structure in the Prophetic Writings*. Ed. by P.R. Davies, & D.J.A. Clines. Sheffield: Sheffield Academic Press (1993) 55–59 (JSOT.S 144).

Barth, H., "Israel und das Assyrerreich in den nichtjesajanischen Texten des Protojesajabuches. Eine Untersuchung zur produktiven Neuinterpretation der Jesajaüberlieferung". Unpublished Th.D. diss. Hamburg: Evangelical Theological Faculty 1974.

Barton, J., "History and Rhetoric in the Prophets", *The Bible as Rhetoric. Studies in Biblical Persuasion and Credibility*. Ed. by M. Warner. London & New York, New York: Routledge (1990) 51–64.

——, "Intertextuality and the 'final form' of the Text", *Congress Volume Oslo 1998*. Ed. by A. Lemaire & M. Sæbø. Leiden: Brill (2000) 33–37 (VT.S 80).

——, "Reading the Bible as Literature", *JLT* 1 (1987) 135–153.

——, *Understanding Old Testament Ethics: Approaches and Explorations*. Louisville, Kentucky: Westminster John Knox Press 2003.

Baumann, E., "Zwei Einzelbemerkungen", *ZAW* 21 (1901) 266–268.

Becker, U., *Jesaja—von der Botschaft zum Buch*. Göttingen: Vandenhoeck & Ruprecht 1997 (FRLANT 178).

Begrich, J., "Jesaja 14, 28–32. Ein Beitrag zur Chronologie der israelitisch-judäischen Königszeit", *ZDMG* 86 (1933) 66–79.

Bentzen, Aa., *Jesaja*. København: G.E.C. Gads 1944.

Ben Zvi, E., *A Historical-Critical Study of the Book of Zephaniah*. Berlin/New York: Walter de Gruyter 1991 (BZAW 198).

Berlin, A., "Introduction to Hebrew Poetry", *NIntB*. Vol. 4. Ed. by L.E. Keck & al. Nashville, Tennessee: Abingdon Press (1996) 301–315.

——, *Poetics and Interpretation of Biblical Narrative*. Sheffield: The Almond Press 1983 (BiLiSe 9).

——, *The Dynamics of Biblical Parallelism*. Bloomington, Indiana: Indiana University Press 1985.

————, "Zephaniah's Oracle against the Nations and an Israelite Cultural Myth", *Fortunate the Eyes that See. Essays in Honor of David Noel Freedman in Celebration of His Seventieth Birthday*. Ed. by A.B. Beck, A.H. Bartelt & al. Grand Rapids, Michigan/Cambridge: William B. Eerdmans Publishing Company (1995) 175–184.

Best, T.F. (ed.), *Hearing and Speaking the Word: Selections from the Works of James Muilenburg*. Chico, California: Scholars Press 1984 (SPHS 7).

Beuken, W.A.M., "Isaiah 30: A Prophetic Oracle Transmitted in Two Successive Paradigms", *Writing and Reading the Scroll of Isaiah. Studies of an Interpretive Tradition*. Vol. 1. Ed. by C.C. Broyles & C.A. Evans. Leiden: E.J. Brill (1997) 369–397 (VT.S 70/1. Formation and Interpretation of Old Testament Literature 1/1).

————, *Jesaja deel 2A*. Nijkerk: G.F. Callenbach 1979 (PrOT).

————, *Jesaja deel 2B*. Nijkerk: G.F. Callenbach 1983 (PrOT).

————, *Jesaja deel 3A*. Nijkerk: G.F. Callenbach 1989 (PrOT).

————, *Jesaja deel 3B*. Nijkerk: G.F. Callenbach 1989 (PrOT).

————, "Jesaja 33 als Spiegeltext im Jesajabuch", *EThL* 67 (1991) 5–35.

————, "The Confession of God's Exclusivity by All Mankind: A Reappraisal of Is. 45:18–25", *Bijdr.* 35 (1974) 335–356.

Beyse, K.-M., "המם", *ThWAT* 2 (1977) 1045–1050.

Bjørndalen, A.J., *Untersuchungen zur allegorischen Rede der Propheten Amos und Jesaja*. Berlin/New York: Walter de Gruyter 1986. (BZAW 165).

Black, C.C., "Keeping up with Recent Studies XVI. Rhetorical Criticism and Biblical Interpretation", *ET* 100 (1989) 252–258.

Black, M., *Models and Metaphors. Studies in Language and Philosophy*. Ithaca, New York & London: Cornell University Press 1962/1981.

Blenkinsopp, J., *Isaiah 1–39. A New Translation with Introduction and Commentary*. New York, New York: Doubleday 2000 (AncB 19).

Bons, E., "שקף", *ThWAT* 8 (1995) 449–454.

Borowski, O., *Agriculture in Iron Age Israel*. Winona Lake, Indiana: Eisenbrauns 1987.

Botterweck, J.G., "בהמה", *ThWAT* 1 (1973) 523–536.

Brandes, E., *Jesaja oversat fra hebraisk*. København: Gyldendalske Boghandels Forlag (F. Hegel & Søn) 1902.

Brangenberg, J.H., "A Reexamination of the Date, Authorship, Unity and Function of Isaiah 13–23". Unpublished Ph.D. diss. Ann Arbor, Michigan: Golden Gate Baptist Theological Seminary 1989.

Braun, J., *Music in Ancient Israel/Palestine. Archaeological, Written, and Comparative Sources*. Translated by D.W. Scott. Grand Rapids, Michigan: Eerdmans Publishing Company 2002.

Brichto, H.C., *Toward A Grammar of Biblical Poetics. Tales of the Prophets*. Oxford, New York: Oxford University Press 1992.

Brown, F., Driver, S.R., Briggs, C.A., *The New Brown—Driver—Briggs—Gesenius Hebrew and English Lexicon with an Appendix Containing the Biblical Aramaic*. Peabody, Massachusetts: Hendrickson Publishers 1979.

Bruce, F.F., "Travel and Communication. The New Testament World", *ABD* 6. Ed. by D.N. Freedman & al. New York, New York: Doubleday (1992) 648–653.

Brueggemann, W., *Isaiah 1–39*. Louisville, Kentucky: Westminster John Knox Press 1998.

Buhl, F., "Jesaia 21, 6–10", *ZAW* 8 (1888) 157–167.

————, *Jesaja oversat og fortolket*. København: Gyldendalske Boghandel 1894.

————, *Jesaja oversat og fortolket*. København: Gyldendalske Boghandel 1912.

Cañellas, G., "El universalismo en el Deuteroisaias", *CuBi* 35 (1978) 3–20.

Carr, D.M., "Reaching for Unity in Isaiah", *JSOT* 57 (1993) 61–80.

Carroll, R.P., *When Prophecy Failed. Reactions and Responses to Failure in the Old Testament Prophetic Traditions*. London: SCM Press Ltd 1979.

Casson, L., *Ships and Seamanship in the Ancient World*. Baltimore, Maryland & London: John Hopkins University Press 1971/1995.

————, *Travel in the Ancient World*. Baltimore, Maryland & London: The John Hopkins University Press 1994.

Ceresko, A.R., "A Rhetorical Analysis of David's 'Boast' (1 Sam 17:34–37)", *CBQ* 47 (1985) 58–74.

————, "Janus Parallelism in Amos's 'Oracles Against the Nations' (Amos 1:3–2:16)", *JBL* 113 (1994) 485–490.

Cheyne, T.K., *Einleitung in das Buch Jesaja*. Giessen: J. Rickersche Buchhandlung 1897.

————, *The Book of the Prophet Isaiah. Critical Edition of the Hebrew Text Arranged in Chronological Order and Printed in Colors Exhibiting the Composite Structure of the Book with Notes*. Leipzig: J.C. Hinrichs'sche Buchhandlung 1899. (SBONT 10).

————, "The Nineteenth Chapter of Isaiah", *ZAW* 13 (1893) 125–128.

Childs, B.S., *Introduction to the Old Testament as Scripture*. London: SCM Press 1979.

————, *Isaiah*. Louisville, Kentucky: Westminster John Knox Press 2001 (OTL).

————, *Isaiah and the Assyrian Crisis*. London: SCM Press 1967 (SBT 2. Ser. 3).

————, *Myth and Reality in the Old Testament*. London: SCM Press 1960.

Clements, R.E., "Beyond Tradition-History. Deutero-Isaianic Development of First Isaiah's Themes", *JSOT* 31 (1985) 95–113.

————, *Isaiah and the Deliverance of Jerusalem. A Study of the Interpretation of Prophecy in the Old Testament*. Sheffield: JSOT Press 1980 (JSOT.S 13).

————, *Isaiah 1–39*. Grand Rapids, Michigan: Eerdmans 1980/1994 (NCBC).

————, "OT 'Woe' Oracles", *ABD* 6. Ed. by D.N. Freedman & al. New York, New York: Doubleday (1992) 945–946.

————, "Zion as Symbol and Political Reality: A Central Isaianic Quest", *Studies in the Book of Isaiah. Festschrift Willem A.M. Beuken*. Ed. by J. Van Ruiten & M. Vervenne. Leuven: University Press (1997) 3–17 (BEThL 132).

Clifford, R.J., *Fair Spoken and Persuading. An Interpretation of Second Isaiah*. New York: Paulist Press 1984 (TI).

————, "Rhetorical Criticism in the Exegesis of Hebrew Poetry", *SBL.SP* 19 (1980) 17–28.

————, *The Cosmic Mountain in Canaan and the Old Testament*. Cambridge, Massachusetts: Harvard University Press 1972 (HSM 4).

————, "The Unity of the Book of Isaiah and Its Cosmogonic Language", *CBQ* 55 (1993) 1–17.

————, "The use of Hôy in the Prophets", *CBQ* 28 (1966) 458–464.

Clines, D.J.A., "Deconstructing the Book of Job", *The Bible as Rhetoric. Studies in Biblical Persuasion and Credibility*. Ed. by M. Warner. London & New York, New York: Routledge (1990) 65–80.

————, (ed.), *DCH*. Vols. 1–5. Sheffield: Sheffield Academic Press 1993ff.

Collins English Dictionary. The Authority on Current English. Glasgow: Harper Collins Publishers (1979/1994).

Coulson, J. & al. (eds.), *The New Oxford Illustrated Dictionary*. Sydney: Bay Books in association with Oxford University Press 1978.

Craven, T., *Artistry and Faith in the Book of Judith*. Chico, California: Scholars Press 1983 (SBL.DS 70).

Culley, R.C., *Oral Formulaic Language in the Biblical Psalms*. Toronto, Canada: University of Toronto Press 1967 (NMES 4).

Davidson, R., "Universalism in Second Isaiah", *SJTh* 16 (1963) 166–185.

Davies, G.I., "The Destiny of the Nations in the Book of Isaiah", *The Book of Isaiah. Le livre d'Isaïe. Les Oracles et les relectures. Unité et complexité de l'ouvrage*. Ed. by J. Vermeylen. Leuven: Leuven University Press (1989) 93–120 (BEThL 81).

Deist, F.E., *The Material Culture of the Bible. An Introduction*. Sheffield: Sheffield Academic Press 2000/2002 (BiSe 70).

Delitzsch, F., *Commentar über das Buch Jesaia*. Leipzig: Dörffling & Franke 1889 (BC 3).

————, *Die Lese- und Schreibfehler im Alten Testament nebst den dem Schrifttexte einverleibten*

Randnoten klassifiziert. Ein Hilfsbuch für Lexicon und Grammatik, Exegese und Lektüre.
Berlin & Leipzig: Walter de Gruyter 1920.
———, *Jesaja.* Giessen: Brunnen Verlag 1984 (BC).
Die heilige Schrift nach der deutschen Übersetzung Martin Luthers. Berlin: Britische und
Ausländische Bibelgesellschaft 1929.
Dietrich, W., *Jesaja und die Politik.* München: Chr. Kaiser Verlag 1976 (BEvTh 74).
Dillmann, A., *Der Prophet Jesaja.* Leipzig: S. Hirzel 1890.
Dion, P.E., *Hebrew Poetics.* Mississauga, Ontario: Benben Publications 1992.
Dodd, C.H., *The Parables of the Kingdom.* Glasgow: Collins/Fontana Books 1935/1961
(FB).
Donner, H., *Israel unter den Völkern. Die stellung der klassischen Propheten des 8. Jahrhunderts v.
Chr. Zur Aussenpolitik der Könige von Israel und Juda.* Leiden: E.J. Brill 1964 (VT.S 11).
Dozeman, T.B., "Rhetoric and Rhetorical Criticism. Old Testament Rhetorical
Criticism", *ABD.* Ed. by D.N. Freedman & al. New York, New York: Doubleday
5 (1992) 712–715.
Driver, G.R., "Birds in the Old Testament", *PEQ* (1954–1955) 129–140.
———, "Difficult Words in the Hebrew Prophets", *Studies in Old Testament Prophecy.
Presented to Professor Theodore H. Robinson by the Society for Old Testament Study on
His Sixty-fifth Birthday, August 9th 1946.* Ed. by H.H. Rowley. Edinburgh:
T. & T. Clark (1957) 52–72.
———, "Hebrew Scrolls", *JThS* 2 (1951) 17–30.
———, "Isaiah 1–39: Textual and Linguistic Problems", *JSSt* 13 (1968) 36–57.
Duhm, B., *Das Buch Jesaia übersetzt und erklärt.* Göttingen: Vandenhoeck & Ruprecht
1892 (HK 3,1).
Duke, R.K., *The Persuasive Appeal of the Chronicler. A Rhetorical Analysis.* Sheffield: The
Almond Press 1990 (BiLiSe 25).
Eaton, J.H., "Music's Place in Worship: A Contribution from the Psalms", *Prophets,
Worship and Theodocy. Studies in Prophetism, Biblical Theology and Structural and Rhetorical
Analysis and on the Place of Music in Worship. Papers read at the joint British-Dutch
Old Testament Conference held at Woudschoten 1982.* Ed. by A.S. van der Woude.
Leiden: E.J. Brill (1984) 85–107 (OTS 23).
Eichrodt, W., *Der Herr der Geschichte. Jesaja 13–23 und 28–39.* Stuttgart: Calwer Verlag
1967 (BAT 17/2).
Eide, T., Hägg, T. & al. (eds.), *Fontes Historiae Nubiorum. Textual Sources for the History
of the Middle Nile Region between the eighth century BC and the sixth century AD. From
the eighth to the mid-fifth century BC.* Vol. 1. Bergen: John Grieg AS 1994.
——— (eds.), *Fontes Historiae Nubiorum. Textual Sources for the History of the Middle Nile
Region between the eighth century BC and the sixth century AD. From the mid-fifth to the
first century BC.* Vol 2. Bergen: John Grieg AS 1996.
——— (eds.), *Fontes Historiae Nubiorum. Textual Sources for the History of the Middle Nile
Region between the eighth century BC and the sixth century AD. From the first to the sixth
century AD.* Vol. 3. Bergen: John Grieg AS 1998.
Eidevall, G., *Grapes in the Desert. Metaphors, Models, and Themes in Hosea 4–14.* Stockholm:
Almqvist & Wiksell International 1996 (CB.OT 43).
Eising, H., *Das Buch Jesaja.* Düsseldorf: Patmos-Verlag 1970 (GS.AT 2/1).
Eitan, I., "A Contribution to Isaiah Exegesis. (Notes and Short Studies in Biblical
Philology)", *HUCA* 12/13 (1937/38) 55–88.
Erlandsson, S., *The Burden of Babylon. A Study of Isaiah 13:2–14:23.* Lund: CWK
Gleerup 1970 (CB.OT 4).
Even-Shoshan, A., *A New Concordance of the Bible.* Jerusalem: Kiryat Sepher Publishing
House 1983 [Hebrew].
Fabry, H.-J., "נס", *ThWAT* 5 (1986) 468–473.
Feldmann, F., *Das Buch Isaias übersetzt und erklärt.* Münster in Westfalen: 1925 (EHAT
14).

Ferrie, J.J., Jr., "Singing in the Rain: A Meteorological Image in Isaiah 42:10–12", *Imagery and Imagination in Biblical Literature. Essays in Honor of Aloysius Fitzgerald, F.C.S.* Ed. by L. Boadt & M.S. Smith. Washington, D.C.: The Catholic Biblical Association of America (2001) 95–104 (CBQ.MS 32).

Ficker, R., "מלאך", *THAT* 1 (1971) 900–908.

Firmage, E., "Zoology", *ABD* 6. Ed. by D.N. Freedman & al. New York, New York: Doubleday (1992) 1109–1167.

Fisch, H., "The Analogy of Nature, A Note on the Structure of Old Testament Imagery", *JThS.NS* 6 (1955) 161–173.

———, *Poetry with a Purpose. Biblical Poetics and Interpretation.* Bloomington & Indianapolis, Indiana: Indiana University Press 1988/1990 (ISBL).

Fishbane, M., "Types of Biblical Intertextuality", *Congress Volume Oslo 1998.* Ed. by A. Lemaire & M. Sæbø. Leiden: Brill (2000) 39–44 (VT.S 80).

Fischer, J., *Das Buch Isaias.* Bonn: Peter Hanstein Verlagsbuchhandlung 1937 (HSAT 7).

Fischer, T. & Rüterswörden, U., "Aufruf zur Volksklage in Kanaan (Jesaja 23)", *WO* 13 (1982) 36–49.

Fohrer, G., *Das Buch Jesaja Kapitel 1–23.* Vol. 1. Zürich & Stuttgart: Zwingli Verlag 1960/1966 (ZBK.AT).

———, *Das Buch Jesaja Kapitel 24–39.* Vol. 2. Zürich & Stuttgart: Zwingli Verlag 1962/1967 (ZBK.AT).

———, "Zum Text von Jes. xli 8–13", *VT* 5 (1955) 239–249.

Fokkelman, J.P., "The Cyrus Oracle (Isaiah 44:24–45:7) from the Perspectives of Syntax, Versification and Structure", *Studies in the Book of Isaiah, Festschrift W.A.M. Beuken.* Leuven: Leuven University Press (1997) 303–323.

Follis, E.R., "Sea", *ABD* 5. Ed. by D.N. Freedman & al. New York, New York: Doubleday (1992) 1058–1059.

Fox, M.V., "The Rhetoric of Ezekiel's Vision of the Valley of the Bones", *HUCA* 51 (1980) 1–15.

Franke, C., *Isaiah 46, 47, and 48: A New Literary-Critical Reading.* Winona Lake, Indiana: Eisenbrauns 1994 (BJudSt v. 3).

Freedman, D.N., "Another Look at Biblical Hebrew Poetry", *Directions in Biblical Hebrew Poetry.* Ed. by E.R. Follis. Sheffield: Sheffield Academic Press (1987) 11–28. (JSOT.S 40).

Freedman, D.N., & Willoughby, B.E., "מלאך", *ThWAT* 4 (1984) 887–904.

Friman, G., *Profeten Jesaja.* Stockholm: Svenska Kyrkans Diakonistyrelses Bokförlag 1917 (HBib.).

Futato, M.D., "Sense Relations in the 'Rain' Domain of the Old Testament", *Imagery and Imagination in Biblical Literature. Essays in Honor of Aloysius Fitzgerald, F.C.S.* Ed. by L. Boadt & M.S. Smith. Washington, D.C.: The Catholic Biblical Association of America (2001) 81–94 (CBQ.MS 32).

Geller, S.A., *Parallelism in Early Biblical Poetry.* Missoula, Montana: Scholars Press 1979 (HSM 20).

Gemser, B., "Be'ēver hajjardēn: In Jordan's borderland", *VT* 2 (1952) 349–355.

Gemünden, P. von, *Vegetationsmetaphorik im Neuen Testament und seiner Umwelt. Eine Bildfelduntersuchung.* Freiburg/Göttingen: Universitätsverlag/Vandenhoeck & Ruprecht 1993 (NTOA 18).

Gerstenberger, E., "The Woe-Oracles of the Prophets", *JBL* 81 (1962) 249–263.

Gesenius, W., *Hebräisches und Chaldäisches Handwörterbuch über das Alte Testament. 9. Auflage.* Leipzig: F.C.W. Vogel 1883.

———, *Hebräisches und Aramäisches Handwörterbuch über das Alte Testament. 17. Auflage.* Berlin: Springer-Verlag 1962.

———, *Hebräisches und Aramäisches Handwörterbuch über das Alte Testament. 18. Auflage.* Berlin: Springer-Verlag 1987ff.

———, *Philologisch-kritischer und historischer Commentar über den Jesaia.* Leipzig: F.C.W. Vogel 1821.

————, *Thesaurus Philologicus Criticus Linguae Hebraeae et Chaldaeae Veteris Testamenti.* Lipsiae 1842.

————, *Thesaurus Philologicus Criticus Linguae Hebraeae et Chaldaeae Veteris Testamenti.* Lipsiae 1829–1853.

Gileadi, A., *The Literary Message of Isaiah.* New York, New York: Hebraeus Press 1994.

Gitay, Y., *Prophecy and Persuasion. A Study of Isaiah 40–48.* Bonn: Linguistica Biblica 1981 (FThL 14).

————, "Rhetorical Analysis of Isaiah 40–48: A Study of the Art of Prophetic Persuasion". Unpublished Ph.D. diss. Ann Arbor, Michigan: Emory University 1978.

Glück, J.J., "Paronomasia in Biblical Literature", *Semitics* 1 (1970) 50–79.

Goldhammer, K., "Die heilige Fahne. Zur Geschichte und Phänomenologie eines religiösen Ur-Objectes", *Tribus. Zeitschrift für Ethnologie und ihre Nachbarwissenschaften* 4/5 (1954/1955) 13–55.

Goshen-Gottstein, M., *R. Judah Ibn Bal'am's Commentary on Isaiah. The Arabic Original according to M.S. Firkovitch (Ebr-arab I 1377) with a Hebrew Translation, Notes and Introduction.* Ramat Gan: Bar-Ilan University Press 1992 [Hebrew].

Gosse, B., "Isaiah 8:23b and the Three Great Parts of the Book of Isaiah", *JSOT* 70 (1996) 57–62.

————, *Isaïe 13:1–14:23 dans la tradition littéraire du livre d'Isaïe et dans la tradition des oracles contre les nations.* Göttingen: Vandenhoeck & Ruprecht 1988 (OBO 78).

————, "Isaïe 14:24–27 et les oracles contre les nations du livre d'Isaïe", *BN* 56 (1991) 17–21.

————, "Isaïe 17:12–14 dans la redaction du livre d'Isaïe", *BN* 58 (1991) 20–23.

————, "Isaïe 21:11–12 et Isaïe 60–62", *BN* 53 (1990) 21–22.

Gottwald, N.K., *All the Kingdoms of the Earth. Israelite Prophecy and International Relations in the Ancient Near East.* New York, New York: Harper & Row 1964.

————, *The Politics of Ancient Israel.* Louisville, Kentucky: John Knox Press 2001 (LAI).

Gradwohl, R., *Die Farben im Alten Testament. Eine terminologische Studie.* Berlin: Verlag Alfred Töpelmann 1963 (BZAW 83).

————, "Zum verständnis von Ex. XVII 15f.", *VT* 12 (1962) 491–494.

Gray, G.B., *A Critical and Exegetical Commentary on the Book of Isaiah.* Edinburgh: Morrison and Gibb 1962 (ICC 1).

Greene, J.T., *The Role of the Messenger and Message in the Ancient Near East. Oral and Written Communication in the Ancient Near East and in the Hebrew Scriptures: Communicators and Communiques in Context.* Atlanta, Georgia: Scholars Press 1989 (BJSt 169).

Greenstein, E.L., "How Does Parallelism Mean?", *A Sense of Text. The Art of Language in the Study of Biblical Literature. Papers from a Symposium at the Dropsie College for Hebrew and Cognate Learning May 11, 1982.* Winona Lake, Indiana: Published for Dropsie College by Eisenbrauns (1983) 41–70 (JQR.S 1982).

Guthe, H., *Palästina.* Bielefeld: Velhagen & Klasing 1927 (MzE 21).

Görg, M., "Der Altar—theologische Dimensionen im Alten Testament", *Freude am Gottesdienst. Aspekte ursprünglicher Liturgie. Festschrift für Weihbischof Dr. Josef G. Plöger zum 60. Geburtstag.* Ed. by J. Schreiner. Stuttgart: Verlag Katholisches Bibelwerk (1983) 291–306.

————, "Nes—ein Herrschaftsemblem?", *BN* 14 (1981) 11–17.

Haak, R.D., "'Cush' in Zephaniah", *The Pitcher is Broken. Memorial Essays for Gösta W. Ahlström* Ed. by S.W. Holloway & L.K. Handy. Sheffield: Sheffield Academic Press: (1995) 238–251 (JSOT.S 190).

Hagelia, H., *Coram Deo. Spirituality in the Book of Isaiah, with Particular Attention to Faith in Yahweh.* Stockholm: Almqvist & Wiksell International 2001 (CB.OT 49).

Haller, M., "Die Kyros-Lieder Deuterojesajas", ΕΥΧΑΡΙΣΤΗΡΙΟΝ. *Studien zur Religion und Literatur des Alten und Neuen Testaments. Hermann Gunkel zum 60. Geburtstage, dem 23. Mai 1922.* Ed. by H. Schmidt. Göttingen: Vandenhoeck & Ruprecht (1923) 261–277 (FRLANT 19).

Hallo, W.W. (ed.), *The Context of Scripture. Canonical Compositions from the Biblical World.*
    Vol. 1. Leiden: Brill 1997.
────── (ed.), *The Context of Scripture. Monumental Inscriptions from the Biblical World.*
    Vol. 2. Leiden: Brill 2000.
────── (ed.), *The Context of Scripture. Archival Documents from the Biblical World.* Vol. 3.
    Leiden: Brill 2002.
Hamborg, G.R., "Reasons for Judgement in the Oracles Against the Nations of the
    Prophet Isaiah", *VT* 31 (1981) 145–159.
Hamlin, E.J., "The Meaning of 'Mountains and Hills' in Isa 41:14–16", *JNES* 13
    (1954) 185–190.
Hasel, G.F., "כרת", *ThWAT* 4 (1984) 355–367.
Hausmann, J., "קיץ", *ThWAT* 7 (1993) 26–29.
──────, "קצר I", *ThWAT* 7 (1993) 106–112.
Hays, J.D., "The Cushites: A Black Nation in Ancient History", *BS* 153 (1996)
    270–280.
Hayes, J.H., "Amos's Oracles Against the Nations (1:2–2:16)", *RExp* 92 (1995)
    153–167.
Hayes, J.H. & Irvine, S.A., *Isaiah, The Eight-century Prophet: His Times and His Preaching.*
    Nashville, Tennessee: Abingdon Press 1987.
Herbert, A.S., *The Book of the Prophet Isaiah. Chapters 1–39.* Cambridge: Cambridge
    University Press 1973 (CNEB).
Herder, J.G. von, *Vom Geist der ebräischen Poesie 1 & 2.* Carlsruhe: Bureau der
    deutschen Classiker 1827.
Herrmann, W., "Eine notwendige Erinnerung", *ZAW* 104 (1992) 262–264.
Hidal, S., "The Land of Cush in the Old Testament", *SEÅ* 41–42 (1977) 97–106.
Hillers, D.R., "*Hôy* and *Hôy*-Oracles: A Neglected Syntactic Aspect", *The Word of
    the Lord Shall Go Forth. Essays in Honor of David Noel Freedman in Celebration of His
    Sixtieth Birthday.* Ed. by C.L. Meyers & M. O'Connor. Winona Lake, Indiana:
    Eisenbrauns (1983) 185–188.
Hoffmann, H.W., *Die Intention der Verkündigung Jesajas.* Berlin/New York: Walter de
    Gruyter 1974 (BZAW 136).
Hollenberg, D.E., "Nationalism and 'the Nations' in Is. 40–55", *VT* 19 (1969) 23–36.
Holmberg, B., "עב", *ThWAT* 5 (1986) 978–982.
Holt, E.K., "The meaning of an *inclusio*: A Theological Interpretation of the Book
    of Jeremiah MT", *SJOT* 17 (2003) 183–205.
Holter, K., "Africa in the Old Testament", *Yahweh in Africa. Essays on Africa and the
    Old Testament.* New York, New York: Peter Lang (2000) 93–106 (BibThA 1).
──────, "Is Israel Worth More to God than Cush? An Interpretation of Amos 9:7",
    Yahweh in Africa. Essays on Africa and the Old Testament. New York, New York:
    Peter Lang (2000) 115–125 (BibThA 1).
──────, *Second Isaiah's Idol-Fabrication Passages.* Frankfurt am Main: Peter Lang 1995.
    (BET 28).
House, P.R. *Zephaniah. A Prophetic Drama.* Sheffield: The Almond Press 1988 (BiLiSe 16).
Hrushovski, B., "Prosody, Hebrew", *EJ* 13 (1972/1974) 1195–1240.
Huber, F., *Jahwe, Juda und die anderen Völker beim Propheten Jesaja.* Berlin: Walter de
    Gruyter 1976 (BZAW 137).
Hurvitz, A., "Wisdom Vocabulary in the Hebrew Psalter: A Contribution to the
    Study of 'Wisdom Psalms'", *VT* 38 (1988) 41–51.
Huwyler, B., *Jeremia und die Völker. Untersuchungen zu den Völkersprüchen in Jeremia 46–49.*
    Tübingen: Mohr Siebeck 1997 (FAT 20).
Høgenhaven, J., *Gott und Volk bei Jesaja. Eine Untersuchung zur Biblischen Theologie.*
    Leiden: E.J. Brill 1988 (AThD 24).
──────, "The Prophet Isaiah and Judean Foreign Policy under Ahaz and Hezekiah",
    JNES 49 (1990) 351–354.

Intertextuality and the Bible. Semeia 69/70. Ed. by G. Aichele & G.A. Phillips. Atlanta, Georgia: Scholars Press 1995.

Irsigler, H., *Zefanja*. Freiburg: Verlag Herder 2002 (HThK.AT).

Iser, W., *The Act of Reading. A Theory of Aesthetic Response*. London & Henley: Routledge & Kegan Paul 1978.

Jacob, I. & Jacob, W., "Flora", *ABD* 2. Ed. by D.N. Freedman & al. New York, New York: Doubleday (1992) 803–817.

Jakobson, R. & M. Halle, *Fundamentals of Language*. The Hague/Paris: Mouton 1975 (JL.SM 1).

James, T.G.H., *A Short History of Ancient Egypt. From Predynastic to Roman Times*. Baltimore, Maryland & London: The John Hopkins University Press 1995/1998.

Janzen, W., *Mourning Cry and Woe Oracle*. Berlin/New York: Walter de Gruyter 1972 (BZAW 125).

Jenkins, A.K., "The Development of the Isaiah Tradition in Isaiah 13–23", *The Book of Isaiah. Le livre d'Isaïe. Les Oracles et les relectures. Unité et complexité de l'ouvrage*. Ed. by J. Vermeylen. Leuven: University Press (1989) 237–251 (BEThL 81).

Jenner, K.D., "The Big Shofar (Isaiah 27:13): A Hapax Legomenon", *Studies in Isaiah 24–27. The Isaiah Workshop—De Jesaja Werkplaats*. Ed. by H.J. Bosman & H. Van Grol & al. Leiden: Brill (2000) 157–182.

Jenni, E., "Die Rolle des Kyros bei Deuterojesaja", *ThZ* 10 (1954) 241–256.

———, "חוֹי", *THAT* 1 (1971) 474–477.

Jensen, J., *Isaiah 1–39*. Wilmington: Michael Glazier 1984 (OTMes 8).

Jeppesen, K., *Græder ikke saa saare. Studier i Mikabogens sigte*. Vol. 1–2. Aarhus: Aarhus Universitetsforlag 1987.

———, *Jesajas Bog fortolket*. København: Det Danske Bibelselskab 1988.

Jeremias, J., *Der Gottesberg. Ein Beitrag zum Verständnis der biblischen Symbolsprache*. Gütersloh: Bertelsmann 1919.

Jones, B.C., *Howling over Moab. Irony and Rhetoric in Isaiah 15–16*. Atlanta, Georgia: Scholars Press 1996 (SBL.DS 157).

Jones, I.H., "Musical Instruments", *ABD* 4. Ed. by D.N. Freedman & al. New York, New York: Doubleday (1992) 934–939.

Jonker, L.C., "Communities of Faith as Texts in the Process of Biblical Interpretation", *Skr.K* 20 (1999) 79–92.

———, *Exclusivity and Variety. Perspectives on Multidimensional Exegesis*. Kampen: Kok Pharos s.a. [1996] (CBET 19).

Kaiser, O., *Der Prophet Jesaja. Kapitel 13–39 übersetzt und erklärt*. 3., durchgesehene Auflage. Göttingen: Vandenhoeck & Ruprecht 1983 (ATD 18).

Kapelrud, A.S., "The Main Concern of Second Isaiah", *VT* 32 (1982) 50–58.

Katsnelson, J., "Dew", *EJ* 5 (1974) 1600–1602.

Katzenstein, H.J., *The History of Tyre. From the Beginning of the Second Millennium B.C.E. until the Fall of the Neo-Babylonian Empire in 538 B.C.E.* Jerusalem: The Schocken Institute for Jewish Research of the Jewish Theological Seminary of America 1973.

Kautzsch, E. (ed.), *Gesenius' Hebrew Grammar as Edited and Enlarged by the late E. Kautzsch*. Second English Edition Revised in accordance with the Twenty-eighth German Edition (1909). Reprinted lithographically. Oxford: The Clarendon Press 1910/1970.

——— (ed.), *Wilhelm Gesenius' hebräische Grammatik völlig umgearbeitet von E. Kautzsch*. Kleine Ausgabe der 28. vielfach verbesserten und vermehrten Auflage. Leipzig: F.C.W. Vogel 1909.

——— (ed.), *Wilhelm Gesenius' hebräische Grammatik völlig umgearbeitet von E. Kautzsch*. Reprografischer Nachdruck der 28. vielfach verbesserten und vermehrten Auflage Leipzig 1909. Hildesheim: Georg Olms Verlagsbuchhandlung 1962.

Kienpointner, M., "Linguistics", *Encyclopedia of Rhetoric*. Ed. by T.O. Sloane. Oxford, New York: Oxford University Press (2001) 426–449.

Kilian, R., *Jesaja 1–39*. Darmstadt: Wissenschaftliche Buchgesellschaft 1983. (EdF 200).

Kinnier Wilson, J.V., "A Return to the Problems of behemoth and leviathan", *VT* 25 (1975) 1–14.

Kissane, E.J., *The Book of Isaiah*. Vol. 1. Dublin: Browne and Nolan Ltd 1960.

Kittel, R., "Cyrus and Deuterojesaja", *ZAW* 18 (1898) 149–162.

Klein, R.W., "Going Home—A Theology of Second Isaiah", *CThMi* 5 (1978) 198–210.

Knobel, A., *Der Prophet Jesaia*. Leipzig 1843 (KEH 5).

Koch, K., *The Prophets. The Assyrian Period*. Vol. 1. London: SCM Press 1982.

Koffmahn, E., "Sind die altisraelitischen Monatsbezeichnungen mit den kanaanäisch-phönikischen identisch?", *BZ* 10 (1966) 197–219.

Kolari, E., *Musikinstrumente und ihre Verwendung im Alten Testament. Eine lexikalische und kulturgeschichtliche Untersuchung*. Helsinki: Tekijä 1947.

Korpel, M.C.A., *A Rift in the Clouds. Ugaritic and Hebrew Descriptions of the Divine*. Münster: Ugarit-Verlag 1990 (UBL 8).

Krantz, E. Strömberg, *Des Schiffes Weg mitten im Meer. Beiträge zur Erforschung der nautischen Terminologie des Alten Testaments*. Lund: CWK Gleerup 1982 (CB.OT 19).

Kratz, R.G., *Die Komposition der erzählenden Bücher des Alten Testaments. Grundwissen der Bibelkritik*. Göttingen: Vandenhoeck & Ruprecht 2000 (UTBW 2157).

———, *Kyros im Deutero-Jesaja-Buch*. Tübingen: J.C.B. Mohr (Paul Siebeck) 1991. (FAT 1).

Krause [sic], H.-J., "*hôj* als prophetische Leichenklage über das eigene Volk im 8. Jahrhundert", *ZAW* 85 (1973) 15–46.

Kristeva, J., *Desire in Language. A Semiotic Approach to Literature and Art*. Ed. by L.S. Roudiez. Tr. by T. Gora, A. Jardine & L.S. Roudiez. New York, New York: Columbia University Press 1980.

Kugel, J.L., *The Idea of Biblical Poetry. Parallelism and Its History*. Baltimore, Maryland & London: The John Hopkins University Press 1981/1998.

Kuntz, J.K., "The Contribution of Rhetorical Criticism to Understanding Isa 51:1–16", *Art and Meaning: Rhetoric in Biblical Literature*. Ed. by D.J.A. Clines & al. Sheffield: JSOT Press (1982) 140–171 (JSOT.S 19).

Kutsch, E., "חרף I", *ThWAT* 3 (1982) 217–223.

Kutscher, E.Y., *The Language and Linguistic Background of the Isaiah Scroll (1Q Isaᵃ)*. Leiden: E.J. Brill 1974 (StTDJ 6).

Koehler, L. & Baumgartner, W. (eds.), *Lexicon in Veteris Testamenti Libros*. Leiden: E.J. Brill 1958.

———, *Hebräisches und Aramäisches Lexikon zum Alten Testament*. Leiden: E.J. Brill 1967.

Köhler, L., "Baza' = fortschwemmen", *ThZ* 6 (1950) 316–317.

König, E., *Das Buch Jesaja eingeleitet, übersetzt und erklärt*. Gütersloh: C. Bertelsmann 1926.

———, *Stilistik, Rhetorik, Poetik in Bezug auf die biblische Litteratur*. Leipzig: Dieterich'sche Verlagsbuchhandlung 1900.

Laato, A., *"About Zion I will not be silent". The Book of Isaiah as an Ideological Unity*. Stockholm: Almquist & Wiksell International 1998 (CB.OT 44).

Lakoff, G., *Women, Fire, and Dangerous Things*. Chicago, Illinois & London: The University of Chicago Press 1987.

Lakoff, G. & Johnson, M., *Metaphors We Live By*. Chicago, Illinois & London: The University of Chicago Press 1980.

Lakoff, G. & Turner, M., *More than Cool Reason. A Field Guide to Poetic Metaphor*. Chicago, Illinois & London: The University of Chicago Press 1989.

Leene, H., "Universalism or Nationalism? Isaiah XLV 9–13 and Its Context", *Bijdr.* (1974) 309–334.

Lemaire, A., "Note épigraphique sur la pseudo-attestation du mois '*šḥ*'", *VT* 23 (1973) 243–245.

Levenson, J.D., *Sinai and Zion. An Entry into the Jewish Bible*. Minneapolis, Minnesota: Winston Press 1985.

——, "Zion traditions", *ABD* 6. Ed. by D.N. Freedman & al. New York, New York: Doubleday (1992) 1098–1102.

Levi, J., *Die Inkongruenz im biblischen Hebräisch*. Wiesbaden: Otto Harrassowitz 1987.

Lilley, J.P.U., "By the River-side", *VT* 28 (1978) 165–171.

Lisowsky, G., *Konkordanz zum Hebräischen Alten Testament*. 2nd ed. Stuttgart: Deutsche Bibelgesellschaft 1981.

Lowth, R., *Isaiah. A New Translation with a Preliminary Dissertation and Notes. Critical, Philological, and Explanatory*. Vol. 1–2. London: T. Cadell 1795.

——, *Lectures on the Sacred Poetry of the Hebrews*. Vol. 1–2. Translated by G. Gregory. London: Routledge/Thoemmes Press 1995.

Lubetski, M., "Beetlemania of Bygone Times", *JSOT* 91 (2000) 3–26.

Lugt, P. van der, *Rhetorical Criticism and the Poetry of the Book of Job*. Leiden: E.J. Brill 1995 (OTS 32).

Lundbom, J.R., *Jeremiah: A Study in Ancient Hebrew Rhetoric*. Missoula, Montana: Society of Biblical Literature and Scholars Press 1975 (SBL.DS 18).

——, *Jeremiah. A Study in Ancient Hebrew Rhetoric. Second Edition*. Winona Lake, Indiana: Eisenbrauns 1997 [With a new, introductory chapter].

Lundbom, J.[R.], "נטשׁ", *ThWAT* 5 (1986) 436–442.

Lutz, H.-M., *Jahwe, Jerusalem und die Völker. Zur Vorgeschichte von Sach 12:1–8 und 14:1–5*. Neukirchen-Vluyn: Neukirchener Verlag 1968.

Macintosh, A.A., *Isaiah xxi. A palimpsest*. Cambridge: Cambridge University Press 1980.

Macky, P.W., *The Centrality of Metaphors to Biblical Thought. A Method for Interpreting the Bible*. Lewiston, New York: The Edwin Mellen Press 1990 (SBEC 19).

Mafico, T.L.J., "Judge, Judging", *ABD* 3. Ed. by D.N. Freedman & al. New York, New York: Doubleday (1992) 1104–1106.

Manahan, R.E., "The Cyrus Notations of Deutero-Isaiah", *GrJ* 11 (1970) 22–33.

Mandelkern, S., *Veteris Testamenti Concordantiae Hebraicae Atque Chaldaicae*. Lipsiae 1896, repr. in Israel 1971.

Marcus, R., "The 'Plain Meaning' of Isaiah 42:1–4", *HThR* 30 (1937) 249–259.

Marti, K., *Das Buch Jesaja*. Tübingen: J.C.B. Mohr (Paul Siebeck) 1900 (KHC 10).

Martin-Achard, R., "Esaïe 47 et la tradition prophétique sur Babylone", *Prophecy. Essays Presented to G. Fohrer on His Sixty-fifth Birthday 6 September 1980*. Berlin: Walter de Gruyter (1980) 83–105 (BZAW 150).

Meier, S.A., *The Messenger in the Ancient Semitic World*. Atlanta, Georgia: Scholars Press 1988 (HSM 45).

Melugin, R.F., "Israel and the Nations in Isaiah 40–55", *Problems in Biblical Theology. Essays in Honour of Rolf Knierim*. Ed. by H.T.C. Sun & K.L. Eades & al. Grand Rapids, Michigan & Cambridge: William B. Eerdmans Publishing Company (1997) 249–264.

——, "The Conventional and the Creative in Isaiah's Judgement Oracles", *CBQ* 36 (1974) 301–311.

Merwe, C.H.J. van der, & al., *A Biblical Hebrew Reference Grammar*. Sheffield: Sheffield Academic Press 1999/2002.

Merwe, C.H.J. van der, "Old Hebrew Particles and the Interpretation of Old Testament Texts", *JSOT* 60 (1993) 27–44.

Mettinger, T.N.D., *The Dethronement of Sabaoth. Studies in the Shem and Kabod Theologies*. Lund: CWK Gleerup 1982 (CB.OT 18).

——, "YHWH SABAOTH—The Heavenly King on the Cherubim Throne", *Studies in the Period of David and Solomon and Other Essays: Papers Read at the International Symposium for Biblical Studies, Tokyo, 5–7 December, 1979*. Ed. by T. Ishida. Tokyo: Yamakawa-Shuppansha (1982) 109–138.

Meyer, R., *Hebräische Grammatik. Mit einem bibliografischen Nachwort von Udo Rüterswörden.* Berlin: Walter de Gruyter 1992 (GrSt).

Meynet, R., *Rhetorical Analysis. An Introduction to Biblical Rhetoric.* Sheffield: Sheffield Academic Press 1998 (JSOT.S 256).

Michelsen, E., *Profeten Esaias.* Kristiania: Lutherstiftelsens Boghandel s.a. (BibMF 4).

Miscall, P.D., *Isaiah.* Sheffield: JSOT Press 1993 (RNBC).

Moor, J.C. de, "Cloud", *IDB.S.* Ed. by K. Crim & al. Nashville, Tennessee: Abingdon Press (1976) 168–169.

Mosely, H.R., "The Oracles Against the Nations", *TEJTM* 52 (1995) 37–45.

Moulton, R.G., *The Literary Study of the Bible. An Account of the Leading Forms of Literature Represented in the Sacred Writings.* Revised and partly rewritten. Boston, Massachusetts: D.C. Heath & Co. 1895/1899.

Muilenburg, J., "Form Criticism and Beyond", *JBL* 88 (1969) 1–18.

———, "The Book of Isaiah: Chapters 40–66", *IntB* 5. Ed. by G.A. Buttrick & al. Nashville, Tennessee: Abingdon Press (1956) 381–418, 422–773.

Mulzer, M., "Döderlein und Deuterojesaja", *BN* 66 (1993) 15–22.

Müller, C.G., *Gottes Pflanzung—Gottes Bau—Gottes Tempel. Die metaphorische Dimension paulinischer Gemeindetheologie in 1 Kor 3:5–17.* Frankfurt am Main: Verlag Joseph Knecht 1995 (FuSt; 5).

Müller, H.-P., "כרם", *Theologisches Wörterbuch zum Alten Testament* 4 (1984) 334–340.

Möller, K., *A Prophet in Debate. The Rhetoric of Persuasion in the Book of Amos.* London: Sheffield Academic Press 2003 (JSOT.S 372).

Nielsen, K., "Intertextuality and Hebrew Bible", *International Organization for the Study of the Old Testament: Congress Volume 1998.* Ed. by A. Lemaire & M. Sæbø. Leiden: Brill (2000) 17–31 (VT.S 80).

———, "Old Testament Imagery in John", *New Readings in John. Literary and Theological Perspectives. Essays from the Scandinavian Conference on the Fourth Gospel Århus 1997.* Ed. by J. Nissen & S. Pedersen. Sheffield: Sheffield Academic Press (1999) 66–82 (JSNT.S 182).

———, *There is Hope for a Tree. The Tree as Metaphor in Isaiah.* Sheffield: JSOT Press 1989 (JSOT.S 65).

Noegel, S.B., "Drinking Feasts and Deceptive Feats: Jacob and Laban's Double Talk", *Puns and Pundits. Word Play in the Hebrew Bible and Ancient Near Eastern Literature.* Ed. by S.B. Noegel. Bethesda, Maryland: CDL Press (2000) 163–179.

Nysse, R., "Keeping Company with Nahum: Regarding the Oracles Against the Nations as Scripture", *Word & World* 15 (1995) 412–419.

O'Connell, R.H., *Concentricity and Continuity. The Literary Structure of Isaiah.* Sheffield: Sheffield Academic Press 1994 (JSOT.S 188).

———, "Deuteronomy 8:1–20: Asymmetrical Concentricity and the Rhetoric of Providence", *VT* 40 (1990) 437–452.

———, "Isaiah XIV 4B-23: Ironic Reversal through Concentric Structure and Mythic Allusion", *VT* 38 (1988) 407–418.

———, *The Rhetoric of the Book of Judges.* Leiden: E.J. Brill 1996 (VT.S 63).

O'Connor, D., *Ancient Nubia. Egypt's Rival in Africa.* Philadelphia, Pennsylvania: The University Museum of Archaeology and Anthropology, University of Pennsylvania 1993.

O'Connor, M., *Hebrew Verse Structure.* Winona Lake, Indiana: Eisenbrauns 1980/1997.

Oorschot, J. van, *Von Babel zum Zion. Eine literarkritische und redaktionsgeschichtliche Untersuchung.* Berlin: Walter de Gruyter 1993 (BZAW 206).

Oosterhoff, B.J., "Tot een licht der volken (Is 42:6)", *De Knecht. Studies rondom Deutero-Jesaja door collega's en oud-leerlingen aangeboden aan Prof. Dr. J.L. Koole.* Kampen: Kok (1978) 157–172.

Orelli, C. von, *Die Propheten Jesaja und Jeremia.* München: C.H. Beck'sche Verlags-buchhandlung 1891.

Oswalt, J.N., "מכון", *TWOT*. Vol. 1. Chicago, Illinois: Moody Press (1981) 433–434.
———, *The Book of Isaiah. Chapters 1–39*. Grand Rapids, Michigan: Eerdmans 1986.
   (NIC).
Otto, E., "ציון", *ThWAT* 6 (1989) 994–1028.
Otzen, B., "טל", *ThWAT* 5 (1982) 344–352.
Pardee, D., *Ugaritic and Hebrew Poetic Parallelism. A Trial Cut ('nt I and Proverbs 2)*.
   Leiden: E.J. Brill 1988 (VT.S 39).
Parmelee, A., *All the Birds of the Bible. Their Stories, Identification and Meaning*. London:
   Lutterworth Press 1959.
Patrick, D. & Scult, A., *Rhetoric and Biblical Interpretation*. Sheffield: Almond Press
   1990 (JSOT.S 82).
Payne, D.F., "A Perspective on the Use of Simile in the Old Testament", *Semitics*
   1 (1970) 111–125.
Petersen, D.L. & Richards, K.H., *Interpreting Hebrew Poetry*. Minneapolis, Minnesota:
   Fortress Press 1992 (GBS.OT).
Petersen, D.L., "The Oracles Against the Nations: A Form-Critical Analysis", *SBL.SP*
   1 (1975) 39–61.
Pfeiffer, R.H., *Introduction to the Old Testament*. London: Adam and Charles Black
   1953.
Polan, G.J., *In the Ways of Justice Toward Salvation: A Rhetorical Analysis of Isaiah 56–59*.
   New York, New York: Peter Lang 1986 (AmUSt.TR 13).
———, "Zion, the Glory of the Holy One of Israel: A Literary Analysis of Isaiah
   60", *Imagery and Imagination in Biblical Literature. Essays in Honor of Aloysius Fitzgerald,
   F.C.S.* Ed. by L. Boadt & M.S. Smith. Washington, D.C.: The Catholic Biblical
   Association of America (2001) 50–71 (CBQ.MS 32).
Poland, L., "The Bible and the Rhetorical Sublime", *The Bible as Rhetoric. Studies in
   Biblical Persuasion and Credibility*. Ed. by M. Warner. London & New York, New
   York: Routledge (1990) 29–47.
Power, E., "The Prophecy of Isaias against Moab (Is 15:1–16:5)", *Bib*. 13 (1932)
   435–451.
Prickett, S., *Words and The Word. Language, Poetics and Biblical Interpretation*. Cambridge:
   Cambridge University Press 1986/1989.
Pritchard, J.B. (ed.), *ANET*. Third Edition with Supplement. Princeton, New Jersey:
   Princeton University Press 1950/1969.
Procksch, O., *Jesaia I übersetzt und erklärt*. Leipzig: A. Deichertsche Verlagsbuchhandlung
   D. Werner Scholl 1930 (KAT 9).
Raabe, P.R., *Psalm Structures. A Study of Psalms with Refrains*. Sheffield: JSOT Press
   1990 (JSOT.S 104).
———, "Why Prophetic Oracles Against the Nations?", *Fortunate the Eyes that See.
   Essays in Honor of David Noel Freedman in Celebration of His Seventieth Birthday*. Ed.
   by A.B. Beck, A.H. Bartelt & al. Grand Rapids, Michigan & Cambridge:
   William B. Eerdmans Publishing Company (1995) 236–257.
Rad, G. von, *Theologie des Alten Testaments. Band II. Die Theologie der prophetischen Über-
   lieferungen Israels*. München: Chr. Kaiser Verlag 1962.
Regt, L.J. de, *Participants in Old Testament Texts and the Translator. Reference Devices and
   their Rhetorical Impact*. Assen: Van Gorcum 1999 (SSN 39).
Reimer, D.J., *The Oracles Against Babylon in Jeremiah 50–51. A Horror Among the Nations*.
   San Francisco, California: Mellen Research University Press 1993.
Reinhartz, A., "Anonymity and Character in the Books of Samuel", *Semeia* 63 (1993)
   117–141.
Rendtorff, R., "Between Historical Criticism and Holistic Interpretation: New Trends
   in Old Testament Exegesis", *Congress Volume Jerusalem 1986*. Leiden: E.J. Brill
   (1988) 298–303 (VT.S 40).
———, "The Book of Isaiah: A Complex Unity: Synchronic and Diachronic Reading",

Prophecy and Prophets. The Diversity of Contemporary Issues in Scholarship. Ed. by Y. Gitay. Atlanta, Georgia: Scholars Press (1997) 109–128 (SBL.SS).

Renz, J., *Die althebräischen Inschriften. Teil 1, Text und Kommentar.* Darmstadt: Wissenschaftliche Buchgesellschaft 1995 (HEp.).

Reymond, P., *L'eau, sa vie, et sa signification dans l'Ancien Testament.* Leiden: Brill 1958 (VT.S 6).

Rice, G., "The African Roots of the Prophet Zephaniah", *JRT* 36 (1979) 21–31.

Richards, I.A., *The Philosophy of Rhetoric.* New York: Oxford University 1936/1965.

Ricoeur, P., *Interpretation Theory: Discourse and the Surplus of Meaning.* Fort Worth, Texas: The Texas Christian University Press 1976.

Rignell, L.G., *A Study of Isaiah ch. 40–55.* Lund: C.W.K. Gleerup 1956 (AUL; 52:5).

Rimbach, J.A., "Animal Imagery in the Old Testament. Some Aspects of Hebrew Poetics". Unpublished Ph.D. diss. Ann Arbor, Michigan: John Hopkins University 1972.

Ringgren, H., "ים", *ThWAT* 3 (1982) 645–657.

———, "נבט", *ThWAT* 5 (1986) 137–140.

———, "שופר", *ThWAT* 7 (1993) 1195–1196.

Roberts, J.J.M., "Double Entendre in First Isaiah", *CBQ* 54 (1992) 39–48.

Robinson, A., "Zion and Ṣāphôn in Psalm XLVIII 3", *VT* 24 (1974) 118–123.

Ross, J.F., "The Prophet as Yahweh's Messenger", *Prophecy in Israel. Search for an Identity.* Ed. by D.L. Petersen. Philadelphia, Pennsylvania: Fortress Press & London: SPCK (1987) 112–121 (IRT 10).

Rowe, J.C., "Structure", *Critical Terms for Literary Study.* Ed. by F. Lentricchia & T. McLaughlin. Chicago, Illinois & London: The University of Chicago Press (1995) 23–38.

Rudolph, W., *Jeremia. Second Edition.* Tübingen: Verlag von J.C.B. Mohr (Paul Siebeck) 1958 (HAT 12).

———, "Jesaja xv–xvi", *Hebrew and Semitic Studies Presented to Godfrey Rolles Driver in Celebration of His Seventienth Birthday 20 August 1962.* Ed. by D. Winton Thomas & W.D. McHardy. Oxford: The Clarendon Press (1963) 130–143.

———, *Micha—Nahum—Habakuk—Zephanja. Mit einer Zeittafel von Alfred Jepsen.* Gütersloh: Gütersloher Verlagshaus Gerd Mohn 1975 (KAT 13/3).

Ryken, L., Wilhoit, J.C. & al. (eds.), *DicBI.* Downers Grove, Illinois & Leicester: Inter Varsity Press 1998.

Ryou, D.H., *Zephaniah's Oracles Against the Nations: A Synchronic and Diachronic Study of Zephaniah 2:1–3:8.* Leiden: E.J. Brill 1995 (BibIS 13).

Sachar, A.L., *A History of the Jews.* New York: Knopf 1966.

Sadler, R.S., "Can a Cushite Change His Skin? An Examination of Race, Ethnicity, and Othering in the Hebrew Bible". Unpublished Ph.D. diss. Ann Arbor, Michigan/Durham: Duke University 2001.

Sawyer, J.F.A., "'Blessed be my People Egypt', (Isaiah 19:25): The Context and Meaning of a Remarkable Passage", *A Word in Season. Essays in Honour of W. McKane.* Ed. by J.D. Martin & P.R. Davies. Sheffield: JSOT Press (1986) 57–71 (JSOT.S 42).

Scharbert, J., *Der Schmerz im Alten Testament.* Bonn: Peter Hanstein 1955 (BBB 8).

Schipper, B.U., *Israel und Ägypten in der Königszeit. Die kulturellen Kontakte von Salomo bis zum Fall Jerusalems.* Freiburg: Universitätsverlag 1999 (OBO 170).

Schmitt, J.J., "The City as Woman in Isaiah 1–39", *Writing and Reading the Scroll of Isaiah. Studies of an Interpretive Tradition.* Ed. by C.C. Broyles & C.A. Evans. Vol 1. Brill: Leiden (1997) 95–119 (VT.S 70/1. Formation and Interpretation of Old Testament Literature 1/1).

Schmidt, H., *Der heilige Fels in Jerusalem. Eine archäologische und religionsgeschichtliche Studie.* Tübingen: J.B.C. Mohr (Paul Siebeck) 1933.

Schottroff, W., "Das Weinberglied Jesajas (Jes 5:1–7). Ein Beitrag zur Geschichte der Parabel", *ZAW* 82 (1970) 68–91.

Schultz, C., "עד", *TWOT*. Vol. 2. Chicago, Illinois: Moody Press (1981) 647–648.
Schwarzenbach, A.W., *Die geographische Terminologie im Hebräischen des alten Testamentes*. Leiden: E.J. Brill 1954.
Scott, R.B.Y., "Isaiah XXI 1–10; The Inside of a Prophet's Mind", *VT* 2 (1952) 278–282.
———, "Meteorological Phenomena and Terminology in the Old Testament", *ZAW* 64 (1952) 11–25.
Seidel, H., *Musik in Altisrael. Untersuchungen zur Musikgeschichte und Musikpraxis Altisraels anhand biblischer und außerbiblischer Texte*. Frankfurt am Main: Peter Lang 1989 (BEAT 12).
Seitz, C.R., "How is the Prophet Isaiah Present in the Latter Half of the Book? The Logic of Chapters 40–66 within the Book of Isaiah", *JBL* 115 (1996) 219–240.
———, *Isaiah 1–39*. Louisville, Kentucky: John Knox Press 1993 (ITP).
Shaw, C.S., *The Speeches of Micah. A Rhetorical-Historical Analysis*. Sheffield: SJOT Press 1993 (JSOT.S 145).
Sheppard, G.T., "More on Isaiah 5:1–7 as a Juridical Parable", *CBQ* 44 (1982) 45–47.
Ska, J.L., *"Our Fathers Have told Us". Introduction to the Analysis of Hebrew Narratives*. Roma: Editrice Pontificio Institutio Biblico 1990 (SubBi 13).
Slotki, I.W., *Isaiah. Hebrew Text and English Translation with an Introduction and Commentary*. London & Bournemouth: The Soncino Press 1949 (SBBS 8).
Smith, M., "II Isaiah and the Persians", *JAOS* 83 (1963) 415–421.
Smith, P.A., *Rhetoric and Redaction in Trito-Isaiah. The Structure, Growth and Authorship of Isaiah 56–66*. Leiden: E.J. Brill 1995 (VT.S 62).
Smith, R., "A New Perspective on Amos 9:7a", *JITC* 22 (1994) 36–47.
Smith, R.L., *Micah-Malachi*. Waco, Texas: Word Books 1984 (WBC 32).
Snijders, L.A., *Jesaja deel 1*. Nijkerk: G.F. Callenbach N.V. 1969 (PrOT).
———, "נהר", *ThWAT* 5 (1986) 283.
Snijders, L.A., "סור", *ThWAT* 5 (1986) 803–810.
Snodgrass, K., *The Parable of the Wicked Tenants. An Inquiry into Parable Interpretation*. Tübingen: J.C.B. Mohr (Paul Siebeck) 1983 (WUNT 27).
Soggin, J.A., "Zum wiederentdeckten altkanaanäischen Monat צח", *ZAW* 77 (1965) 83–86.
Soskice, J.M., *Metaphor and Religious Language*. Oxford: Clarendon Press 1985.
Speiser, E.A., "The Rivers of Paradise", *Festschrift Johannes Friedrich zum 65. Geburtstag am 27. August 1958 gewidmet*. Ed. by R. von Kienle, A. Moortgat & al. Heidelberg: Carl Winter Universitätsverlag (1959) 473–485.
Stadelmann, L.I.J., *The Hebrew Conception of the World. A Philological and Literary Study*. Rome: Pontifical Biblical Institute 1970 (AnBib; 39).
Staerk, W., *Das assyriche Weltreich im Urteil der Propheten*. Göttingen: Vandenhoeck & Ruprecht 1908.
Stansell, G., "Isaiah 28–33: Blest be the Tie that Binds (Isaiah together)", *New Visions of Isaiah*. Ed. by R.F. Melugin & M.A. Sweeney. Sheffield: Sheffield Academic Press (1996) 67–103 (JSOT.S 214).
Steck, O.H., "Aspekte des Gottesknechts in Deuterojesajas 'Ebed-Jahwe-Liedern'", *ZAW* 96 (1984) 372–390.
———, *Gottesknecht und Zion. Gesammelte Aufsätze zu Deuterojesaja*. Tübingen: J.C.B. Mohr (Paul Siebeck) 1992 (FAT 4).
Stolz, F., "ציון", *THAT* 2 (1976) 543–551.
Stordalen, T., "'Bibel og litteratur' i nyere GT-forskning", *TTK* 2 (1992) 113–128.
———, *Echoes of Eden. Genesis 2–3 and Symbolism of the Eden Garden in Biblical Hebrew Literature*. Leuven: Peeters 2000 (CBETh 25).
Stähli, H.-P., "עבר", *THAT* 2 (1976) 200–204.
Svensen, Å., *Tekstens mønstre. Innføring i litterær analyse*. Oslo: Universitetsforlaget 1985.

Sweeney, M.A., *Isaiah 1–4 and the Post-Exilic Understanding of the Isaianic Tradition*. Berlin: Walter de Gruyter 1988 (BZAW 171).
———, *Isaiah 1–39 With an Introduction to Prophetic Literature*. Grand Rapids, Michigan & Cambridge: Eerdmans Publishing Company 1996 (FOTL 16).
———, *Zephaniah. A Commentary*. Minneapolis, Minnesota: Fortress Press 2003 (Hermeneia).
Talmon, S., "הר", *ThWAT* 2 (1977) 459–483.
———, "Har and Midbār: An Antithetical Pair of Biblical Motifs", *Figurative Language in the Ancient Near East*. Ed. by M. Mindlin & al. London: School of Oriental and African Studies (1987) 117–142.
———, "Prophetic Rhetoric and Agricultural Metaphora", *Storia e tradizioni di Israele. Scritti in onore di J. Alberto Soggin*. Brescia: Paideia Editrice (1991) 267–279.
———, "צח", *ThWAT* 6 (1989) 983–986.
Tanghe, V., "Dichtung und Ekel in Jesaja 28:7–13", *VT* 43 (1993) 235–260.
Teixidor, J., "Bulletin d'épigraphie sémitique", *Syr.* 44 (1967) 163–195.
Then, R., *"Gibt es denn keinen mehr unter den Propheten?" Zum Fortgang der alttestamentlichen Prophetie in frühjüdischer Zeit*. Frankfurt am Main: Peter Lang 1990 (BEAT 22).
[Théodoret of Cyrus] Théodoret de Cyr, *Commentaire sur Isaïe*. Vol. 2. Paris: Les Éditions du Cerf. 1982 (SC 295). [Introduction, textual criticism and notes by Jean-Noel Guinot].
Thomas, D.W., "'A Drop of a Bucket?' Some Observations on the Hebrew Text of Isaiah 40:15", *In Memoriam Paul Kahle*. Ed. by M. Black & G. Fohrer. Berlin: Verlag Alfred Töpelmann (1968) 214–221 (BZAW; 103).
Thrall, W.F. & Hibbard, A., *A Handbook to Literature. Revised and enlarged by C.H. Holman*. New York, New York: The Odyssey Press 1962.
Torrey, C.C., *The Second Isaiah. A New Interpretation*. Edinburgh: T. & T. Clark 1928.
Trible, P., *Rhetorical Criticism. Context, Method, and the Book of Jonah*. Minneapolis, Minnesota: Fortress Press 1994 (GBS.OT).
Trigger, B.G., Kemp, B.J. & al., *Ancient Egypt. A Social History*. Cambridge: Cambridge University Press 1983.
Török, L., *The Kingdom of Kush. Handbook of the Napatan-Meroitic Civilization*. Leiden: Brill 1997 (HOr. 31).
Ullendorff, E., *Ethiopia and the Bible*. London: Oxford University Press 1968 (SchL; 1967).
Van Winkle, D.W., "The Relationship of the Nations to Yahweh and to Israel in Isaiah 40–55", *VT* 35 (1985) 446–458.
Vermeylen, J., "L'unité du livre d'Isaïe", *The Book of Isaiah. Le livre d'Isaïe: Les oracles et leurs relectures. Unité et complexité de l'ouvrage*. Ed. by J. Vermeylen. Leuven: Leuven University Press (1989) 11–53 (BEThL 81).
Vinje, E., *Tekst og tolking. Innføring i litterær analyse*. Oslo: Ad Notam Gyldendal 1993.
Vogels, W., "A Structural Analysis of Ps 1", *Bib.* 60 (1979) 410–416.
———, "L'Égypte mon peuple—L'Universalisme d'Is 19, 16–25", *Bib.* 57 (1976) 494–514.
Vogt, E., "'eber hayyarden = regio finitima Iordani", *Bib.* 34 (1953) 118–119.
Wales, H.G.Q., *The Mountain of God. A Study in Early Religion and Kingship*. London: Bernard Quaritch 1953.
Walsh, C.E., *The Fruit of the Vine: Viticulture in Ancient Israel*. Winona Lake, Indiana: Eisenbrauns 2000 (Harvard Semitic Museum Publications. HSM 60).
Wanke, G., "אוי und הוי", *ZAW* 78 (1966) 215–218.
Watson, D.F. (ed.), *Persuasive Artistry. Studies in New Testament Rhetoric in Honor of George A. Kennedy*. Sheffield: Sheffield Academic Press 1991 (JSNT.S 50).
Watson, W.G.E., *Classical Hebrew Poetry. A Guide to its Techniques*. Sheffield: JSOT Press, 1984/1986 (JSOT.S 26).
———, "Internal or Half-line Parallelism in Classical Hebrew again", *Poetry in the*

Hebrew Bible. Selected Studies from VT. Compiled by D.E. Orton. Leiden: Brill (2000) 198–220 (BRBS 6).

———, *Traditional Techniques in Classical Hebrew Verse.* Sheffield: Sheffield Academic Press 1994 (JSOT.S 170).

———, "Tribute to Tyre (Is. 23:7)", *VT* 26 (1976) 371–374.

Watts, J.D.W., *Isaiah 1–33.* Waco, Texas: Word Books 1985 (WBC 24).

———, *Isaiah 34–66.* Waco, Texas: Word Books 1987 (WBC 25).

Watts, J.W., "Text and Redaction in Jeremiah's Oracles Against the Nations", *CBQ* 54 (1992) 432–447.

Webb, B.G., "Zion in Transformation. A Literary Approach to Isaiah", *The Bible in Three Dimensions. Essays in celebration of forty years of Biblical Studies in the University of Sheffield.* Ed. by D.J.A. Clines & al. Sheffield: Sheffield Academic Press (1990) 65–84 (JSOT.S 87).

Weinfeld, M., *Deuteronomy and the Deuteronomic School.* Oxford: The Clarendon Press 1972.

Weippert, H., *Die Prosareden des Jeremiabuches.* Berlin: Walter de Gruyter 1973. (BZAW 132).

———, "Feldzeichen", *BRL.* Ed. by K. Galling. Tübingen: J.C.B. Mohr (Paul Siebeck) (1977) 77–79.

Weippert, M., "Archäologischer Jahresbericht", *ZDPV* 80 (1964) 150–193.

———, "'Heiliger Krieg' in Israel und Assyrien. Kritische Anmerkungen zu Gerhard von Rads Konzept des 'Heiligen Krieges im alten Israel'", *ZAW* 84 (1972) 460–493.

Weis, R.D., "A Definition of the Genre Massa' in the Hebrew Bible". Unpublished Ph.D. diss. Ann Arbor, Michigan: University Microfilms International/Claremont Graduate School 1986.

Weiser, A., *Das Buch der zwölf kleinen Propheten I.* Göttingen: Vandenhoeck & Ruprecht 1959 (ATD 24).

Wensinck, A.J., *The Ideas of the Western Semites Concerning the Navel of the Earth.* Amsterdam: Johannes Müller 1916.

Westermann, C., *Basic Forms of Prophetic Speech.* Translated by Hugh Clayton White. Cambridge: The Lutterworth Press & Louisville, Kentucky: Westminster/John Knox Press 1991.

———, "Das Heilswort bei Deuterojesaja", *EvTh* 24 (1964) 355–373.

———, *Genesis 1–11.* Neukirchen-Vluyn: Neukirchener Verlag 1974 (BK 1/1).

———, *Sprache und Struktur der Prophetie Deuterojesajas. Mit einer Literaturübersicht "Hauptlinien der Deuterojesaja-Forschung von 1964–1979", zusammengestellt und kommentiert von Andreas Richter.* Stuttgart: Calwer Verlag 1981 (CThM 11).

Westphal, G., *Jahwes Wohnstätten nach den Anschauungen der alten Hebräer. Ein alttestamentliche Untersuchung.* Gießen: Verlag von Alfred Töpelmann 1908 (BZAW 15).

Widyapranawa, S.H., *The Lord is Saviour: Faith in National Crisis. A Commentary on the Book of Isaiah 1–39.* Grand Rapids, Michigan: Eerdmans Publishing Company 1990 (ITC).

Wiklander, B., *Prophecy as Literature. A Text-Linguistic and Rhetorical Approach to Isaiah 2–4.* Stockholm: CWK Gleerup 1984 (CB.OT 22).

Wildberger, H., *Jesaja 1–12.* 2. rev. ed. Neukirchen-Vluyn: Neukirchener Verlag 1980 (BK 10/1).

———, *Jesaja 13–27,* Neukirchen-Vluyn: Neukirchener Verlag 1978 (BK 10/2).

———, *Jesaja 28–39.* Neukirchen-Vluyn: Neukirchener Verlag 1982 (BK 10/3).

Wilke, F., *Jesaja und Assur. Eine exegetisch-historische Untersuchung zur Politik des Propheten Jesaja.* Leipzig: Dieterich (Theodor Weicher) 1905.

Williamson, H.G.M., *The Book Called Isaiah. Deutero-Isaiah's Role in Composition and Redaction.* Oxford: Clarendon Press 1994.

Willis, J.T., "The Genre of Isaiah 5:1–7", *JBL* 96 (1977) 337–362.

Wilson, A., *The Nations in Deutero-Isaiah. A Study on Composition and Structure.* Lewiston, New York: The Edwin Mellen Press 1986 (ANETS 1).

Winckler, H., *Alttestamentliche Untersuchungen.* Leipzig: E. Pfeiffer 1892.

Wolf, H.M., *Interpreting Isaiah. The Suffering and Glory of the Messiah.* Grand Rapids, Michigan: Zondervan Publishing House 1985 (Ac.B).

Wolff, H.W., *Dodekapropheton 1. Hosea.* Neukirchen-Vluyn: Neukirchener Verlag 1961 (BK 14/1).

———, *Dodekapropheton 2. Joel und Amos.* Neukirchen-Vluyn: Neukirchener Verlag 1969 (BK 14/2).

Wong, G.C.I., "Isaiah's Opposition to Egypt in Isaiah 31:1–3", *VT* 46 (1996) 392–401.

Wutz, F., "Abweichende Vokalisationsüberlieferung im hebr. Text", *BZ* 21 (1933) 7–21.

Yee, G.A., "A Form-Critical Study of Isaiah 5:1–7 as a Song and a Juridical Parable", *CBQ* 43 (1981) 30–40.

Young, E.J., *The Book of Isaiah. The English Text, With Introduction, Exposition, and Notes.* Grand Rapids, Michigan: William B. Eerdmans Publishing Company 1965/1978 (NIC 1–3).

Zakovitch, Y., "Miracle", *ABD* 4. Ed. by D.N. Freedman & al. New York, New York: Doubleday (1992) 845–856.

Zapff, B.M., *Schriftgelehrte Prophetie—Jesaja 13 und die Komposition des Jesajabuches. Ein Beitrag zur Erforschung der Redaktionsgeschichte des Jesajabuches.* Würzburg: Echter 1995 (FzB 74).

Zapletal, V., "Der Spruch über Moab: Is. 15 und 16", *Alttestamentliches.* Freiburg: Universitaets-Buchhandlung (1903) 163–183.

Ziegler, J., *Isaias.* Würzburg: Echter-Verlag 1948 (EB).

Zobel, H.-J., "הוי", *ThWAT* 2 (1977) 382–388.

Zobel, H.-J., "צבאות", *ThWAT* 6 (1989) 876–892.

Zohary, M., *Plants of the Bible. A Complete Handbook to All the Plants with 200 Full-Color Plates Taken in the Natural Habitat.* Cambridge: Cambridge University Press 1982.

Zorell, F., *Lexicon Hebraicum et Aramaicum Veteris Testamenti.* Roma: Pontificium Institutum Biblicum 1968.

Zyl, A.H. van, *The Moabites.* Leiden: E.J. Brill 1960 (POS 3).

INDEX OF AUTHORS

INDEX OF PASSAGES

SUPPLEMENTS TO VETUS TESTAMENTUM

13. Roth, W.M.W. *Numerical sayings in the Old Testament.* A form-critical study. 1965. ISBN 90 04 02336 4
14. Orlinsky, H.M. *Studies on the second part of the Book of Isaiah.* — The so-called 'Servant of the Lord' and 'Suffering Servant' in Second Isaiah. — Snaith, N.H. Isaiah 40-66. A study of the teaching of the Second Isaiah and its consequences. Repr. with additions and corrections. 1977. ISBN 90 04 05437 5
15. *Volume du Congrès* [International pour l'étude de l'Ancien Testament]. *Genève 1965.* 1966. ISBN 90 04 02337 2
17. *Congress Volume, Rome 1968.* 1969. ISBN 90 04 02339 9
19. Thompson, R.J. *Moses and the Law in a century of criticism since Graf.* 1970. ISBN 90 04 02341 0
20. Redford, D.B. *A Study of the Biblical Story of Joseph.* 1970. ISBN 90 04 02342 9
21. Ahlström, G.W. *Joel and the Temple Cult of Jerusalem.* 1971. ISBN 90 04 02620 7
22. *Congress Volume, Uppsala 1971.* 1972. ISBN 90 04 03521 4
23. *Studies in the Religion of Ancient Israel.* 1972. ISBN 90 04 03525 7
24. Schoors, A. *I am God your Saviour.* A form-critical study of the main genres in Is. xl-lv. 1973. ISBN 90 04 03792 2
25. Allen, L.C. *The Greek Chronicles.* The relation of the Septuagint I and II Chronicles to the Massoretic text. Part 1. The translator's craft. 1974. ISBN 90 04 03913 9
26. *Studies on prophecy.* A collection of twelve papers. 1974. ISBN 90 04 03877 9
27. Allen, L.C. *The Greek Chronicles.* Part 2. Textual criticism. 1974. ISBN 90 04 03933 3
28. *Congress Volume, Edinburgh 1974.* 1975. ISBN 90 04 04321 7
29. *Congress Volume, Göttingen 1977.* 1978. ISBN 90 04 05835 4
30. Emerton, J.A. (ed.). *Studies in the historical books of the Old Testament.* 1979. ISBN 90 04 06017 0
31. Meredino, R.P. *Der Erste und der Letzte.* Eine Untersuchung von Jes 40-48. 1981. ISBN 90 04 06199 1
32. Emerton, J.A. (ed.). *Congress Volume, Vienna 1980.* 1981. ISBN 90 04 06514 8
33. Koenig, J. *L'herméneutique analogique du Judaïsme antique d'après les témoins textuels d'Isaïe.* 1982. ISBN 90 04 06762 0
34. Barstad, H.M. *The religious polemics of Amos.* Studies in the preachings of Amos ii 7B-8, iv 1-13, v 1-27, vi 4-7, viii 14. 1984. ISBN 90 04 07017 6
35. Krašovec, J. *Antithetic structure in Biblical Hebrew poetry.* 1984. ISBN 90 04 07244 6
36. Emerton, J.A. (ed.). *Congress Volume, Salamanca 1983.* 1985. ISBN 90 04 07281 0
37. Lemche, N.P. *Early Israel.* Anthropological and historical studies on the Israelite society before the monarchy. 1985. ISBN 90 04 07853 3
38. Nielsen, K. *Incense in Ancient Israel.* 1986. ISBN 90 04 07702 2
39. Pardee, D. *Ugaritic and Hebrew poetic parallelism.* A trial cut. 1988. ISBN 90 04 08368 5
40. Emerton, J.A. (ed.). *Congress Volume, Jerusalem 1986.* 1988. ISBN 90 04 08499 1
41. Emerton, J.A. (ed.). *Studies in the Pentateuch.* 1990. ISBN 90 04 09195 5
42. McKenzie, S.L. *The trouble with Kings.* The composition of the Book of Kings in the Deuteronomistic History. 1991. ISBN 90 04 09402 4
43. Emerton, J.A. (ed.). *Congress Volume, Leuven 1989.* 1991. ISBN 90 04 09398 2
44. Haak, R.D. *Habakkuk.* 1992. ISBN 90 04 09506 3

45. BEYERLIN, W. *Im Licht der Traditionen*. Psalm LXVII und CXV. Ein Entwicklungs-zusammenhang. 1992. ISBN 90 04 09635 3
46. MEIER, S.A. *Speaking of Speaking*. Marking direct discourse in the Hebrew Bible. 1992. ISBN 90 04 09602 7
47. KESSLER, R. *Staat und Gesellschaft im vorexilischen Juda*. Vom 8. Jahrhundert bis zum Exil. 1992. ISBN 90 04 09646 9
48. AUFFRET, P. *Voyez de vos yeux*. Étude structurelle de vingt psaumes, dont le psaume 119. 1993. ISBN 90 04 09707 4
49. GARCÍA MARTÍNEZ, F., A. HILHORST and C.J. LABUSCHAGNE (eds.). *The Scriptures and the Scrolls*. Studies in honour of A.S. van der Woude on the occasion of his 65th birthday. 1992. ISBN 90 04 09746 5
50. LEMAIRE, A. and B. OTZEN (eds.). *History and Traditions of Early Israel*. Studies presented to Eduard Nielsen, May 8th, 1993. 1993. ISBN 90 04 09851 8
51. GORDON, R.P. *Studies in the Targum to the Twelve Prophets*. From Nahum to Malachi. 1994. ISBN 90 04 09987 5
52. HUGENBERGER, G.P. *Marriage as a Covenant*. A Study of Biblical Law and Ethics Governing Marriage Developed from the Perspective of Malachi. 1994. ISBN 90 04 09977 8
53. GARCÍA MARTÍNEZ, F., A. HILHORST, J.T.A.G.M. VAN RUITEN, A.S. VAN DER WOUDE. *Studies in Deuteronomy*. In Honour of C.J. Labuschagne on the Occasion of His 65th Birthday. 1994. ISBN 90 04 10052 0
54. FERNÁNDEZ MARCOS, N. *Septuagint and Old Latin in the Book of Kings*. 1994. ISBN 90 04 10043 1
55. SMITH, M.S. *The Ugaritic Baal Cycle. Volume 1*. Introduction with text, translation and commentary of KTU 1.1-1.2. 1994. ISBN 90 04 09995 6
56. DUGUID, I.M. *Ezekiel and the Leaders of Israel*. 1994. ISBN 90 04 10074 1
57. MARX, A. *Les offrandes végétales dans l'Ancien Testament*. Du tribut d'hommage au repas eschatologique. 1994. ISBN 90 04 10136 5
58. SCHÄFER-LICHTENBERGER, C. *Josua und Salomo*. Eine Studie zu Autorität und Legitimität des Nachfolgers im Alten Testament. 1995. ISBN 90 04 10064 4
59. LASSERRE, G. *Synopse des lois du Pentateuque*. 1994. ISBN 90 04 10202 7
60. DOGNIEZ, C. *Bibliography of the Septuagint – Bibliographie de la Septante (1970-1993)*. Avec une préface de PIERRE-MAURICE BOGAERT. 1995. ISBN 90 04 10192 6
61. EMERTON, J.A. (ed.). *Congress Volume, Paris 1992*. 1995. ISBN 90 04 10259 0
62. SMITH, P.A. *Rhetoric and Redaction in Trito-Isaiah*. The Structure, Growth and Authorship of Isaiah 56-66. 1995. ISBN 90 04 10306 6
63. O'CONNELL, R.H. *The Rhetoric of the Book of Judges*. 1996. ISBN 90 04 10104 7
64. HARLAND, P.J. *The Value of Human Life*. A Study of the Story of the Flood (Genesis 6-9). 1996. ISBN 90 04 10534 4
65. ROLAND PAGE JR., H. *The Myth of Cosmic Rebellion*. A Study of its Reflexes in Ugaritic and Biblical Literature. 1996. ISBN 90 04 10563 8
66. EMERTON, J.A. (ed.). *Congress Volume, Cambridge 1995*. 1997. ISBN 90 04 106871
67. JOOSTEN, J. *People and Land in the Holiness Code*. An Exegetical Study of the Ideational Framework of the Law in Leviticus 17–26. 1996. ISBN 90 04 10557 3
68. BEENTJES, P.C. *The Book of Ben Sira in Hebrew*. A Text Edition of all Extant Hebrew Manuscripts and a Synopsis of all Parallel Hebrew Ben Sira Texts. 1997. ISBN 90 04 10767 3
69. COOK, J. *The Septuagint of Proverbs – Jewish and/or Hellenistic Proverbs?* Concerning the Hellenistic Colouring of LXX Proverbs. 1997. ISBN 90 04 10879 3

70,1 Broyles, G. and C. Evans (eds.). *Writing and Reading the Scroll of Isaiah*. Studies of an Interpretive Tradition, I. 1997. ISBN 90 04 10936 6 (*Vol. I*); ISBN 90 04 11027 5 (*Set*)

70,2 Broyles, G. and C. Evans (eds.). *Writing and Reading the Scroll of Isaiah*. Studies of an Interpretive Tradition, II. 1997. ISBN 90 04 11026 7 (*Vol. II*); ISBN 90 04 11027 5 (*Set*)

71. Kooij, A. van der. *The Oracle of Tyre*. The Septuagint of Isaiah 23 as Version and Vision. 1998. ISBN 90 04 11152 2

72. Tov, E. *The Greek and Hebrew Bible*. Collected Essays on the Septuagint. 1999. ISBN 90 04 11309 6

73. García Martínez, F. and Noort, E. (eds.). *Perspectives in the Study of the Old Testament and Early Judaism*. A Symposium in honour of Adam S. van der Woude on the occasion of his 70th birthday. 1998. ISBN 90 04 11322 3

74. Kassis, R.A. *The Book of Proverbs and Arabic Proverbial Works*. 1999. ISBN 90 04 11305 3

75. Rösel, H.N. *Von Josua bis Jojachin*. Untersuchungen zu den deuteronomistischen Geschichtsbüchern des Alten Testaments. 1999. ISBN 90 04 11355 5

76. Renz, Th. *The Rhetorical Function of the Book of Ezekiel*. 1999. ISBN 90 04 11362 2

77. Harland, P.J. and Hayward, C.T.R. (eds.). *New Heaven and New Earth Prophecy and the Millenium*. Essays in Honour of Anthony Gelston. 1999. ISBN 90 04 10841 6

78. Krašovec, J. *Reward, Punishment, and Forgiveness*. The Thinking and Beliefs of Ancient Israel in the Light of Greek and Modern Views. 1999. ISBN 90 04 11443 2.

79. Kossmann, R. *Die Esthernovelle – Vom Erzählten zur Erzählung*. Studien zur Traditions- und Redaktionsgeschichte des Estherbuches. 2000. ISBN 90 04 11556 0.

80. Lemaire, A. and M. Sæbø (eds.). *Congress Volume, Oslo 1998*. 2000. ISBN 90 04 11598 6.

81. Galil, G. and M. Weinfeld (eds.). *Studies in Historical Geography and Biblical Historiography*. Presented to Zecharia Kallai. 2000. ISBN 90 04 11608 7

82. Collins, N.L. *The library in Alexandria and the Bible in Greek*. 2001. ISBN 90 04 11866 7

83,1 Collins, J.J. and P.W. Flint (eds.). *The Book of Daniel*. Composition and Reception, I. 2001. ISBN 90 04 11675 3 (*Vol. I*); ISBN 90 04 12202 8 (*Set*).

83,2 Collins, J.J. and P.W. Flint (eds.). *The Book of Daniel*. Composition and Reception, II. 2001. ISBN 90 04 12200 1 (*Vol. II*); ISBN 90 04 12202 8 (*Set*).

84. Cohen, C.H.R. *Contextual Priority in Biblical Hebrew Philology*. An Application of the Held Method for Comparative Semitic Philology. 2001. ISBN 90 04 11670 2 (In preparation).

85. Wagenaar, J.A. *Judgement and Salvation*. The Composition and Redaction of Micah 2-5. 2001. ISBN 90 04 11936 1

86. McLaughlin, J.L. *The Marzēaḥ in sthe Prophetic Literature*. References and Allusions in Light of the Extra-Biblical Evidence. 2001. ISBN 90 04 12006 8

87. Wong, K.L. *The Idea of Retribution in the Book of Ezekiel* 2001. ISBN 90 04 12256 7

88. Barrick, W. Boyd. *The King and the Cemeteries*. Toward a New Understanding of Josiah's Reform. 2002. ISBN 90 04 12171 4

89. Frankel, D. *The Murmuring Stories of the Priestly School*. A Retrieval of Ancient Sacerdotal Lore. 2002. ISBN 90 04 12368 7

90. Frydrych, T. *Living under the Sun*. Examination of Proverbs and Qoheleth. 2002. ISBN 90 04 12315 6

91. KESSEL, J. *The Book of Haggai*. Prophecy and Society in Early Persian Yehud. 2002. ISBN 90 04 12368 7
92. LEMAIRE, A. (ed.). *Congress Volume, Basel 2001*. 2002. ISBN 90 04 12680 5
93. RENDTORFF, R. and R.A. KUGLER (eds.). *The Book of Leviticus*. Composition and Reception. 2003. ISBN 90 04 12634 1
94. PAUL, S.M., R.A. KRAFT, L.H. SCHIFFMAN and W.W. FIELDS (eds.). *Emanuel*. Studies in Hebrew Bible, Septuagint, and Dead Sea Scrolls in Honor of Emanuel Tov. 2003. ISBN 90 04 13007 1
95. VOS, J.C. DE. *Das Los Judas*. Über Entstehung und Ziele der Landbeschreibung in Josua 15. ISBN 90 04 12953 7
96. LEHNART, B. *Prophet und König im Nordreich Israel*. Studien zur sogenannten vorklassischen Prophetie im Nordreich Israel anhand der Samuel-, Elija- und Elischa-Überlieferungen. 2003. ISBN 90 04 13237 6
97. LO, A. *Job 28 as Rhetoric*. An Analysis of Job 28 in the Context of Job 22-31. 2003. ISBN 90 04 13320 8
98. TRUDINGER, P.L. *The Psalms of the Tamid Service*. A Liturgical Text from the Second Temple. 2004. ISBN 90 04 12968 5
99. FLINT, P.W. and P.D. MILLER, JR. (eds.) with the assistance of A. Brunell. *The Book of Psalms*. Composition and Reception. 2004. ISBN 90 04 13842 8
100. WEINFELD, M. *The Place of the Law in the Religion of Ancient Israel*. 2004. ISBN 90 04 13749 1
101. FLINT, P.W., J.C. VANDERKAM and E. TOV. (eds.) *Studies in the Hebrew Bible, Qumran, and the Septuagint*. Essays Presented to Eugene Ulrich on the Occasion of his Sixty-Fifth Birthday. 2004. ISBN 90 04 13738 6
102. MEER, M.N. VAN DER. *Formation and Reformulation*. The Redaction of the Book of Joshua in the Light of the Oldest Textual Witnesses. 2004. ISBN 90 04 13125 6
103. BERMAN, J.A. *Narrative Analogy in the Hebrew Bible*. Battle Stories and Their Equivalent Non-battle Narratives. 2004. ISBN 90 04 13119 1
104. KEULEN, P.S.F. VAN. *Two Versions of the Solomon Narrative*. An Inquiry into the Relationship between MT 1 Kgs. 2-11 and LXX 3 Reg. 2-11. 2004. ISBN 90 04 13895 1
105. MARX, A. *Les systèmes sacrificiels de l'Ancien Testament*. Forms et fonctions du culte sacrificiel à Yhwh. 2005. ISBN 90 04 14286 X
106. ASSIS, E. *Self-Interest or Communal Interest*. An Ideology of Leadership in the Gideon, Abimelech and Jephthah Narritives (Judg 6-12). 2005. ISBN 90 04 14354 8
107. WEISS, A.L. *Figurative Language in Biblical Prose Narrative*. Metaphor in the Book of Samuel. 2006. ISBN 90 04 14837 X
108. WAGNER, T. *Gottes Herrschaft*. Eine Analyse der Denkschrift (Jes 6, 1-9,6). 2006. ISBN 90 04 14912 0
109. LEMAIRE, A. (ed.). *Congress Volume Leiden 2004*. 2006. ISBN 90 04 14913 9
110. GOLDMAN, Y.A.P., A. van der Kooij and R.D. Weis (eds.). *Sôfer Mahîr*. Essays in Honour of Adrian Schenker Offered by Editors of *Biblia Hebraica Quinta*. 2006. ISBN 90 04 15016 1
111. WONG, G.T.K. *Compositional Strategy of the Book of Judges*. An Inductive, Rhetorical Study. 2006. ISBN 90 04 15086 2
112. HØYLAND LAVIK, M. *A People Tall and Smooth-Skinned*. The Rhetoric of Isaiah 18. 2006. ISBN 90 04 15434 5
113. REZETKO, R., T.H. LIM and W.B. AUCKER (eds.). *Reflection and Refraction*. Studies in Biblical Historiography in Honour of A. Graeme Auld. 2006. ISBN 90 04 14512 5
115. BERGSMA, J.S. *The Jubilee from Leviticus to Qumran*. A History of Interpretation. 2006. ISBN-13 978 90 04 15299 1. ISBN-10 90 04 15299 7